American Cinema of the 1920s

AMERICAN CULTURE / AMERICAN CINEMA

Each volume in the Screen Decades: American Culture/American Cinema series presents a group of original essays analyzing the impact of cultural issues on the cinema and the impact of the cinema in American society. Because every chapter explores a spectrum of particularly significant motion pictures and the broad range of historical events in one year, readers will gain a continuing sense of the decade as it came to be depicted on movie screens across the continent. The integration of historical and cultural events with the sprawling progression of American cinema illuminates the pervasive themes and the essential movies that define an era. Our series represents one among many possible ways of confronting the past; we hope that these books will offer a better understanding of the connections between American culture and film history.

LESTER D. FRIEDMAN AND MURRAY POMERANCE
SERIES EDITORS

André Gaudreault, editor, *American Cinema, 1890–1909: Themes and Variations*

Charlie Keil and Ben Singer, editors, *American Cinema of the 1910s: Themes and Variations*

Lucy Fischer, editor, *American Cinema of the 1920s: Themes and Variations*

Ina Rae Hark, editor, *American Cinema of the 1930s: Themes and Variations*

Wheeler Winston Dixon, editor, *American Cinema of the 1940s: Themes and Variations*

Murray Pomerance, editor, *American Cinema of the 1950s: Themes and Variations*

Barry Keith Grant, editor, *American Cinema of the 1960s: Themes and Variations*

Lester D. Friedman, editor, *American Cinema of the 1970s: Themes and Variations*

Stephen Prince, editor, *American Cinema of the 1980s: Themes and Variations*

Chris Holmlund, editor, *American Cinema of the 1990s: Themes and Variations*

American Cinema of the 1920s

Themes and Variations

EDITED BY
LUCY FISCHER

RUTGERS UNIVERSITY PRESS
NEW BRUNSWICK, NEW JERSEY, AND LONDON

LIBRARY OF CONGRESS CATALOGING-IN-PUBLICATION DATA

American cinema of the 1920s : themes and variations / edited by Lucy Fischer.
p. cm. — (Screen decades)
Includes bibliographical references and index.
ISBN 978–0–8135–4484–7 (hardcover : alk. paper)
ISBN 978–0–8135–4485–4 (pbk. : alk. paper)
1. Motion pictures—United States—History. 2. Motion pictures—United States—Plots, themes, etc. I. Fischer, Lucy.
PN1993.5.U6A85734 2009
791.430973—dc22

2008029193

A British Cataloging-in-Publication record for this book is available from the British Library.

Visit our Web site: http://rutgerspress.rutgers.edu

Manufactured in the United States of America

In memory of my aunt Emma Fischer Pinkus
and my uncle Reuben Levine,
who both were young in the 1920s

CONTENTS

ACKNOWLEDGMENTS

I would like to thank the editors of the Screen Decades series, Lester Friedman and Murray Pomerance, for inviting me to edit this volume and for providing me assistance in its formulation. I would also like to thank all the contributors to the volume for their hard work and patience in seeing the book through to publication. Additionally, I would also like to express my gratitude to Leslie Mitchner of Rutgers University Press, with whom I have worked before on several projects and who always makes such collaboration a fruitful experience, and to Eric Schramm for his careful work editing the manuscript.

At the University of Pittsburgh, I would like to thank Film Studies Administrative Assistant Jennifer Florian for her help in preparing the volume for publication, as well as the following graduate student assistants for their research aid: Julie Wade, Sangeeta Mall, Nathan Koob, Katherine Field, and Jason Bittel. Finally, I am indebted to my graduate students in the seminar The Jazz Age in Cinema for all their stimulating ideas and input.

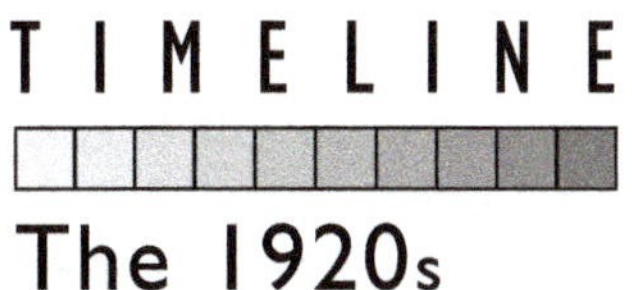

The 1920s

1920

10 JANUARY The League of Nations is established in Geneva, Switzerland; the Treaty of Versailles is ratified by Germany.

16 JANUARY The Eighteenth Amendment to the U.S. Constitution goes into effect, prohibiting the making, selling, possession, and consumption of alcoholic beverages. It would be repealed in 1933.

28 MARCH The marriage of Mary Pickford and Douglas Fairbanks, after a three-year affair, is a Hollywood sensation.

18 AUGUST The Nineteenth Amendment to the U.S. Constitution is ratified, giving women the right to vote.

28 SEPTEMBER The "Black Sox" scandal rocks Major League Baseball when eight Chicago White Sox players are indicted on charges of fixing the 1919 World Series.

2 NOVEMBER The Republican ticket of Warren G. Harding and Calvin Coolidge defeats Democrats James M. Cox and Franklin Roosevelt in the U.S. presidential election.

1921

31 MAY–1 JUNE Race riots in Tulsa, Oklahoma.

14 JULY Italian immigrant anarchists Nicola Sacco and Bartolomeo Vanzetti are convicted of first-degree murder in Massachusetts.

30 AUGUST The Federal Trade Commission (FTC) sues Famous Players–Lasky for violating antitrust laws by refusing to allow independent films to play in its theaters.

5 SEPTEMBER Comic actor Roscoe "Fatty" Arbuckle injures Virginia Rappe during a sexual encounter. She later dies of acute peritonitis.

7 SEPTEMBER The first Miss America Pageant is held in Atlantic City, New Jersey.

2 OCTOBER Babe Ruth finishes the baseball season with a record fifty-nine home runs.

1922

2 FEBRUARY Forty-five-year-old film director William Desmond Taylor is found murdered in Los Angeles with a bullet in his back.

19 MAY American inventor Charles Francis Jenkins makes the first laboratory transmission of a television picture signal.

30 MAY Built at a cost of $3 million, the Lincoln Memorial opens on the Mall in Washington, D.C.

27 SEPTEMBER *The Power of Love*, the first 3-D feature film, plays to a paying film audience. It is projected dual-strip in the red/green anaglyph format, making it both the earliest known film that utilized dual strip projection and the earliest known film in which anaglyph glasses were used.

26 NOVEMBER King Tut's tomb is found in the Valley of the Kings by British Egyptologists George Carnarvon and Howard Carter.

26 NOVEMBER *The Toll of the Sea*, directed by Chester M. Franklin for Metro Pictures, is the first two-color Technicolor film released. The two strips, made of film stocks thinner than regular film, were then cemented together base to base to create a projection.

1923

3 MARCH *Time*, the first weekly newsmagazine, is published by Henry Luce and Briton Hadden.

4 APRIL The four Warner brothers' film distribution and production business is incorporated and called Warner Bros. Pictures Inc.—one of the first large film studios.

15 APRIL Lee de Forest shows the first "talkies" at the Rivoli Theatre in New York using the Phonofilm system, projecting a series of short musical films featuring vaudeville performers. He was forced to show his films in independent theaters such as the Rivoli, since Hollywood movie studios controlled all major theater chains.

5 JULY The Kodak Model A film camera and Model A motorized Kodascope projector—the first complete 16 mm system—are introduced in the United States.

2 AUGUST President Warren Harding dies of bronchial pneumonia in a San Francisco hotel room. He is succeeded by Calvin Coolidge.

25 OCTOBER The Teapot Dome scandal comes to public attention. It would result in the conviction of Harry F. Sinclair of Mammoth Oil, and later Secretary of the Interior Albert B. Fall, the first cabinet member in American history to go to jail. The scandal, named

for the Teapot Dome oil reserves in Wyoming, involved Fall secretly leasing naval oil reserve lands to private companies.

1924

24 JANUARY C.B.C. Film Sales Company (founded by brothers Jack and Harry Cohn, and Joseph Brandt) officially changes its name to Columbia Pictures Corporation.

3 FEBRUARY Former president Woodrow Wilson dies.

17 APRIL Metro and Goldwyn combine to form the Metro-Goldwyn studio.

2 JUNE Native Americans are declared U.S. citizens under the Snyder Act.

2 JULY The Immigration Act of 1924 limits the number of immigrants from any particular country to 2 percent of the number of people from that country who were already living in the United States according to the Census of 1890. It thus excludes Asian immigration to the United States.

4 NOVEMBER Calvin Coolidge is elected to a full term as president.

1925

21 FEBRUARY Harold Ross publishes the first issue of the *New Yorker*.

18 MARCH The worst tornadoes in U.S. history kill about 700 people in the Midwest (Missouri, Illinois, and Indiana).

22 MAY Vitagraph, one of the oldest studios, sells out to Warner Bros., who inherit all the research undertaken by Vitagraph in the field of sound (Vitaphone).

21 JULY John Scopes is found guilty of teaching evolution in Dayton, Tennessee.

8 AUGUST Fifty thousand Ku Klux Klansmen march on Washington.

28 NOVEMBER The "Grand Ole Opry," a weekly American radio program featuring live country and western music, begins broadcasting. The nation's oldest continuous radio show, it was first broadcast on Nashville's WSM as an amateur showcase.

1926

16 MARCH Robert H. Goddard launches the first liquid fuel rocket in Auburn, Massachusetts.

6 AUGUST Gertrude Ederle becomes the first woman to swim the English Channel.

6 AUGUST In New York, Warner Bros. debuts *Don Juan*—the first Vitaphone film (developed by Bell Telephone Laboratories in 1926) and the first publicly shown sound film—starring John Barrymore. It is the first mainstream film that successfully coordinates audio sound on a recorded disc synchronized to play in conjunction with a projected motion picture. The sounds in the film consist of effects and music, but no dialogue.

23 AUGUST Film star Rudolph Valentino dies at thirty-one of septicemia after surgery for a perforated gastric ulcer.

9 SEPTEMBER NBC, the National Broadcasting Company, is incorporated in the United States as an offshoot of the Radio Corporation of America (RCA).

31 OCTOBER Magician Harry Houdini dies of gangrene and peritonitis that develops after his appendix ruptures.

15 NOVEMBER NBC is inaugurated as a radio network, comprising twenty-four stations, with a 4½-hour program hosted from the Waldorf-Astoria Hotel in New York and involving feeds from Chicago (soprano Mary Garden) and Independence, Kansas (Will Rogers).

1927

11 MAY The Academy of Motion Picture Arts and Sciences is founded by Louis B. Mayer. Its first president is Douglas Fairbanks.

18 MAY Grauman's Chinese Theater, later famed for hand- and footprints of various film stars and celebrities, opens in Hollywood.

20–21 MAY Cheers greet *The Spirit of St. Louis* when Charles Lindbergh lands his plane in Paris. He makes the first nonstop solo transatlantic flight in the history of aviation, flying 3,600 miles in over thirty-three hours from New York to Paris, forsaking a radio for additional gasoline.

30 SEPTEMBER In baseball, Babe Ruth sets a new record, hitting his sixtieth home run in a season. The record will stand for thirty-four years.

6 OCTOBER *The Jazz Singer*, a part-talking film, opens.

27 OCTOBER Fox Movietone News premieres the first sound newsreel in New York.

1928

15 AND 18 MAY Mickey Mouse debuts in the silent cartoon *Plane Crazy* and in *Steamboat Willie*, the first fully synchronized sound cartoon.

28 MAY All major Hollywood studios adopt sound-on-film systems, rejecting Warner Bros.'s Vitaphone sound-on-disc format.

17–18 JUNE Amelia Earhart becomes the first woman to fly across the Atlantic (as a passenger).

6 JULY Warner Bros.'s *The Lights of New York* premieres as the first all-talking feature-length motion picture.

31 JULY For the first time, Metro-Goldwyn-Mayer films start with a logo of a roaring lion shown in a frame, accompanied by MGM's new motto, "Ars gratia artis" (Art for art's sake). The logo was based on the original Goldwyn Pictures logo and the Lion was called Slats.

3 SEPTEMBER Penicillin is discovered.

6 NOVEMBER Republican Herbert Hoover, secretary of commerce in the Coolidge administration, is elected the thirty-first president of the United States, defeating New York governor Al Smith.

1929

14 FEBRUARY The St. Valentine's Day Massacre, a gangland "hit," takes place in a Chicago garage. Seven are killed.

16 MAY The first Academy of Motion Picture Arts and Sciences awards ceremony (the Academy Awards) is held at the Roosevelt Hotel in Hollywood to honor the films of 1927 and 1928.

28 MAY *On with the Show!*, the first all-color, all-talking picture, premieres.

27 JUNE Bell Laboratories makes the first U.S. public demonstration of color television in New York. The images they show are those of roses and an American flag.

24 AND 29 OCTOBER The stock market crash begins with "Black Thursday" and "Black Tuesday."

2 NOVEMBER The first news cinema—the Embassy on Broadway in New York City—opens. It would close in 1949 due to competition from television.

American Cinema of the 1920s

Foolish Wives (1922). Count Karamzin (Erich von Stroheim) romances Mrs. Hughes (Miss DuPont) on the porch of a European hotel.

INTRODUCTION

Movies and the 1920s

LUCY FISCHER

"It was an age of miracles, it was an age of art, it was an age of excess . . ."
—F. Scott Fitzgerald

An Age of Miracles

Writing in November 1931, F. Scott Fitzgerald stated: "It is too soon to write about the Jazz Age with perspective" (13). It may have been then, but it is not now. Furthermore, there are many aspects of the decade that make it an especially fascinating one to chronicle—both in terms of American cultural and film history.

As for the first realm, it was an age of great drama, book-ended, as it was, between two cataclysmic events—World War I and the stock market crash. Beyond that, it begins and ends with a depression (though the earlier crisis is less spectacular than the later). Furthermore, the decade has been seen as a highly representative one. As Joseph Wood Krutch noted at the decade's finale: "The 1920s illuminates fundamental issues of the twentieth century" (12). Years later, Nathan Miller came to a similar conclusion: "It is indeed a judgment call to select one decade to describe the warp and woof of American history, but the 1920s present themselves admirably for such treatment. To an astonishing extent, the 1920s resemble our own era, at the turn of the twenty-first century. . . . Much of what we consider contemporary actually began in the Twenties" (1). Likewise, the classical Hollywood cinema also had its roots in the twenties: the studio and star systems, talking pictures, color photography, bona fide theaters, and the movies' status as a major American industry. In fact, ever since, the fates of American society and the movies have been inextricably entwined.

The twenties began on the heels of the Great War—a momentous global conflict pitting the United States and her allies (France, Britain, Russia, Italy) against the Central Powers (Germany, Austria-Hungary, and Turkey). This international catastrophe was to cast a long shadow on the decade that followed. As Frederick Lewis Allen observed at the time: "Since 1919 the circumstances of American life have been transformed" (1). Clearly, this metamorphosis entailed an end to American isolationism. As Ronald Allen Goldberg later noted: "For the first time in history, the mass of Americans had been brought into contact with events abroad and the previous nineteenth-century insular American view of the world was under serious challenge" (2). In part, such internationalism was disillusioning. Allen observed that, for some, there was a sense that "life was futile and nothing mattered much" (67). For F. Scott Fitzgerald, "the events of 1919 left [people] cynical" but simultaneously emboldened. As he remarked: "We were the most powerful nation. Who could tell us any longer what was fashionable and what was fun?" (14).

Though a few American films tackled wartime subjects early on (notably *Hearts of the World*, directed by D. W. Griffith, and *Heart of Humanity*, directed by Allen Holubar, both from 1918), it was not until the mid- to late-twenties that a series of significant works on the topic emerged. One of the most notable was Paramount's *Wings* (1927), directed by William Wellman, which focused on American pilots overseas—their camaraderie and the tragedy of lives lost. One lighthearted sequence in the film, however, contrasts naive Americans with their sophisticated European counterparts, in line with the era's song lyric: "How You Gonna Keep 'em Down on the Farm after They've Seen Paree?" (1919). Following a hard-fought battle, American soldiers are given leave in France's capital, which is represented as a gleeful site of mass debauchery (in contrast to the Puritanical USA). Once in the city, the doughboys frequent a café where, unlike Prohibition-era America, liquor flows freely. The film's hero (played by Charles "Buddy" Rogers) immediately gets drunk and hallucinates bubbles floating before his eyes. Beyond inebriates, the club is populated by women in shocking, low-cut gowns as well as by lesbians garbed in masculine attire. While war news brought Americans closer to their allies (the French and English), at home German Americans were suddenly suspect, which is clear from the treatment of a character in *Wings*. Herman Schwimpf (El Brendel), a U.S. soldier, must constantly prove his patriotism to distrustful anti-Prussian platoon mates. The title of the film also foregrounds American aviation of the period, an important aspect of the fighting corps in World War I; Wellman, who had been a pilot, was the perfect director for the project. Beyond the battlefield, American aviation saw great progress on the commercial front—with Charles Lindbergh's nonstop flight from New York to Paris in May 1927 and Amelia Earhart's journey as the first transatlantic female airplane passenger in June 1928.

As the twenties dawned, America also experienced massive social change. As Robert Sklar writes in *The Plastic Age*: "American culture was newborn" (1). While some have seen this transformation as a compensatory reaction to the shock of worldwide conflagration, others have found it prefigured in the teens (Dumenil 3). One of the major alterations was a shift from rural to metropolitan life. As Allen notes, the decade saw the "conquest of the whole country by urban tastes and urban dress and the urban way of living" (152). This change is articulated in numerous ways in the films of the decade. First, there is the avant-garde "city symphony," almost always set in New York. *Manhatta* (1921), made by photographer Paul Strand and painter Charles Sheeler, is a realist but poetic paean to the beauty and majesty of the city—its ports, skyscrapers, automobiles, bridges, and trains. Similarly, Robert Flaherty's *Twenty-four-Dollar Island* (1926) is a documentary "Camera Impression" of New York that casts the metropolis as its "central character." Some works, however, were more experimental in expressing their love affair with the city. Fox News released a "Loony Lens" series. Some footage, shot by cameraman Al Brick between 1924 and 1927, displays anamorphic images of the city, spinning views, and split screen shots that make it look like buildings are collapsing into one another. As an intertitle quips, New York is a "dizzy" place that is "all a whirl." There were those cultural critics, however, who took a more cynical view of the urban terrain—emphasizing the alienation of the anonymous masses. As Harold Stearns noted:

> Consider . . . the average city man's daily routine. He gets up. . . . He shaves and washes his teeth, using a standardised razor and soap and tooth-brush. He gets into standardised clothes and eats a more or less standardised breakfast. Then he comes to his office by train or subway, reading his morning newspaper; which again hundreds of thousands of others are doing at that same moment of time. . . . At his office he goes through the routine of his business, sharing the crowd-assumptions of the organisation of which he is a part, and in general sharing the wider assumptions of the whole business-world in which his particular organisation functions. After a hasty lunch eaten with the crowd he goes back to the afternoon routine; and then goes home with the crowd. . . . Thus he spends the larger part of the day as a member of a crowd. (59–60)

Even *Manhatta* referenced intimidating crowds in its view of hordes of people exiting a ferry at rush hour and in titles that spoke of a "million footed Manhattan" that, when "unpent, descends to its pavements." But feature films like Paul Fejos's *Lonesome* (1928) take this critique of the city to a higher level through its portrait of two working-class youths—a man and woman—who each toil separately at their respective jobs (machinist and phone operator). Isolated and anonymous in the harsh city, they are desperately lonely until they meet in Coney Island only to realize that they have lived in the same rooming house all along. Here, we are reminded of a statement by journalist/sociologist Agnes Smedley, who recalled her early days in New York in the 1920s as "vast, impersonal [and] merciless": "Always before I had felt like a person, an individual, hopeful that I could mold my life according to some desire of my own. But here in New York I was ignorant, insignificant, unimportant—one in millions whose destiny concerned no one. New York did not even know of my existence. Nor did it care" (234–35).

Significantly, while much of urban space was seen as cold and alienating, the amusement park was regarded as a site of pleasure and excitement, not only in *Lonesome* but in *The Crowd* (1928) and *Sunrise* (1927). In several such films couples travel to Coney Island by subway (or, in the case of *Sunrise,* by trolley). Here, we are reminded that the twenties was the age in which electricity became ubiquitous in urban America. As David Kyvig notes, by 1920, some 24 million homes were electrified—a factor primary in "differentiat[ing] urban from rural life" (56, 45). Starting in the twenties, in fact, electrical appliances began to appear on the consumer market: sewing and washing machines, toasters, refrigerators, and vacuum cleaners (the latter being an object that the hero of *The Crowd* half-heartedly sells door-to-door). Indicative of this, filmed advertisements for electrical products became commonplace in the era, as is clear from one made in 1926 (by the Electric League of Pittsburgh) promoting a refrigerator available at a local store. Similarly, the instructional film *De-Light: Making an Electric Light Bulb* (1920), produced by the Ford Motor Company, touts the marvels of modern-day lighting. Even a fiction film took on the subject. James Young's *Welcome Stranger* (1924) tells the story of a Jewish man who moves his family to a Christian New England town and overcomes provincial prejudice by bringing the town prosperity through investing in a local electric light factory.

While America had enjoyed a boom economy during wartime (since Europe was in chaos and its commercial and agricultural resources decimated), the immediate postwar period brought a mild depression that affected farmers most of all. As the twenties progressed, however, succeeding business-friendly Republican presidential administrations (those of Warren Harding [1921–1923] and Calvin Coolidge [1923–1929]) brought "seven years of unparalleled plenty" (Allen 138). Between 1922 and 1927 the purchasing power of American wages increased at a rate of 2 percent annually. Among the industries responsible for the boom were those producing automobiles, radio, rayon, cigarettes, refrigerators, telephones, cosmetics, electrical devices, and movies (Allen 140–44). Much of this output was due to the continued industrialization of America.

With consumerism on the rise (as spurred by an emphasis on salesmanship), the department store became a major commercial site (Allen 144). Fred Newmeyer's and Sam Taylor's *Safety Last* (1923) is set in one such establishment, with Harold Lloyd cast as a salesman. As the story proceeds, Lloyd tries to impress his supervisors by proposing an exciting promotional publicity stunt to bring business to the emporium: having someone scale its tall façade. Though he means for his friend to execute the feat, he ends up having to do it himself—the source of much comedy. As Allen notes, "Never before [the twenties] had such pressure been exerted upon salesmen to get results" (146).

It was the affluence of the period (and what Fitzgerald deemed its attendant "excesses") that earned the decade the moniker of "Roaring Twenties." Not surprisingly, countless films depicted scenes of wealth and glamour, with well-dressed socialites partying in smartly appointed rooms—works like Harry Beaumont's *Our Dancing Daughters* (1928) and Jack Conway's *Our Modern Maidens* (1929). In many of these, people are seen drinking liquor despite Prohibition, which lasted the entire decade. In the depiction of such luxurious settings, the high production values of Hollywood were fully marshaled—with each studio employing a stable of chic costumers (like Adrian, Orry-Kelly, Travis Banton, and Max Rée) and set designers (like Cedric Gibbons, Joseph Urban, Richard Day, and William Cameron Menzies).

But it was not only the economy that "roared" in the twenties. Women were empowered by their new voting rights, sanctioned in the Nineteenth Amendment to the Constitution in 1920. As Miller observed: "The emancipated woman was the standard-bearer of the modern age" (46). On screen, however, the decade began with some rather conventional portrayals of female characters. In *Way Down East* (1920), D. W. Griffith (a director associated with codes of nineteenth-century melodrama) revived an old theatrical standard concerning a Victorian heroine (Lillian Gish) duped into false marriage and made pregnant by her "groom." Thereafter, she faces the stigma of being an unwed mother, despite the fact that she has lost her child. Even here, however, there is a moment of rebellion as the young maid accuses men of perpetrating a double standard, by which they are blameless for their sexual intrigues while women are culpable. But it is the "flapper" who constitutes the most notorious feminine icon of the period—the young woman (often middle or upper-middle class) who revolts against the trappings of Victorian propriety by wearing short skirts, smoking, applying makeup, dancing, drinking, and partying. It is such a figure we see embodied by Joan Crawford and her girlfriends in *Our Dancing Daughters* or by Clara Bow and her fellow coeds in *The Wild Party* (1929). Given this hedonism it is no surprise that Fitzgerald sees the era characterized by a "general decision to be amused" (15). But the focus on female liberation took other more serious forms in the twenties. In *Wings*, Clara Bow plays an ambulance driver in World War I Europe. On the home front, however, the number of women working increased as countless single girls came to the city to find employment in offices and stores. Reflecting this situation, in John W. Harkrider and Millard Webb's *Glorifying the American Girl* (1929), Gloria Hughes (Mary Eaton) plays a young woman who works in the sheet music section of a department store before she succeeds as a performer.

Associated with the flapper was a burgeoning "youth culture." Fitzgerald proudly claimed that the "wildest of all generations" (by which he meant that which had come of age during "the confusion of the War") had "danced" its way "into the limelight." As he continued: "The old America groaned in his sleep as he waited to be poisoned . . . [as] we had things our way at last" (14–15). With some 23 million passenger cars on the roads by 1929 (Allen 141), youngsters were driving automobiles and venturing beyond the family terrain, especially when it came to romantic encounters. Thus, we are not surprised to find that the car (with what Fitzgerald called its "mobile privacy" [14]) plays a major role in many films: *Our Dancing Daughters*, *Wings*, Lois Weber's *The Blot* (1921), and Cecil B. DeMille's *Manslaughter* (1922).

As for gender roles, the twenties also saw the rise of the so-called New Woman—a more mature figure than the flapper or shop girl, one who demanded equality on the sexual as well as the sociopolitical front. As might be expected, however, Hollywood focused most on the former front—with sophisticated stars like Greta Garbo personifying the modern liberated female. Thus, in works like John Robertson's *The Single Standard* (1929), the heroine demands what the title indicates (rather than a double standard) and (like a man) has a passionate affair. Garbo's character does the same in Jacques Feyder's *The Kiss* (1929)—even going so far as to inadvertently murder her husband. Similarly, in works such as Erich von Stroheim's *Foolish Wives* (1922), a woman vacationing in Europe is "forgiven" for flirting with a Continental cad (von Stroheim) because her gauche American husband ignores her and denies her an emotionally and sexually satisfying relationship. Significantly, only four years later, Margaret Sanger publishes *Happiness in Marriage* (Miller 264). While many applauded the sexual freedom of the twenties, others raised a cautionary note. As Joseph Wood Krutch remarked: "When the consequences of love were made less momentous, then love itself became less momentous too, and we have discovered that the now-lifted veil of mystery was that which made it potentially important as well as potentially terrible. Sex, we learned, was not so awesome as once we had thought. . . . Love is becoming so accessible, so unmysterious and so free that its value is trivial" (69).

Von Stroheim, of course, did not simply *play* a European in *Foolish Wives* and other films; he *was* one, and thus joined a fraternity of émigré directors working in Hollywood: Jacques Feyder, F. W. Murnau, Benjamin Christensen, Victor Sjöström, and Mauritz Stiller, among them. Many of these artists had been wooed to California in the wake of a wave of critically acclaimed European art films (for example, *Metropolis* [1927], *The Last Laugh* [1924], *The Passion of Joan of Arc* [1928]), as the movie moguls tried to lend a touch of class to the American film industry, that bastion of commerce. Similarly, in the silent era (when mastering English was not required), many foreign-born actors flourished in Hollywood, not only von Stroheim and Garbo but Nils Asther, Emil Jannings, Pola Negri, and Lars Hanson.

Europe held great fascination for Americans at this time. On one level, it was seen as the center of style—with the influential Paris *Exposition des artes décoratifs and industriels modernes* of 1925 heralding avant-garde movement of fashion and design. For others, Europe was the hub of intellectual and artistic consciousness. Hence many American literary figures (such as Ernest Hemingway, T. S. Eliot, and Gertrude Stein) lived there as expatriates, causing Harold Stearns to decry "the steady denudation of the United States of its imaginative and adventurous and artistically creative" young people (158). Similarly, Allen mentions a *Harper's* article about American talent abroad entitled "Babes in the *Bois*" (207). Furthermore, within the discourse of Hollywood narrative, Europe was seen as an exotic playground for wealthy Americans in a new age of deluxe ocean travel. Thus, in Frank Borzage's *They Had to See Paris* (1929), the family of a newly rich Kansas City oil man (played by Will Rogers) goes to France in order to get "culture," "meet the right people," and gain a "different point of view."

Meanwhile, sensational scandals began to envelop Hollywood. Actor Wallace Reid, celebrated for having played a moneyed American who voyages to Monte Carlo to party and gamble while simultaneously decrying Continental aristocratic culture in James Cruze's *Hawthorne of the U.S.A.* (1919), became addicted to painkillers after treatment for an on-set injury and, after checking into a clinic for detoxification in 1922, died the following January. Also in 1922, director William Desmond Taylor was found murdered. To make matters worse, these unsavory occurrences followed on the heels of another film-colony tabloid incident. In 1921, comic star Roscoe "Fatty" Arbuckle attended a three-day "orgy" in a San Francisco hotel at the end of which a young woman (Virginia Rappe) was found dead. Arbuckle was tried for her rape and murder and, although acquitted, his film career was ruined by the bad publicity he had received. As a result of such events (as well as risqué representations of sex on screen), the public called for increased movie censorship. Attempting to forestall government regulation, the industry instituted a policy of self-control and, in 1922, hired William Hays (former postmaster general of the United States and ex-chair of the Republican National Committee) to head the Motion Picture Producers and Distributors of America (MPPDA). He included moral clauses in actor's contracts and authored a Production Code that would guide the making of Hollywood films for decades. Of course, the scandals did not cease with Hays's arrival; in 1924, Charles Chaplin married sixteen-year-old Lita Grey, an adolescent he had impregnated. In the same year, producer Thomas Ince died of mysterious circumstances aboard the yacht of William Randolph Hearst (Miller 242).

Such scandals, of course, would not have held much interest for the public had the film industry not already created a vast "star system," and among the most popular of the era were Rudolph Valentino, John Gilbert, John Barrymore, Joan Crawford, Gloria Swanson, Clara Bow, and Lillian Gish. With actors under contract to particular studios, the latter had great control over their employees' lives. They could change their names (from Lucille LeSuer to Joan Crawford, from Greta Louisa Gustafsson to Greta Garbo, from Asa Yoelson to Al Jolson), arrange for them to undergo plastic surgery, tell them whom to date, decide what screen roles they would play, and launch publicity campaigns to control their image (with requisite magazine interviews, articles, and photographs). If one were a superstar (like Chaplin), one might have one's own studio, as did he on La Brea and Sunset Avenues. Furthermore, in 1919, Chaplin, along with Mary Pickford, D. W. Griffith, and Douglas Fairbanks, had started their own film company, United Artists.

But a "stable" of performers was only one part of a studio's capital in the twenties. Organized like an industrial assembly plant based on Ford's prototype, the studios had departments of screenwriting, cinematography, editing, costume design, art direction, and construction—as is clear from a promotional documentary, *MGM Studio Tour* (1925), which shows off stars (including Joan Crawford), costumers (Erté), writers (Elinor Glyn), and directors (Josef von Sternberg, Erich von Stroheim, and Christy Cabanne). Other production companies of the era were Paramount, Universal, Fox, and Warner Bros. Studios were also engaged in ongoing technological research and development. Lighting advances were made in the era, and

MGM Studio Tour proudly presents Tod Browning shooting illuminated night scenes for *The Mystic* (1925) instead of utilizing daytime shots printed on blue stock. The twenties also saw the introduction of the two-strip Technicolor process, used in sequences of Rupert Julian's *The Phantom of the Opera* (1925) and von Stroheim's *The Wedding March* (1928).

Of course, the watershed technical innovation of the twenties was the coming of sound. But in truth it was a misnomer because silent films were almost always accompanied by live music and/or theatrical sound effects. What was new in the mid-twenties was that sound was now recorded along with the film image (either on a disc or on the film strip) and mechanically synchronized to the print. While the coming of sound is usually dated to 1926–1927, there were earlier sound-on-film movies (1924–1925) made as tests by Theodore Case, an electrician who worked with Lee de Forest on developing the technology. A few present Case talking to the camera, trying out his sibilant *s*'s; others depict one man playing a harmonica, another playing a harp, a Chinese man in folk costume singing a popular American song in Chinese, and Gus Vesser and His Singing Duck, who quacks each time Vesser sings the word *Ma* in the song "Ma, He's Makin' Eyes at Me."

The first feature silent film released with a synchronized score was Alan Crosland's *Don Juan* (1926). The first "part-talking" feature was the same director's *The Jazz Singer* (1927), starring Al Jolson, a work that alternated between sequences of mimed silence and synchronized singing and dialogue. The first "all-talking" picture was Bryan Foy's *Lights of New York* (1928). All were produced by Warner Bros. The arrival of sound issued in a new crew of movie actors. Some entered from the Broadway stage: "legitimate" players like Melvyn Douglas and Helen Hayes, comedians like the Marx Brothers, and hoofers like Fred Astaire. Others came from radio, which "was an even more powerful medium of mass cultural diffusion than movies [because it] was accessible to a much larger audience—to the ill and the infirm, the very young and the very old, those who could not easily go out to enjoy the pleasures of a movie or an auto ride" (Sklar, *Plastic* 77). The first radio station opened in Pittsburgh in 1920 and, within short order, people spoke of a "radio craze" (Allen 67, 71). By 1927, there were some six million radio sets in the country with their owners listening one to two hours per day (Sklar, *Plastic* 90). Radios also show up on screen. In Ernst Lubitsch's *So This Is Paris* (1926), when an American woman abroad cannot attend a Parisian ball with her husband, she listens to it on the hotel wireless.

While *The Jazz Singer* propagated a version of white jazz (and a racist one encapsulated in the song "Mammy"), the coming of sound also allowed black performers to have opportunities in film that went beyond the usual

The Jazz Singer opened at New York City's Warners' Theatre on 6 October 1927.

stereotypical roles. Clearly, such advances mirrored those of the contemporaneous Harlem Renaissance, a movement that drew attention to black artists (be they musicians, poets, novelists, or painters). Hence such jazz entertainers as Bessie Smith appeared in shorts like Dudley Murphy's *St. Louis Blues* (1929).

While the Hollywood drama was showing off its latest technical innovation (the sound film) and celebrating modernity in general, another genre of cinema—the documentary—was focusing, in a contradictory and nostalgic fashion, on the last bastions of the world of "Primitivism." The nonfiction feature film saw its birth with the commercial success of Robert Flaherty's *Nanook of the North* (1922), which presented the life of an Inuit family in northern Canada. Flaherty followed this success with *Moana* (1926), which depicted the universe of Polynesian islanders in the South Seas. Then, Flaherty collaborated with W. S. Van Dyke on another film set in that region, *White Shadows in the South Seas* (1928), but eventually pulled out for artistic reasons. Finally, the documentary *Grass* (1925), made by Merian Cooper and Ernest Schoedsack (the team that would later direct *King Kong* in 1933), concerns the Bakhtiari people of the Middle East who make a grueling annual trek with their families and livestock from one grazing area to another. All these works fall short of nonfiction in the true sense of the term, blending documentary material and staged or restaged action. Beyond a longing for pre-industrial times, the era's fascination with the Exotic was fueled by colonialism, expanded ocean and air travel, and the unearthing of King Tut's tomb in Egypt in 1922.

While the documentary was decidedly outside the mainstream of commercial film production, the most marginal genre was the experimental film, which nonetheless took off in the 1920s both in Europe and the United States. One from 1925 is entitled *Cockeyed Gems from the Memory of a Nutty Cameraman*. Here, the filmmaker (Alvin Knechtel) uses nonfiction footage to play with the medium, breaking away from realism to test out bizarre cinematic special effects. In *The Life and Death of 9413, a Hollywood Extra* (1928), Robert Florey and Slavko Vorkapich use graphic cut-outs and models to create an abstract Expressionist portrait of the tragedy and travails of an anonymous actor who comes to Hollywood expecting success in the entertainment industry, only to find failure, poverty, and death. *The Loves of Zero* (1927), also involving a collaboration between Florey and Vorkapich, is another Expressionist drama (influenced by the German film *The Cabinet of Dr. Caligari* [1920]), made for only $200. It depicts (with distorted sets, canted camera angles, symbolic objects, split-screens, and prismatic photography) a heartrending love affair between a man and a woman that ends in the latter's death. *Hands—The Life and Loves of the Gentler Sex* (1927–28), made by Stella Simon and Miklos Bandy (with music composed and performed by Mark Blitzstein), is a drama enacted entirely with people's arms and hands set against an abstract background; it seeks to portray the tense and combative world of male-female relations. (Significantly, in James Thurber's and E. B. White's 1929 satirical book *Is Sex Necessary?* the glossary defines the word "attack" as "Man's method of showing interest in women" [189].) Two experimental works of 1928 adapt Edgar Allan Poe short stories: *The Fall of the House of Usher* (1928), made in Rochester by James Sibley Watson and Melville Webber, and *The Telltale Heart* (1928) by Charles Klein. Both show the Expressionist influence of *Caligari* with their shadowplay, angular, distorted sets, and interest in visually representing insanity. Another film, *In Youth, Beside the Lonely Sea* (1925), of unknown authorship, employs a triptych of contiguous "screens" to visualize a 1907 poem by Thomas Aldrich Bailey. Finally, Dudley Murphy's *The Soul of the Cypress* (1921) employs documentary footage of Point Lobos, California, to depict the legend of a musician who becomes enamored of a nymph who lures him to an ocean death. Stylistically, it utilizes starkly silhouetted trees and rocks, superimposition, and color tinting to lend the tale a supernatural aura.

An "Unhappy Time"

> "As for this present unhappy time, haunted by ghosts from a dead world and not yet at home in its own, its predicament is not . . . unlike the predicament of the adolescent who has not yet learned to orient himself. . . . He still seeks in the world of his experience for the values he had found there, and he is aware only of a vast disharmony." (Krutch 18)

While many aspects of the twenties were heady and uplifting (its economic boom, its liberal morality, its new roles for women, its booming film industry, its technical advances), others were less salutary. The plot of *The Jazz Singer* signals one of these features, since it concerns the son of an immigrant Jewish cantor who feels he must renounce his religion and change his name to meet success in the world of American popular culture. Clearly, ethnic poverty and prejudice were central problems in the twenties, following on the heels of a huge wave of eastern and southern European immigration to the United States begun in the 1890s. By 1924, the backlash against immigrants was so great that laws were changed to delimit America's "open-door" policy. In fact, the National Origins Act pushed the base period for determining national immigration quotas back to 1890, thus favoring northern Europeans (Miller 147).

Contributing to this counterattack was the infamous Sacco and Vanzetti case. In 1920 a Massachusetts paymaster and guard were killed during a robbery and two Italian immigrants with alleged anarchist leanings were charged with the crime. Nicola Sacco and Bartolomeo Vanzetti were found guilty in 1921 and executed in 1927, though the case against them was considered to have been biased from the start. Anti-Italian prejudice was also seen in response to one of the major film stars of the era, Rudolph Valentino, who immigrated to the United States from Castellaneta in 1913. Some films of the twenties considered the plight of the immigrant: E. Mason Harper's *Hungry Hearts* (1922), Edward Sloman's *His People* (1925), Sidney Olcott's *Salome of the Tenements* (1925), and Frank Capra's *The Younger Generation* (1929). While these works concentrated on Jews, they often portrayed other ethnic groups. In *His People*, the Jewish family's best friends are their Irish neighbors across the courtyard; and in Phil Rosen's *Rose of the Tenements* (1926), an Italian girl is adopted by an elderly Jewish couple. Clearly, such works were a countervailing force to the virulent antisemitism of the era, fueled by a series of articles in the *Dearborn Independent* (industrialist Henry Ford's newspaper), later retitled *The International Jew: The World's Foremost Problem*.

If immigrants had a difficult time being accepted in the twenties, it was even harder for African Americans, former slaves. The postwar era saw their migration to northern urban centers, which created tensions and rivalry with white workers. Not surprisingly, the decade saw an increase in race riots, the most notable in Greenwood, Oklahoma, a black enclave of Tulsa (Miller 94). The twenties also saw the revival of the Ku Klux Klan, and on 9 August 1925, the organization held a huge rally in Washington, D.C. (Miller 29). Despite blacks being celebrated on screen for their sophisticated music and dance, in most films they were demeaned by racist portrayals. For example, in Max and Dave Fleischer's comic film *Chemical Ko-Ko* (1929), a black janitor drinks a magic potion that turns him white. As soon as this happens, he puts down his mop and pail, no longer willing to work at a menial job. With such insulting cinematic portrayals, black audiences turned to "race movies"—films with all-black casts that dealt with subjects relevant to African American life (residing in the North versus the South, the specter of lynching, the "uplift" movement, the role of religion). While some of these films were produced or directed by white men (such as Frank Peregini's *The Scar of Shame* [1927]), others were created by black filmmakers—most notably Oscar Micheaux—who made some twenty films in the decade, among them *Within Our Gates* (1920) and *Body and Soul* (1925). On rare occasions, Hollywood made a film that focused on African American characters, like Paul Sloane's *Hearts in Dixie* (1929), which concerns an elderly man who tries to save his grandson from his shiftless father (played by Stepin Fetchit).

The twenties was also an era of labor unrest in America. Numerous steel strikes took place in 1920, as did a bombing on Wall Street near the House of Morgan (Allen 40, 62). Often, labor organizers were viewed as traitorous Communists. Attorney General A. Mitchell Palmer (who conducted numerous raids in 1920) had, in fact, predicted a Bolshevik coup for the same year. Often radical politics were associated with particular ethnicities—especially with Jews from Eastern Europe who were tainted by the shadow of the Russian Revolution. As Allen reports, Americans "were listening to ugly rumors of a huge radical conspiracy against the government and institutions of the United States. They had their ears cocked for the detonation of bombs and the tramp of Bolshevist armies. They seriously thought . . . that a Red revolution might begin in the United States the next month or next week" (39).

Given that Hollywood's depiction of activists was pejorative, some leftist groups joined together to craft their own alternative films, such as *The Passaic Textile Strike* (1926), about an actual labor dispute in New Jersey. Made by Sam Russak, it starred nonprofessional actors from the worker community and intermixed scripted and documentary footage. Despite the force of anti-radical rhetoric, some Americans were troubled by the Palmer raids and their attendant restrictions of rights. As Katherine Fullerton Gerould wrote in a 1922 issue of *Harper's Magazine*:

> [The USA] is no longer a free country, in the old sense; and liberty is, increasingly, a mere rhetorical figure. . . . No thinking citizen, I venture to say, can express in freedom more than a part of his honest convictions. I do not of course refer to convictions that are frankly criminal. I do mean that everywhere, on every hand, free speech is choked off in one direction or another. The only way in which an American citizen who is really interested in all the social and political problems of his country can preserve any freedom of expression, is to choose the mob that is most sympathetic to him, and abide under the shadow of that mob. (qtd. in Allen 53–54)

In many films (like *The Big Parade*, which contained a comic scene of GIs inebriated and partying in Paris), the excesses of youthful drinking during Prohibition were treated lightly. As Will Rogers once quipped: "Prohibition is better than no liquor at all." In other works, however, the consequences of overindulgence were given a tragic spin. In *Our Dancing Daughters*, for example, a tipsy young woman falls to her death down a steep flight of stairs. Significantly, while the bar of the pre-Prohibition era was a decidedly male bastion, the speakeasy catered to both sexes (Allen 86; Miller 102). Prohibition (1920–1933) also ushered in a crime wave with such notable outlaws as Al Capone, the mastermind behind the sensational St. Valentine's Day Massacre of 1929. Reflecting this milieu, gangster films became popular. Howard Higgin's *The Racketeer* (1929), for instance, tells the story of an elegant mobster who circulates in high society. Alternately, Roland West's *Alibi* (1929), a more inspired work, focuses on working-class thugs and draws on Expressionist techniques that anticipate 1940s film noir. Prohibition was, of course, a multi-determined phenomenon. In part, it was an attack on immigrant populations and their alleged saloon cultures. On the other hand, it was tied to a resurgence of religious fundamentalism that reacted against the perceived loss of sacred authority to popular culture and science. As Krutch noted: "Illusions have been lost one by one. God, instead of disappearing in an instant, has retreated step by step and surrendered gradually his control of the universe. . . . Man is left more and more alone in a universe to which he is completely alien" (Krutch 7). Significant, in this regard, was the infamous Scopes trial, which began on 10 July 1925, whereby a school teacher was prosecuted and convicted for instructing students about evolution versus creationism (Krutch 7).

Finally, a few movies of the period aimed a skeptical eye at the American Stock Exchange, the very institution that would crash in October 1929, bringing a close to the Roaring Twenties. A 1920 Keaton film entitled *The Saphead* (directed by Herbert Blaché for Metro) is set on Wall Street and involves a speculator who tries artificially to lower the dividend price of a mining stock for his own monetary gain, just the kind of fraud that helped topple the market some nine years later (Allen 145). Similarly, in *The Kiss,* released on 15 November 1929 (only seventeen days after the stock market crash), a character faces dire financial straits due to some market catastrophe. When he dies, people assume his financial loss has led him to suicide. Significantly, F. Scott Fitzgerald says that the Jazz Age "leaped to a spectacular death in October 1929" (13).

Hooray for Hollywood

> "It is impossible now to even think of the saturation point for motion pictures. . . . It can hardly fail to become as universal an experience as reading from the printed page." (Halsey 214)

Throughout the boom and bust of the twenties the American film industry continued to grow and prosper, finding ways to sell movies that celebrated the nation's victories (war, prosperity, technology) and exploited its lapses (crime, Prohibition, scandal). A financial publication of 1926 reported the following statistics about American cinema: the nation had 20,000 movie theaters (two-fifths of the world's total) (Halsey 172). Many of these were so-called "picture palaces," beautifully appointed motion picture showplaces, like the Chicago Theater in Illinois (1921), the Loew's Penn in Pittsburgh (1925), and Grauman's Chinese (1927) and Egyptian (1922) in Los Angeles. The combined seating capacity of all American theaters was 18 million. About 100 million Americans attended the movies each week, close to the total population of the United States (Halsey 183). The income gleaned from these admissions came to some $750 million (Halsey 184). Investment in the American film industry reached about $1.5 billion, with the sector employing some 350,000 people (Halsey 172–73). Most studios produced some fifty films each year and supplied 90 percent of the world's movies (Halsey 176, 179).

As we know, from today's perspective, though the American film industry was grand in the 1920s, it was still in its infancy. Yet, observers realized, even then, that it was already a dominant world force. As the anonymous author of Halsey, Stuart and Company's financial report wrote in 1926: "It does not seem extravagant to prophesy that the motion pictures will come to be regarded as almost as necessary to healthful living as the food which . . . people eat [and] the clothes they wear. The industry behind all this promises to be and will long continue [to be] one of the most serviceable to mankind" (188–89). In so stating, he might well have borrowed Al Jolson's famous line from *The Jazz Singer* and proclaimed to the world: "You ain't seen nothin' yet."

And, of course, it hadn't.

The Decade in Review

The essays that follow examine the decade of the twenties on a year-by-year basis, discussing important themes of the era that intersect with the history of American film.

In his chapter on 1920 ("Movies, Margarine, and Main Street"), Michael Aronson places certain films within the context of their exhibition. Rather than focus on the big city, he examines the practice in five small American towns in Pennsylvania, Ohio, Michigan, and Wisconsin. In so doing, he draws on local newspapers to track which films were shown as well as how they were received and advertised. Among the works he discusses is *Billions,* featuring Russian actress Alla Nazimova and set designs by Natacha Rambova (later to become Mrs. Rudolph Valentino). The narrative concerns the fate of a wealthy émigré princess living in America and her melodramatic amorous entanglements. Alternately, in *Sex,* Louise Glaum plays a "vamp" (a favorite stereotype of the period), whom a Monessen, Pennsylvania, newspaper critic deemed an "alluring home wrecker." In *Pollyanna,* Mary Pickford incarnates her established role as "little Mary," despite being twenty-six at the time. As the title indicates, she plays a perennially optimistic girl who, though paralyzed, triumphs merrily over adversity. *Suds* (which ran in Coshocton, Ohio) gives Pickford a chance at a less sunny role as Amanda, a London laundress whose dreams of being saved by an imaginary Prince Charming come to naught. Pickford's new husband, Douglas Fairbanks, also appears in a film of the year—*Zorro*—which gives him an opportunity to display his athletic skills in yet another swashbuckling adventure. All three Pickford/Fairbanks movies were produced by their recently formed production company United Artists. Finally, Aronson examines a film by a master of silent comedy, Buster Keaton. In *The Saphead* (which showed in Van Wert, Ohio, a scant month after its New York premiere), Keaton plays a wealthy but dull young man who accidentally manages to save his family from financial ruin on the stock market floor. Given that this was Keaton's first feature film, the ad in the Van Wert newspaper focuses more on the author of the literary source than on the screen performer.

In "Movies and Personality," Mark Lynn Anderson surveys 1921 for the manner in which the films of the year (including their reception and cultural context) bespeak a new fascination in America with celebrity and the "unusual person"—an interest fanned by the nation's 2,335 daily newspapers. Clearly, such concern included Hollywood stars, especially when (as in the case of Fatty Arbuckle) they were enmeshed in titillating scandals. Some films of the year (like *The Affairs of Anatol*) bring issues of wealth, hedonism, and sexual license to the screen—topics for which Cecil B. DeMille would become known. Others took a more critical tack, for instance *The Ace of Hearts*, which (drawing on news stories of the day) concerns a radical group that assassinates rich individuals who fail to remedy rampant social ills. Also critical of American society is director Lois Weber (one of a few established female filmmakers of the era), who questions the growing materialist culture by taking on the subject of genteel poverty in *The Blot*—inquiring why the American intelligentsia are so poorly paid (in comparison to the country's "cruder" merchants). The issue of star personality comes crashing to the surface in *The Sheik*, featuring Rudolph Valentino, one of the major heartthrobs of the period who frequently (as in this film) embodied exotic roles (often of a non-Caucasian cast). The film became a national phenomenon, setting attendance records in New York City and around the nation.

In "Movies and the Perilous Future," Sara Ross considers 1922, which she sees as a "pivot point between the traditional and the modern." On an industrial level, the Hollywood industry expands international distribution and moves toward vertical integration with the purchase of additional movie theaters. On the film front, Ross finds evidence of the import of the flapper generation in such comic films as *Bobbed Hair*, in which the heroine plays out her fantasy of bohemianism only to return to the bourgeois marital fold. The drama *Manslaughter* (directed by DeMille) offers a more extreme vision of the contemporary woman, but, once again, her wildness (fast driving, partying, and so on) must eventually be tamed. Modernity of a different kind is satirized in *The Electric House*, a Keaton farce that mocks the newly automated home. At the opposite end of the spectrum (and evincing a certain nostalgia for ages past) is a documentary like Robert Flaherty's *Nanook of the North*, which investigates a society viewed as "primitive" in Western eyes, specifically a family of Inuits in Canada's arctic region.

Marcia Landy's subject in "Movies and the Changing Body of Cinema" is 1923, which she views as a year of transition, with the disappearance of certain stars and directors, the emergence of new ones, and transformations of film genre. In the works she examines, however, her focus is on issues of sexuality and corporeality. In Chaplin's *A Woman of Paris*, dramatic conventions of the "fallen woman" story are confounded, as the central character "flouts expectations of long suffering and . . . redeemed womanhood." Similarly, in the highly experimental *Salome* (based on Oscar Wilde's play), Natacha Rambova plays the infamous biblical character, a *femme fatale,* who punishes men who resist her desires. Utilizing art nouveau sets, the film is a mix of "ballet, biomechanics [and] dream." Another European émigré actress, the Polish-born Pola Negri, appears in *The Spanish Dancer*—where she plays an exotic Gypsy. On the one hand, Negri embodies "uninhibited female sexuality," but does so without challenging American middle-class values. On the masculine front, there are westerns, like *The Covered Wagon,* starring J. Warren Kerrigan as Banion, a defender of women and children during the pioneers' trek westward. Male deformity (vs. rugged heroism) is at the core of *The Hunchback of Notre Dame,* featuring Lon Chaney, who came to specialize in those kinds of roles. Biblical masculinity (and its modern-day counterparts) is at play in *The Ten Commandments,* as is historical heroism (set in the French revolution) in *Scaramouche,* with Ramon Novarro cast as a radical law student.

In considering 1924, Jennifer Bean examines the relation between "Movies and Play." Once more, Douglas Fairbanks appears as a major star in *The Thief of Bagdad,* an exotic adventure (based on *Arabian Nights*) that gives him ample opportunity to show off his exuberant and "relentless motility" as he morphs from thief to prince. A ludic sense also informs various Hal Roach "Our Gang" comedies, a series that follows a group of mischievous boys as they "derange the ordinary world through inventive, physical play." In *Sunshine Limited,* for example, they pretend to be engineers and design a train out of discarded parts, using a caged dog to assure its locomotion. Equally impish is the character of Felix the Cat, who appeared in cartoons created by animator Otto Messmer for Paramount. As Bean notes, "At once irrational and recognizable, the world Felix inhabits plays wildly with physical logic." Thus, in *Felix Finds 'em Fickle,* he must scale a precipice to pick a flower for the feline he fancies. Buster Keaton, now firmly entrenched in making feature films, released one of his greatest that year, *Sherlock Jr.,* a highly self-conscious work in which he plays a film projectionist who falls asleep on the job and imagines that he enters the screen (and the film narrative) in order to play a brilliant sleuth. Like Fairbanks, Keaton performs many deft physical stunts in the process of getting his laughs.

According to Gwenda Young, the movies of 1925 reflected "a year of change." *The Plastic Age* (whose very title signals modernity) tells a tale of college life (reflecting the twenties concern with youth culture) and follows the progress of a young man at "Prescott College" as he achieves athletic and romantic success. Significantly, his paramour is played by popular star and "It" girl Clara Bow. Also invoked in the film is a theme that would characterize the decade: the clash between generations. Cultural shifts in romance and the working woman are at play in *Smouldering Fires*, featuring established actress Pauline Frederick and rising star Laura La Plante. It takes on (in an ambivalent fashion) a controversial subject: a businesswoman's infatuation with a younger man who is also her employee. Similarly, *The Home Maker* considers a more traditional subject, that of woman as keeper of the domestic flames, but treats it in a novel fashion. The film's heroine feels trapped by her conventional role and, when her husband becomes disabled, she takes a job as a saleswoman in a department store and he stays home to mind the children. Based on a notorious murder case from 1922, *The Goose Woman* tells the tale of a has-been opera singer who witnesses a homicide and is transformed by the prosecuting attorney into a respectable matron so that she will be more impressive at trial—a feat accomplished thanks to the acquisition of plentiful consumer goods. Finally, in *Stella Dallas* (a maternal melodrama to be remade numerous times in film history), we find a sympathetic portrait of a lower-class woman who sacrifices happiness for the benefit of her child. Given the film's success, it would seem that such a traditional attitude was endorsed by the moviegoing public.

For Maureen Turim, 1926 was a year of "Movies and Divine Stars, Defining Genres," and one of its melancholy signal moments was the death of matinee idol Rudolph Valentino, who had appeared earlier that year in *Son of the Sheik*. In order to explore the topic of stardom, she first focuses on two prominent (but opposing) actresses of import that year: Lillian Gish and Greta Garbo. While in *La Boheme* and *The Scarlet Letter* (both based on literary works), Gish continues to specialize in portrayals of suffering, melodramatic heroines (roles honed in works by D. W. Griffith), in *The Torrent* (Garbo's debut American film), the Swedish player formulates a new kind of screen woman: sophisticated, headstrong, alluring, and independent. Turim also considers masculine film genres of the year in her examination of *Beau Geste*, directed by Herbert Brenon and featuring Ronald Colman. A tale of the French Foreign Legion, the film "celebrates male bravado and mythologizes the colonial enterprise." Hence, she sees the movies of the year as struggling to "define gender," oscillating between a variety of cinematic heroines and the nationalist male hero.

The "New Woman as Consumer" is Sumiko Higashi's interest in discussing the works of 1927. But, of course, the major consumerist change to hit the Hollywood industry was the so-called coming of sound, with the release of the first part-talkie: *The Jazz Singer* starring Al Jolson. As Higashi points out, however, the film was not immediately viewed as a decisive break with the past by viewers or producers, since experimentation with sound had been a frequent exhibition novelty since the mid-twenties. Higashi's focus in her essay is on new female roles (as opposed to new technology)—specifically the New Woman who replaced the Victorian "Angel in the House" in the twenties. F. W. Murnau's *Sunrise* contrasts the noxious City and the wholesome Country Woman, and shows the latter voyaging to the metropolis where she enjoys the unfamiliar pleasures of restaurants, amusement parks, nightclubs, and photography studios. *It,* on the other hand, shows consumerism from within, as seen from the perspective of a department store salesgirl played by Clara Bow, who sets her cap for the boss's son. While the City Woman in *Sunrise* is an extreme and unredeemable version of the female vamp, Greta Garbo's incarnation of a seductress in *Flesh and the Devil* is a more nuanced figure. Issues of consumerism surface again since she is surrounded by luxury, not only a fabulous wardrobe but "high ceilings, pilasters, chandeliers, paneled and coffered doors, arched windows, floor-to-ceiling drapery, rich upholstery, paintings, and statuary." Quite the opposite female portrayal is realized by Mary Pickford in *My Best Girl,* where she once more depicts an idealized and sentimentalized screen heroine.

Angela Dalle Vacche sees a world unaware of impending economic disaster in America of 1928. *The Docks of New York,* directed by Austrian émigré director Josef von Sternberg, is about the unlikely romance (on the seamy side of town) of a tough sailor and a suicidal blond. Yet it is ultimately a highly poetic film with a depth that belies its melodramatic structure. *The Wind* is another work by a European filmmaker—the Swedish Victor Sjostom. It stars Lillian Gish, as already demonstrated, a luminary of the American silent cinema. Set in the American West and Expressionistic in tone, it concerns the travails of a young woman who is sent there from the east only to endure loneliness and abuse on the vast, harsh plains. Paul Leni, another European émigré, directs *The Man Who Laughs,* a historical film based on a Victor Hugo novel. *The Crowd,* directed by King Vidor (which Dalle Vacche sees as a central text of the year), is highly critical of contemporary urban society and of the American Dream. While its hero attempts to get ahead and raise a family, he is ultimately defeated by a modern, bureaucratic culture that treats people like cogs in a vast machine. Everything, however, was not entirely bleak on the screen that year. Buster Keaton's *Steamboat Bill Jr.* and Walt Disney's *Steamboat Willie* (which helped launch the character of Mickey Mouse) certainly appealed to the public's sense of humor.

Our Modern Maidens (1929). Kentucky Strafford (Anita Page), the mistress of Gil Jordan (Douglas Fairbanks Jr.), in the *moderne* apartment he provides for her.

As I demonstrate in "Movies, Crashes, and Finales," 1929 was the year in which the "coming of sound" (heralded in 1926) truly came of age. While the year continued to see the production of silent films outfitted with musical scores, and the release of both silent and sound versions of the same work, one of its major developments was the burgeoning of the musical genre. In truth, the form was divided into numerous subcategories. On some level, certain silent films with accompaniment had been proto-musicals. Jack Conway's *Our Modern Maidens* focuses on wealthy Jazz Age youth so that scenes of partying and dancing are central. As for bona fide sound films, there was the variety-show subgenre, exemplified by Charles Reisner's *The Hollywood Revue,* which comprised multiple vaudeville acts (songs, dances, acrobatics, dramatic readings, slapstick routines) strung together by the comic commentary of an emcee. There was the conventional backstage musical like Harry Beaumont's *The Broadway Melody,* which told a Horatio Alger tale of ingénues and their rise to success. There were also the more realistic musical dramas, like Rouben Mamoulian's *Applause,* which explored the tawdry side of burlesque while simultaneously pioneering sound technique. While these films routinely cast white performers in lead roles, the year also saw an influx of black entertainers to the movies. Shorts like Dudley Murphy's *Black and Tan* set a performance by famous jazz artist Duke Ellington within a narrative frame that was merely an excuse to display his musical skills. Alternately, a groundbreaking feature film, King Vidor's *Hallelujah,* employed an all-black cast of unknown actors to tell a heartrending tale of the plight of sharecroppers in the American South and utilized work songs, folk songs, and gospel pieces to augment its narrative.

Hence, in retrospect, the twenties was an era that saw the development and apotheosis of the silent film, only to witness its ultimate demise.

1920

Movies, Margarine, and Main Street

MICHAEL ARONSON

A Very Cold and Somewhat Urban Nation

Not surprisingly, it was cold at the beginning of January: that first Friday morning of the New Year would turn out to be particularly frigid across much of the Northeast and Midwest ("1 January"). But regardless of the bitter weather, enumerators in the towns of Monessen, Pennsylvania; Van Wert and Coshocton, Ohio; Bessemer, Michigan; and Waukesha, Wisconsin, had a job to do, and along with some 90,000 others around the country, they set out from their homes, portfolios of schedules under their arms and fountain pens in their pockets, duly instructed to take the 14th Census of the United States. A few months later, the official results of their collective tally would show that for the very first time in the country's history the majority of American's (51.4 percent) were now living within an "urban" environment (Hill). This population milestone represented a recent acceleration of a general trend that had begun in earnest more than seventy years ago. The shift from a rural to urban state, widely noted that year in both popular reports and academic analysis of the census, helped solidify America's sense of itself as a modern industrialized state, but it is important to understand that the government's statisticians defined "urban" as an incorporated residential center of only 2,500 people. The reality was that this year much of the American population continued to live not in big cities, but in what we envisage and typically describe as towns, both large and small, places just like Monessen, Van Wert, Coshocton, Bessemer, and Waukesha.

This chapter concentrates on the first year of the decade in these various towns, focusing in particular on their experiences with the movies as made visible in their respective newspapers.[1] Daily newspapers allow film historians access to contemporary local reviews and advertising within the context of the everyday existence of a community's social, political, and economic life. As such, the chapter pays due heed to both the many stories and stars that filled the screen this year, as well as to where, when, and how the movies were presented and consumed by American audiences.

One reason to concentrate on moviegoing in towns such as these five is that the spectacle of Hollywood and its accompanying history of American cinema have too often been associated with life in the big city. This metropolitan bias is perhaps particularly true of the 1920s, a decade in which we see the swift and literal rise of the picture palace—opulent places like the Uptown Theater in Chicago, Grauman's Egyptian in Los Angeles, and New York City's Roxy. These grand spaces, each seating many thousands, were built on such a dramatic scale that if you were able to pick up one of these theaters and set it down in an empty spot of land in the Ohio countryside or a cleared plot of Michigan timberland, it would statistically qualify as an urban space all to itself. But these dream palaces were really the exhibition exception, not the rule, and only found in the biggest cities. Most Americans would have known about such cinematic grandeur, but this is not where most of them saw their movies. While the populations of all five of the towns in question here fall easily to the right of the census's rural/urban divide—ranging in populace from fewer than 3,000 (Bessemer) to almost 20,000 (Monessen) residents—they each offer up a much different kind of encounter with the movies than what was likely in places like Chicago, Los Angeles, or New York. While we cannot assume that Coshocton, Monessen, Van Wert, Bessemer, or Waukesha are truly representative of all American towns, or even those of similar size in the Northeast or Midwest, they offer a more typical range of moviegoing experiences that were available to most Americans in this first year of the decade, experiences with movies seen on Main Street rather than Broadway.

A Bad Year for Anarchists and John (Barleycorn)

If those same census enumerators had taken a moment to glance at their morning newspapers before heading out onto the main streets of their respective towns, they would have read of a number of issues and events set in motion the year before but that would remain front-page news for a considerable time to come. It would, from its very first days, for instance, be a significantly troubling year for American anarchists, communists, socialists, or even labor union members. The *Monessen Daily Independent*, the *Van Wert Daily Bulletin*, the *Bessemer Herald*, and the *Waukesha Daily Freeman* all shared similar headlines New Year's morning, announcing that Attorney General A. Mitchell Palmer had declared the year an "open season" on any and all radicals who might "preach the doctrine of unrest" ("1920 Open"). In fact, on the very same day the census takers first hit the streets, so did hundreds of Palmer's agents and local lawmen, as simultaneous raids of communist party offices, Industrial Workers of the World (IWW) union halls, and "known" meeting places of "radical cults" in more than thirty cities across the country resulted in the mass arrest of more than 4,000 people. At or near the top of the raiders' list of potential human targets was radical unionist "Big Bill" Hayward (1869–1928). One of the founders and leaders of the IWW, or Wobblies, Hayward was one of the few true fugitives sought by the law that day, having recently jumped bail while out on appeal for violating the Espionage Act ("Chicago"). According to the reports that morning, federal and local agents believed that Hayward would be found hiding in Chicago. But unbeknownst to Palmer's men, Hayward was already long gone, having fled the country to Russia, where he would end up living as an expatriate the rest of his life.

Unlike Hayward's often violent approach to unionism, American Federation of Labor president Samuel Gompers (1850–1924) was less interested in subverting the system itself and more concerned with gaining better wages and job security for his more craft-oriented union members. As such, Gompers had both publicly supported the country's participation in World War I and often actively spoken out against socialism. Perhaps it is not surprising, then, that on the day of the raids, the *Van Wert Bulletin* prominently carried Gompers's "promise" to the country that "America's workers stand ready in the New Year as in the past to do their duty as American citizens" ("America"). Gompers's patriotic avowal in the press was a politic attempt to distance the AFL from subversive "foreign" organizations like the Wobblies, as well as even more radical elements present on the American scene, particularly the Italian Galleanists, who sought to overthrow capitalism itself, by any means necessary, including terrorism. Later that fall, on 16 September during a busy weekday Wall Street lunch hour, a horse-drawn carriage pulled up across from the New York headquarters of financier J. P. Morgan. A moment later the horse and wagon were gone, vaporized in the explosion of a hundred pounds of dynamite and five hundred pounds of lead slugs made from window-sash weights, a bomb designed to cause maximum damage to life and property at the symbolic heart of American capitalism. George Weston, an Associated Press reporter who witnessed the blast, called it "an unexpected, death-dealing bolt, which in a twinkling turned into a shamble the busiest corner of America's financial center"

("Arrest"). The attack killed thirty-eight individuals, mostly clerks, secretaries, and passersby, and injured more than four hundred others. Almost immediately, blame in the daily reports in the newspapers centered on anarchist groups, suspicions soon corroborated by a printed message found in a mailbox that same morning a few hundred yards from the explosion, proclaiming "Free the political prisoners. Or it will be sure death for all of you. American Anarchist Fighters." Although no one was ever charged with the Wall Street attack, it was likely not a coincidence that on the day prior to the bombing, Galleanist anarchists Nicola Sacco and Bartolomeo Vanzetti had been indicted in Massachusetts for bank robbery and murder.

Although less well remembered than these domestic Red Scare battles, the American government was at the same time actively fighting revolutionaries far outside its own national borders. Articles in all the town newspapers the first week of the year reported on American military participation in the ongoing war in Russia. January found a contingent of more than 13,000 U.S. soldiers fitfully continuing their role in an allied invasion of the newly socialist country, a military incursion intended, in part, to assist British, Czech, and "White" Russian forces attempting to overthrow the still-shaky Bolshevik government. While all the papers offer generally supportive rhetoric for Palmer's raids and the "local drive on Bolsheviks," their headlines and general reportage reveal, in comparison, a less sympathetic attitude toward the continued use of American soldiers in a post-Armistice foreign conflict ("Reds"). With dozens of recent casualties, and with a large group of Michigan National Guardsmen engaged in difficult battles in northern Siberian towns with unpronounceable names, the *Bessemer Herald* was particularly critical of this lingering war, and later that spring President Woodrow Wilson would end all American participation in the Russian conflict, bringing the last of the troops home in late May (Mills).

Unfortunately, by the time they returned, the only way these soldiers could celebrate their homecoming with a stiff drink would be to do so illegally. On 16 January, the Eighteenth Amendment—prohibiting the manufacture, transportation, and sale of alcohol—went into effect, beginning thirteen years of a nationwide ban. With Palmer and the war in Russia front and center in the news, at least one of the local papers humorously linked the impending national dry law with the government's fight against radical elements: "Another 'red' is being deported today. At midnight he will be sent from American shores, while thousands of his friends bewail his departure. 'Red rye' alias John Barleycorn is the only deportee who is nationally mourned today" ("Few Shed"). In particular, many in the movie industry were not sad to see Barleycorn go, although their position appears largely driven by profits. According to Hiram Abrams, then managing director of United Artists, "Ignoring entirely pro and con discussion of prohibition . . . and looking at it solely from the standpoint of the industry, no one can question for a moment that it will bring millions of dimes and quarters to the box office. The family at the films will enjoy the money which formerly went to the saloon" (Aronson). But not all citizens were thrilled with the prospect of a dry life, and at least one popular song of the day declared, "It's the smart little feller who stocked up his cellar . . . that's getting the beautiful girls." While more than one million gallons of liquor were removed by its owners from government-bonded warehouses in the month leading up to Prohibition, the Volstead Act made the actual consumption or sale of that stocked liquor illegal, and more than 10,000 Americans would be arrested for violating the law by the end of the year (Sann).

A Better Year for Women and Warren (Harding)

One right lost, another gained, and in the only year of the twentieth century to see the implementation of two different federal constitutional amendments, the Nineteenth ("suffrage") Amendment declared that "the right of citizens of the United States to vote shall not be denied or abridged by the United States or by any State on account of sex." National ratification came with the success of a closely fought floor battle in the Tennessee legislature on 18 August, after which thirty-six states had passed the amendment, making it the law of the land. In the next day's *Waukesha Daily Freeman*, the leader of Wisconsin's suffrage forces, Mrs. Henry M. Youman, was quoted on the front page as saying that she believed the amendment's passage to be "the most advanced step society has taken in years—equal in importance to the founding of representative government and the abolition of slavery" ("Suffrage"). A few months later, on 2 November, women across the country were among those who went to the polls and helped elect in a landslide Ohio senator Warren G. Harding as the twenty-ninth president of the United States. Harding, a dark-horse conservative candidate for the Republican nomination, largely campaigned on a postwar "return to normalcy" and ran what became known as the classic "front porch campaign," speaking most often to press and public from his home in Marion, Ohio. Although home radio receiver sets were still few and far between, Ohioans, as well as most anyone listening up and down the East Coast, would have had for the first time the option of hearing the presidential election results arrive through the ether, announced on a commercial AM radio station:

KDKA, which chose to broadcast its initial public show that night from a shack built on the roof of the Westinghouse corporate office in Pittsburgh, Pennsylvania ("KDKA").

A Profitable Year for Loew, Griffith, and Fox

Harding's "front porch" campaign was one of the first presidential campaigns to be heavily covered by the press and to receive widespread newsreel attention, but it was also the first modern campaign to use the power of Hollywood and its stars, who traveled to Marion for photo opportunities with Harding and his wife. Al Jolson, Lillian Russell, Douglas Fairbanks, and Mary Pickford were among the more conservative-minded luminaries to make a pilgrimage to central Ohio. Jolson even wrote Harding a campaign song:

> We think the country's ready
> For another man like Teddy.
> We need another Lincoln
> To do the country's thinkin'
> (Chorus) Mis-ter Har-ding
> You're the man for us! ("Al Jolson")

While Jolson was busy stumping for the future president, others in Hollywood were busy furthering their own prospects. In that busy first week of January, Marcus Loew, "hitherto concerned only with [movie] theatre management," would acquire, for around $3 million, total ownership of Metro Pictures Corporation, "and so make his entry into the field of picture producing" ("Marcus"). Loew's purchase of this company, and its accompanying national exchange system, was a function of two major economic trends occurring within the still-developing industry, "the entry on a large scale of Wall St. big financial interests with consequent efforts to control both the producing and distributing ends of the business," as well as the initial movement toward wide-scale vertical integration by the industry's various owners (Aronson). Acquisition of Metro, funded by a combination of public stock offerings by Loew's Inc. and a sizeable loan from Wall Street banking syndicates, was specifically a competitive reaction by Loew to Adolph Zukor's obtainment of his own chain of theaters, designed to show the movies of his successful studio, Famous Players Company. For Loew's millions, he obtained under the Metro banner the product of a number of secondary studios that had previously been bought up by Metro's former owners and their bevy of mostly lesser known talent. The one major exception in his newly acquired cadre of stars would be the flamboyant actress

Alla Nazimova. Nazimova, a Russian immigrant and a theatrical ingénue, had been a significant Hollywood presence for a number of years and is immodestly described in an ad promoting *Billions*, one of four films she would release this year, as "The World's Greatest Actress" (*Billions*). At forty-one years old, Nazimova was still a top-tier star with one of the highest paychecks in Hollywood ($13,000 a week) and with considerable creative authority over her work, including contractual approval of every script, director, and leading man she performed with. But "the fourth most popular actress" was probably a more realistic description of her stature in Hollywood's pecking order, at least according to the annual *Photoplay* popularity poll. Although her first picture of the year, *Stronger Than Death*, would be the most profitable of the four released during the year, *Billions*, a modest failure, is in many ways a more typical production for Nazimova, who prided and promoted herself as being involved in every significant aspect of her movies, from designing the sets to titling and assembling the film.

In the case of *Billions*, the film's credited production designer would actually be Natacha Rambova, the future Mrs. Rudolph Valentino who, although born Winifred Shaughnessy in Salt Lake City, Utah, had already developed at the age of twenty-three into an eroticized figure of fascination for the Hollywood community. The puerile interest in the young designer would grow with Rambova's collaborative artistic, and possibly intimate, relationship with Nazimova, but it first began with her tumultuous love affair with the well-known Russian dancer and choreographer Theodore Kosloff, who shot her in the leg with a rifle when she announced her departure from his life and ballet troupe. Rambova's stylish and influential art deco designs for *Billions*, the first of a number for Nazimova dramas, surround a story adapted by Nazimova and her "husband" Charles Bryant from a successful 1914 French stage play, *L'Homme Riche*.[2] The couple's film version transports the action from Paris to America while adapting a lead role and narrative to take advantage of Nazimova's exotic star text, as well as the broader current media attention to and fear of all matters red and revolutionary. In *Billions*, "which as the title implies has to do with wealthy people," the film concerns Princess Triloff (Nazimova), a recent émigré from Czarist Russia who escapes to America where she becomes a patron of the arts ("*Nazimova*"). The princess falls in love with the poetry of an impoverished writer, Owen Carey (played by Charles Bryant), and becomes his anonymous benefactor. But Owen, in a melodramatic twist of coincidence, soon inherits his own fortune from "a rich Uncle" and, for reasons unexplained in the now lost film, assumes his benefactor's name, Krakerfeller, bestowing his own real identity upon his friend, Frank Manners (William J. Irving).

"Nazimova the Incomparable," California Theatre advertisement for *Billions*, starring "the fourth most popular actress" in Hollywood.

The princess, Carey/Krakerfeller, and Manners/Carey all come together at a "fashionable winter resort in California" where the princess becomes, under false pretenses, enamored with the wrong Carey. In due time the truth is revealed and the right couple falls in love, but unfortunately a series of misadventures leads to the rescinding of Carey's inheritance. Ashamed of his rags-to-riches-to-rags-again story, Carey leaves the resort to bitterly sulk in his artist's garret. But the film, of course, ends happily with a final reunion between the star-crossed couple, when the princess discovers that she too is now equally destitute, her fortune lost, confiscated back home by the Bolsheviks and their revolution.

Loews-owned Metro heavily promoted Nazivoma and her film, and in Waukesha, Wisconsin, it was booked to play three straight days at Saxe's Park Theater. This was the town's newest theater, built that year, with seating for 400; upon opening it quickly became Waukesha's most luxurious place for moviegoing. The town of 12,500, a traditional site of regional tourism related to its proximity to mineral springs, already supported three other medium-sized movie theaters, the Unique (seating 350); the Colonial, offering a mix of pictures and vaudeville; and the Auditorium, another 400-seater just one block down from the Unique on Main Street. The Park, across from its namesake, Cutler Park, was one of forty-five theaters operated by Saxe Amusement Enterprises, a Milwaukee-based theater chain owned by Midwest exhibitor pioneers Thomas and John Saxe ("Garfield"). The brothers would hire a local man, Loren F. Thurwacher, a celebrated Great War veteran and former army captain, to manage the Park for them. Trained by the Saxes in the art of movie theater promotion, even before the actual opening of the Park, Thurwacher worked to situate the new theater as a central site of local entertainment and community. Prior to the theater's "grande" December opening, Thurwacher placed a series of large advertisements in the *Freeman* that presented a long list of "the best pictures at present on the market so that the people of Waukesha may select the picture for the opening program." A cutout ballot was supplied alongside the list, and the movie that garnered the most votes would win the premiere time slot, allowing the town's participants "to feel that it is their theater and that the management is doing . . . everything in its power to please the Waukesha public" ("Choose"). Nazimova's *Billions* was one of more than sixty choices available to the town's citizens, but it did not garner enough votes to go first, and was later shown about a month into the theater's opening. Along with the Nazimova feature, the Park offered a traditional mix of accompanying short films, including a "news weekly" and a "hand colored review." But, in addition, on the first night of the show, manager Thurwacher had a special event designed to capture the imagination and pocketbooks of his local audience, a personal appearance by Edith May, "America's Most Beautiful Salesgirl." Miss May was attractive to the eye, but a large part of her promotional appeal for manager Thurwacher must have been her background, for "not on the city's boulevard [would you] find this prettiest girl; not in a gilded palace nor clothed in priceless silks and laces . . . and [she] has never seen a Parisian frock nor a Fifth Avenue hat." Miss May, rather, hailed from small-town Monroe, Wisconsin, the daughter of a "village blacksmith" who was taught by both her parents to "work like a switch engine" (May "My Dream").

This "diligent" seventeen-year-old "charming brunette," whose bodily measurements were detailed in a number of midwestern newspapers (5'2", 136 lbs, 32" chest, 25" waist, 22" thighs, 32" hips, and 8" ankles), provided Thurwacher with the perfect corporal text with which to promote his theater and its delights as providing small-town wholesomeness while still offering the pleasures of big-city glamour. For while May still was a "salesgirl" in title and Midwest in her origins, her life and labor had been transformed by the beauty contest win, having "jumped from the quiet obscurity of a backwoods Wisconsin village to the heart of hectic Broadway overnight, landing backstage in the famous Zeigfeld girl shows—first the Follies then the Midnight Frolic" ("My Adventures"). May, in both role and rhetoric, was thus an ideal figure to help sell the movies in a small town. Her activities in Waukesha on the day leading up to her appearance at the Park included, not surprisingly, a professional courtesy call on the town's two biggest department stores, the McCoy and the Enterprise, a brief stopover at the popular Waukesha Mud Baths for an introduction to the benefits of "restoring health by means of mud," and a touching personal visit to Resthaven, a convalescent hospital and home for injured local veterans, where she "conversed [with] some of the war heroes and prevailed upon them to relate to her their war experiences" ("Edith May").

In the many newspaper accounts of Edith May's dramatic transformation from shopgirl to showgirl, she remains throughout described as a simple, if beautiful, rural outsider, naively looking in on the seductive, if perilous, urban environment of life in the big city. In one supposedly self-authored article written while temporarily in the employment of Florenz Ziegfeld, May describes this mix of fear and desire in her first encounter with a very unfamiliar kind of village, Greenwich Village: "I had heard of this place back home and that it was very queer—and wicked. We went into a basement place for dinner. There was sawdust on the floor and the tables were bare and the air was choked with smoke. Then my dream of naughtiness was realized—ALL THE WOMEN WERE SMOKING! Two of them had sandals on instead of shoes. And another's lips were so red I thought she had been in an accident" ("My Adventures"). If May offered contemporary women one model of female identity and desire, one shaped largely by discourses of the hard-working girl and her growing role within mass consumption, her "dream of naughtiness" point to another, very different (if related) female "type" visible in some basement restaurants and on many more moving picture screens, the "vamp."

Although Theda Bara is now the best-known exemplar of this erotic predatory figure of femininity, this year it was instead, in the words of *Photoplay* columnist Herbert Howe, "Louise Glaum, another vamp making the world safe for sin" (Lowry). Glaum (1894–1970), unlike Nazimova, was born in America, in Baltimore, and began her early acting career in a Los Angeles stock theater performance of the aptly titled *Why Girls Leave Home*. Her screen debut in an unknown film for American Pathé occurred while she was still a teenager, but her vamping potential first became evident in Thomas Ince's *Hell's Hinges* (1916), where at the age of twenty-one, playing the barmaid Dolly, her character gets the Reverend Robert (Jack Standing) drunk, seduces him, and then ruins him by letting the townspeople discover him in her bed. *Hinges* was a western vehicle for Ince's upright cowboy star William S. Hart, but the vamp, smoking, with feet exposed and lips so red, is a figure more typically defined by the environs of the big city. The instrument that would give Glaum her vampire crown would take place in just such an urban locale, on similar stages in New York City, the same city where Edith May had first realized her dreams and her newfound theatrical fame. The film, in which Glaum would "give to the screen one of the most perfect vampire characterizations," would be the bluntly titled *Sex*, a seven-reel "special feature" directed by Fred Niblo and produced by J. Parker Read Jr. at Ince Studios in Hollywood-adjacent Culver City (Fox and Silver). The photoplay of *Sex*, penned by C. Gardner Sullivan, Ince's highly respected writer and studio script supervisor, tells the story of Adrienne Renault (Glaum), the queen of the Midnight Follies at the Frivolity Theater, a character described in the *Monessen Daily Independent* as "a dazzling, alluring home wrecker . . . who never had a qualm of conscious about taking another's husband" ("Sex").

As the film's story begins, Adrienne's current conquest is Phillip Overman (William Conklin), a self-satisfied baron of business who sits in his luxurious private box, simultaneously savoring champagne and his lover's performance of the "Spider Dance." The opening theatrical number is set within a faerie-like woodland and begins with Glaum's dramatic entrance, dressed as a black widow spider. In her first moment, she appears floating above the Frivolity stage, clad in a translucent cloak of webs wrapped cloak-like around a body-hugging shimmering black sheath. Literally in the spotlight, she descends slowly to the stage's forest floor, a sequence intercut with images of the theater audience's wild adulation. The newspaper's

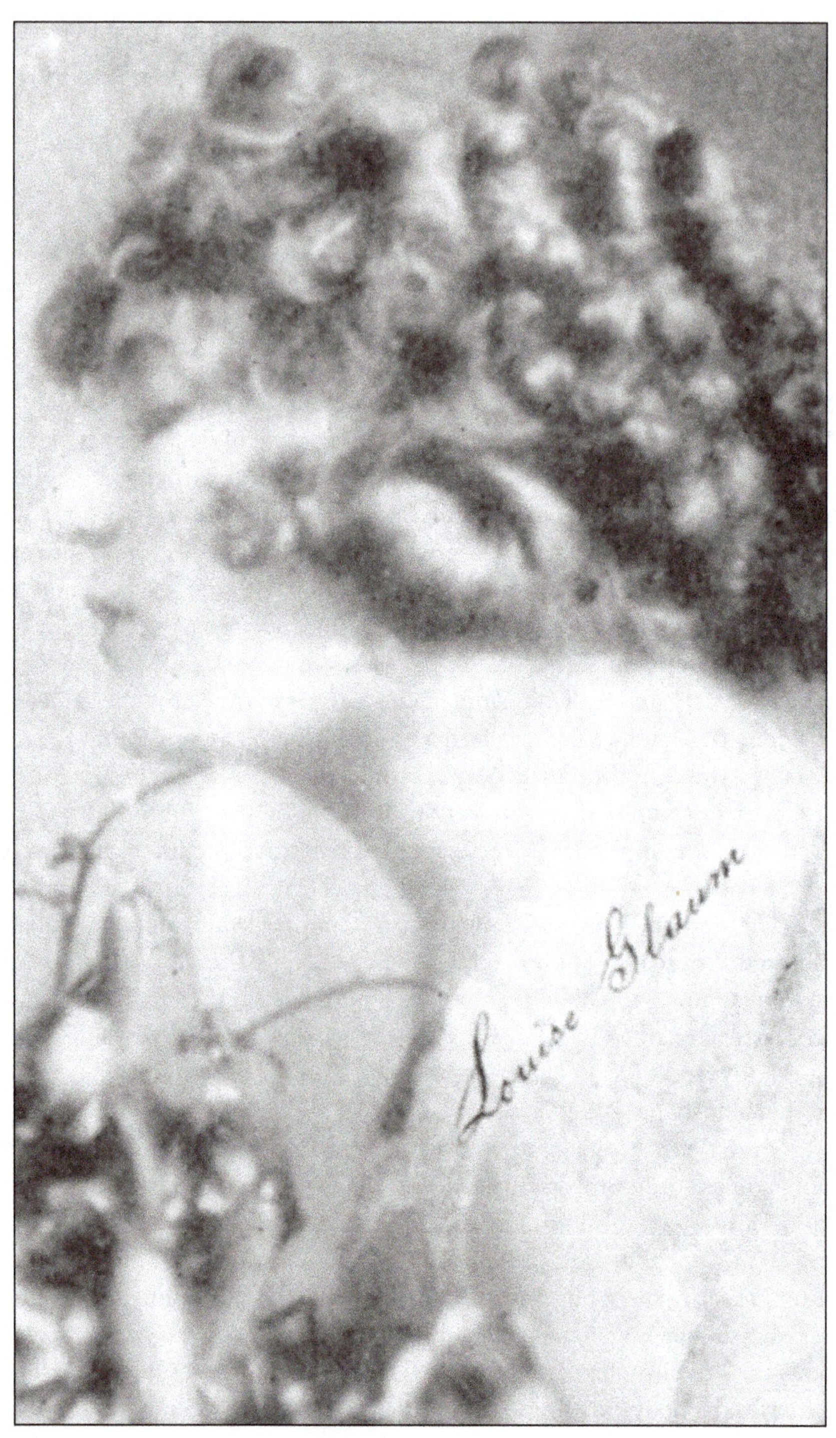

Louise Glaum, "another vamp making the world safe for sin," pictured on a Blue Ribbon Tea trading card.

reviewer aptly critiques the odd performance of Adrienne's arachnid-like movements that follow her earthly touchdown. Deeming Glaum "strangely beautiful," the writer, nonetheless, notes that she "was never made to be a dancer, and it seems that she realizes this fact herself" ("Sex"). Contrasted with this crowded scene of a group of men adoring a dangerous female is another of Mrs. Overman (Myrtle Stedman) "spending the evening alone . . . as usual" in her cavernous and empty manor. When Mrs. Overman learns of Adrienne's hold on her husband through a private detective she has hired, she pleads to the vamp's sense of "fair play" to free her man from her powerfully erotic grasp. Adrienne, of course, refuses. Meanwhile, young chorine Daisy Henderson (Peggy Pierce), a fictional version of Edith May recently removed from rural life, "still dazed by the fact she is now a member of the Frivolity beauty squad," is shocked by the Machiavellian behavior of her new colleague. But Adrienne, in a sequence of wild bacchanalia and table dancing, instructs the new small town ingénue in the ways of handling married men. Adrienne, however, soon ends up casting Overman aside when she falls for self-effacing but "rich as sin" Pittsburgh industrialist David Wallace (Irving Cummings). She is caught, according to the film's intertitles, in "a web of love [that] aroused within her the instinct of the nest-builder." In the fourth reel Adrienne marries Wallace and withdraws from her former theatrical life, taking on the role of dutiful, if extravagantly attired, wife. Unfortunately for Adrienne, she schooled Daisy a bit too well in the vampire's art, and she soon learns that her new husband is having an affair of his own, with the once innocent village maiden, now herself the reigning queen of Broadway. In the penultimate scene of the film, Adrienne goes begging to Daisy, like Mrs. Overman not so long ago had done to her, pleading for her own husband's release. But Daisy, in a dramatic two-shot that draws the two women's faces into a single close-up, rejects Adrienne's desperate appeal, repeating back to her the very philosophy Adrienne had taught her in the first reel. Despondent and alone, Adrienne boards a ship bound for Europe, only to find the Overmans on a second honeymoon, now happily reunited. As the sun sets into the sea, and the film reaches its unusually unhappy conclusion, the lesson of the vamp's life is made explicit in a final intertitle: "The standards of morality eternally demand that the naked soul of Sex be stripped of its falsehoods—which can only be atoned for through bitter tears."

Although *Sex* would have its national premiere in the spring, on 11 April, at the Fabian Garden Theatre in Paterson, New Jersey, it would not reach Monessen's Star Theater until more than six months later, arriving with a new and lengthier title, *Sex Crushed to Earth*. This oddly prosaic designation was a courtesy, or rather a requirement, of the Pennsylvania State Board of Motion Picture Censors. The title change, necessary for exhibition of the movie anywhere in the state, was in addition to a number of unknown alterations and deletions to the film itself required by the censors. The Pennsylvania Board, notorious as one of the most severe of the various motion picture censor groups around the country, proscribed the film's new title with the intention of clarifying the pedagogical nature of its narrative, to make clear the lesson learned concerning the immorality of Adrienne's onscreen life. Additionally, by adding the depressive phrase "Crushed to Earth," the censors hoped to remove any exploitive "prurient" possibility the original title might have allowed for exhibitors promoting the film. If the potential sexual deviance of the vamp figure was modified and downplayed by the censors for its Pennsylvania exhibition, W. Roy McShaffrey, the owner of the Star, could still promote the film "as the most 'lavish' picture to appear in Monessen," as well as reminding his audience of the existing star text of Glaum as an object of erotic desire. In the ads and notices in the newspaper leading up to the Star's three-day exhibition of the film, primary attention is given to the wardrobe, particularly the twenty-four "gorgeous gowns" worn by Glaum and promoted by McShaffrey as costing $500,000 (Adv. for *Sex*).

McShaffrey, who had first begun his career as a showman putting on traveling tent shows around the region, had recently reopened and enlarged the Star Theater after a fire the previous year severely damaged the building, increasing its now-upholstered seating to just under a thousand, including a new 300-seat balcony. To create an exhibition environment to match the excessive spectacle of the movie itself, McShaffrey chose to promote *Sex Crushed to Earth* with an "out of the ordinary" display both on and around the theater's exterior and inside the playhouse, "decorating the lobby for the occasion with cut flowers and plants . . . and building a special stage setting . . . with a gorgeous display of chrysanthemums arranged by M. Irwin of Irwin Flower store" ("Gorgeous"). Despite any potential disruptions to the narrative or promotional limitations caused by the censors' required changes, the film was a "smash" in Monessen and did good business for McShaffrey's Star, which would go on to exhibit at least two other Louise Glaum pictures this year.

A Year of (Re)Marriages and Remakes

While onscreen Glaum's vamp character in *Sex* would be punished for the immoral act of stealing fictional husbands from fictional wives, the greatest matrimonial drama of the year would occur offscreen, involving two of Hollywood's biggest stars, Mary Pickford and Douglas Fairbanks. Pickford and Fairbanks had fallen in love and been having an adulterous affair for a number of years, but Fairbanks had recently received a divorce from his wife, the socialite Anne Beth Sully, and was now pushing hard for Mary to do the same and leave her husband, the actor Owen Moore. While "Little Mary" had agreed to a professional union, joining Fairbanks along with Charlie Chaplin and D. W. Griffith in the formation of United Artists the year before, it was not until early this spring that Pickford would consent to leave Moore and marry Fairbanks. According to statistics, only one in seven marriages ended in divorce this year, and Pickford, a Catholic, was extremely concerned about the potential damage to her "sweetheart" image that annulment or divorce and, more important, remarriage might cause to her established star text. But by the new year, Pickford had agreed to risk it all for love, and in the middle of February "moved" to a resort ranch in Minden, Nevada, to begin two weeks of an elaborately staged sequence of events. They included Moore "coincidentally" showing up in a nearby mountain town "with a cameraman to take snow pictures for a coming picture" so that he could easily be served with divorce papers. The Nevada divorce from Pickford's accommodating husband on the grounds of "cruel treatment, habitual intoxication and desertion" ("Mary Pickford Wins") was announced in the press around the world at the beginning of March, and before the month was up, in a small ceremony with mostly family present, she was married to Douglas Elton Fairbanks ("Mary Pickford Weds").[3] Despite Pickford's private worries that her rapid change of spouses might negatively affect her career, such that she publicly claimed in her interviews right after the divorce that "she never would marry again and would devote the rest of her life to the films," as a couple Doug and Mary were quickly transformed by the press into the "King and Queen of Hollywood," collectively achieving a popular following unprecedented in the history of entertainment ("Douglas"). Soon after the wedding they would move into Pickfair, the former Beverly Hills hunting lodge that Fairbanks had bought for $35,000, thus fusing their public identities (Morrison).

Between the divorce, the marriage, and moving into Pickfair, it is perhaps not surprising that Pickford's output of films would slow this year to only two feature releases. But her fears that marital issues would damage her reputation or box office appeal would turn out to be unfounded. *Pollyanna* was both her first release following divorce and remarriage as well as her first film distributed by United Artists Corp. The star-owned

Postcard of "the King and Queen of Hollywood," Douglas Fairbanks and Mary Pickford, at their new Beverly Hills home, Pickfair.

distribution company, already falling behind its intended release schedule, needed a surefire success, and although Pickford was, at age twenty-six, reluctant to play happy "little Mary" once again, *Pollyanna* was purposefully designed to capitalize on her well-established role as the optimistic young girl who always triumphs in the face of overwhelming adversity. In *Pollyanna,* Pickford plays the title character, whose credo, the film's intertitles tell us, is "Just be glad." Pollyanna remains unrelentingly positive throughout the film, even after being run over by a car and subsequently becoming paralyzed, and so teaches "cranky old Aunt Polly" and the rest of the town to rejoice in their own good fortune. By the film's final reel her paralysis is cured by the doctor who teaches Aunt Polly to love again, and in "the last lingering love-lock with which all orthodox movies must end," Pollyanna herself weds the town's now grown orphan Jimmie Bean, played by Howard Ralston. *Pollyanna,* which was released at the beginning of January, earned $1.1 million in its domestic release, and although the *New York Times* claimed that its success was proof that Pickford could/should "no more grow up than Peter Pan," her next film of the year, *Suds,* would offer her a significant departure in both character and story.

Suds would not arrive in Coshocton, Ohio, a town of 10,000 in the coal-rich region of eastern Ohio, until early October, on the same weekend as the annual county fair. Perhaps because most of the town folk would likely be spending the majority of their leisure funds at the fair this week instead of at the town's movie theater, the manager of the Pastime Theater decided to use what might otherwise be a slow few days at the box office to lend his support to his local community, in this case, "The Ladies of the Episcopal Church." Tickets for the weekend show would be sold directly by the church's women's auxiliary and directly profit their own charitable causes. *Pollyanna*, which was exhibited in the United States largely prior to Pickford's exchange of husbands, was highly praised both by the National Board of Review of Motion Pictures for its positive moral message, but the later *Suds* appears to have also suffered no collateral moral damage from Pickford's very public divorce and rapid remarriage.

Suds was adapted from a one-act play called *'Op o' Me Thumb* (1905) starring Maude Adams, a well-known English stage actress with whom Pickford was often compared in the press of this period. The story's main character, Amanda Afflick, is a clumsy and plain young woman who works in a laundry in the London slums. Her active fantasy life keeps the other laundresses in stitches and helps her survive the harsh realities of daily existence. The imagined tales Amanda constructs, which she at first appears to believe herself, revolve around one Horace Greensmith (Albert Austin), a well-to-do customer who once left a shirt for cleaning. Amanda imagines a future of romance and wealth when "'Orace" would return and sweep her away from her grim life. But illusion and reality collide when Horace does eventually show up to collect his shirt, and clearly does not share Amanda's dreams. Left without her nourishing fantasy, wretched and alone, Amanda collapses on the laundry steps and weeps.

Pickford was very pleased to assume an atypical unhappy role, but understood that a Mary Pickford film had to have some sense of humor to mix with its pathos. The film's scenarist, Waldemar Young, was charged with bringing a bit of comedy to the original story via the addition of slapstick sequences, and in fact, the Pastime Theater ad in the *Coshocton Tribune* foregrounds the physical comedy and prominently features an illustration of Mary's character upside down in a laundry basket, limbs wildly akimbo. Besides the pratfalls, Young also gave Amanda, who is devastatingly alone in the play, friends, including Ben (Harold Goodwin), a kind delivery boy, and Lavender (an ex-polo pony according to the credits), a scrawny horse the laundress saves from the glue factory. Young also made a slight change to the otherwise desolate finale. The film ends as the play does, with Amanda grieving on the laundry steps, but now Ben, who has watched the scene between Horace and Amanda, sadly stands outside the laundry with a romantic bouquet he brought for her. Happiness with Ben may lie in Amanda's future, but at the fadeout, Amanda cannot see it or him. This is how *Suds* concluded—until its New York premiere and the reviews from critics who found the end too ambiguous, "a tragedy . . . too deliberately sentimental . . . too obviously 'different'" ("Screen" [June]).

Pickford, ever conscious of her own place with the public, must have worried that this reaction might result from such an untraditional ending, because after the premiere United Artists offered national exhibitors a different final reel with a clearly upbeat ending. This is very likely the version that the Pastime manager showed and promoted in the newspaper as Pickford's "new joy bringing picture" (Adv. for *Suds*). According to trade reports of the additional footage, in the revised reel a scene was added to the picture (after the original fadeout) showing Amanda and Ben sharing a playful day in the country with Lavender. Despite the additional "glad girl" ending, unlike her experience with *Pollyanna,* Pickford was not prepared to totally sacrifice her creative desires. American exhibitors, or at least the exchanges, were offered both endings by United Artist and they decided which version to showcase based on their box office needs. Although the film would be profitable for United Artists, it would not do nearly as well as *Pollyanna,* and Pickford would soon return to her more typical "glad girl" roles that had first made "little Mary" a star.

But if this year was primarily one of personal change for Pickford and for her new husband, it was also a moment of significant professional remaking. A former Broadway actor, now thirty-seven years old with almost thirty films under his belt, Douglas Fairbanks was already a star with a box office appeal that came close to rivaling both his UA actor partners, Chaplin and Pickford. His established screen persona of good-humored (American) optimism tied to a bounding body of graceful vitality was displayed to profitable effect up until the fall of this year, in largely romantic and situational comedies that took place in the milieu of contemporary industrial life. His first film of the year, *The Mollycoddle,* in which he humorously plays "a man surrounded by supercivilization" who must relearn a more American (natural) form of masculinity, falls well within the mold of his previously established canon of work. But after his second film of the year, *The Mark of Zorro,* Fairbanks would cease to be associated with contemporary characters and narratives of modernity and instead become overwhelmingly identified with the historically based costume-adventure picture, the "swashbuckler." Fairbanks himself, using his pseudonym Elton Thomas, would adapt *Zorro*'s scenario from the story "The Curse of Capistrano" by Johnston McCulley, which was originally published as a five-part series in *All-Story Weekly.* Produced by Fairbanks for United Artists and directed by Fred Niblo, who also directed Glaum's performance in *Sex, Zorro* tells the tale of Don Diego Vega, a wealthy rancher of the early nineteenth century who returns from Spain to his family's estate in Old California only to discover that the despotic governor Alvarado (Sidney De Grey) and his military have the western territory in their tyrannical grip. While most of the populace is cowed by the governor, Vega works to restore justice to his countryside. Taking on the outward persona of a foppish and lazy aristocrat, he secretly masquerades as Zorro, masked swordsman and champion of the oppressed, his true identity remaining known only to his faithful servant Bernado (Tote du Crow). Zorro bests his foes with his remarkable displays of swordsmanship, forcing the evil governor to abdicate his power and wittily winning the affections of the beautiful Lolita (Marguerite De La Motte), who is, in the last reel, delighted to learn that Vega is no simpering fop at all, but instead a dashing hero.

The film had its national premiere in early November at the Capital Theater in New York, where almost 20,000 people paid $11,708 to see it on the first day, the largest single-day gross in movie history up to that time ("Douglas"). Samuel "Roxy" Rothafel's Capital was then the largest movie theater in the country, with a capacity of more than 5,000 for a single show; in contrast, in the small Upper Peninsula town of Bessemer, Michigan (population 2,550), the Rex Beautiful, the iron-mining town's single movie theater, could only accommodate 300 patrons, and *Zorro* would not arrive there for almost another year. But the film's eventual booking for a two-day run in late October 1921 was still heavily promoted in the town newspaper, *The Bessemer Herald,* by the theater's manager, D. J. Kulazekwiez. The Rex ads for *Zorro* promote the film as offering its viewers both "rapid fire action [and] appealing romance," and show a press book illustration of "Doug" as the masked Zorro in his "latest United Artists production," laughing with sword casually in hand as he confidently leans against a large cask of (now prohibited) wine. Alongside the image of the self-amused *Zorro* and county probate notices are other local ads offering "Home Grown Potatoes, $1.25 per Bushel" for sale at the Finnish Mercantile Stock Co. and "1000 Cords of Dry Wood . . . ideal for use in your kitchen stove" available for delivery "while roads are good" from Bessemer Lumber (*Zorro*).

Like most of the features shown at the Rex, *Zorro* would be exhibited along with another, typically shorter, film. In this case, Fairbanks's film was programmed with a two-reel comedy, *Torchy's Millions,* part of the recently introduced "Torchy" series starring Johnny Hines, described in one trade ad of the period as "An American Go-getter" always finding himself in a bit of "good clean trouble" (Dannenberg). In addition to, and probably in return for, the Rex advertisements, the *Herald* also offered its readers a number of articles (likely written by a studio press agent) about the upcoming Fairbanks film, including a short piece titled "His Wife Laughed at His Appearance" on the subject of Pickford's amused reaction to seeing her husband first "cut his capers" as the "weary, uninterested Don Diego Vega" in such "strong contrast to those antics undergone by the strenuous 'Doug'" ("His Wife"). Bessemer was too small to support a daily newspaper—the *Herald* was instead published once every three days—and two days before the film's arrival the newspaper's front page reported in a boxed item above the fold that the first Thursday evening show of *Zorro* would be earlier than usual, 6:45 P.M., to accommodate the town's "biggest pep meeting of the week" for that Saturday's high school football game against the nearby archrivals of Ironwood. Besides opening his theater to "one of the largest audiences ever seen at a meeting here" Kulazekwiez, who acted as master of ceremonies, also provided the gathering with his regular four-piece "orchestra" for musical accompaniment to the team's "cheers and yells," whose words "were flashed on screen" with slides produced for the occasion by the theater's manager ("*Plans*"). Much as we have seen in Waukesha and Coshocton, manager Kulazekwiez actively worked to make his local patrons understand the Rex Beautiful as an integral and productive part of their small community.

Bessemer, Michigan, was (and remains) a small (if statistically urban) town in the farthest reaches of the state's Upper Peninsula, and so it is not too surprising that a popular movie like *Zorro* took so long to arrive at its only theater. Van Wert, Ohio, on the other hand, was a busy county seat of more than 8,000 residents in a prosperous agricultural region with direct rail service to a number of nearby larger cities, including Toledo, Ohio, and Fort Wayne, Indiana. This proximity to the wider world helped make potatoes cheaper—only seventy-five cents a bushel at C. S. Allen & Son's grocery—and movies more current. *The Saphead* arrived at the Van Wert Strand Theatre a little more than a month after it premiered in New York City (*Saphead*).

The Saphead was the second movie remake of a successful 1913 Broadway play, *The New Henrietta*, in which Douglas Fairbanks, "exceeding pleasant expertation [*sic*]" as Bertie Lamb, first propelled himself to theatrical stardom ("Much to Please"). The initial movie adaptation was also Fairbanks's first film, *The Lamb* (1915), and the second one was originally offered to him as well. But as the story's rights were owned by Loew's Metro, and Fairbanks was now only working for himself and his United Artists partners, Fairbanks suggested in his stead his friend Buster Keaton, a two-reeler comedian who had just begun his own production company that coincidentally already distributed its films through Metro.

In this year's version, Bertie van Alstyne (Keaton), the saphead, son of Nicholas Van Alstyne, a wealthy New Yorker (William H. Crane, who had previously played against Fairbanks in the original Broadway production), is in love with Agnes Gates (Beulah Booker), a ward of Van Alstyne's. Bertie adores Agnes and does his best to win her interest. He succeeds, but in the process he disgusts his father, who kicks Bertie out the house with only a million dollars, charging him with making something of himself before he weds Agnes. Meanwhile, the man married to Bertie's sister, Mark Turner (Irving Cummings), receives temporary power of attorney from Van Alstyne, but the son-in-law has a dark secret—a former lover, Henrietta. Henrietta has died leaving a young child fathered by Mark and secret letters revealing the fact that show up just as Bertie and Agnes are to be married. But Mark swiftly accuses Bertie of being the author of the letters. Bertie is too much of a sap to realize what has happened and the nuptials are called off. Mark is a liar and a bad investor to boot, and nearly ruins the family business by selling off Van Alstyne's stock at too low a price. Bertie accidentally comes to the family's rescue on the trading floor of the exchange and unwittingly manages to save the day, allowing his marriage to Agnes to go blissfully forward.

At seven reels *The Saphead* would be Keaton's first feature-length film, something that is quite evident in the advertisements for the film's two-day showing at the Van Wert Strand that foreground neither the film's title nor Keaton's name. Instead, the ad's lead and largest space is given over to what now seems a curious question: "Do You Remember the Play 'David Harum'?" Originally, a popular homespun novel published in 1898 by Edward Noyes Westcott, a country banker turned novelist, the book was translated into a successful Broadway production in 1900, starring William H. Crane in the title role, a small-town sage who solves everyone's problems while having humorous troubles of his own. Rather than Keaton, it is Crane, born in 1845 and best known for his domestic stage comedies, who receives star billing in the *Van Wert Bulletin*. According to Lewis C. Strang's 1899 *Famous Actors of The Day*: "Although Mr. Crane's versatility and his talent for impersonations are limited, his comedy powers . . . are exceptionally authoritative. His humor is broad, unctuous, and perfectly understandable. . . . There is neither bite nor sting to the fun that he invokes" (179).

So it is apparent that *The Saphead*, a film that now is conceived as primarily a Keaton comedy about a bumbling spoiled big-city millionaire, is in Van Wert, Ohio, predominately promoted for its links to a turn-of-the-century play dealing with small-town life starring a seventy-five-year-old thespian. Why might this make sense? In part, it reveals that Keaton was not yet the star that he would soon become, but what might the other ads and articles on the same page of the *Van Wert Bulletin* tell us about the role of the movies in the town's daily life? Van Wert is a place where a regular column on "News of the County" reveals to its readers which family "took Sunday supper" with their friends, who recently visited their parents from Bowling Green, and whose "little babe is very ill." In a county whose primary economy is agriculture, we find mostly classified ads for the sale of "early cabbage plants" and "fertile" acreage, as well as an article entitled "If a Farmer Had to Pay His Wife" that describes a study by the University of Nebraska that analyzes the hypothetical cost of paying a farmer's wife a "living wage" for her labors ($4,000 a year). It's the kind of place where, in addition to those cheap potatoes, the grocer sells gunpowder by the pound (sixty cents) and lists the prices for bulk staples such as flour, beans, and soap (thirteen different kinds). Yet Van Wert is big enough in its numbers and its consumer desires to offer at least some of its citizens the kind of life that might require a man to buy a $35 "trouser suit," one advertised by the Van Wert Clothing Company, nothing too flashy, mind you, just "smart Browns Blues and Greys" ("Van Wert"). That suit could then be "dry cleaned" at Crescent Laundry, a new and somewhat dangerous convenience, preceding by some years the use of a process employing a less-flammable solvent produced specifically for dry cleaning (Fabricare). In many ways, then, this single page from a small-town newspaper reflects many of the possibilities and anxieties of American modern life at this moment, and the context from which the people of Van Wert, and many other "urban" places around the country, saw their movies—promotion for mass entertainment blending with prices and pitches for industrialized consumer culture—Campbell's Soup, Quaker Oats, and the "miracle science" of Nutto-Oleo Margarine—alongside everyday issues of life and death, work and leisure. Within this swirling set of modern discourses it is, of course, purely coincidental that the Strand's ad would claim *The Saphead* as "good clean fun" adjacent to ads for dry cleaning and more than a dozen brands of soap. But it is no accident that, much like the use of Edith May in Waukesha, the foregrounding of Crane and his previous performance as village wise man allows the Strand's owners to promote the movie as acceptable small-town entertainment, even when the story it tells is about the wealthy excesses of big city life. If this type of seeming contradiction made perfect sense for Van Wert, as well as the many other towns discussed in this chapter, it would be silly in New York, where "Roxy" Rothafel would choose to advertise *The Saphead* much differently. Here, at his picture palace, the (aptly named) Capital, whose grand space was large enough to accommodate the entire town of Bessemer, Michigan, with plenty of seats leftover, Rothafel had no need to disguise the debauched metropolitan life of Keaton's character Bertie. Instead, Roxy promotes the film's fantastical excesses, teasingly asking his potential audience: "How Would You Spend a Million?" ("Screen" [February]). Although in the official eyes of the new census, towns like Van Wert and cities like New York were equally "urban," they offered their residents very different experiences at the movies, even when the movie shown was exactly the same.

NOTES

1. All research materials for this chapter (with the exception of the films themselves) were located and accessed using only Internet resources that fit into three approximate categories: free-public access web sites (such as the National Oceanic and Atmospheric Library), low-cost commercial databases (Newspaperarchive.com), and various academic database collections of the type typically available from most university and public library systems (Proquest). The purpose of this historiographic experiment, of artificially limiting myself to writing about a year in the past from the digital present, was to explore what the rapidly expanding online archive could offer, and what its potential might be to reshape both the production of and access to American history.

2. Charles Bryant (1879–1948), a successful Broadway actor and director, was gay, privately out but publicly "married" to Nazimova from 1912 to 1925. This marriage was never legally officiated, and Nazimova was, in fact, still married to another man, Sergei Golovin, a Russian she had met as a young actress before immigrating to the United States.

3. The Nevada state attorney would, upon hearing of Pickford's marriage to Fairbanks, sue to nullify her divorce to Moore, on the grounds that Pickford never intended to become a permanent resident of Nevada, a legal requirement of the state divorce law. Although it would take more than two years, the divorce and subsequent marriage would stand.

1921

Movies and Personality

MARK LYNN ANDERSON

The films made this year and the performers who starred in them participated in a relatively new popular interest in the secret strangeness of the familiar personality. The stories the movies now told bore the traces of a significant cultural transition: from a Progressive Era concern with finding happiness through solving life's problems to a new but sustained fascination with the experiences and fate of the unusual person. For some, this development marks the transition from a socially conscious cinema to one of mere entertainment, but it also announces the arrival of the contemporary media personality, one of the principal categories through which we now experience the world. Several films released during the year—*Enchantment, Footlights, Her Face Value, Hickville to Broadway, Reputation, A Small Town Idol*—dealt both seriously and humorously with the complicated lives of fictionalized popular performers. This new fascination with celebrity differed from the traditional admiration of historically significant individuals such as great artists, thinkers, and statesmen. Instead, the new personality was more likely to be any ordinary individual who had, because of some peculiar personal characteristic or particular circumstance, arbitrarily entered upon the world stage. In September, Margaret Gorman, a "Mary Pickford look-a-like" and the newly crowned Miss Washington, D.C., won the first intercity beauty pageant held on the boardwalks of Atlantic City (Allen 80; "1,000 Bathing Girls"). Apparently, a relatively ordinary individual could now achieve unprecedented renown overnight, solely through the possession of some unusual quality or through involvement in some sensational event.

Sales of musical records peaked at a level the recording industry would not see again until World War II. While radio and sound movies would eventually become the principal mechanisms for the promotion of popular songs, phonograph records and sheet music remained important components of a mass culture devoted to the promulgation of personalities. Songwriters James F. Hanley and Grant Clarke witnessed the composition they penned for the *Ziegfeld Follies* become a national sensation, but the appeal of "Second Hand Rose" was inextricably tied to its performer, Fanny Brice, who sang the song at the Follies during the summer. Brice had become a star attraction because of her comedic turns at musical parody and her performance of "ethnic" numbers. Unlike other Jewish performers, Brice exploited her working-class origins by travestying high cultural forms of dance and by singing mock romantic songs in Yiddish dialect. As theater historian Linda Mizejewski points out, Brice's identity not only contrasted with "the outrageous fabrication" (8) of whiteness and Anglo-ancestry of the typical Glorified American Girl on display in the *Follies*, but also "situated [her] in the ambiguous intersection of stardom and contempt" (133). Yet as Brice was saving the seemingly indistinguishable bevy of Ziegfeld beauties from conformity to a single standard of American feminine desirability, she also created a popular appeal for her own difference. If public interest in Brice sometimes took the form of ridicule, it also often constituted a cultural appreciation of the comedienne as a compelling figure whose biography and art could provide valuable insight into contemporary life.

"Second Hand Rose" was received as a biographical gloss on Brice's own impoverished upbringing, and with her ability to inject heartfelt pathos into the most comic of songs, the public easily recognized the emotional costs of the struggle to keep up appearances in an increasingly consumerist society: "Second hand pearls I'm wearing second hand curls / I never get a single thing that's new / Even Jake the plumber, he's the man I adore / Had the nerve to tell me he's been married before / Ev'ry one knows that I'm just second hand Rose / From Second Avenue."[1] Second Avenue was the center of the Jewish theatrical district and was known during the early decades of the century as "Jewish Broadway." Here, the song's very connection to Brice's own background opens upon a series of contemporary issues including fashion systems, premarital sex, divorce, class mobility, and the difficulties of ethnic assimilation, making Brice herself a salient interpreter of contemporary America society. The real success of the song's appeal, however, is its insistence on inevitable failure. By claiming that "Ev'ry one knows" the real identity of Rose, the song describes the public's own involvement in the construction and deconstruction of modern personalities whose glamorized surfaces were valued precisely because they lead into new processes of discovery.

Another source for promoting popular personalities were the nation's 2,335 daily newspapers, with an aggregate circulation of over thirty million (Park 64). The newly elected president, Warren G. Harding, had come to politics as a successful newspaper publisher from Marion, Ohio. Harding had exploited the media's new interest in the private lives of public figures by campaigning from the front porch of his home in Marion in the 1920 race. Newspapers and newsreels had given his campaign extensive coverage and free publicity, especially when Mr. and Mrs. Harding were visited by well-known stage and screen personalities such as Al Jolson, Mary Pickford, Douglas Fairbanks, Texas Guinan, Conway Tearle, or *Photoplay* editor James R. Quirk ("Actors to Go to Marion").

The Republicans came to power on a platform of isolationism, probusiness policies, and anti-radicalism. If postwar society was to be remade, it was going to be remade as a fully "American" society. The Republicans promoted a vast platform of Americanization, seeking to assure that traditional cultural values and social relations would be preserved as big business expanded and the new consumer economy flourished. The ideology of Americanization found support within white supremacist organizations, as well as providing much of the rationalization for anti-immigrant policies such as the Emergency Quota Act, passed by the Congress in May to limit the number of immigrants allowed into the United States according to ethnicity and race. Membership in the Ku Klux Klan was at an all-time high, and the newspapers provided the country with seemingly daily coverage of the Klan's vigilante violence, not only in the South, but also in New York, Ohio, Indiana, and Michigan. A race riot in Tulsa, Oklahoma, left an inestimable number of black citizens murdered with impunity. During the summer, the national press turned its attention to the controversial trial in Boston of two Italian anarchists charged with murdering a pair of retail clerks during a payroll robbery. Their widely contested conviction this year, their subsequent appeals, and their eventual execution in 1927 made Nicola Sacco and Bartolomeo Vanzetti emblematic of the anti-radical xenophobia often imputed to the decade.

While Hollywood steadfastly avoided the topics of racial inequality, segregation, or lynching, the white-owned and independent Reol Corporation released as many as six black-cast race features, with *The Burden of Race* going so far as to promote the legitimacy of miscegenation, which was still outlawed in the majority of states. In both *The Land of Hope* and *Puppets of Fate*, the majors did, however, attempt to deal sensitively with the plight of European immigrants. The Great War also remained an important event for dramatizing international relations, as in Frances Marion's *The Love Light* and Rex Ingram's *The Four Horsemen of the Apocalypse*. The cinematic rumination on modern marriage begun by Cecil B. DeMille continued with comedies such as George Marshall's *Why Trust Your Husband?*, melodramas such as Lois Weber's *What Do Men Want?* and *Too Wise Wives*, and DeMille's own *The Affairs of Anatol*. Wallace Reid contributed to his popular series of automobile racing films with *Too Much Speed*, but was joined by daredevil Bebe Daniels in *The Speed Girl* and even by cowboy Tom Mix in *The Road Demon*. One of the most highly praised and successful films of the year was a bucolic coming-of-age story filmed in rural Virginia. As a refreshing alternative to Hollywood's obsession with sex and the city, Henry King's *Tol'able David* apparently played well in heartland theaters because of its nostalgic celebration of old-time rural values; the film did just as well, however, in urban centers, mostly due to twenty-six-year-old Richard Barthelmess's endearing portrayal of the adolescent title character. Barthelmess had risen to stardom just two years before in the role of a disillusioned Chinese immigrant in D. W. Griffith's *Broken Blossoms*, and, after his performance in *Tol'able David*, he was widely considered one of the screen's finest actors.

One of the year's most popular films appeared in early February. While *The Kid* conferred immediate stardom upon six-year-old actor Jackie Coogan, Charles Chaplin had been an international celebrity for over five years before releasing his first feature-length motion picture. Taking nearly nine months to complete and costing over half a million dollars, the film was an immediate critical and popular success. Additionally, the movie helped cement the idea that Chaplin was a serious, even intellectual filmmaker, an identity that would become a central component of the enduring Chaplin mythos (Maland 59). *The Kid* featured Chaplin's perennial tramp character as an accidental father who discovers an infant abandoned among the garbage. Through numerous small details of their frugal domestic lives, Chaplin depicts the relationship between the kid and the tramp as one of deep affection, two figures bound together because of the world's indifference to their fates. The film was praised for its brilliant combination of comic and tragic elements, and, throughout the year, was regularly pronounced the most important motion-picture comedy ever made, an artistic achievement possessing "integrity," "genius," and "literary charm" (Carr "Charlie"; Kingsley). Chaplin had long been adding pathos and psychological depth to the tramp character in order to broaden that figure's appeal and to promote his own status as an artist. The paradox of the tramp's longing for love and his isolation, his emotional proximity and his social distance, resonated well with the contemporary understanding of the media personality as dependent upon the public's own interest and emotional investment in the lives of persons with whom they had no other organic social relation.

Her Picture in the Papers: Public Opinion and *The Ace of Hearts*

While Hollywood was expanding the public's interests in its stars, modern personalities were also increasingly available for public consumption in the overlapping media of newspapers, magazines, musical recording, and radio, but the terms and ultimate ends of the public's interests in media celebrities were still largely unregulated. In March, ordinary citizen Adelaide Doane sent New York governor Nathan Miller a letter calling on him to broaden the state's power of censorship to include not only motion pictures but the press as well, a medium she believed constituted a similar but more dangerous threat to the social order. While this letter was only one of several hundred received by the governor on the issue of film censorship, it points to an important relation between the movies and the newspapers that was obtaining at that time, a relation that might be generally defined as the two media vying for the public's attention. Doane writes:

> The people who are so concerned about purifying the "movies" seem to think that they cater to the lowest tastes of our young people, but has it ever occurred to them that people have to go out of their houses to go to the movies but the daily mail comes into every home to be read by every member of the family. I hold no brief for the movies for I seldom go, but I am sick of the "free speech" and "free press" which have been exploited ad infinitum, ad nausea.

As the mass media sought to exploit a newly imagined social force called "public opinion," different institutions and different sectors of the citizenry understood and responded to the situation differently; nevertheless, public opinion provided a model of address that made the public an entity deeply interested in itself, in its own processes, and in its possibilities. Before the domain of public opinion was alienated from the public—that is, before it became the principal concern of a professional class who studied it, theorized it, and sold it—the public had to be won over and made to take an active interest in itself *as a social force*. This was a project potentially dangerous for traditional interests, as Doane's letter to the governor bears witness.

Doane included a clipping from one of the many New York newspapers as evidence for her concern. The clipping reports on the recently disclosed charges of complaint in the Stillman divorce, a case that would occupy the nation's headlines throughout the spring and summer, and that would leave a lasting impression on public opinion throughout the decade. When James Stillman filed for divorce from his wife, Anne, he was the president of the

National City Bank, in which he and the Rockefeller family owned the controlling shares. At the height of the divorce suit that summer, Florence Leeds, a former chorus girl named by Mrs. Stillman as one of her husband's many dalliances, was rumored to have been planning to "star" in a Hollywood production about the Stillman affair. There was also apparently talk in the industry that Mrs. Stillman herself might attempt to perform in motion pictures ("Mrs. Stillman Bars Exile"). Of course, most sectors of the film industry mounted an intense effort to halt the screen appearances of individuals who had achieved notoriety because of involvement with famous divorce and murder cases. However, the Stillman affair was only one of many such cases discussed by the press during the first half of the year. Numerous individuals were reportedly seeking to use their unfortunate connections with public scandals to launch careers as screen celebrities.

These cases suggest that the movies had the possibility of functioning in tandem with newspapers as another way for the public to experience media personalities whose appeal had nothing to do with their status as film artists. Their appeal rested on something else, something related to the star system but outside of it. When she requested that Governor Miller extend motion picture censorship to apply to the press as well, Doane glimpsed the several points of convergence between the motion picture and the newspaper around the public's interest in sensational crimes, divorce cases, and scandalous exposés. What she saw was the real potential for the newspaper to play a role in the organization of a mass society, a potential that would quickly be contained and redirected by the separation of the mass media into distinct tasks: entertainment and reportage.

However, a film such as William Worsley's *The Ace of Hearts* demonstrates that while mainstream films might seek to avoid politics through vague topicality, the cinema remained intertwined with modes of address created by the headlines of the day. *The Ace of Hearts* tells the story of a radical organization dedicated to assassinating wealthy individuals who have done nothing to alleviate society's ills. This secret society is composed of eight men and one woman, Lilith (Leatrice Joy), a revolutionary so committed to the organization's cause that she has no time for romance. The group's perfected means of attack is the planting of bombs in public places. Such story elements clearly called to mind news events of the preceding two years, including the numerous insurrectionary bombings that targeted capitalists and politicians during the spring and summer of 1919, the bombing of Wall Street in September of 1920, and the federal deportations of the anarchists Emma Goldman and her lover, Alexander Berkman. Nevertheless, the film refuses to reference these events directly, emphasizing instead the clandestine nature of the organization's activities through a low-key lighting style presciently like film noir.

Randomly dealt the ace of hearts by the group's leader, Forrest (John Bowers) is lucky enough to carry out the next bombing, gaining Lilith's admiration and her pledge to marry him if it will help him serve the cause more fervently. Lon Chaney's celebrated skill at conveying intense psychological torment enhances his performance of Farralone, Forrest's rival for Lilith's attention. Lilith and Forrest wed the day before the planned attack, but after a night of nuptial bliss, both begin to lose their resolve for political violence. Forrest will, in fact, change his mind after wistfully observing a young couple that would likely be unintended casualties of the blast. Subsequently, Farralone, in an act of violent self-sacrifice, aids Lilith and Forrest in escaping from the organization to an idyllic life in the wilderness. Before this resolution, however, the film's suspense turns upon whether Forrest will detonate the bomb in a crowded restaurant where the targeted man regularly breakfasts. We see the members of the secret society waiting for word of the mission's completion. Startled by the cries of a hawking newsboy outside, they look for word of the assassination in the relatively rapid means of communication provided by the daily papers. A member of their group just arriving on the scene purchases a paper and inspects its headlines before joining the others indoors. The headlines he observes on the street are withheld from the audience until he arrives upstairs and opens the paper for Lilith and Farralone to inspect. The insert of the newspaper that follows contains several items with which the public was already deeply familiar. Underneath a banner announcing an unspecified "President's Message to Congress" are displayed headlines of labor strikes, radical agitation, and, finally, the Stillman divorce, one of the very subjects the industry was so keen to keep off the screen just a few months before the film's release. Showing the audience an insert in which the narrative information that is looked for is absent suggests that the bombing only has meaning for the secret society if it appears in the paper. Such publicity would not only give them certainty about the result, but produce a particular effect of terror by exploiting the mass media's purchase on the public's attention. By presenting motion picture audiences with actual headlines recognizable outside the fiction, the film suggests that the newspaper is bound to the cinema, not as a source of topical information but as a mode of mass communication. Of course, the narrative of *The Ace of Hearts* is taking a particular turn at this moment, one away from these headlines and toward the isolation of the romantic couple in a state of nature, far outside the spreading communication networks of modernity.

No news is plenty when Mrs. Stillman makes her screen debut in this insert from *The Ace of Hearts* (William Worsley, Goldwyn). Frame enlargement courtesy of George Eastman House Motion Picture Department Collection.

Sinful Hollywood: Scandal and *The Affairs of Anatol*

The ascendancy of the tabloid press resonated well with the motion picture industry's own promotion of its stars as ordinary people who led extraordinary lives both onscreen and in the newest American colony known as Hollywood. Thus, the relation between the cinema and the press at this time was complicated by their overlapping projects of exploiting the public's interest in the lives of fascinating people. The arrest in September of the popular film comedian Roscoe Arbuckle on a charge of raping and murdering a young actress named Virginia Rappe was the first in a series of scandals that would forever change Hollywood's relation to the nation's newspapers. But while Arbuckle's arrest and subsequent trials have become the most discussed of the early scandals, his notoriety in the headlines was only the continuation of a series of developing contradictions in the creation and dissemination of modern personalities by the press and by the movies. At the time, Arbuckle had a three-year contract with Famous Players–Lasky, the production wing of Paramount, and was earning a salary of $3,500 a week, plus 25 percent of each of his picture's profits ("Scandal Hits"). After news of the arrest broke, the scandal and its sordid details remained prominent in the nation's newspapers for over a year and a half. Communities across the country banned Arbuckle's films, and three sensational criminal trials were held consecutively before the third finally led to an acquittal. Perhaps unfairly, the Arbuckle fiasco quickly become the most iconic early Hollywood scandal and has remained so ever since.

Arbuckle's arrest occurred as the industry was already facing a mounting crisis over the perceived immorality of its pictures, particularly with respect to matters of promiscuous sexuality. After the Great War, reformers of different stripes had intensified their calls for increasing regulation of motion pictures at local, state, and federal levels. The studios were promising to pursue self-regulation and to cooperate with anyone seeking to improve the moral tenor and artistic quality of motion pictures. They argued that most films were more or less wholesome entertainment and that those few lurid and sensational pictures causing such public alarm were typically products of small, fly-by-night film companies over whom majors had little or no control.

Thus, the industry was proposing that the improvement of the motion picture lay in further industrial consolidation, an outcome already well underway as Paramount head Adolph Zukor had been aggressively acquiring control over the country's important theater chains. Zukor's rapid pursuit of vertical integration (controlling film production, distribution, and exhibition) at the beginning of the decade quickly became the business model for the entire American film industry. As Douglas Gomery notes, the Federal Trade Commission (FTC) concluded that by this year over a quarter of all theaters in the United States were showing Paramount pictures exclusively (19–20), a situation that led the FTC to bring an anti-trust suit against Paramount less than two weeks before the Arbuckle scandal broke. A public discourse soon emerged identifying the enormous financial power of the major studios as the principal cause of star immorality. As an editorial appearing in the *New York Times* argued, "The immense vogue of the movies has rapidly created a large number of the newly rich. They are proverbially the class from which lavish roisterers are mainly recruited. . . . The movies have made some people rich who do not know what money is for, except . . . to be spent in the gratification of barbarian and brutish tastes" ("Sudden Affluence"). While the luxurious lifestyles of the stars had furnished the industry with a concrete demonstration of Hollywood's transformative potential to elevate both taste and standards of living, the scandals pointed to the corruptive possibilities of this new form of class mobility and leisured consumption. A compact between America and the film colony had seemingly been broken by the Arbuckle affair, so much so that by the start of 1922, the New York State Motion Picture Commission was seeking to prohibit not only objectionable film content but objectionable film personalities as well ("Walker Fights Bar").

In light of this situation, the release of Paramount's *The Affairs of Anatol* in September might appear poorly timed given the film's promotion of the studio's most important stars in a risqué story about opulent consumption, marital infidelity, and extravagant parties. Instead, the success of the film exemplifies Hollywood's ability to defuse complaints about its inhabitants and its products through demonstrating that the transformations of personality made possible by fashionable consumption were not substantive but pleasurable, precisely because they were playful, artificial, or even fantastical. *The Affairs of Anatol* was the sixth and last of an immensely successful series of sex comedies staring Gloria Swanson that Cecil B. DeMille directed from 1919 through this year. Like its predecessors, *The Affairs of Anatol* presented itself as a lighthearted treatise on marriage and the contemporary crisis in the relation between the sexes, a crisis observable in the rapidly rising rate of divorce. These films promoted the new consumerism and the new social freedoms for women as significant social advances that could save the institution of marriage by transforming it. DeMille's endorsement of companionate marriage, both on screen and in the pages of the fan magazines, urged wives to take an active interest in the leisure pursuits of their husbands and to offer themselves as playmates on equal footing in the enjoyment of the expanding consumer marketplace. Similarly, husbands were instructed to let go of preconceived notions about self-sacrificing wives and their duty to provide for home and family, and to honor a woman's right to pleasure. The command to "know thy wife" was a particular instantiation of the modern personality in that it required one to participate in a process of discovery by appreciating fashionable consumption as a means of communication within matrimony.

The sex comedies of DeMille were, therefore, illustrations of fashion as an expression of personality, a situation that required a new relation to the visible. Appearances in themselves no longer bespoke an underlying identity but an attitude, a momentary relation to the world, or what we might now recognize, somewhat reductively, as "a fashion statement." Sumiko Higashi has argued that *The Affairs of Anatol* represented a "collapse of sign systems based on coded distinctions between private and public spheres," a collapse in which "appearances no longer functioned as a reliable index of character and breeding. Discourse in fan magazines implied that stars like Gloria Swanson assumed new personalities whenever they changed their wardrobes" (Higashi, *DeMille* 174). But for all its radical implications, this particular version of the modern personality was placed in the service of reestablishing traditional values and institutions by repeatedly staging a rediscovery of the remarkably familiar beneath all the exoticism of modern fashions. As Richard Koszarski observes in relation to Swanson, "DeMille realized that he had found an average American girl who could wear clothes. . . . Swanson proved to be the one actress, even more than Bebe Daniels, whom DeMille could cloak in worldliness without obscuring the homelier American virtues underneath" (295). With its half-dozen major Hollywood stars wearing exquisitely designed costumes and inhabiting the luscious sets created in nascent art-deco style by Parisian designer Paul Iribe, *The Affairs of Anatol* represents one of the most graphically extravagant productions of the entire decade. Release prints were elaborately tinted, toned, and color stenciled.

Jeanie Macpherson based her scenario for the film rather loosely on a short play by Viennese writer Arthur Schnitzler. Schnitzler depicted the serialized romantic infatuations of a young hedonist whose intense and singular devotions to various young women were astonishingly short-lived. Much of the play's humor comes from Anatol's insouciant exaggerations of his tormented passions, as he confides the details of recent heartbreaks to his best friend, Max. Although Macpherson's scenario for the film version of *The Affairs of Anatol* retains some of the play's minor elements, the character of Anatol has been transformed from an aesthete European bachelor to an American newlywed bent on rescuing young women from the vices of modern life. Matinee idol Wallace Reid brings an All-American boyishness to the role quite at odds with the sardonic wit and cynicism of Schnitzler's original characterization. The loyal Max becomes the confidante of Anatol's wife, Vivian (Gloria Swanson), remaining a trusted and understanding companion to whom she can express her frustrations with matrimony. The film begins with what had become a celebrated convention of DeMille's comedies during the period: an elaborate bathing scene showcasing exquisitely designed bathrooms of immense proportions with fanciful fixtures and the latest in toilet accoutrements. Anatol de Witt Spencer enters such a bathroom to express his annoyance at having to wait for breakfast while his wife completes her morning pedicure. From behind a screen, Vivian playfully instructs the chambermaid to inform her husband that he will have to be patient with his new bride. Glancing at his watch, Anatol's vexation is further increased when Vivian calls him forth for a small kiss. These newlyweds already exhibit the central problem of modern marriage according to DeMille: the wife is insensitive to the interests of her husband outside of the marriage, while the husband is unresponsive to the wife's need for playful affection. The complications that follow from this initial situation do not significantly develop it further, but instead reiterate the ideas that modern sensuality is not a wicked thing in itself, and that its pleasures are most profitably enjoyed within the free and open relationship of companionate marriage. Without fully considering his wife's needs, Anatol will pursue his interests in saving young women from moral or physical ruin, while Vivian will suspect her husband of dissembling virtuous intent in order to secure romance outside of the marriage. They each err in seeking to check the other's pursuit of pleasures, not fully appreciating the nature of the other's personality. Yet, in a nod to modern psychology, the film also hints that Anatol's investments in moral guardianship may, indeed, have an erotic basis unknown to himself, while Vivian's relationship to Max belies the mutual sublimation of desires.

Anatol's compulsion to rescue young women finally leads Vivian to leave him. "I'll share my purse, and my food, and my home—but I'm through sharing you," she later explains. This separation provides Anatol and Vivian an excuse for a vengeful competition to see who can spend the most sinful evening on the "Great Gay Way." While Vivian's night on the town is only briefly depicted, we later learn that whatever promiscuity occurred went no further than her passing another evening with dear old Max, who seems only remotely capable of acting on his highly guarded passions. Anatol, on the other hand, encounters Satan Synne (Bebe Daniels) at a rooftop cabaret where, in a state of undress, she scandalously performs in a tableaux vivant entitled "The Unattainable." After the performance, she invites Anatol to a rendezvous at her abode, "The Devil's Cloister."

The set for Satan Synne's vampish seduction of Anatol represents the film's most outlandish art direction, where the hedonistic drives of consumerist excess are mocked through the details of Satan's orientalist boudoir, rendered in expressionistic low-key lighting. Upon arriving, Anatol is met by a servant dressed in pseudo-Egyptian slave attire, who leads him beneath a curtained archway inscribed with the legend "He Who Would Sup with the Devil Must Have a Golden Spoon." Satan rises from her vanity to reveal a flowing cape in the shape of a large black octopus, accentuated with diaphanous fabric and rows of giant pearls. In what is clearly the sartorial climax of the entire film, Satan raises her arms to embrace Anatol, and the cape spreads before the camera to reveal its playfully macabre design. This gown and all the other details of ersatz decadence—her pink monogrammed cigarettes, her ornamental absinthe decanter, the leopard she keeps tied to her bed—figure the presumed dissipative effects of fashion, luxury consumption, and sensual leisure as entirely lacking in substance, even as they provide for a new language of sumptuous display as

Bebe Daniels reveals her designs upon Wallace Reid in *The Affairs of Anatol* (Cecil B. DeMille, Famous Players–Lasky). Digital frame enlargement.

personal expression. Indeed, Anatol quickly learns that Satan is seeking three thousand dollars in order to pay for the surgical operation required to save her husband's life. As it turns out, her husband is one of the thousands of "forgotten" veterans wounded in the last war. Thus, the woman who appears the wickedest and participates in the most provocative forms of erotic display is revealed to be the most sacrificing, patriotic, and dutiful woman in the film. After giving Satan the funds she needs, Anatol returns home to find Vivian still out on the town.

The casting of Bebe Daniels as Satan Synne is a fine example of the way personality was being refigured by Hollywood as infinitely transformable because of modern conditions of media, travel, and fashion. Like Swanson, Daniels had gained renown as a comedienne before becoming a regular fixture of romantic comedies at Famous Players–Lasky, where she was promoted as an "American girl" who, in words attributed to DeMille, "is the most perfect type of Oriental womanhood I have ever known" (Cheatum 32). The fan magazines and the films in which she appeared made Daniels a compelling personality because of the non-alignment of her presumed Anglo whiteness with the sartorial expression of that identity. As Daniels claimed quite bluntly, "I am just a Texan, not an Oriental at all, but I love,

love everything Oriental" (Cheatum 123). Hollywood turned Daniels into a star by providing her the means to express herself within a broadly modernist idiom of fashionable consumption that simultaneously allowed the public to learn more about her. While Anatol comes to view Synne's performance of the predatory vamp as a mere deception, concocted only to save her dying husband, the audience is prompted to understand that performance as the expression of Satan's unflagging devotion to her marriage, and as an instance of Daniel's taste in fashion. The fact that the husband's illness is the result of war injury is not an arbitrary detail, for the turn toward consumption in the early 1920s, though often seen as an escape from the trauma of the war years, was also figured as a justified response to the many depravations Americans endured during the war.

"Character" versus "Personality": Jazz Age Reform and *The Blot*

Culturally daring but politically conservative, American society was repeatedly depicted as having successfully conducted its "revolution in morals" only to arrive at a comfortable, even cozy, mediocrity. In Sinclair Lewis's *Main Street*, the year's best-selling novel, the complacency and self-assuredness of the folks populating the small town of Gopher Prairie, Minnesota, stood in for the nation: "Such a society functions admirably in the large production of cheap automobiles, dollar watches, and safety razors. But it is not satisfied until the entire world also admits that the end and joyous purpose of living is to ride in flivvers, to make advertising-pictures of dollar watches, and in the twilight to sit not talking of love and courage but of the convenience of the safety razor" (267). The wide popularity of the novel's critique of mass society resulted, in part, from its gentle reassurances about both the inevitability of standardization, as well as the mass media's ability to afford each individual a means of overcoming that standardization through self-fashioning.

She was one of the most widely admired and highest-paid directors of the late 1910s, but by the time *The Blot* appeared this year, Lois Weber's critical fortunes had greatly diminished. Weber's reputation for writing and directing powerful social message dramas had already begun to cast her as a somewhat old-fashioned remnant from the Progressive era, a meddling parent increasingly out of step with the youthful exuberance of a dawning Jazz Age. Whether these assessments were accurate or not, Weber was aware of such characterizations of her work, and even laudatory reviews of her films of the early 1920s tended to be defensive about the director's investments in social issues. *Variety*'s reviewer of *The Blot*, for instance, reassured exhibitors by praising the director's ability to covey "a moral without offensive preaching" (35).

The Blot appeared at the end of the summer, the first of Weber's independent productions to be released by F. B. Warren Company, a small, newly formed distributor that also handled the films of Nell Shipman and May Tully, two other women producer/directors of the era. Weber, who had been an independent producer since 1917, signed a lucrative distribution agreement with Paramount in 1919 for a series of Lois Weber Productions. Anthony Slide suggests that this distribution relationship eventually faltered in February 1921 when, after an advance private screening, Paramount decided not to distribute Weber's meditation on straying husbands, *What Do Men Want*? (112). While films on infidelity and companionate marriage were certainly serving well enough the likes of DeMille, Swanson, and Paramount, Weber's refusal to feature big-name stars or to glamorize consumerist excess placed her work outside emerging Hollywood formulas.

The Blot is a comparative study in social class, consumption, and cultural values that pits the historical fates of three families against one another: the Griggs family, whose middle-class standard of living is deteriorating because of the low salary Professor Griggs receives as a college professor; the Wests, whose long-established wealth allows the young Paul West Jr. (Louis Calhern) to indulge in the most extravagant sorts of pleasures then available for youthful dissipation; and the newly if modestly affluent Olsens, an immigrant family of eight "making good" in the new consumerist economy because Mr. Olsen makes fashionable "high-priced shoes that ruin the feet of the women who wear them." While the film's social message ostensibly calls attention to the low salaries paid to American educators, the drama centers on attempts by Mrs. Griggs (Margaret McWade) to maintain her family's well-being in the face of increasing deprivations, thereby speaking to the plight of a larger body of professionals and their families who constituted the traditional and emerging middle classes, and whose spending power was diminished by postwar inflation. The complex motivations behind her struggle to retain her family's social standing in a period of rapid cultural transformations makes Mrs. Griggs by far the most complicated and richly drawn character, at least until late in the film when her daughter, Amelia (Claire Windsor), begins making the important decisions affecting her family's sustainability.

Because the film is ultimately concerned with the preservation of this middle-class family, it works as affective melodrama; yet it creates its pathos through a meditation on the suffering of this class in relation to the new affluence of the working class and the obliviousness of the wealthy, and thus presents a pressing social problem. As Shelley Stamp has observed, Weber's films of the early 1920s neatly combined the commitments to social reform that occupied her Progressive Era filmmaking with an attention to the demands of the new entertainment that emerged in the postwar period. This emergent cultural environment, with its deepening participation in the emergent style systems that were driving advertising, mass communications, and the new consumerist economy, becomes in *The Blot* a new social situation threatening to disadvantage if not destroy those sectors of the nation charged with maintaining and reproducing societal health: the so-called "brain workers" whose ranks included academics, social workers, civil planners, the clergy, journalists, community organizers, medical professionals, and homemakers.

The film begins with Paul and two wealthy friends disrupting a lecture by Professor Griggs. While each exhibit signs of immaturity, Paul is quickly revealed as the most robust and healthiest of the bunch, actively drawing caricatures of Professor Griggs and revealing an appreciation for visual expression. From the beginning, Louis Calhern's athletic stature and fair complexion mark his performance of Paul as a compelling and dynamic personality worthy of our attention. It comes as no surprise, then, when we are soon made aware of Paul's attraction to Griggs's daughter, Amelia, who works behind the circulation desk of the public library. If a professor's daughter must work to supplement her family's income, a library job seems entirely consistent with the family's station and social charge. Yet Amelia's work places her in mildly dangerous situations where she is subject to the advances of strange men and exposed to an unregulated public. Her work at the library affords Paul several opportunities to flirt with her by feigning an interest in literature, a pretense that Amelia easily unmasks. Yet for all her common sense and precaution, she cannot effectively control the two young girls who chat in the open doorway of the library, creating the cold draft that will lead to Amelia's illness. Thus, even before the comparative analysis of living standards begins, *The Blot*'s exposition aligns the *public* library with a dangerous proximity to disease and sexual promiscuity. Even while the threat of contagion posed by this seemingly respectable civic institution is extremely understated, it is crucial to the film's overall ideological investments in protecting class boundaries through recourse to culturally ascendant arguments about racial purity. Here, the free circulation of books at the public library will be distinguished from the more meaningful appreciation of rare books in the private collections of Professor Griggs and his close friend, the young clergyman, Reverend Gates (uncredited).

The class comparisons begin in earnest when Reverend Gates accompanies the professor home. As the two quietly converse on the sidewalk, Professor Griggs invites the reverend in for tea with a promise that Amelia might soon return. Mrs. Griggs is restrainedly vexed by the clergyman's visit, since she considers the expense of tea an extravagance the family can hardly afford. Quietly, she surveys the shoddiness of her home's worn upholstery, torn carpets, and the hole in the sole of her husband's shoe, all provided in close-up through point-of-view inserts. Weber apparently sought to film *The Blot* in sequence and in actual locations, and critics of the day often praised the film's unusual naturalism. This somber homecoming of Professor Griggs is intercut with the arrival of his next-door neighbor in a new Model T, the most affordable car on the market at a time when only about 10 percent of American households owned a car, a statistic that would dramatically increase during the decade. As Mr. Olsen parks the automobile in front of his house, numerous children and Mrs. Olsen spill across the lawn, squealing with excitement as they run to get a closer look at the family's latest purchase. The commotion draws the attention of the Mrs. Griggs who, in medium close-up, expresses a mixture of envy and disdain at this boisterous display, while Professor Griggs and Reverend Gates exhibit only mild bemusement. Such worldly matters do not seem to preoccupy these two men as much as they do Mrs. Griggs, who must provide the comforts of home for her family. Mrs. Olsen, who thinks the Griggs family is "stuck up," waves from the curbside in a mock-friendly manner designed to taunt her neighbors, but it is only Mrs. Griggs who seems to suffer the indignity.

While the film continues such sociological comparisons by alternating scenes depicting the differing behaviors, affluence, and cultural values of these two families, as well as by alternating these with scenes of the more extravagant diversions of the moneyed class to which Paul West belongs, the message fundamentally remains the same: the white-collar professional classes represented by the Griggs family suffer unfair degradation while those immigrant working classes who have benefited from Fordism have more than they need, but devote their earnings and energies to frivolous popular amusement. Likewise, the wealthiest classes can afford the most exclusive lifestyles that often lead to decadence and to a happy unawareness of the plights of those less fortunate. In other words, the pain of contemporary social transformations are felt only or most significantly by that sector of the American middle class represented by Reverend Gates and the Griggs family, people who have, because of their callings, devoted themselves to a set of cultural and spiritual values more permanent than the latest popular songs that the Olsens sing after dinner, or the thrills of fast cars purchased by the youthful rich of Paul West's crowd. Between blissful ignorance and numb oblivion lies the truth of timeless values. Weber makes no attempt to portray the contempt that Mrs. Olsen holds for the Griggs family as anything but childish competition and willful pride. Refusing to allow the Griggs's cat to eat from the garbage can in her backyard, Mrs. Olsen is shown to be not only uncharitable, but mean-spirited. There is no sense that she has had to suffer any significant indignities or exclusions because of her own class or immigrant status. Similarly, the privilege of the wealthy is seemingly unconnected to any real social antagonisms, and Paul West, at the end of the film, is able to alert his father about the plight of college professors by showing him an article on the problem in the *Literary Digest*. Members of other classes only gain moral weight in the narrative once they take an interest in the problems of the middle class, as Paul does once he learns of Amelia's poverty.

Against this societal portrait, the central drama of *The Blot* concerns the competition between Paul West and Reverend Gates for Amelia's affection. When Amelia falls ill, each man pays a visit to the Griggs home, and Weber provides another study in contrasts. While both Paul and the reverend are properly appreciative of Amelia's charms and her character, Paul has the advantage of wealth. He arrives to visit Amelia first, much to the delight of Mrs. Griggs, who quickly ducks out of the house with what little money she has to buy fancy sweets and cream for Paul's visit. When Mrs. Griggs returns, entering the parlor with a tray of expensive treats, she is horrified to discover that Reverend Gates has replaced Paul. Though she may respect and identify with the earnest Reverend Gates, she is committed to matching Amelia to the wealthier suitor who might relieve her daughter of the daily struggles she herself must endure.

If Mrs. Griggs's preference in a son-in-law is forgivably practical, her attempt to impress Paul with expensive confections turns out to have been a colossal lapse in judgment, because after Amelia's condition worsens, the doctor advises feeding her nourishing food. Unable to get credit at the local grocery, Mrs. Griggs becomes distraught, remorseful for having succumbed to the easy lure of consumer culture, squandering the last of her precious money on foolish trifles. Matters worsen when Mrs. Griggs decides upon stealing one of the chickens that Mrs. Olsen always places at her kitchen window so that the neighbors might appreciate the Olsen's bounty. Stalking over to the neighbor's house and cowering below the kitchen window, Mrs. Griggs quickly snatches a chicken, only to replace the bird a few moments later, overcome with shame at having performed such a reprehensible act. Unbeknownst to Mrs. Griggs, Amelia witnesses her mother's thievery, but not her return of the chicken, and Weber uses a quickly paced shot/reverse shot to dramatize the scandal. Subsequently, Amelia refuses to eat what she believes to be an ill-gotten meal, and returns to work at the library the next day even though she is still not well—her aim being to make enough money to repay Mrs. Olsen and humbly apologize for her mother's transgression. When Amelia presents the money and begs her for forgiveness, Mrs. Olsen is so deeply impressed by Amelia's sincerity and sense of honor that she undergoes a dramatic change in attitude toward her neighbors. Sensing a quality in her she has never known before, Mrs. Olsen comforts Amelia by reassuring her that no chickens have gone missing. The film ends with Paul betrothed to Amelia, the Olsens reconciled with the Griggs family, and Professor Griggs being paid to provide Paul and his friends with evening tutorials. Weber keeps the issue of middle-class poverty open by ending the film with the image of Reverend Gates walking forlornly away from the Griggs home, without Amelia and with no foreseeable change in his immediate prospects.

What Mrs. Olsen discovers in Amelia is a quality Jennifer Parchesky identifies as "character," an essential trait of the traditional middle classes whereby an individual's moral value is grounded in the legacy of an ancestral stock (44). Character thus understood is essentially a racial category in the service of naturalizing class identity. Amelia's essential goodness shines through despite her dire circumstances, and in reclaiming her mother's reputation through an act of humility, she is continuing the work of generation: manifesting an essential character that guarantees the integrity of her class. Character was an effective response to Hollywood's promotion of personality since it countered the latter's celebration of self-fashioning with an insistence on authoritative values not amenable to commodification or transmittable through mass cultural forms. In the social critique at work in *The Blot,* the very suffering of the class who possesses these values furnishes the proof of their social significance. When the Second International Congress of Eugenics took place at the American Museum of Natural History in New York in September, Henry Fairchild Osborne welcomed the attendees by promoting "character" against the "melting pot theory," and by proclaiming it a crucial category for scientific thinking about heredity: "The true spirit of American democracy that *all men are born equal with equal rights and duties* has been confused with the political sophistry that *all men are born with equal character and ability to govern themselves and others,* and with the educational sophistry that education and environment will offset the handicap of heredity" (*Eugenics* 2; emphasis in the original). Whatever Weber's

In *The Blot* (Lois Weber, Lois Weber Productions), Mrs. Griggs (Margaret McWade) darkens her character in the eyes of her daughter by stealing a chicken. Digital frame enlargement.

personal relation to the eugenics movement might have been, *The Blot*'s ideological project is startlingly commensurate with its insistence on policing class and racial boundaries. Many commentators have noted that Weber makes the Olsens Nordic immigrants and thereby avoids representing those ethnic groups most troubling to nativists, yet the film's emphasis on the Olsens' fecundity, their corpulent bodies, their vivacity, and their dynamic movements all work to pose a specific type of threat that is not racially innocent. And while thoroughly motivated by the narration, making "chicken stealing" the moment of Mrs. Griggs's self-betrayal calls upon the existing cultural recognition of such an act's provenance.[2] The theft is certainly a lapse in moral integrity, but it is also a flaw of racial character, an unfortunate blot on the family's name, a stain to be removed only by a daughter's redemptive act of purity.

Leaving Home: Encountering *The Sheik*

At the height of Americanization, a new Hollywood star emerged whose seemingly exotic ethnicity was exploited by the studios in order to create a media sensation. An unexceptional Italian immigrant whose exceptional good looks and dancing ability turned him into a celebrity of unprecedented fame, Rudolph Valentino embodied the very contradictions of the new celebrity culture. He attracted the scorn of racists as well as the fascination of millions by departing from the conventions of white, heteronormative masculinity. His stardom was secured by his portrayal of Julio Desnoyes in Metro's prestige production of *The Four Horsemen of the Apocalypse*, released in March. As Gaylyn Studlar notes, Valentino's role in that film established a narrative pattern that would be repeated throughout his short career (176–77). A key early scene presents Julio, bullwhip in hand, passionately dancing the tango with a prostitute, to the bemusement of the assembled demimonde in a rundown saloon. Valentino would be closely associated with this dance throughout his career, and scenarist June Mathis supposedly chose Valentino for the role based upon his skill and experience as a tango dancer. This scene remains a privileged instance of the Valentino "mystique" in that it presents the star as both sexual menace and object of erotic contemplation, an alternation of roles indicative of the tango itself. Julio moves to Paris, where he pursues the decadent life of a studio artist and has a scandalous affair with a married woman. After the outbreak of world war, he eventually comes to recognize his moral duty as a Frenchman, and, absolving himself of his past transgressions, dies honorably on the battlefield. This story of geographical displacements that ends with the Valentino character reclaiming moral integrity after leading a rather suspect and dissolute life is repeated in many of his subsequent films, though they rarely end with his character's death.

The Sheik was the first film Valentino made under his new contract with Famous Players–Lasky, and it was the last of the Valentino films released this year. It became a national phenomenon after its November premiere, setting attendance records at several important downtown theaters in New York. While motion pictures dealing with Bedouin culture and desert settings were not entirely unusual during the period, *The Sheik* established something of a craze for Arab-inspired themes and fashions, and it also introduced the word "sheik" into American parlance to describe the male version of the seductive vamp. Filmed on location less than a hundred miles from Hollywood, in the plains and sand dunes near Oxnard, California, *The Sheik*'s stunning desert landscapes are often devoid of geographical markers, providing fairly abstract exteriors for this story about a young adventuress's vertiginous crossing of various cultural boundaries.

Lady Diana Mayo (Agnes Ayers) resides in Briska, an old British colonial town near the Sahara desert where we find her declining a young Englishman's proposal of matrimony and pronouncing marriage to be only a modern form of "captivity." For the time being, she has decided to assert her independence by commencing a tour of the Sahara with a hired Arab guide. The night before her departure, Sheik Ahmed Ben Hassan (Valentino) arrives in town, and Diana takes an ethnographer's interest in this commanding tribal leader and the exclusive "marriage fair" he is conducting at a nearby casino, where young Arab women are offered as prizes to Arab men of various ages. Convinced of Ahmed's brutal "savagery," but also intrigued upon hearing of his Parisian education, Diana disguises herself as a Bedouin dancer and steals away to witness this unusual cultural ritual for herself. Thus, the film begins with Diana rejecting conventional gender expectations, and claiming the masculine imperial privilege of visually penetrating the secluded spaces of the Arab world in order to witness their esoteric practices, a right more typically figured as Western access to the colonial harem. The film's pleasures are offered as an extended encounter with an imaginary non-Western culture, one made possible, in part, by the gender deviance of the English heroine whose audacity places her at risk of not only losing her independence but of forfeiting her European identity altogether. When she is chosen to present herself for auction at the casino, Ahmed immediately detects her difference from the other women and, reversing a familiar colonialist trope, tears away her veil to reveal "the pale hands and golden hair of a white woman." Immediately, Ahmed's erotic interest in the defiant Diana is expressed by his removal of her outer garment and by the slow downward scan of her body until his eyes rest upon the loaded revolver she holds at her waist. With lascivious grin and bulging eyes, Ahmed expresses an unnatural desire for Diana in her very transgression of identity categories, for it is not simply Diana's white skin that excites him, but this vision of her white skin in Arab garb, her unauthorized presence at a proscribed site, as well as her phallic posturing with the revolver.

Here the type of ethnic disguise that Hollywood was famously promoting as a form of self-expression allows Diana to become an ethnographic observer, but it also transforms her into a perverse object of Arab male interest. Later, after kidnapping her and taking her to his desert camp, Ahmed observes that she makes "a very charming boy" in her riding boots and jodhpurs, adding, "but it was not a boy I saw two nights ago in Briska." In many ways, the question of just whom Ahmed saw and whom he thought he saw in their first encounter is the erotic engine of the film's suspense. While stories exploiting the threat/fantasy of captivity and rape were certainly nothing new in American cinema, *The Sheik* combines this narrative with a process of discovery initiated by the heroine through her donning of alien signifiers. Here ethnic disguise creates peril, but it also provides an opportunity for self-discovery and, of course, romance. The film proposes that there is something worthwhile in Europeans living like Arabs and Arabs living like Europeans.

In its details, the film sticks close to novelist E. M. Hull's hugely successful popular romance of 1919, even amplifying the fantasy elements of the original through the overly expressive posing of Valentino and Ayers, particularly within the interior of Ahmed's tent, with its numerous hanging carpets and orientalist furnishings. The anti-naturalism of the film is similarly heightened by the extensive use of irises for medium close-ups, as well as by shooting much of the interior action through the doorways of tents and other structures, thereby creating a series of arabesque mattes framing the scenes and making them appear as so many tableaux. *The Sheik* also places a lot of emphasis on skin color, continually contrasting Valentino's brown hands with Ayers's alabaster complexion, as it supports an ideology that skin is a measure of civilization. When Diana is kidnapped by Omair (Walter Long), a rival Arab leader, the threat of rape is heightened by representing him and his followers as significantly darker and, therefore, more barbaric. Ahmed's relatively restrained libidinal investments in Diana are made more acceptable by contrast with Omair's brutality, and when Ahmed is severely wounded rescuing Diana from Omair's stronghold, he redeems himself by turning against one of his own kind in defense of a white woman. It comes as no surprise then, even to Diana, when Ahmed is revealed to have been of European ancestry and only raised as an Arab. Ahmed is a good object then, not because he turns out to be European, but because he turns out to be a European who travels with Arabs. The importance of such a role for Valentino's stardom cannot be underestimated. He too was a suave European, a dark Italian immigrant who seemed naturally adept at playing various ethnicities and races. Valentino was one of the most extreme expressions of the new media personality. The same sorts of pleasures and experiences that Ahmed Ben Hassan makes possible for Lady Diana, Valentino was also making possible for various audiences by his appearance in the cinema. This is why he was such a fascinating and controversial star. Valentino was, in short, captivating.

* * *

While the film industry had long promoted the cinema as a unique means for appreciating celebrities, the year's films both registered and participated in the fairly rapid ascendancy of personality as one of the principal categories for understanding the modern world. The new class antagonisms occasioned by a growing white-collar workforce, the expanding role of the media in mass society, the challenges to matrimony occasioned by the new morality, the alarm among the traditional guardians of culture confronting a simmering American "melting pot"—all these were now topics that could be engaged through the biographies of real or fictional individuals experiencing modernity in dynamic, exciting, and, often, tragic ways. Whether exceptional or ordinary, any individual could be made compelling for a mass audience of newspaper readers and cinema spectators willing to interest themselves in the intimate details of a life lived in public view and discussed by the nation. While Hollywood stars had moved from the entertainment pages to the front pages of the nation's dailies, the movies were providing audiences glimpses into the headlines through their promotion of fashionable personalities who were now something more than just interesting characters in a story or popular screen performers. Hollywood had become news, and the new personalities on display at the movies had become signs of the times.

NOTES

1. Brice further inscribes her ethnicity into the number when she recorded the song for Victor in the fall, changing the lyric "Even Jake the plumber" to "Even Jackie Cohen."

2. As Jacqueline Stewart remarks in relation to preclassical films, "A white voyeuristic look is perhaps more conventionally structured in fiction films that explicitly enable fantasies of surveillance by constructing scenarios in which Black subjects are unaware of watching white eyes watching them. Many fiction films produced during this period situate the camera as a recorder of typical Black activities, which can catch Blacks stealing white property—most frequently chickens and watermelons—and then record their apprehension by whites within the diegesis" (73). Interestingly, though Mrs. Olsen had earlier displayed dressed chickens in her kitchen window to taunt her neighbors, in this scene, for the first time, we are shown a large, fenced-in chicken pen next to the Olsens' house, providing a familiar mise-en-scène for the conventional chicken-stealing narrative.

1922

Movies and the Perilous Future

SARA ROSS

"The world broke in two in 1922 or thereabouts . . ."

—Willa Cather, *Not Under Forty*

In a surprising number of spheres, this year may be regarded as a pivot point between the traditional and the modern. Political forces that would shape the rest of the twentieth century were coming to the fore. The United States was emerging as the preeminent first-world military power as the old model of political control gave way to economic control over the third world, and thus the postcolonial era began. Future foes of both the Second World War and the Cold War appeared, as Mussolini and his Fascisti took power in Italy and the young Soviet Union made its first international diplomatic appearances (North 7). Two years after women finally obtained the right to vote, a woman became a U.S. senator for the first time. And President Warren Harding's secretary of the interior, Albert Fall, took illegal payoffs in exchange for awarding the lease of the Teapot Dome oil fields to Mammoth Oil without competitive bidding, establishing a hallmark of modern politics: political scandal over government corruption and complicity with big oil.

The year marked the beginning of seven years of tremendous prosperity, during which America accumulated two-fifths of the world's wealth and domestic purchases boomed, creating the full-blown modern consumer economy. White collar work was on the rise for both men and women. College enrollment expanded rapidly, feeding the need for corporate workers. The numbers of household servants such as cooks, laundresses, and maids was in sharp decline, and many women instead took positions as secretaries and shop assistants. Male office workers spent long hours with female support staff, and the concept of the "office wife" was born. Skilled manual labor was pushed to the margins as the everyday lives of Americans grew more intertwined with machines (Nye 217). Machines replaced human servants, as millions of homes were wired for electricity. Car purchases led the consumer boom, and the speed of life grew faster. Media attention to the generation gap exacerbated the impression that the younger generation was pushing relentlessly at the boundaries of socially sanctioned behavior, rejecting the constraint of their outraged elders. These trends challenged the figure of the unquestioned patriarch who provided for his family through his physical skill.

The rate of change in so many spheres of life must have been disorienting and threatening. In *Middletown,* the famous study of social trends conducted in Muncie, Indiana, sociologists Robert and Helen Lynd described the period from the 1890s to the mid-1920s as "one of the eras of greatest rapidity of change in the history of human institutions. . . . A citizen has one foot on the relatively solid ground of established institutional habits and the other fast to an escalator erratically moving in several directions at a bewildering variety of speeds" (Lynd and Lynd 497).

In the face of modernity's onslaught, there was a strong thread of fascination with the "primitive" and the exotic running through the social fabric of the year. The Orientalism of the teens continued, as demonstrated by the opening of Grauman's Egyptian theater in Hollywood in October. The Orientalist craze was powerfully reinvigorated by Howard Carter's discovery of the tomb of the young pharaoh Tutankhamen in November. The discovery did for ancient Egyptians what *Nanook of the North* did for "Eskimos," giving rise to what Michael North calls "the first truly modern media event" (North 19). The world clamored for news and images of the pharaoh's plundered treasure, which was not wrenched from the tomb fast enough to satisfy the immediacy of the modern news cycle. A fad for ancient Egyptian motifs in clothing and architecture sprang up, and the smart set danced to the "Tutankhamen Rag." The Egyptian elements in art deco architecture inspired by Tut's discovery had a lasting impact on design.

The Modern Media

The year also marked significant turning points in the realm of literature, as the voice of the disillusioned "Lost Generation" reached full volume. North has argued that, with the publication of James Joyce's *Ulysses* and T. S. Eliot's *The Wasteland,* literary modernism "arrived as a commonly accepted public fact." Modernist poet Ezra Pound claimed that the Christian Era ended with the completion of *Ulysses* and proposed a new calendar in which this became year one of a new era (North 3). F. Scott Fitzgerald chronicled the upheavals of modern youth in both a serious novel,

The Beautiful and Damned, and a collection of popular short stories, *Tales of the Jazz Age*, and his name for the period stuck. The Harlem Renaissance had its beginnings as well, in the publication of Claude McKay's *Harlem Shadows* and James Weldon Johnson's *Book of American Negro Poetry*.

In Sinclair Lewis's *Babbitt*, the title character, a successful businessman, is awakened to his conformity and his separation from the world. Lewis writes of Babbitt that "he beheld . . . his way of life as incredibly mechanical. Mechanical business. . . . Mechanical religion . . . mechanical friendships. . . . He saw the years, the brilliant winter days and all the long sweet afternoons which were meant for summery meadows, lost in such brittle pretentiousness" (178–79). The impulse of disillusionment with modern life and nostalgia for a simpler past resonated with readers, who propelled *Babbitt* to the top ten best-seller list for the year. In a more sensational vein, Warner Fabian's *Flaming Youth*, which this year was serialized in the *Metropolitan Magazine* before its release as a book the following January, stirred up controversy with its story of young flapper sisters skinny-dipping at parties and having premarital sex. *Flaming Youth* was issued by the maverick young publishing house Boni and Liveright (B&L), which pioneered many of the strategies of modern publishing, including using aggressive advertising and employing Edward Bernays, who this year would coin the term "public relations" for the new field he was helping to invent.

The other popular media industries partook of the economic boom years as well, making strides toward the pervasiveness and internationalism that would mark the twentieth century. The formation of radio stations in the United States accelerated, and the stage was set for radio as a commercial medium when the first paid radio advertisement was aired in August on WEAF, New York. The Hollywood film industry expanded international distribution, increased theater ownership, and built more movie palaces. First National joined Famous Players–Lasky/Paramount and Marcus Loew among the ranks of the vertically integrated (those companies that controlled production, distribution, and exhibition) when it built a giant studio in Burbank, and Warner Bros. Pictures produced its first films.

Hollywood replicated the rapid pace of change in other cultural spheres by cooperating with the other media. The film and publishing trade papers noted the increasingly rapid turnover of modern plays, short stories, and novels into films, from a couple of years to a few months in many cases, with some publishers selling movie rights in advance of a book's release. In fact, *Manslaughter* came out as a book and as a movie on about the same date in several cities ("Building Sales"). This allowed Hollywood producers to capitalize efficiently on the new aggressive publicity for works of modern literature. The more sensational and notorious the title was in print, the better its box office potential.

In many ways, Warner Bros.' adaptation and promotion of Fitzgerald's *The Beautiful and Damned* exemplifies this practice. In its inaugural production year, all seven of Warner Bros. releases were based on modern novels. In addition to *The Beautiful and Damned,* the roster included adaptations of Charles G. Norris's commentary on modern divorce, *Brass; a Novel of Marriage* (1921), and Sinclair Lewis's *Main Street* (1920). The film adaptation of *The Beautiful and Damned* was released within months of the book. Warner Bros.' marketing took advantage of both the prestige of the book and its sensational aspects, emphasizing Fitzgerald's notoriety as the chronicler of modern youth. One typical advertisement in the film trade paper *Moving Picture World* printed stills from the film in the center of reproductions of two strategically chosen pages of the novel that detail a night of drunken debauchery from the viewpoint of the main flapper character, Gloria. Though such strategies paid off at the box office, the practice raised the difficulty of making modern stories palatable to a conservative audience of film exhibitors, censors, citizens groups, and many general audience members, who followed films with an even keener censorious eye than they did novels or plays. For all that Warner Bros. played up the book's notoriety in its marketing, it was also careful to emphasize the "moral of the story" in its adaptation for the screen.

With gender roles in flux, films confronted the quandary of defining a new masculinity and femininity, and explored the shifting dynamics of power between men and women. Comedians like Buster Keaton and Harold Lloyd played harried but ambitious modern salary men in *Cops* and *Safety Last* (1923), while new women appeared in films like *Nice People* and *The Married Flapper*. Fascination with the exotic and primitive also cropped up in the films of this period, suffused with a nostalgic fantasy of male mastery. Rudolph Valentino's star-making film *The Sheik,* released in November 1921, is one of the most notable examples, as is his *Blood and Sand,* a story of the brutal art of bullfighting. However, with its masochistic and somewhat androgynous hero, *Blood and Sand* didn't hit quite the same note as *The Sheik*. Valentino's graceful dancing, posing mannerisms, and bullfighter's pigtail made his machismo suspect. In one remarkable scene set in his dressing room, as a crowd of male admirers looks on, he performs what nearly amounts to a strip tease, poking his bare limbs out from behind one side of a dressing screen and then the other as he puts on his costume for the arena. Ernst Lubitsch's lavish Orientalist epic *The Wife of the Pharaoh,* released in the United States in May, also features the masterful, primitive male, while old world exoticism suffuses the dominating male character played by Erich von Stroheim in *Foolish Wives*.

Hollywood films of this year are filled with a sense of the emerging modern world as fraught with perils both fascinating and alarming. The "problem" of the new woman tops the list. Comedies like *Bobbed Hair* deal with the new woman by making fun of her "foibles," while *Manslaughter* treats her as a social problem and puts her through a rigorous reformation. Buster Keaton's short *The Electric House* makes nervous comedy out of the alarming rate of technological change, the conveniences of which come at the cost of its encroachment on daily life. On the other hand, *Nanook of the North* and *Down to the Sea in Ships* provide colorful settings for a nostalgic vision of the primal struggle between man and nature, with modernity and its myriad transformations only a repressed subtext to the proceedings. However, in their reactionary retreat from the modern world, these films partake of the anxiety about the pivot into modernity every bit as much as those films that address modern themes more explicitly. Hollywood, with its increasing capacity to bring topical stories to the screen and its burgeoning industrial clout, was proving itself to be ideally positioned this year to mediate the perils of the unknown future, in the process asserting its central position in modern American life.

Rebellious Women: *Manslaughter* and *Bobbed Hair*

"May one offer in exhibit the year 1922! That was the peak of the younger generation," stated F. Scott Fitzgerald in "Echoes of the Jazz Age," speaking of this year as when the "wildest of all generations, the generation which had been adolescent during the confusion of the war . . . danced into the limelight." His metaphor suggests the qualities with which youth in this year were most associated: dancing, jazz, sex, speed, and a passion for center stage. The excesses of youth, real or imagined, consumed the attention of the popular media, and the flapper emerged as the figurehead of the young generation. She would be criticized from all sides as fast, shallow, apolitical, and hedonistic. However, in her complex balance of sexuality and innocence, artifice and frankness, "femininity" and assertiveness, she was not only endlessly fascinating; she set a model for the future.

The new generation defined itself in large part through the use to which it put the outpouring of consumer products in the post–World War I period and, above all, through the burgeoning popular culture. Among other media, young people proved to be a significant market for motion pictures, and, much to the consternation of their parents, producers and exhibitors increasingly catered to these young sensation seekers. Film trade papers often commented on whether films had sufficient appeal for young women. For example, *The Married Flapper* was praised as "the sort of material that is particularly well liked by the younger element—the 'flapper' crowd" ("Married Flapper"). On the other hand, the more traditional mystery *Face in the Fog* was said to have been "given a great hand by critics, but never caught regular flapper clientele, probably because it lacked youthful star" ("Estimates for Last Week").

While catering to the young generation with flapper stories, however, producers and theater owners had to keep in mind the attitudes of their elders. Acceptance of film going among respectable middle-class women, in particular, had been hard won in the preceding decade. In April, one Chicago theater manager reported that he made decisions about whether to book a film that portrayed the younger generation on the basis of what "the mothers" might think of it. "A slight thing will often bring their voluble condemnation," the manager stated. "I recently decided not to book a popular picture now on the market, because of the heroine's insatiable desire for cigarettes" ("Around Chicago"). Women's groups might also succeed in boycotting or bringing censorship pressure to bear on films that they found unacceptable. Offending the older generation had very real financial consequences for producers and theater owners. It was their difficult job to mediate the desires of the "flapper crowd" and the fears of the larger audience.

By now, Hollywood film producers had been grappling with this problem of how to put the new woman on the screen for several years, making films centered on rebellious "madcaps," "feminists," "baby vamps," and even a handful of "flappers." This was the year, however, when a successful formula for "new woman" stories finally congealed into the flapper film. Often adapted from a literary source, these films typically featured an attractive young woman who rebels against her family by doing such things as endorsing free love (though at most she may kiss a man), drinking, smoking, wearing risqué clothes, driving fast in roadsters, going to wild parties, and generally kicking up her heels in ways that were a powerful box office draw for the younger set. To appease anyone who objected to this modern behavior, the young woman was also shown to have a pure heart under her wild exterior, and must learn her lesson and reform her naughty ways by the end of the picture.

In fact, the moral lesson was often a selling point. A trade paper review for *The Beautiful and Damned* stated that "there is a sermon delivered that, carefully handled, should contribute materially in bringing patrons to your box office" ("Beautiful and Damned"). Likewise, *Bobbed Hair* was marketed as "a story for girls who want to be 'different' and for other folks who want to know why" ("Bobbed Hair"). Publicity urged parents to see flapper films so that they could better understand their children and educate themselves on the dangers of "jazzy" behavior. The justification that came to be known as "compensating moral values" was a defense that film producers used consistently and with varying success for the next decade. Within this overall formula, flapper stories fell into two main camps: the comedies that made light of flapper behavior, and the dramas that treated it as a social problem.

The success of this formula solidified the flapper as the preeminent icon of modern youth, on screen and off. Film producers couldn't get flapper stories into production fast enough. Paramount cast screen queen Gloria Swanson as the flapper "Swifty" in *Prodigal Daughters*, and young Clara Bow played her first roles. Producers Security Corporation even revamped an abandoned Dorothy Gish film from 1920, *The Cynic Effect*, as *The Country Flapper*, adding all new intertitles full of flapper slang. Ongoing fascination and fears about where youth were headed assured flapper films significant box office receipts for the remainder of the decade.

Bobbed Hair: Making Light of the Modern Woman

Bobbed Hair provides a good example of how the problem of capitalizing on the controversial flapper could be finessed through comedy. Comedic handling reassured viewers that the character's behavior, though it seemed quite shocking, was silly, superficial, and, above all, a reversible pose of sophistication. As with the majority of films made in this era, which have been lost to destruction, decay, neglect, or lack of restoration funds, there does not appear to be a surviving print of *Bobbed Hair*. However, there is a great deal to be learned about how this subject matter was handled in advertisements, contemporary reviews, and the pressbook for the film prepared by the producer, Realart Pictures.[1] *Bobbed Hair* tells the story of Polly Heath (Wanda Hawley), whose family has arranged a marriage with a prosaic businessman, Dick, who has "no time for romance and poetry." Polly runs away to a bohemian art colony, Carmel-by-the-Sea, where she has her hair bobbed. Soon, she meets a "futurist poet" who lures her to an evening meeting at his studio and tries to seduce her, but Dick, who has pursued her to the colony, intervenes. A chastened Polly is reconciled with Dick, with

In *Bobbed Hair*, with the encouragement of a sculptress friend, Polly (Wanda Hawley, left) runs away to a bohemian art colony, has her hair bobbed, and dons the short smock and sandals worn by its members. Courtesy Photofest.

only her short new hairstyle to remind her of her bohemian sojourn. As an advertisement for the film put it, "Come see her get her fill of 'new thought' and 'new freedom' and thank her stars to be just an old-fashioned girl" ("Bobbed Hair").

Indeed, the bobbed hair of the film's title is the perfect visual symbol of girlish rebellion. It is at once shockingly different and yet superficial enough that its adoption does no lasting damage to her virtue. As the pressbook describes it: "The badge of woman's 'new freedom'—bobbed hair! Free from man-made rules! Freedom to work, to live to—whoa! See what happened to this young goddess of liberty when she tried to live up to her curls and her notions!"

Polly's new hairdo was also an ideal device for promoting the film, situated as it was on the cusp between rebellion and fashion. These two registers were present in two different promotional images of her bobbing her hair. One of these images consists of an apprehensive looking Polly in the act of having her long curls cut off. Disembodied male hands reach into the frame and hold a lock of hair between open scissors. The image transmits both Polly's rebellious act and her lack of wholehearted participation in it, thus economically suggesting the tentative nature of her revolt, and the "happy ending" to come. Another advertising image shows Polly with a pleased expression, holding up her hands to gesture to her bob. Her bobbed hair is thus represented in the two images as both an emblem of rash rebellion and as an attractive fashion choice. A condensed version of this dichotomy appears in one review, which urges, "If your wife wants to cut her hair, and you object, take her to see *Bobbed Hair* . . . and let her see what happened to Miss Hawley after she bobbed hers. If your sweetheart is timid about cutting her locks, and you think it would improve her, take her to see the picture, and let her observe how fetching are all the acolytes—bobbed as to both hair and skirts—of the artist colony."

Bobbed Hair and its promotion thus encapsulate the central contradiction of the flapper character: the gap between a bold surface appearance and innocence of character. When her audacious ideas of emancipation are expressed through fashion choices rather than through active social subversion, the flapper's rebellion can be rendered comical rather than threatening. At the same time, this adroit move channels the desire for rebellion and personal expression into the surging river of our consumer culture, where it has by and large stayed throughout the twentieth and into the twenty-first centuries. The flapper comedy thus relies on the reassuring idea that the flapper's rebellion is a superficial masquerade that is adopted as easily as a new hairdo, and just as easily dropped again when the time comes to "settle down."

Manslaughter: Redeeming the Modern Woman

Dramas of the new woman allowed for more extreme representations of her transgressions than did comedies, but they also required more thorough redemption of the character. In *Manslaughter* (directed by Cecil B. DeMille) the reckless behavior of jazz-mad socialites is both exploited as a spectacle and condemned through DeMille's distinctive storytelling style. *Manslaughter* gives us a healthy taste of the new woman's wild ways in its first thirty or so minutes, before spending another seventy minutes on her punishment and redemption. The conservative view toward the new woman is hyperbolically expressed in the film by District Attorney Dan O'Bannon (Thomas Meighan) during the heroine's trial: "The over-civilized, mad young set of wasters . . . must be STOPPED! Or they will destroy the Nation—as Rome was destroyed, when Drunkenness and Pleasure drugged the Conscience of its Young!"

Parentless and ungovernable Lydia Thorne (Leatrice Joy) is introduced in the film's opening title as "simply 'speed mad' and geared too high." The first shot is a close-up of a speedometer hovering just under fifty-five miles per hour, which dissolves to a close-up of Lydia behind the wheel, her clothing whipping about her and an exhilarated smile on her face. A matte effect provides the illusion that the surrounding countryside is speeding by in a blur. These images stand alone as a statement about Lydia's character, but they are soon brought into the context of the story, as Lydia races with a train and nearly crashes. Continuing to speed down the road, she is pulled over by traffic cop Jim Drummond, but she bribes her way out of a ticket with a diamond bracelet.

The next scene is a fine exemplar of the wild party that was de rigueur in flapper films. Lydia cuts loose at a jazzy New Year's Eve party at a road house. Also there is the disapproving Dan O'Bannon, who, as a title tells us, "loves her for the Girl he thinks she could be—but not for the Girl she is." Party scenes tended to contain the most risqué moments and were high points of flapper films' production values. They were also major selling points of the films. *Manslaughter*'s party is packed with modern fashions and slang and the sort of high society fads, like showering real rose petals on the revelers and having pogo stick races, that studio publicity departments loved. At the same time, these scenes offered an opportunity to show just how badly the young people were behaving and to provide warnings about that behavior.

Throughout the party, characters, titles, and even flashbacks serve to condemn the hedonistic behavior of the partiers, reminding us how naughty it all is even as it dwells on the fascinating details. The shower of rose petals serves double duty as a titillating glimpse of the world of the young and rich and as a symbol of their excesses. Dan is prompted to note that "this Dance—with its booze and license—is little better than a Feast of Bacchus!" The scene then dissolves to one of the lavish Roman orgy scenes for which DeMille was to become famous. The barbaric revels go on much longer than is strictly necessary to make the moral point about the debauchery of modern youth. Lest the comparison to the present day be too subtle, the orgy scene ends with a dissolve into a girl-on-girl boxing match at the modern party, and Dan cries, "You see it's just the same—Gladiators or Prize Fights! Gambling and Booze! The same in a modern Roadhouse, as it was in the House of the Caesars!"

An accumulation of melodramatic incidents brings Lydia to crisis. Her constant partying causes her callously to ignore the plight of the sick son of her maid, Evans, and when the desperate maid steals a ring to try to help him, Lydia allows her to be sent to prison. Meanwhile, Officer Drummond's wife discovers the diamond bracelet with which Lydia bribed him. She insists that he give back the bracelet and arrest Lydia. "And now," says a title over an image of a shining hand with a white pen, "the Great Auditor begins to balance Lydia's account," effectively announcing that we have entered the compensating moral values portion of the film, as well as providing a decidedly corporate era personification of God.

The scene that follows is similar to the opening one, with matte shots of Lydia driving fast and powdering her nose. Officer Drummond begins to pursue her on his motorcycle, but Lydia just smiles and steps on the gas, skidding into a turn that she knows the motorcycle can't duplicate. As Lydia skids, Drummond is flipped over her car and mortally hurt, still clutching the diamond bracelet in his hand. After a dramatic court scene, Dan succeeds in convicting Lydia of manslaughter. In trying her, he effectively puts modern youth on trial as well. He once again raises the comparison to the excesses of ancient Rome, and a second flashback reveals the morning after the wild orgy we have seen earlier. Invaders with winged and horned helmets, bearskin cloaks, and scruffy beards barge in amongst the piles of sleeping Romans, who can offer little resistance when the invading leader tells his men to "loot, plunder and kill." The scene of this assault dissolves back to the courtroom, where O'Bannon declares, "I'm not only considering the debauches of Ancient Rome, but of 1922—with its debauches of Speed, and carelessness of Human Life—of which this Defendant's actions are a daily example!"

Forty-five minutes of screen time later, Lydia's conscience has been awakened and she emerges from prison. Her punishment is complete and her regeneration can begin. Interestingly, the initial "cure" does not lead her straight to marriage and domesticity, as in so many stories of the new woman, but to an earlier version of feminism, as she starts a new life working among the poor. Lydia's new feminine virtue is thus defined in the context of earlier social feminists of the 1880s and 1890s such as Jane Addams. This older generation of crusading feminism was not always portrayed so favorably in flapper stories, which tended to exaggerate the differences between old-school "busy body" feminists and the carefree younger generation. Here, however, it initiates Lydia's journey to redemption.

Meanwhile, Dan has succumbed to his despair at having imprisoned her and has descended to drunken indigence. In a New Year's Eve scene that parallels the party at the opening of the film, Lydia is shown passing out coffee and donuts in the city slum. The new Lydia resists the requests of her old friends, still as gin-soused and heedless as ever, to join them at a roof party. She tells them, "In prison—I learned that keeping time to human heart-beats, is far more important than keeping time to a Saxaphone!" [*sic*]. Dan arrives at her soup kitchen looking for a handout, and Lydia vows to repay him for saving her by saving him in return. Here, a still older model of feminine virtue comes to the fore, as she becomes the embodiment of Victorian true womanhood, also exemplified in the film by Evans and Mrs. Drummond, able to redeem the baser male of the species with her constancy and love. A quick scene communicates Dan's struggle with alcoholism, before an ellipse of three years. During that time, with Lydia as his inspiration, he has regained his old prestige and has run a successful campaign for governor. When Dan is warned that an ex-convict such as Lydia can't preside over the governor's mansion, she proves willing to sacrifice her love, telling him that they must part. He in turn makes a sacrifice for her, resigning his candidacy and giving up his dream of the governorship to be together. The two embrace as the screen irises to black.

Though Lydia's crime is ostensibly manslaughter, it is also her social and sexual license as portrayed in the driving and roadhouse scenes, and her rejection of a meek and nurturing persona. A heavy toll of redemption must be levied in order to clear her account. Few directors were as bold as DeMille about having their cake and eating it too when it came to using spectacles of licentious sexuality as part of a moral lesson. However, the same basic strategy of portraying shocking behavior and then condemning it informed countless flapper stories that followed. Numerous critics, censors, and undoubtedly most audience members saw through this strategy, decrying flapper films' daring incidents and expressing skepticism that girls could behave this way and still be recuperable "good girls." Eventually, the transparency of this strategy would help sink the genre. But this year, it proved a means to push modern youth onto the screen in ways that allowed both generations to have a look.

The Modern Home: *The Electric House*

Near the end of *The Electric House,* Buster Keaton is trying to climb some stairs with a heavy chest on his back. The stairs are mechanized so that they move, escalator style. Unfortunately, the stairs are moving the wrong way, and he becomes a modern Sisyphus, trudging step after step but gaining hardly any ground. When he finally does reach the top and sets the chest down, the stairs catch it and whisk it back to the bottom. The stairs then suddenly reverse direction and hurl the chest up and out a top-floor window and into the swimming pool below. He tries to run down to retrieve his chest, but he's unable to descend the erratic stairs, and finally resorts to sliding down the banister. The unpredictability of the modern "convenience," rather than simplifying his task, renders the age-old structure of the staircase, the center of so many homes, alien, menacing, and, in Keaton's hands, ridiculous.

Electrification was a juggernaut sweeping through America's cities and towns, changing the nature of the American home. Through his struggle with the escalating stairs, Keaton forges a visual metaphor for anxieties about shifts taking place within the domestic space of the early twenties. He uses physical comedy to explore both fascination with and mistrust of rapid technological change.

The Electric House's depiction of the mechanized home played on growing awareness of new electrical technologies. As David E. Nye notes in his study of the electrification of the United States, while many modern electrical appliances were available in the early twenties, including irons, vacuum cleaners, washing machines, and refrigerators, very few people actually owned them. However, this state of affairs was changing rapidly. "The electrification of the domestic market began in earnest only after 1918," writes Nye, "when in a single decade the majority of the homes in the United States were wired and acquired at least a few electrical appliances. One million new residential customers were added in 1921 alone, and by 1924 two million were being added annually" (267, 265, 261).

Families were beginning to learn what electrification would mean for their homes as either they or their neighbors went electric, and the changes went far beyond simply adding electric lights. Electrification required new technological competencies, and the mysterious new danger of electrocution required vigilance to protect oneself and one's children from outlets and other electrical hazards.

Moreover, the introduction of electric lights transformed the very space of the home. The flexible distribution of lights throughout rooms and new open floor plans contributed to the demise of the central hearth, resulting in a dispersion of the family through the house. The introduction of electrical appliances made the modern home, like the modern factory, increasingly mechanized and rational, and less reliant on specific artisanal proficiencies. Electrical appliances also helped blur gender roles in the domestic sphere. At the same time that women were more easily able to enter the industrial work force, single men gained the ability to both manage a house and hold a job. "Bachelors" could care for their own domestic space, and this reduced their reliance on men's boarding houses (Nye 253, 279, 282). The rapidly spreading adoption of electrical lights and appliances was thus a central component of the many perplexing changes Americans were facing, while the pressure to electrify was intense.

The electricity giant General Electric (GE) actively sought to minimize any fears regarding the new technologies and to create a "positive electrical consciousness." The company hired an outside advertising agency, escalating their spending on advertising, with "a goal of reaching every family through two hundred advertisements a year." The ads promoted electrical products as symbols of the advancement of civilization, in the process devaluing physical labor in the home. One GE advertisement asked, "How Civilized Are We?" and quoted Edward Everett Hale: "The extent to which the world has changed the laborer who uses his body into the workman who uses his head is the index of civilization." Electrical appliances were a marker of a home's degree of civilization and the freedom of its occupants from drudgery and reliance on the dwindling servant class (Nye 265, 268, 274).

The Electric House centers on one such "civilized" home, modified by Keaton's character to include a number of devices designed to eliminate all need for physical labor. Keaton may well have derived particular inspiration from the construction of numerous "home electrics," model homes in cities around the country designed by the utilities to showcase electrical devices. Such homes drew over one million curious visitors this year to see their array of modern conveniences. These same curious throngs might have found amusement in *The Electric House*'s satire of upper-class electrification. The devices in the film, though ingenious, are absurd in that most of them perform household tasks that are perfectly easy to do without electrical assistance. The home's dining table, for example, sports an electrified lazy Susan. A tub that moves on tracks even eliminates the need to leave the bedroom when one desires to bathe. Like the escalating stairs, however, each of these devices inevitably goes amiss, propelling Keaton and the house's residents into confusion and physical danger.

The Electric House joins anxieties about electricity with another, related transformative social current of the era, the dramatic increase in college attendance and the professionalization of the workforce. The film opens at a graduation ceremony, where we are introduced to three students earning a cross-section of modern college degrees. Keaton, a botany major, sits next to a young woman getting a degree in "manicure and hair dressing." Beyond her is a grim-faced, newly minted electrical engineer. In the course of the proceedings, the three graduates drop their diplomas and mix them up. When a college official seeks to hire an engineer to electrify his house, the real engineer presents him with the manicurist's diploma and is refused the job. The official then mistakes Keaton for the engineer, and the smiles of his pretty daughter help convince Keaton to let the error stand and take the job.

The college boy was a notable new type in popular culture. John R. Thelin notes that the image of the gentlemanly college man of the late nineteenth century was overtaken in this period by those of the hedonistic college boy and his flapper-like female counterpart, the co-ed (Thelin 205, 211). College boys were suddenly staple characters in literature, such as the writings of F. Scott Fitzgerald and Percy Marks, in cartoons, such as those of John Held, and in a wide variety of films.[2] Keaton and fellow silent comedian Harold Lloyd later made entries into a popular cycle of feature films that centered on that increasingly important phase of youth, the college years.

The film's presentation of Keaton as a college boy notifies us that his character ostensibly fits the category of the "workman who uses his head" rather than the "laborer who uses his body." However, Keaton will of course be compelled to resort to physical prowess to overcome the problems caused by too much misplaced brainpower. The film also satirizes the professionalization of the modern workforce, for which even manicurists must dutifully get their college degrees. Rather than getting their training through an apprenticeship with a family or community member, these college graduates have selected from among an array of options that can be learned in an institution, symbolized by their interchangeable diplomas. Like electricity, higher education was a force in displacing traditional continuities.

Underscoring the arbitrariness of career choices suggested by the diploma gag, when Keaton the botanist arrives at the house he simply sits down on a curb and reads a book, *Electricity Made Easy*, and he is apparently ready to make the switch to engineer. However, when the family arrives back from their vacation, they find that their home has been transformed with a number of devices of questionable utility and precarious functionality. In the kitchen, there is even, as the title notes, "something for the housewife," an electric dishwasher with a conveyor belt to transport the dishes.

Despite several malfunctions during Keaton's demonstration of his devices, the family seems to be reasonably pleased, as they soon invite several friends over to see their new devices, certainly a realistic plot development given the popularity of the "home electrics." At the same time, the real engineer arrives on the scene, vowing to take his revenge on Keaton for stealing his job. Ensconcing himself in a room with the wiring, he begins switching the connections, causing the devices throughout the house to go haywire and unleashing chaos.

The Electric House satirizes the professionalization of the modern workforce. Buster Keaton stars as a college boy, the "workman who uses his head." Courtesy the Wisconsin Center for Film and Theater Research.

There is a dual pleasure in each device in the film, both delight in its clever functioning but also mirth at its malfunctions and their consequences. An example is provided by the devices in the dining room designed to serve the family's food. When Keaton first shows them off, they work like a charm. The bemused cook sets bowls onto an electric train and a door to the dining room springs open. The soup course runs along the tracks around the table and is thereby delivered to each family member. However, when the maid tries to serve the next course, Keaton accidentally uncouples the railroad tracks, and the derailed entrées are dumped into the lap of the lady of the home. Later, after the vengeful engineer arrives on the scene, the woman and her visiting friends are whimsically using the device to transport kittens around the table. Keaton bursts into the room, in the middle of a chase, and leaps over the table, but the lazy Susan catches him up and spins him around, throwing him off the other side. Like the escalating stairs, the device takes on a physical menace disproportionate to the modest convenience it offers when operating correctly.

The problems created by these machines would certainly have been variations on a familiar theme to any Keaton fan. He was well known for using absurd mechanical devices, from simple to complex, to create the gags and stunts in his films. In his world, train ties, waterfalls, and clotheslines become levers, fulcrums, and slingshots for propelling him through space. His work appeals to what Neil Harris terms the "operational aesthetic," which, as film scholar Tom Gunning explains, "reflected a fascination with the way things worked, particularly innovative or unbelievable technologies" (88). Gunning notes: "This fascination with the way things come together, visualizing cause and effect through the image of the machine, bridges the end of the nineteenth century and the beginning of the twentieth, shaping many aspects of popular culture" (100).

Keaton's short *The Scarecrow* (1920) perhaps bears closest comparison to *The Electric House* in that it, too, features a home tricked out with clever gadgets for everything from washing the dishes to getting the table scraps to the pigs. However, the devices in *The Scarecrow* are primarily based on simple, hand-powered machines. Indeed, much of the pleasure in seeing these devices unfold lies in the fact that, though unexpected, their workings are simple and entirely legible to the eye. The technologies featured in *The Electric House* are more inscrutable. The electrical system powering the devices is the realm of the college-trained specialist and can only be visualized by the engineer in his room full of wires, switching them all about. While in his films Keaton often extracts himself from a difficult situation by taking elegant advantage of the same mechanics that have gotten him into trouble, here he resorts in frustration to a simple act of sabotage. He dumps armloads of metal pots and pans through the open transom of the wiring room, short-circuiting the devices and shocking the engineer, forcing him out into the open. "In the end," the title offers sarcastically, "electrical engineering proved to be one of his talents."

The Electric House thus displays a deep skepticism about the benefits of electrification and a suspicion of the changes it brought to the American home, particularly its usurpation of humans' physical manipulation of their environment. As Keaton leaps from the intransigent electrified stairs and slides down the banister, he uses the elemental force of gravity to make his elegant getaway from the unexpectedly repressive forces of home mechanization. In so doing, he reestablishes his body as the ultimate dynamic force and substitutes practical labor for the abstractions of an educated engineer.

Primitive Men: *Nanook of the North* and *Down to the Sea in Ships*

There is no question that this year produced texts that looked with a mixture of fascination and trepidation toward the onrushing future. However, at this point in Western history when manual labor was being pushed to the margins, when homes and work spaces alike were being mechanized, and when old gender roles seemed to fall by the wayside, a thick vein of primitivism and nostalgia ran through American popular culture. Two films that exemplify this impulse are *Nanook of the North* and *Down to the Sea in Ships*. These films present as quaint and colorful the fading customs of two communities: the nomadic hunter-gatherers of the Canadian artic and the Quaker whaling community of New Bedford, Massachusetts. The exoticism with which these unfamiliar ways of life are presented is at one and the same time suffused with nostalgia for their embodiment of simple and unquestioned patriarchal mastery. Modernism, mechanization, and the Jazz Age are eliminated from view as these films celebrate the ability of men to face down the eternal forces of nature and provide for their families with bare hands and remarkable skill.

On the surface, *Nanook of the North* and *Down to the Sea in Ships* couldn't be more dissimilar. *Nanook* is renowned as a pioneering feature film documentary of timeless fascination, while *Down to the Sea* is every inch a fictional period melodrama of its day. Upon closer examination, the films reveal not only a shared fascination for fading ways of life, but a surprising number of shared filmic strategies for validating their material. Both films trade on the authenticity of their representation of an elemental lifestyle and suppress the reality that modern life has overtaken their subjects. Both films invoke an interesting combination of exoticism and nostalgia for an imagined artisanal past. And, both films contain extended sequences showing documentary footage of men performing real if somewhat anachronistic tasks, underscoring their dexterity and resourcefulness in the absence of modern machines or formal schooling.

Nanook of the North was the result of a collaboration between explorer and prospector Robert Flaherty and an Inuit "family" assembled by Flaherty; they served as his subjects and suggested actions for him to film during shooting in 1920–21. Flaherty obtained funding from the fur company Révillon and distribution from the independent Pathé exchange, which released the film to theatrical audiences with great success.

Along with other "exotic" cultures such as those of ancient Egypt and Japan, the Eskimo's mode of living was the subject of fascination in the early 1920s even before *Nanook*'s release, in part because of ongoing public interest in Arctic explorers such as Roald Amundsen. Eskimo practices were also brought to public attention in this year by a study and book by Johns Hopkins professor Elmer Verner McCollum, which reported on the health benefits of the Eskimo diet, prompting a *Los Angeles Times* columnist to protest, "We do not envy the Eskimo anything he has, neither his climate nor his feasts of blubber, nor even his perplexing health."

Fascination with the Eskimo also suffused popular culture. Jokes circulated about the Eskimos' love of the cold and their supposed propensity for eating blubber. Plays, operas, numbers in musical reviews, parade floats, and even society parties took on Eskimo themes, sporting floating icebergs, dancing polar bears, and northern light effects ("Pantages Pictures," "Eskimo Opera," "Eskimo Babies," "Musical Parade"). In 1921, Christian Kent Nelson trademarked the name "Eskimo Pie" for his frozen confection of ice cream and chocolate, so that by now the trademarked smiling Eskimo on its wrapper and advertisements was a familiar image. When *Nanook* was released on 11 June, the public had been well primed for its vision of the "kindly, brave, simple Eskimo," as the film's opening titles put it.

Few discussions of *Nanook of the North* fail to mention Flaherty's notorious "salvage ethnography." When shooting the film, Flaherty eliminated elements that would reveal the modernization of his subjects' lifestyle, such as their use of guns and Western-style clothing and housing, in favor of walrus ivory knives, fur parkas, and hand-built igloos. While the episodes in the film are presented as real events, they are clearly carefully staged to provide the ideal camera angle to capture actions such as Nanook racing to join a walrus hunt and sneaking up on a trapped fox. The most obvious example is the cutaway igloo that the subjects built so that Flaherty could shoot the family "going to sleep." In the final scene of the film, Flaherty cuts between the sled dogs outside during a storm at dusk and the family settling into the igloo, with bright daylight streaming in through the openings.

The very obviousness of the construction of these scenes belies an attempt to deceive the audience. The film's claims of authenticity are quite openly couched in terms of its dramatization of events and its generation of iconic images. The film's full title is *Nanook of the North: A Story of Life and Love in the Actual Arctic*; the setting, it indicates, is "real," but the film presents a constructed story within that setting. Similarly, the film's last title declares the iconic nature of the image: "The shrill piping of the wind, the rasp and hiss of driving snow, the mournful wolf howls of Nanook's master dog typify the melancholy spirit of the North." Flaherty wishes to show what he believes to be the essential characteristics of his subject, whether or not this requires some creative reenactment.

Nanook does, however, seek to provide its audience with evidence of the authenticity of the work performed by its subjects. Flaherty's camera dwells on details of the handiwork of the women Nyla and Cunayou, and above all Nanook. The film's celebrated sequences include Nanook fishing on an ice flow and building an igloo from the ground up. Film theorist André Bazin has attributed the impact of these scenes to the fact that Flaherty often uses long shots that incorporate several elements of an action in a single frame, rather than assembling different aspects of the action through montage. He praises Flaherty's "respect for the spatial unity of an event at the moment when to split it up would change it from something real into something imaginary. . . . It is inconceivable," Bazin says, "that the famous seal hunt in *Nanook* should not show us hunter, hole, and seal all in the same shot" (50). For Bazin, it would not be significant that the other end of the rope that Nanook holds was reportedly being pulled not by a seal but by some friends offscreen. Rather, he argues, "what is imaginary on the screen must have the spatial density of something real."

Nanook himself is presented as the embodiment of the intrepid spirit of the North. Low angle shots repeatedly place him in the top left of the frame, standing at the top of hills of ice, a dark, heroic figure silhouetted against white, surveying the landscape. He is identified in titles as a leader and a great hunter, upon whose skill and bravery the lives of those around him depend. Scenes portraying his skills are balanced by those in which he is presented as a devoted family man, such as the scene in which he teaches his son to shoot a bow and arrow, and the comical opening scene in which one family member after another crawls out of the recesses of his kayak like clowns from a trick car. Perhaps the most troubling scene to modern viewers, however, is that in which a puzzled Nanook bites a record after a demonstration of the phonograph at the trading post, reaffirming the stereotype of the "savage" man as a noble but infantilized figure, the antithesis of the modern man. But even here the stereotype is undone by Nanook himself who, in feigning ignorance about the record player, is in fact self-consciously performing a scene for the movie camera, to which he plays with great success throughout the film.

The films' fascination with the hunting and slaughtering of animals and the groups' eating habits also contributes to the representation of the Eskimos as "noble savages." At the end of the walrus and seal hunts, the camera dwells on Nanook and his companions cutting open the animals, slicing off slabs of bloody meat and chewing them with gusto. The alien image of Nanook eating raw meat straight off his kill is contradicted by a title that attempts to connect his actions to the familiar. "The 'blubber-eating Eskimo' is a misconception. Blubber they use as we use butter."

The characters' willingness to put something unexpected in their mouths is a related motif. The punch line of the boy Alleggoo's visit to the trading post, where he eats too much sea biscuit and lard, is his lip-smacking reaction to the spoonful of castor oil he is given to settle his stomach. In a shot of the family in the igloo, a title draws our attention to Nyla, at the left of the frame, chewing Nanook's boots to soften them after they have stiffened overnight. These episodes play with a juxtaposition of the cozy familiarity of family life—children gorging on treats, a wife's solicitude for her husband's comfort—with the incongruous—a delighted reaction to castor oil, putting shoes in one's mouth. The final sequence of the film is a poetic homage to the resiliency of the nuclear family (with the interesting but never explicitly commented upon addition of a second adult woman). As the storm howls outside, the family snuggles together in the home that Nanook built, and the final shot shows us the contented, sleeping face of the patriarch. The film thus works to reiterate the importance of the traditional family, with the resourceful and hardworking man at its center, by first exoticizing it and then reasserting its universality.

Down to the Sea in Ships is a delirious hodgepodge of filmic devices that were prominent at that time. Set in nineteenth-century New Bedford, Massachusetts, the film was shot by the independent production company Whaling Film Corporation. The plot is full-on blood-and-thunder melodrama, replete with sinister villains, threatened innocence, and epic battles of man against nature. It tells the story of Allan (Raymond McKee), a college boy just returned home to the whaling town of New Bedford, who loves Patience (Marguerite Courtot), the daughter of a Quaker whaler, Charles W. Morgan (William Walcott). The college boy must go to sea to prove himself as a whaleman, successfully harpoon a whale, and lead a counter-mutiny after the nefarious first mate kills the rightful captain and kidnaps Morgan's young niece Dot (Clara Bow), who has stowed away on the ship.[3] No sooner are Dot and the ship saved than Allan must race back in time to rescue Patience from Samuel Siggs, a sinister, generically Asian interloper who passes himself off to Morgan as a Quaker. The film is also notable as the first screen appearance of Clara Bow as the feisty Dot. Despite her inexperience, Bow steals every one of her short scenes with a lively performance style that makes the other performers look comparatively stuffy. This brief synopsis can't begin to do justice to the many subplots and melodramatic situations that pack the film. At its core, however, *Down to the Sea* shares *Nanook's* celebration of primitivism, integrating an anthropological fascination with the practices of a fading culture into its melodrama.

Many of *Down to the Sea's* titles share a similar function with those in *Nanook* that serve to authenticate and render iconic the images with which they are juxtaposed. A title near the film's opening, for example, insists, "Whalers continue to go out from New Bedford on similar voyages to the one portrayed in this picture. The brawny boatsteerer still throws the hand harpoon." The film was in fact shot within a couple of years of the last whaling expedition out of New Bedford.

The film devotes several long sequences to details of the whaling operation, as when the ship comes upon a dead whale and the crew butchers it. The sequence has a marginal narrative justification as part of the hero's progression toward becoming a real whaleman. However, as the camera dwells upon the details of the slaughtering process, the titles take on a frankly educational tone, identifying the "blanket piece" and the spermaceti, noting the number of teeth and the size of the whale's jaws, and so on. The interest of the scene, like that of the slaughtering scenes in *Nanook*, is largely that of witnessing the process by which the flesh of the large and alien creature is disassembled by hand into useable parts, though whale oil for lamps was a product whose utility had almost faded.

The activities of the Quakers are subject to the same documentary gaze as the whaling expedition. As with the Eskimo's, the Quakers, with their quaint rituals and clothing, are put on display, and yet their religious "discipline" is also expressive of traditional values. Scenes set in the Quaker meeting house present various facets of their religious practices for the audiences' examination. They worship silently, separate the men and women with a partition to conduct their business meeting, and "read a young man 'out of meeting' for marrying a girl who is not a Quaker," emphasizing the discipline of the young. The childlike "loving obedience" of Patience to her father as he prepares to dispose of her to Siggs against her wishes, which is characterized as typically Quaker, is smoothly incorporated into the film's overarching melodramatic conventions of the virtuous, passive heroine and the last-minute rescue by the hero. As with *Nanook*, the exotic treatment of this way of life is at the same time suffused with nostalgia for its embodiment of simple and unquestioned patriarchal control.

Consistent with the centrality of male physical valor to these films, both feature a climactic battle of the protagonist against a creature of the sea. More than any other point in each of the films, these sequences meld the fascination of documentary footage of an actual kill with a drama centering on the hero's larger struggle: Allan's need to prove himself among the whalemen and win Patience, and Nanook's need to bring food home to his hungry family during the lean winter months. In each case, however, the fight itself is difficult to visualize. The opponents of the men are underwater for most of the struggle, and, poor creatures, are primarily engaged in trying to get away. In *Down to the Sea* we can at least see the occasional whale surface, but in *Nanook* all we can see of the opponent is a small hole in the ice with a rope disappearing down it. Both films therefore use cinematic devices common in fiction films to enhance the suspense of the struggle. For the seal hunt in *Nanook,* Flaherty begins with a single shot of Nanook trying to pull the rope that is (ostensibly) attached to the seal out of the hole. He staggers back, only to be pulled forward on his belly, and performs a flip onto his back in his dramatization of his struggles to land the seal. When the permutations of the rope-pulling struggle seem to be exhausted, Flaherty cuts to a different framing in which Nanook's family, with the dog sled, is visible in the distant background. Nanook tries to get the family's attention while still struggling with the rope, and a classic race to the rescue commences, handled entirely through staging. There is no need to crosscut to the family approaching, as we can see the dog sled rushing closer across the flat surface of the ice, and we are led to wonder if it will arrive in time to help, as the seal seems to be prevailing. The scene climaxes with help arriving, the successful landing of the seal and the family's feast.

Similarly, the scene of Allan's battle with the harpooned whale must rely in large part on showing the effects of the struggle on the human end of a line that disappears down into the water. Repeated shots show Allan and his companions in their small boat being dragged along at high speed, with spray splashing up over the sides. However, the director, Elmer Clifton, takes a more editing-dependent approach to creating a suspenseful battle. He cuts to subjective, blurred shots of water rushing by to indicate the whalers' point of view and inserts close-ups of the rope rapidly playing out of the boat. At the end of the sequence he constructs several events out

Down to the Sea in Ships celebrates male physical valor. Raymond McKee, former college boy, takes up whaling and becomes a "laborer who uses his body." Courtesy Photofest.

of pure montage, as the whale turns on the boat, upsetting it, and one whaler is fatally attacked by a shark. Although the film crew appears to have gotten some footage of whale flukes overturning a boat, the whale and shark attacks are otherwise purely fabricated out of rapidly cut shots joining the space of the men and that of the sea creatures through eyeline matches and other tricks of continuity editing.

Despite the different cinematic traditions of documentary and melodrama, these films share their captivation with the physicality of primitive men. Both films incorporate lengthy displays of their male heroes working on the world around them without the aid of mystifying mechanical apparati. They are members of a dying breed of "laborers who use their bodies," and, rather than deriding this as uncivilized, the films offer a reactionary celebration of their difference from the callow college boys and mechanized Babbitts of the modern corporate world. The women in these two films are submissive helpmeets of their men with none of the tendencies of the troubling new woman. The one exception is Clara Bow's little hoyden, Dot, whose nascent rebellion against her authoritarian grandfather, thanks to Bow's performance, provides a vivid splash of modern spirit that will not be repressed. For all these films' nostalgia for an idealized past, as 1922 rolled forward into 1923, the momentum had turned toward Bow and her Jazz Age contemporaries.

NOTES

1. A pressbook was a document developed by the producer/distributor for exhibitors in order to promote a film. Materials typically included articles and "reviews" that could be placed in papers, advertisements, posters, and lobby cards, and suggestions for exploitation stunts and bally-hoo, such as parades, letter-writing campaigns, tie-ins with others businesses such as bookstores and department stores, and so on.

2. For example, the main character in *Down to the Sea in Ships* is a college boy who returns home and must put aside his book learning and prove himself in the realm of traditional physical labor.

3. Rudolph Valentino played a similar role that year in *Moran of the Lady Letty* as a bored and jaded socialite who is shanghaied by smugglers and discovers the joys of hard labor and a simple life aboard a sailing vessel.

1923

Movies and the Changing Body of Cinema

MARCIA LANDY

Embodiment—national, global, cultural, and personal—shifts and transforms on many levels at once this year. In Washington, one of the most corrupt presidential administrations in U.S. history is presided over by Warren G. Harding, who, after his death on 2 August, leaves a legacy of scandal involving disastrous political judgment (Teapot Dome), cronyism, extramarital affairs, and alcoholism (Prohibition notwithstanding). Despite public exposure of shady government and business interests, selling off of private lands, privatization of railroads, pending legislation to restrict immigration, Ku Klux Klan organizing, and labor unrest, the country witnesses an unprecedented economic upswing with the spectacular growth of private wealth and technology in "the rising new industries in electrical appliances, automobiles, motion pictures, and the radio" (Goldberg, *Discontented* 153–59, 80, 127, 40) and the expansion of a culture of consumption.

Before this year, no one knew the unique taste of a Milky Way or Butterfinger candy bar, licked a Popsicle, spread Welch's Grape Jelly on her peanut butter, bought frozen food from Birdseye, drank commercially canned tomato juice, or sipped Sanka. No slugger used a Schick magazine razor, no hostess wore a Maidenform bra. But now people did all these and more, with frenzy, humming, "Yes, We Have No Bananas" (thanks to Frank Silver and Irving Cohn) or "Who's Sorry Now?" (written by Ted Snyder, Bert Kalmar, and Harry Ruby), listening to Bessie Smith's legendary recording of "Down Hearted Blues," muttering the inspiring lines of Robert Frost's "Stopping by Woods on a Snowy Evening," or meandering through Kahlil Gibran's *The Prophet* or Martin Buber's *I and Thou*. The American economy was growing and flowering—the advertising company Young and Rubicam was founded to tout it, and to create the image of hungry men and women in the process. For dad, Walter P. Chrysler came out with a new car and Hertz started renting to those who wanted to "Drive-Ur-Self." Mom, empress-to-be of domesticity, could see George Bernard Shaw's *Saint Joan* onstage or listen to Jean Sibelius's Sixth Symphony or Darius Milhaud's *La Création du Monde*, or watch a performance of William Walton's *Façade*. For the middlebrow crowd, George Gershwin's tunes thickly populated *George White's Scandals* on Broadway. And for baseball fans everywhere, one of the great monuments to the game, Yankee Stadium, opened in the Bronx on 19 April, with Babe Ruth hitting a three-run homer in the third and pointing the Yanks toward their first World Series victory in the fall.

At the same time America was facing a world community, a kind of embodied human family, confronted with stark changes. The Union of Soviet Socialist Republics was founded on 6 July, for example, and an earthquake and fire destroyed Tokyo and Yokohama on 1 September. Jordan became autonomous, the Turkish Republic was founded, and Germany was in a state of pervasive collapse: Adolf Hitler, a politician on the rise, staged a beer hall putsch in Munich. Throughout the country, the Deutschmark was tumbling. By September it had fallen from 7,260 to the American dollar to 13 million, then to 130 billion in November and 4.2 trillion by Christmas.

The movie industry changed, too, and captured the conflicts and contradictions of the age. This year saw the culmination of the "Fatty" Arbuckle trials, with the comedian finally acquitted though his career now in ruins. The publicity given the Arbuckle scandal, coupled with the death of actor Wallace Reid from a drug overdose related to his morphine addiction, helped to legitimize the role of Will H. Hays as the industry's regulator of film censorship. The film industry was also confronted with the threat of losing profits. Fortunately, economic expansion was evident, even if studio output fell to 1,179 titles, improving its efficiency, personnel, and circulation. For writers, technicians, directors, and actors film had become a big business that offered immense wealth and fame. This burgeoning industry was to play a major role in the "creation of a new leisure class" that became "the fifth largest in the United States" (Goldberg, *Discontented* 87). While it is hard to quantify and delimit the "influences movies exerted on their audiences," there is consensus that they were important in the formation of new and conflicting values concerning wealth, sexuality, and gender, if not of social class.

The films produced this year reveal an industry in transition evident in the disappearance of certain directors and stars, the appearance of new talent, and the transformation of genre forms. For example, while the western was a familiar genre, it took on new life and popularity with *The Covered Wagon*, directed by James Cruze. Comedies had been a staple in the era of the short film but were in trouble with the coming of lengthier comedy forms. The comedy stars of the teens were in a process of transition from one- and two-reelers to feature-length films that demanded a situation-oriented form of narration, as in Harold Lloyd's *Safety Last!* and Buster Keaton's *The Three Ages*, a parody of D. W. Griffith's epic *Intolerance* (1916). Comedian Ben Turpin starred in a spoof of Valentino, *The Shriek of Araby*, produced by prolific comedy writer Mack Sennett. These films were evidence of the popular appeal of the films, directors, and stars that they parodied. Griffith satirized the ubiquitous image of the vamp in *The White Rose* with Mae Marsh, who, though popular in the teens, was soon to see the end of her moment of ascendancy.

The extremely innovative but controversial Erich von Stroheim—in legend a monstrous ego who antagonized and demoralized his actors—was to find his extravagant talents as director unwanted in Hollywood. Griffith continued to make films (besides *The White Rose*, also *Mammy's Boy* with Al Jolson), but his career was in decline. Lillian Gish, who had been his prime star, now appeared in films by other directors, most notably *The White Sister*, filmed by Henry King in Italy. Another major star, "America's Sweetheart" Mary Pickford, was to step out of her innocent little girl image and appear in *Rosita*, a romantic comedy directed by Ernst Lubitsch (his first American film) in which she portrays an adult, feisty, and witty entertainer. Gloria Swanson continued to perform in such films as the comedy *Bluebeard's Eighth Wife* and the melodrama *Prodigal Daughters*, both directed by Sam Wood, and another melodrama, *Zaza*, directed by Allan Dwan. Despite negative attitudes to underworld pictures on the part of the censorious Hays Office, they were popular with audiences, none more so at this time than Dwan's *Big Brother*. Unlike directors von Stroheim and Rex Ingram, neither of whom could accommodate to changes in production, Wood and Dwan were to remain within the Hollywood studio system for decades.

Film genres (comedies, westerns, melodramas, historical films, and social uplift dramas) were now creating challenging images of the male and female body in the cinematic landscape. By focusing on exemplary films, it is possible to evaluate the tenor of continuities and discontinuities in production practices and in the types of personnel responsible on- and off-screen for film product. Such a focus can show the forms that the cinematic body, masculine and feminine, assumes in narrative types, in stars' physical appearance, in styles of directing and acting, and in uses of spectacle. Literature on the era often emphasizes the figures of the vamp and the flapper, but how pervasive were these images in the films? And were the women stars "more central to the myths of the period" than men (Haskell, qtd. in MacCann 55)? A sampling of films—*A Chapter in Her Life, A Woman of Paris, Salome, The Spanish Dancer, The Covered Wagon, The Hunchback of Notre Dame, The Ten Commandments,* and *Scaramouche*—can help address these questions. These productions, with the exception of *A Chapter in Her Life* and *Salome,* appeared on lists of the ten best pictures of the year as rated in daily newspapers, and *The Spanish Dancer* was one of the "outstanding box office attractions" ("Spanish Dancer" 123). They offer telling portraits of femininity and masculinity in a diverse range of genre forms.

Remembering Female Architects of Silent Cinema

Such writers and directors as Frances Marion, Adela Rogers St. Johns, Jeanie Macpherson, Elinor Glyn, Anita Loos, and June Mathis, among others, were critical to the success of films at this time, working closely with studio executives to create narratives that could transform the folklore of gender and sexuality. Marion has been credited overall with "writing 325 scripts covering every conceivable genre" (Beauchamp 11), but she, like Jeanie Macpherson, who became an integral part of Cecil B. DeMille's filmmaking team, had accumulated experience in other aspects of the movie business, having acted and (if only for a brief time) directed. Occupying the increasingly prominent position accorded to stars in the 1920s (for example, Pola Negri, Alla Nazimova, Constance and Norma Talmadge, and Clara Bow), women writers treated a range of themes (marital conflict, sexual transgression, courtship, unrequited love), ensuring the increasing popularity of stars. In tandem with producers, these writers had learned how to gauge the temper of audiences and insinuate their philosophical or political ideas into the scripts they wrote, even, sometimes, realizing them on film: Dorothy Davenport Reid was responsible for writing, directing, and acting in several films after the tragic death of her film star husband Wallace on 18 January. Most notable is her personal and didactic *Human Wreckage.*

The figure of Lois Weber is particularly instructive for situating the contributions of women to Hollywood cinema and their effect upon the myths and realities of femininity and masculinity in the 1920s. Like other women writers of the decade, Weber had by now appeared in films for years; now she had turned to directing, formed her own independent company, and even developed a lighting system that enabled her to shoot "interior scenes in natural locations rather than on a studio set" (Slide 104). With H. C.

Caulfield as general manager, W. H. Carr as studio manager, and Arthur Ford as business manager, Weber Productions was set to produce films that have been termed "light domestic dramas" (Slide 105). As a maker of stars, she was responsible for building the reputation of Mildred Harris (then Charles Chaplin's wife), as well as that of Anita Stewart. Thanks to the work of film critics in the last two decades, Weber's career has begun to be reevaluated for its contributions to the history of the silent cinema.

An "Angel" in the House: *A Chapter in Her Life*

Weber's *A Chapter in Her Life,* remade from *Jewel* (1915), takes place in the home of the wealthy and dysfunctional Everingham family, headed by a bitter paternal figure (Claude Gillingwater) who is disappointed in his offspring (one son deceased and the other a recovering alcoholic). Included are a snobbish and domineering aunt, Madge Everingham, the widow of Everingham's son, and her grown daughter, Eloise (Jacqueline Gadsden). Eloise leads a miserable existence. Generally unwanted, unable to express her discontents (except through her piano playing), she has been restrained from marrying below her financial and social status. Depressed and angry, she aloofly shuns Everingham's granddaughter Jewel (Jane Mercer), who has come to stay temporarily in the house while her parents take a business trip to Europe. Completing the menage is the arrogant and tyrannical housekeeper Mrs. Forbes (Eva Thatcher), burdened with an incorrigible alcoholic son. Although she is seen in only one vignette, Jewel's mother, a "working-class woman," is by contrast portrayed as an "angel" in a humble domestic setting. She is a source of ethical and affective values that add to Jewel's creative fantasy life. The fact that alcoholism, in symptoms or in memory, plays so repetitive a role in this film is not surprising, given that the era of Prohibition was just underway and by now firmly on the audience's mind.

Her imaginative power and the nurture Jewel has received enable her to resist the indifference and harsh treatment of the Everingham family in "Castle Discord," as she describes the place. She is able to release her grandfather, Eloise, Mrs. Forbes ("the giantess"), and her son from their imprisonment in rage, resentment, and hopelessness. Jewel lives in a "fairy tale world" in which she herself must undergo a number of trials in order to sustain belief in the transformative power of love. The male figures in the film—the reformed Everingham son, the lonely old patriarch, and the alcoholic son of Mrs. Forbes—are all symptomatic of maimed masculinity linked to the disabling effects of overpowering maternal figures. But their conversion is through the redemptive power of the young girl untainted by despair.

The film's visual portrait of "Castle Discord" relies on a claustrophobic treatment of space. The action is set largely in interiors: the sitting room, the dining room, grandfather's office, and Jewel's bedroom at home and in the mansion. A few outdoor shots include the garden where the child plays alone and the stables where she encounters young Forbes. Physical objects are prominent in this drama of conversion, signifying the frustrations and desires of the characters. Jewel's doll, her link to her mother, from which she is never separated and to which she recounts her distress, becomes expressive of her desire for affection and communications, as do the letters she receives from her parents that sustain her in this hostile environment. Reiterated shots of Eloise in the mansion's large sitting room frame her, set apart from other family members and oblivious to them, as she plays a spinet piano that evokes her striving for freedom (reinforced by an intercut of her running outdoors in a windy landscape). The mug in which the housekeeper's son places the onions that he eats to hide the smell of his drinking from his domineering mother is his sign of rebelliousness.

What we see in *A Chapter in Her Life* is a hermetic bourgeois world centering on imprisoned femininity, with fantasy and fairy tale used to portray emotional discontent. Though Anthony Slide describes this film as "nothing more than a program picture" (129), close consideration of its images and style reveal that the film is more than that. Its visionary uses of montage—such as contrasts between claustrophobic indoor and expansive, brightly lit outdoor scenes; inserted episodes to visualize escape; Eloise's dreamlike image of herself in a natural landscape; and Jewel's image of her parents buffeted by a storm at sea as a consequence of Mrs. Forbes's malicious reference to the possibility of their being endangered in their journey—reveal that rather than being merely didactic, the film is instrumental in exploring the interior world of its characters and alternatives to their discontents. While the movie follows a familiar scenario of conversion at the hands of a precocious child (innocence points the pathway to salvation for lost souls), and while it could be related to the era's concerns with moral uplift, the sanctity of the family, and the dangers of alcoholism, its dramatic investments center on the affective forms of generational, familial, and sexual tyranny. In its use of the child as agent of transformation, the film also works (self-consciously) as a utopian fantasy, with the young girl serving as magical guide through the conflicted landscape of the middle-class family.

The Single Female, European Style: *A Woman of Paris*

A Woman of Paris: A Drama of Fate is testimony not only to Charles Chaplin's innovativeness as a director but also to his daring challenge to prevailing nineteenth-century versions of femininity. The familiar melodramatic image of the "fallen" woman in the sinful city is dramatically transformed in this film, with its female protagonist far from a portrait of chaste and innocent womanhood tragically subjected to a hostile, rapacious, and violent world threatening the moral and social order. In Chaplin's "drama of fate," with its unconventional style, mode of character portrayal, and acting, the central character flouts expectations of long-suffering and then redeemed womanhood.

The "woman" of the film's title is played by Edna Purviance, who was familiar to audiences of the time from her other roles in Chaplin films. At the opening of the narrative, Marie St. Clair lives in a motherless home in "a village somewhere in France" under a tyrannizing father who keeps her imprisoned to guarantee her chastity. To escape this dreary and morally rigid world, she plans to elope to Paris with provincial Jean Millet (Carl Miller). When the father discovers that she has managed to climb out a window, he locks her out when she seeks to return. Similarly, the father of her fiancé refuses to allow her to stay the night in his house. Alone, she goes to the train station to wait for Jean, who does not appear: due to a broken telephone connection, she is unaware that his father has had a heart attack. Standing in the darkly lit dingy station (where Chaplin makes a brief appearance as a porter), she takes the train to Paris.

The film does not provide scenes that detail her entry into the Parisian demimonde, but we next encounter her as kept mistress of a wealthy man about town, Pierre Revel (Adolphe Menjou). The elegant and sophisticated world of the upper classes is portrayed in a scene where Marie, dressed in the height of fashion, enters a classy restaurant with Pierre, who casually displays his proprietary rights over her as the clientele rudely looks on. We see not only a vignette of upper-class snobbery but also views of the kitchen staff mimicking Pierre's self-important behavior—when Pierre consults with the chef about his order for dinner (champagne truffles), the kitchen workers can be seen rudely imitating him behind his back.

Pierre is not a stereotypic villain but a sophisticated and hedonist figure devoted to gastronomic and sexual enjoyment. His attitude toward Marie is that she may remain his playmate, providing spectacle, sex, and

Edna Purviance as the stylish "Woman of Paris." Courtesy Photofest.

company as long as she does not interfere with his pleasures and social class duties. The newspaper announcement of his engagement to a wealthy woman of his own class is equated with his stock market returns. He tosses both aside indifferently. When Marie learns of the engagement from a "well-intentioned" friend, her reaction is fatalistic resignation rather than rage. It is only when Pierre arrives as usual to take her out, and she learns that he intends to maintain the relationship with her after his marriage, that her despondency emerges.

The acting in this pivotal scene is different from conventional melodramatic histrionics. Marie's response is not conveyed through excessive gestures, extreme posturing, or facial contortions. Instead, the interactions and responses of the aristocrat and his woman rely on their physical control of emotion as manifested onscreen through a focus on objects: the handkerchief that Pierre takes from Marie's chest of drawers in casual, proprietary fashion; the reflection of Marie as, unseen by Pierre, she stands before the mirror drawing another handkerchief from her bodice to wipe her eyes; and Pierre's picking up his hat and making a business-like exit. This scene, like the rest of the film, thwarts any expectation of a heavily emotive confrontation between the two protagonists and elides any potential portrayal of Marie alone and bereft. Nor is the audience given a picture of a woman's descent into despair. Her life continues in its usual manner, thanks to Pierre's financial generosity.

In this "drama of fate" (as the title announces), the ill-timed or unsuccessful telephone call plays a significant role as a trope to convey emotion or to explore causality. It serves as the agent of fate in Marie's separation from Jean early in the film. Fate further intervenes by way of a phone call from a friend who invites Marie to a party in the Latin Quarter. Confused as to the address, she knocks on the wrong apartment door and finds none other than her former love, Jean, who, having come to Paris to study painting, is residing with his widowed mother in cramped and shabby quarters. Overwhelmed to find her, he asks to paint her picture and Marie agrees. Their romance is again ignited.

The party that Marie never attends is intercut with the scenes in Jean's apartment. Its bright lighting and risqué revelers, taken out of portraits of the Roaring Twenties, contrast with the darkly lit corridor and Jean's abode, a space reminiscent of the village world abandoned by Marie. At one point the rowdy group of revelers drinking champagne at the party gathers to observe the dancing of a woman who is swathed in bandages like a mummy, while a man slowly unwinds the cloth from her and turns it around himself. Much as it handles Marie's relationship to Pierre, the film treats the eroticism of the party routine in an understated manner: the dancer's nude body is registered only by the enthusiastic responses of the spectators and by a woman's covering the eyes of the man next to her. Until this moment, the film has treated eroticism much as it has handled Marie's relationship to Pierre, matter-of-factly, through humor, and challenging moral censorship concerning sexuality and marriage. This scene is different, however. The viewer can appreciate the orgiastic character of a scene that relies on the exposure of the female body for the entertainment of upper-class males, albeit without a moral commentary in intertitles. Sexual morality is differently evoked as Jean learns of Marie's "immoral" life when he comes to her apartment to help her choose a dress for the portrait, and the maid, seeking a matching scarf from a chest, accidentally drops Pierre's collar. The collar serves to differentiate Marie's life from Jean's, whose provincial dress and rigid behavior bear the marks of his and his family's repressive and unyielding moral values.

Once again, "fate" intervenes for Marie. Although an ultimate union between her and Jean might reasonably have been expected, their relationship is disrupted by a chance visit she pays to Jean's apartment to see the progress on her portrait. Standing outside his door, she overhears part of a conversation in which Jean reassures his mother that he does not intend to marry her. Marie returns to her life with Pierre, until, remorseful and angry at being abandoned, Jean arrives at a café with a gun, planning to kill Pierre. He fails; but standing before a nude statue in the anteroom to the café, he shoots himself. Ultimately, then, in his appearance and gestures Jean repeats the violent roles of his family and of Marie's father, and his acting (like that of his mother) conforms to familiar melodramatic gestures. The other characterizations, however, evince a mode of performance that relies on restrained, worldly, and modern responses.

Cinematographer Roland Totheroh's lighting is critical to our understanding of how the film undermines traditional melodramatic oppositions between country and city life. The darkly lit scenes of village life that open the film show a harsh, judgmental, and vindictive world (Maland 71) unfavorable to women's sexuality. By contrast, the city scenes are brightly lit except for the interior of Jean's apartment. Having juxtaposed the rural and petit-bourgeois values, the film returns in its conclusion to a rural world, but a different one, more brightly lit and set in a more expansive landscape. Marie has assumed the role of an unmarried nurturing figure to orphans, aided by the church and by Jean's mother. Even in this ending, the film refuses to reproduce stereotypes of femininity, landscape, acting, and narrative conventions: "For audiences of 1923 . . . it was startling to have a film which showed a courtesan as sympathetic, a play boy as charming, intelligent, tolerant, and generous, a mother who was jealous and vindictive, a hero who was weak and mother-smothered" (Robinson, *Chaplin* 222). This unusual and nonjudgmental treatment of character may account for the film's poor success at the box office, but also for its praise by critics then and now and especially for its appeal to later filmmakers such as Michael Powell (Smith 69). *A Woman of Paris* can be said to belong to a European mode of filmmaking in its sympathetic if critical treatment of female characters that eschews judgmentalism in both narrative and style.

Alternative Hollywood: *Salome*

Salome undertakes a radical experimental treatment of cinematic form and acting, in a style considerably different from that of *A Woman of Paris*. Critics praised both films, though *Salome* was a distinct financial failure. J. Hoberman, reviewing a retrospective of the film, described it as an "intimation of an alternative Hollywood [that] fits into American film history somewhere between the 'Fall of Babylon' episode from D. W. Griffith's 1916 *Intolerance* and the lysergic *Sunset Boulevard* dress-up Kenneth Anger concocted some four decades later in *Inauguration of the Pleasure Dome*" (*Salome*, imdb.com). The film was the creation of Natacha Rambova, although the credits for directing went to Charles Bryant, her companion of many years. The Salome narrative has, of course, been reproduced many times through opera, novel, drama, and film. An earlier *Salome* starring Theda Bara had been banned in many parts of the country.

Rambova's version of the myth was based on Oscar Wilde's play and on the illustrations of Aubrey Beardsley in the Wilde text. Rambova designed the sets and costumes and cast Alla Nazimova as Salome. Nazimova's character was far removed from rural America and from most feminine portraits of the decade: not, to be sure, from the energy of the Jazz Age, or from the penchant for exoticism, or from the fascination with the female body. Nazimova, Russian by birth and known for her work as a musician in both theater and films and for her ultramodern views on marriage and child rearing, declared in an interview, "A woman living a creative life is bound necessarily to do things sometimes defiant to convention. In order to fulfill herself, she should live freely. Children bring fear, and in that way arrest personal development" (Morris 80). Equally unconventional, Rambova, a dancer and set designer, also played a dominating role in the career and legend of Rudolph Valentino (Morris 15). These two highly distinctive personalities contributed to the film's "decorative decadence" (Card 80).

Subtitled a "historical phantasy," the film is an ensemble of ballet, biomechanics, dream, and psychological exploration of seductive and rebellious femininity, shrouded in mystery and ambiguity in "the non-realistic aesthetic of art nouveau" (Mayer 22). Religion takes a back seat to the conflict between King Herod's incestuous desire for his daughter and her taunting defiance of him. Her sexual attraction to John the Baptist/Jokaanan becomes the instrument for conveying her "wildness of will." Many of the titles (derived from Wilde's text) are aphoristic: "She kills the things she loves. She loves the things she kills"; and "The mystery of love is greater than the mystery of death." Salome's paradoxical character, her willfulness, are conveyed through the scant, glittering, and diaphanous costumes she wears and through her childlike, trim, lithe, and androgynous body that communicates both adolescence and burgeoning sexuality, reminiscent of the contemporary flapper. Before she sports her spectacular gossamer and layered costume for the Dance of the Seven Veils, she is clothed in a short sparkling dark tunic, clinging closely to her body and allowing her freedom of movement. Her hair is covered with shiny small balls, like bubbles, that glitter as she moves her head.

By contrast, her father Herod (Mitchell Lewis) is made up garishly, his face whitened and rouged, his corpulent body covered by a silken toga and a cape that covers one shoulder. Her mother, Herodias (Rose Dione), with wild streaming hair like a Medusa's, claws at Herod to pull him from his trance as he gazes at Salome in a drama of Oedipal triangulation—and, in more mundane terms, of the unholy family. The sets are sparse with different areas demarcated—the banquet table with the assorted courtiers grouped behind it, the terrace containing a tubular cover made of iron bars that resembles a bird cage and covers Jokaanan's subterranean prison, a simple ledge (serving as a wall separating the palace from the world outside) where Salome stretches her body, and an open space between the terrace and the banquet table where she confronts and does her dance for Herod. Through manipulating his guard, she has Jokaanan removed from his prison so that she may observe, confront, and attempt to seduce him. This space is where she also performs her erotic dance for Herod. Since the Wilde text takes place at night, the film was shot indoors with "seventy spotlights, a certain number of arc lamps, and about twenty-five large mercury-vapor ceiling lights" (Morris 89), giving the film an enhanced surreal and dream-like aura.

Jokaanan is clothed in nothing more than a furry loin cloth, his extremely thin body swaying toward and away from Salome as she circles him. Her attraction for and repulsion from the prophet is conveyed by her intense scrutiny of him and by her sinuous movements. The scene alternates between extreme close-ups and medium or medium-long shots. The close-ups of Salome staring at him are tied to a dominant overarching motif of the film, the dangers of looking, articulated by Herodias to Herod: "You must not look at her! You are always looking at her!" It is not only Salome's curious, taunting, seductive, and fateful gaze at Jokaanan but also the

Nazimova as Salome, adolescent temptress of Jokaanan (Nigel De Brulier). Courtesy Photofest.

court's collective gaze upon her as, clothed in a short white shimmering tunic, a white wig, and a long diaphanous cloth, she performs the Dance of the Seven Veils that highlights the fascination and threat of the erotic feminine body. Her final costume is a long black cape with circular designs covering this tunic and a satin turban over her hair. These costumes express her maturation from petulant, even innocent adolescent seductress to murderous temptress.

Looking becomes provocative for the viewer as well. We gaze on not only Salome herself—sexually ambiguous, always moving, even shimmering in the dappled light—but on semi-nude massive black slaves; courtiers with high pointed hats, feathered crowns, and twisted tall braids atop their heads; homosexual seduction scenes; and incestuous glances between stepfather and daughter. However, the viewer is deprived of an image of the prophet's severed head, a central object that is conveyed simply by light emanating from a bowl Salome holds up for all to see. In the use of actors whose gender identification is ambiguous and in the psychologically complex treatment of Salome's seduction of Jokaanan and Herod, the film invites its audience to view a world that defies conformity and that, ironically, uses the biblical text to enhance its transgressiveness. *Salome*'s defiant stance toward sexual morality is occurring while Hollywood conducts its crusade against "offenders" in the film colony, thanks to the strident leadership of Will Hays, newly installed as guardian of respectability at the Motion Picture Producers and Distributors of America. The papers are ablaze with Hollywood scandal (Anger 43–48; Morris 89; Brownlow 40), but *Salome* is an indication of another life emerging in the United States, a life that threatens Hollywood's efforts to create a respectable image of itself for the world.

A European Diva

An import from Europe destined to make an impact in the cinema this year was Pola Negri, born in Poland, a stage and later film actress there and in Germany. Negri was a prime example of the industry's wooing of and receptivity to foreign talent, and of that talent's impact on the American screen. For example, this same year brought Ernst Lubitsch from Germany to begin a highly successful career in Hollywood. Negri's first major film was *The Spanish Dancer* for Paramount, a film that reinforced her image as a passionate and sensual siren both onscreen and off, and which was directed by a prolific filmmaker with four other films in production that same year, Herbert Brenon. In Negri, he could capitalize on an exotic and elusive femininity that was neither frail nor a caricature of "either [feminine] evil or purity" (Card 190).

The film portrays the romance between a gypsy dancer and fortune teller, Maritana, and a Spanish grandee. It begins with her on horseback, traveling with her "lawless, carefree" band of gypsies to the court of Spain, where she has been engaged to dance. Wallace Beery is the dissolute King Philip IV, married to politically ambitious Isabella of Bourbon (Kathlyn Williams), whose aspiration it is to unite France and Spain. Adolphe Menjou plays Philip's scheming courtier and advisor, Don Salluste. At the court festivities, Maritana is ordered to tell the fortune of Don Cesar de Bazan (Antonio Moreno, whose stardom emerges from his incarnating the Latin lover as a competitor to Rudolph Valentino). She refuses to inform the love-smitten man that he is to be arrested and executed, but that before his execution he will marry her, after she is elevated to the rank of a countess. Don Salluste's nefarious plan is to kidnap Maritana after Don Cesar's demise, bring her before the king, who is infatuated with her, and thereby prove to the queen that her husband is unfaithful. Don Cesar appears in time to thwart the intrigue. The kingdom is saved. Don Cesar and Maritana are united. Despite this anodyne scenario, the film succeeds thanks to the understated acting of Negri, Moreno, and Menjou, who bring wit and humor to their roles.

Negri performs with a minimum of histrionics, using the lexicon of stage performance from François Delsarte in the nineteenth century, evolved to suit the limited scope of early camera lenses (Mayer 29). Her acting relies on delicate facial, hand, and body movements and statuesque poses to convey her reactions, with the exception of the climactic scenes in which she is physically and emotionally threatened. No mystical, tortured, or remote diva, she is physically comfortable in her body and accessible in her personality. The fairy tale narrative of a lower-class woman raised to the ranks of aristocracy is tailored to the talents of its female star, who portrays the character with dignity and restraint. The acting of the principals, the costumes, the dancing, and the set design are visually imaginative, thanks to Brenon, who had abandoned British cinema to work in Hollywood, and especially to his cameraman, the innovative James Wong Howe, whose uses of framing, choreography, and lighting gave the film the appearance of a carefully crafted historical reconstruction in concert with the inevitable ingredients of intrigue and romance. Extradiegetic music plays a critical role in this "silent film" and serves to develop the tempo of the action. In the course of filming, Brenon provided accompanying mood music for the actors (Koszarski 131) that may account for the effective and notably realistic performances of the characters.

Negri in particular is photographed so as to highlight her exceptional beauty through close-ups, iris shots, and vignettes that reveal her impact on others, particularly Don Salluste, as they observe her in action or repose. Her dancing is not confined to her performances before the aristocratic court, but is typical of her graceful movements generally. Her character not only emphasizes physical appeal but also vibrant personality and intelligence. Not a vamp or a femme fatale, her persona is consistent with the tendency of the film to present her transformation from a gypsy to an aristocrat, thus stressing her love and devotion to the dashing Don Cesar. According to William K. Everson, Negri became one of the imported stars that "gave new impetus" to this transformative tendency. "As a screen type, she was earthy and tempestuous" (Everson 201), incarnating a form of femininity that overreaches the limitations of her social status whether as a lower-class woman or as nobility.

Given her "un-American" status, Negri's role as a gypsy allows for a portrait of emergent and uninhibited female sexuality without radically threatening residual American middle-class domestic values. In relation to ethnic and immigrant audiences, Maritana's (and Negri's) "foreign-ness" reinforces the fantasy that attaining upward class mobility is a means of assimilating and of overcoming "barriers that may stand in the way of attaining the American dream" (Marchetti 102). The use of European female stars removes them from the quotidian domestic sphere, puritanical morality, and luminous spirituality exemplified by Lillian Gish's role in Henry King's *The White Sister*. Gish's portrait of the American heroine insists on her embattled sexuality and religious commitment. By contrast, Negri's offered a finely tuned amalgam of erotic pleasure and daring that was fascinating and unthreatening at the same time.

Frontier Masculinity: *The Covered Wagon*

The western offered its own portraits of masculinity in the milieu of the American frontier. Its most notable stars were Tom Mix, a rugged adventurer and showman, who made eight films in this year alone, and Fred Thomson, whose blameless reputation as a minister and whose daring acrobatics and showmanship were bright moments in the flagging fortunes of the genre. James Cruze's *The Covered Wagon* helped to restore the western to prominence (Fenin and Everson 75). Cruze was "a peripheral and enigmatic director of the golden age of silent film" (Starman 461). Regrettably, his cinematic achievement during this period has been buried in the enormous critical literature on the western. The success of the film resides in its enactment and celebration of cultural myths of the settlement of the American west, its reanimation of long-enduring gender stereotypes, and its contributions to the romance of empire.

The Covered Wagon was a lavish production. According to the publicity booklet, the film employed the services of one thousand Indians from reservations in Wyoming and Mexico (under the direction of a military officer). The five hundred wild bison in the hunt sequence were hired from a firm known as Buffalo Livestock Corporation. Cowboys managed the animals, including one hundred fifty steers and one thousand horses. Forty thousand feet of canvas were used for the Conestoga wagons. According to Kevin Brownlow, "the filming of the epic western . . . was an epic in itself" (334). Even the intertitles are more than dialogue, description, or explanation: they "gain an almost epic poetry, exactly fitting the mood of the film" (Brownlow 295). In one sense, the film bears comparison to the Wild West shows of the time, and the director, Cruze, a former traveling actor in road shows, was the perfect impresario for this type of spectacle.

The larger drama of the film occurs in the various obstacles entailed in the long and arduous trek westward: the dangerous and dramatic crossing of a deep river by the wagons, buffalo hunting, an attack by Indians, and fights between individuals and factions. Rather than focusing on a psychological treatment of the individuals, the film's "epic" style insists on confronting its protagonists with specific trials: childbirth, death, shortages of food supplies, and dissension among groups, culminating in a split between those who seek gold in California and the "men of the plow" who settle the land. For example, the personal antagonism of Woodhull (Alan Hale) toward Banion (J. Warren Kerrigan) does not overshadow the physical trials confronted by the pioneers. Furthermore, the photography of the landscape is not monumental, eschewing close-ups of high mountains and dangerous waterfalls for dusty, scrubby, and even mucky shots of the land. Through the panoramas, the viewer is given a sense of the vastness of the country and of natural obstacles to be overcome. The choreography of the large cast filmed against this landscape contributes to its grand dimensions; and poses the men and women of the wagon train as larger-than-life gender constructions.

Deformed Masculine Bodies: *The Hunchback of Notre Dame*

In most discussions and reviews of Wallace Worsley's *The Hunchback of Notre Dame*, based on Victor Hugo's novel *Notre Dame de Paris*, the critical emphasis is on Lon Chaney's makeup and acting, the spectacular sets—particularly of the cathedral itself—the choreography of the crowd scenes, and the costuming. Less attention is paid to its portrait of a threatening embodiment of masculinity in the context of stardom that elicits both sympathy and repulsion for physical deformity.

The film offered spectacle not only in its lavish sets but especially in its "portrayal of the grotesque title character" (Schatz 28). Dramatized in the monumental context of the cathedral recreated on the Universal lot, the film focuses on the outrageous exploitation of and brutality toward the lower classes by the upper classes. Physically deformed Quasimodo (Chaney), the "half-blind and deaf" bell ringer and inhabitant of the cathedral, is described in an intertitle as an "inhuman freak, a monstrous joke of nature" who rails against his treatment by the crowds and is exploited by criminal elements. Like the other misfits, Quasimodo elicits our sympathy because of the brutal, inhumane treatment he receives at the hands of virtually everyone; yet his ugliness and animal rage hold us off. His difference is conveyed not only through his garish make-up and animal-like movements to and from his high perch in the cathedral, but also by means of long-lens and high-angle shots of the masses (who at times resemble insects).

Chaney's physical mobility (and that of his stuntman double) was hampered. He had to be weighted down with a seventy-pound device to create his hunchback. As he rings the huge bell and climbs down from his high perch in the cathedral, his movements resemble those of a monkey. The character's freakishness is enhanced by ponderous facial make-up composed of lumps of wax, grease paint, and the covering of one eye to give it a bulbous appearance: this was the antithesis of any culturally dominant version of masculinity. In contrast to the dashing Captain Phoebus de Chateaupers (Norman Kerry, an actor in the mold of Douglas Fairbanks), Quasimodo is a nightmare of malformed and ostracized humanity. He will be redeemed, however, through the compassion of the outcast Esmeralda (Patsy Ruth Miller), stolen from her crib by gypsies and adopted by the king of the underworld.

The film is filled with portraits of social misfits: an impoverished and oppressed poet, denizens of the night, thieves, cutthroats, and gypsies. Through the use of tinting the different groups are distinguished: the massive crowd scenes that take place before the cathedral are black-and-white; the rabble at the "Court of Miracles" is often sepia-toned; scenes at the court of Louis XI are blue, as are critical moments involving the fate of Esmeralda; and a reddish tint is introduced for scenes of treachery. The emphasis on Quasimodo's monstrous appearance is enhanced by alternating shots of the groups and individuals who observe him contemptuously and shots of his perspective on the crowd action taking place below him. Tableau shots and vignettes of the central characters are presented as if from paintings. Quasimodo's ringing of the bell functions throughout to portray his isolation, rage, and, finally, sacrificial death.

Quasimodo's physical deformity prohibits any realization of his desire for Esmeralda; instead he can only gaze on her longingly, regarding his own reflection as loathsome, an image of the "'exposed obscenity of the self'—as Other—as masculinity allowed to be failed and freakish." Thus, his character "may be read as a symptomatic instance of the anxiety surrounding masculinity and the male body during this postwar period of American culture" (Studlar 210). Chaney's role raises the question of how to explain the stardom of a flawed, even perverse figure. Other than accounting for his persona by its timely connection to the popular "freak shows" of the time, his contorted and distorted spectacle of masculinity serves, in Gaylyn Studlar's terms, as a "mad masquerade of masculinity," both threatening and exposing cultural ideals.

Religion for Profit

The Ten Commandments, directed by Cecil B. DeMille, adopts a technique from Griffith's *Intolerance* (and its parody *The Three Ages*) by dividing the narrative into different historical segments to create a parable of modern social and sexual life. The film is a "Janus-faced production that simultaneously looks backward and forward in time," being both "anti-modernist" and traditional as well as "a spectacle in a modern consumer culture" (Higashi, *DeMille* 179). The conventional dimensions are related to "nostalgia for the moral certitude and sense of community associated with small town life," whereas the modern dimensions reside in "the use of color processes, special effects, and colossal set design" (179). Further, the characters juxtapose traditional and modern portraits of masculinity and femininity, allowing DeMille to combine moral uprightness with sexual license as well as to capitalize on the sensational dimensions of the Old Testament for Christian purposes.

Inspired by a newspaper article, the film reflected increasing concerns about film industry morals. An opportunist (like many of his Hollywood colleagues), DeMille was quick to capitalize on popular culture and the biblical narratives to which his Christian background predisposed him, but his choice and treatment of religious topics can be accounted for more complexly as a response to prevailing threats to reigning American values. *The Ten Commandments* reflects American culture and society of this year: its appeal to rural and Christian values; its view of modern urban life as a site of temptation and fascination; corruption in high places; its stance on the threatening role of ethnic outsiders; its sense of the masses as unruly, dangerous, and potentially violent; its notion of the family as an unstable source of moral edification and behavior; and its vision of the fragility and necessity of moral and civic law as restraint. The orchestration of these crisscrossing motifs specifically reveals a cinematic world where ethics and profit are uncomfortably intertwined.

The biblical prologue drew its images from familiar illustrations of the Bible, its language from editions of the Bible known to spectators and conveyed through the intertitles, and its tableaux from popularly circulated Orientalist images (Higashi, *DeMille* 180–81). Most prominent are choreographed views of bondage, notably the dramatic juxtaposition of Pharaoh's entourage against a monumental landscape featuring large sculptures, chariots, and his attendants in contrast to the bedraggled Israelites. The Israelite suffering, posed against the self-indulgent luxury of the Egyptian court, is enhanced by the confrontation of Moses and Pharaoh, the ensuing destruction of the Egyptian firstborn, and then the dramatic exodus, chase, and parting of the sea. The use of color and tinting enhanced the spectacle (Higashi, *DeMille* 184–85), highlighting moments of tension and increasing dramatic contrasts in relation to situation and character (Brownlow 190). As Moses receives the commandments, chiaroscuro lighting conveys his isolation, expectation, and rage, and the presence of God's judgment. The golden calf scenes are intercut with Moses on the mountain, culminating in the breaking of the tablets while all around the lapsed Israelites embrace lasciviously and dance in orgiastic frenzy. The tablets fall, break, and turn to dust, and thus sin and redemption are poised to enter the modern world.

In its ancient sequences the film's confrontation between Pharaoh and Moses is embodied in two modern-day brothers, incarnations of opposing moral views. John (Richard Dix) is pious, resigned to his station in life as a carpenter, while Dan (Rod La Rocque) is a building contractor who disdains religion and worships the golden calf of money. Both men desire Mary (Leatrice Joy), a woman of the streets who finally marries the renegade brother and lives a life of luxury and loneliness as her husband increases his wealth through corrupt business practices that will endanger the safety of building occupants. Two other women in the film are Dan's evangelistic mother, Mrs. McTavish (Edythe Chapman), and Sally Lung (Nita Naldi), with whom he has an affair. The portrait of Mrs. McTavish runs against the grain of the docile, long-suffering idealized maternal figure, being rather an unattractive domineering feminine version of an angry Moses.

Nita Naldi, who performed Sally, was one of a line of duplicitous and immoral Eurasian women who "embody a suspect morality . . . a mysterious seductive sexuality that is seen as difficult to contain within the boundaries of patriarchal domesticity" (Marchetti 70). Naldi had appeared in the same year in *The Glimpses of the Moon* and *Lawful Larceny* (both directed by Allan Dwan), *You Can't Fool Your Wife* (George Melford), and *Don't Call It Love* (William C. de Mille). American-born, she was largely identified with the figure of the vamp: her "Italian surname and vamp persona would situate her at the intersection of two established representational tropes: the predatory female vampire, and the immigrant whose assimilation skills and potential for economic and cultural contribution were uncertain" (Negri 179). By contrast, Mary is the Christian recipient of conversion and regeneration, finally becoming mated to a proper paternal figure, though she, too, is allowed her transgressive moments.

John's sturdy, stern, paternal admonitions (uttered by Richard Dix, a popular actor who appeared in at least six films this year and who was typically typecast as dutiful and dependable) place him in the tradition of the innocent and dutiful American hero, whereas Dan (personified by Rod La Rocque, a romantic matinee idol of the era) is flamboyant, the reprobate who rebels against the religious dictates of the mother. A physically supple figure, Dan is devoted to womanizing and is in league with the underworld through his adulterous relationship with an "oriental" woman. His character embodies the threat of modern relativism and hedonism, thus offering the viewer a relief from the moral strictures embodied by John and Mrs. McTavish, while allowing for a glimpse into forbidden but spectacular delights. *The Ten Commandments* is finally a contrast between two versions of masculinity, exemplified by two brothers who had the same origin: one womanizing, defiant, and unscrupulous, the other gentle, moral, mother-identified, and submissive. The film's premise (to follow the commandments or be broken by them) is illustrated by the demise of both the upright Mrs. McTavish and her wayward son Dan, but then balanced by the Christian family of John and Mary, the holy family at the center of the parable. However, the pleasurable vision of Nita Naldi's vamp, the fashionable image of Mary as Dan's wife, the spectacle of wealth, sexuality, sin, and escape from moral tyranny are an inevitable part of this modern biblical epic. As entertainment, *The Ten Commandments* succeeds by reinforcing the notion that the world of sin is possible and profitable so long as it is accompanied by a biblical disclaimer. But the film also provides contrasting versions of femininity and masculinity that serve to visualize and dramatize reigning splits in the culture between tradition and modernity as related to gender and sexuality. As transgressive desire is introduced into the context of religious piety, morality and sexuality are nobly conjoined.

Aesthetics of the Historical Film

One of the remarkable directors of the silent era, Irish-born Rex Ingram left a legacy of unparalleled cinematic achievement, typified by *Where the Pavement Ends* and *Scaramouche*. Ingram was considered "the great pictorialist and romantic of the cinema of the twenties" (O'Leary x). While in cinema histories Griffith and DeMille are given the lion's share of credit for their spectacular productions, Ingram has undeservedly languished in the background. His films are better known for their artistic innovation and technical expertise. He can also lay claim (along with screenwriter June Mathis) to "discovering" Rudolph Valentino, Alice Terry—who later became his wife—and the Mexican heartthrob Ramon Novarro.

Scaramouche was an "artistic" success that, according to critics and reviewers, was "an epic of vast proportions comparable to *Birth of a Nation* and *Intolerance*" (O'Leary 72). A costume drama set during the French Revolution, and based on Rafael Sabatini's novel of the same name, the film is constructed on a grand scale, relying on paintings of the era to convey a sense of authenticity in the costumes, architecture, statuary, the interior décor of both the Marquis de la Tour d'Azyr's and the Countess de Plougastel's chateaux, and the landscape of the countryside. The sets were elaborate and included a French village built in the San Fernando Valley and in the studio lot on Cahuenga Boulevard in Los Angeles. Using 1,500 extras, *Scaramouche* offered a dazzling display of crowd and tavern scenes, and sequences in the theater where Moreau-Scaramouche (Novarro) performs his plays. The political and romantic drama involves Moreau, a law student, who seeks to avenge the death of a young revolutionary killed by the callous Marquis (Lewis Stone). The film traces Moreau's deepening involvement as a staunch defender of the "rights of man," and we watch him fighting against the corrupt aristocracy in dual roles as an eloquent spokesman for the revolution and as "Scaramouche," a clown in a troupe of traveling players. Alice Terry as Aline de Kercadiou supplies the romance element intrinsic to costume dramas in which the love story parallels and provides an emotive dimension to the historical costume drama. At personal risk, she defends her lover Moreau and hides from the Marquis after he has been wounded during a demonstration. Rather than portraying frivolity and capriciousness, or relying on facial and bodily contortions to convey her reactions to dramatic situations, Terry presents a dignified, restrained, and intelligent portrait of a woman who transfers her affections from the marquis to Moreau. He has saved her from marriage to the aristocrat and from the rage of the revolutionary mob. Statuesque, virginal, a contrast to the mobile erotic vamp, she is onscreen just as described by the British director Michael Powell: "divinely blond," an image of the unattainable, "*la princesse lointaine*" (qtd. in O'Leary 123). Her chiseled and porcelain features, her graceful carriage, and her understated gestures lend her the appearance of a delicate eighteenth-century miniature.

Alice Terry was neither femme fatale nor Victorian angel of the house nor rebel. Nor, as *Scaramouche* demonstrates, is she singled out for exceptional treatment in front of the camera. Ingram did not capitalize on Novarro's dancing abilities or on the stereotype of the Latin lover that he so fully embodied, but focused on the actor's attractive, even mystifying physical appearance, his agility, and his acting ability. Novarro's character here is a significant exception to the stereotypical use of Italian and Latin American actors that would prevail in Hollywood. Furthermore, as the articulate and committed Moreau he is adept at speaking (through intertitles), and at duel-

The "divinely blonde Alice Terry" (Aline) with Ramon Novarro (Moreau) in *Scaramouche*. Courtesy Photofest.

ing, public combat, and oratory when he addresses the National Assembly; however, his persona stands in striking contrast to the swashbuckling heroes of costume dramas with their flamboyant gestures and emphasis on physical action rather than on subtly choreographed physical movement and on verbal dexterity. In Kevin Brownlow's estimation, "The narrative is swiftly flowing but is nevertheless an undercurrent. *Scaramouche* clearly attracted Ingram for its visual qualities rather than for its thrilling story" (qtd. in O'Leary 126). Thanks to the acting, the film does not turn into a vehicle for acrobatic masculinity despite its highlighting of physical action. John Seitz's camera work coordinates the historical and fictional threads of the narrative through thrilling long shots that visualize the aristocratic and plebian milieux, carefully composed vignettes of the principal actors, and close-ups of the characters that resemble eighteenth-century portraiture.

The film's theatricality resides in the varied scenes of duels, public demonstrations, executions, and mob violence, and comes to a focus in Moreau's performance as the actor Scaramouche. Scaramouche serves as a reflection on a form of theater that presents the character as both actor in and observer of events. While the film employs spectacular effects (thanks to Seitz's camera work and Ingram's editing) to render its historical tableaux, it differs from DeMille's *The Ten Commandments* in distancing the audience from strong emotional identification with the characters in favor of a contemplative response that tends to mute melodramatic effects. A further dimension of the film's characterization and of Ingram's concern with historical effect entails his inclusion of historical figures alongside the fictional ones: Louis XVI, Robespierre, Marie Antoinette, Marat. A memorable image is that of Robespierre (Fuerburg De Garcia) filmed in close-up, accentuating his pock-marked face and voluminous wig.

By the late twenties, Ingram had decided to leave Hollywood and pursue his filmmaking in Europe. The heyday of the producer-director-editor was over and the studio system was uncongenial to Ingram's mode of creating cinema—also the case with the prodigious but eccentric Erich von Stroheim. In his outlook on life and filmmaking, Ingram was closer in point of view to European filmmakers. His work, like that of the films of Lois Weber, Chaplin, Bryant-Rambova, Cruze, DeMille, Brenon, and Wallace Worsley, is evidence of the diverse forms of filmmaking offered in this year in terms of genre and spectacle, the innovative construction of masculinity and femininity onscreen, and the creation of stars. Exposed here are transformations in not only narrative styles and forms of acting but also, for better or worse, in the union of art, technology, and commerce and in the ethos of a time of change for American culture, cinema, and society.

■ ■ ■

The embodied transformations visible onscreen were recreating and reflecting gendered shifts and redefinitions in the real world. Like Lois Weber, many women in Hollywood and elsewhere were taking charge of fashioning and supervising productions, creative and otherwise; and like Weber's character Jewel, women were finding in the imaginative life an alternative to the bitter and stringent dictates of patriarchal power. Following Nazimova, women in Hollywood and elsewhere were beginning to see that being "defiant to convention" was a viable way of living a socially valuable life. Watching Pola Negri in *The Spanish Dancer*, women in Hollywood and elsewhere saw that exoticism and elusiveness, identified with vamps, flappers, and females who flout conventions, did not make for a frail femininity, and that delicacy of gesture and attitude could convey strength of conviction; the staid conventions of gender portrayal, in short, were worth breaking.

Nor did masculinity have to be monumental or monolithic to be significant, as was evident in *The Covered Wagon*: men onscreen and off could express their masculinity in confronting the reality of their circumstances, their territory, their conflicted and awkward positions in life even when tormented, like the hunchback of Notre Dame; or when, as in *The Ten Commandments,* they took action with religious principles as their guide; or when, as in *Scaramouche,* they had the supple soft look of Ramon Novarro rather than the tougher façade that had been required in the war years.

In *A Woman of Paris,* audiences—particularly female audiences—could see how it was possible to maintain dignity, poise, and strength even in the face of social class constraints allied to overbearing and persistent male dominance. Perhaps it was sight of a film like this, or of a woman like Chaplin's Marie, that encouraged Alice Paul to spearhead the drafting of an equal rights amendment to the U.S. Constitution that would end discrimination based on sex. It was presented to the Senate on 10 December and to the House of Representatives three days later, the beginning of a long and frustrating road. Passage of the ERA in both the Senate and House, and necessary ratification by the legislatures of thirty-eight states, has yet to come. The cinema has played and continues to play a critical role in embodying and occasionally transforming these gendered conflicts.

1924

Movies and Play

JENNIFER M. BEAN

When static filled the air, it was not for want of trying to eliminate it. On 23 August, the newly formed Radio Broadcasting Association of America sought to abolish interstellar boundaries by relaying a message to Mars (that planet spiraled to within 55.7 million kilometers of Earth this summer day, the closest approach since 1804). Those ever-elusive Martians, alas, did not respond. Even so, radio's communicative capacities triumphed through the live coverage of events from the World Olympic Games in Paris, the first sports broadcast of its kind. It may be for this reason that swimming champion Johnny Weismuller, who won three gold medals at the Parisian games, would so easily slip into celebrity status as a phenomenal screen Tarzan in later years. It may also be that radio's unprecedented media presence played a factor in the landslide electoral victory of President Calvin Coolidge, whose voice reached those gathered around their living room receiver sets on 24 February to hear the first presidential speech, broadcast live, of its kind. Even better, by fall some would sit in a newly wired movie theater to see *and* hear their president speak, his image and voice projecting at the same, synchronic time.

The Phonofilm was the invention of Dr. Lee de Forest, who shot and recorded *President Calvin Coolidge, Taken on the White House Grounds*, during the presidential campaign that fall. While hardly a riveting performance, the speech reveals the crux of Coolidge's campaign platform and political strategy. Beginning with a statistical emphasis on the enormity of the federal debt, and stressing its capacity to undermine the "chief meaning of freedom" for all Americans, Coolidge concludes with a promise to reduce government spending and thus reduce taxation: "When the government affects a new economy," he intones, "it grants everybody a life pension with which to raise the standard of existence. It increases the value of everybody's property, raises the scale of everybody's wages." This sounds good, but the final line is even better, resonant with pith: "One of the greatest favors that can be bestowed upon the American people is economy in government."

Favorable, that is, for some. On one hand, Coolidge supported the Revenue Act of 1924, which sharply reduced income and inheritance taxes, as well as the gift and excise taxes imposed during World War I. On the other, he adamantly refused to use federal economic power to ameliorate the depressed condition of agriculture industries, and effectively killed various farm relief bills that appeared in Congress.[1] Regardless of how one wishes to evaluate the ideological efficacy of this policy of moderation, or what Walter Lippmann described in 1926 as Coolidge's "active inactivity," it obviously appealed to a country suffering from inflation. It also, in Lippmann's opinion, "suits all the business interests which want to be let alone. . . . And it suits all those who have become convinced that government in this country has become dangerously complicated and top-heavy" (www.whitehouse.gov/history/presidents/cc30). Moreover, it suited a country increasingly convinced of government corruption. Indeed, Coolidge's election took place at a moment when the Teapot Dome scandal erupted in the press. Named for the teapot shape of the naval reserve oil fields in Wyoming, the scandal centered on the revelation that Secretary of Interior Albert B. Fall had leased the naval field to private companies in 1921, a lease for which Fall received a hefty and decidedly private sum. Associated with the Harding administration, and specifically with the "Ohio Gang" (so named for the politicians involved, all born in Ohio), the scandal neatly skirted Coolidge, who was born in Vermont, and whose loud cries for government moderation and retraction inevitably gained further appeal.

Multiple scandals of recent vintage had rocked the film industry as well, incurring a strangely similar upshot.[2] Simply put, lean box office profits and a diluted public reputation inspired the major studios to actively practice moderation. A case in point: despite the Phonofilm's popular success in the approximately thirty-four theaters wired for sound on the East Coast, de Forest was unable to interest either Carl Laemmle of Universal or Adolph Zukor of Paramount in his equipment; "talking pictures" were considered an unnecessary expense, a passing fad, a financial gamble. No one wanted to shoot craps this year, with the exception, of course, of inventors like de Forest, and the occasional visionary artist, like independent African American director/producer Oscar Micheaux (*Son of Satan*; *Birthright*) or the legendary artiste Erich von Stroheim.[3]

The saga surrounding the production of von Stroheim's *Greed* proves exemplary in more ways than one. Following the film's wide public release, even von Stroheim's "severest critic," wrote James R. Quirk, "could never accuse him of any ambition to make himself solid with the producers as a good 'commercial director.' He wanted to make pictures for the sake of making them—'art for art's sake' in the finest sense of the word" (27). The word of the Metro-Goldwyn-Mayer Company, however, and particularly that of the twenty-five-year-old boy-wonder producer, Irving Thalberg, was that von Stroheim's art for the sake of art was "too ruthless and too grewsome [*sic*]—too pitilessly faithful to realism" (Carr "Looking at 'Greed'"). It was also about six hours too gruesomely long. Hence, Thalberg opted to cut the forty-five reels down to commercial size, primarily by excising one of the two storylines that von Stroheim had faithfully adapted from Frank Norris's novel *McTeague*. "One [of these stories]," explained the *Los Angeles Times*, "was McTeagues's married life; the other was the horrible episode of the old junk dealer—an insane old miser" (Carr "Junkman's Story"). Suffice it to say: the junkman was junked. Although one editorial for the *New York Times* claimed that von Stroheim took the cutting "calmly," others felt differently (Hall "Persistent von Stroheim"). After seeing the film's December premiere in New York, for instance, Helen Klumph was willing to admit that "they salvaged a remarkably smooth-running short picture out of what was originally a very long one," while loudly pronouncing her preference: "I would gladly have stayed in the theater all day or attended the picture on successive nights in order to see the minor tale of 'Greed' played by Dale Fuller and Cesare Gravina" (C29).

If the miserly cutting of von Stroheim's realist drama registered for some as a sign of commercial "greed," others offered more general complaints about the industry's propensity for moderation, its penchant for following "fads and whims." Even feature-film titles lacked the glow of innovative luster, or so opined reporter Harry Carr: "Just a little while ago, all the movie plays had titles that seemed to have been selected as the result of a prize contest at a firemen's ball. There were 'Flaming Youth' and 'Flaming Barriers' and 'Flaming Passion' and various others kinds of illumination and conflagration. . . . Just now, it's women. 'Unguarded Women,' 'Rejected Wives,' etc." ("Folks Who Name").

Why Carr chose to limit his list is up for speculation. Possible additions spiral onward, ranging from the singular, *This Woman*, to the plural, *Three Women*. The latter film, directed by Ernst Lubitsch, must be acknowledged as a particularly exquisite cinematic gem. But the majority appealed as showcase vehicles for an array of popular female stars: Lillian Gish in *The White Sister*; Mae Murray in *Mlle. Midnight* and *Circe, the Enchantress*; Alla Nazimova in *Madonna of the Streets*; Alma Rubens in *Cytherea*. Some titles, to be sure, flaunted women's relation to the male of the species, as in the Pola Negri vehicle titled simply *Men*, or Gloria Swanson in the more suggestively titled *Manhandled*. Mary Pickford, of course, popularly known as "America's

Sweetheart," never flirted with men in quite the same way, given her girlish star persona and nigh unprecedented appeal as the imago of golden-haired innocence. The country's sweetheart, however, did try something different, jettisoning her little-girl type for a historical costume drama, *Dorothy Vernon of Haddon Hall,* in which "Little Mary" was, give or take a few years, *almost* grown-up.

It was not Pickford's attempt to play a role verging on adulthood, but the diminishment of her capacity to "play" that critic Gilbert Seldes savaged in his "Open Letter to the Movie Magnates." Remembering previous years when "Our Mary" was "a radiant, lovely, childlike girl, a beautiful figurehead, a symbol of all our sentimentality," Seldes demands of the anonymous producers he addresses: "Why did you allow her to become an actress?" (329). It's a curious critique, almost nonsensical when taken out of context, but it is a point that Seldes elaborates in his hope that the "magnates" might remember the simplicity of earlier years of production, when movies offered "players" rather than "actors." These were years in which commercial imperatives and star salaries and attempts to replicate dramatic stage realism were subordinate to simpler plots, to the imaginative use of the camera, and to the movie's most basic and unerring principle, which Seldes describes as "movement governed by light." This fluidity, he opines, has been lost amid the stilted array of dramatic poseurs. "You forgot that the rhythm of the film was creating something, and that this creation adapted itself entirely to the projection of emotion by means *not realistic*; that in the end the camera was as legitimately an instrument of distortion as of reproduction" (339). "Above all," he concludes, "you had something fresh and clean and new; it was a toy and should have remained a toy—something for our delight. You gave us problem plays" (340).

The problem with Seldes's critique lies primarily in what he did not see. It is as if his nostalgia for an earlier period of cinema eclipses his ability to discern the capacity of the moving-image machine to reinvent itself again, and yet again, as a marvelous toy—designed for our delight. In point of fact, notwithstanding von Stroheim's impressively gruesome work of art, the wonder of the year emerges from those who took play seriously. Thus we turn to the mad energy with which "Our Gang" cavorted about on the Hal Roach lot, the insouciant glee of Douglas Fairbanks as a thief bent on adventure, the plasmatic antics of Felix the Cat, and the surreal alchemy conjured by the ever-dexterous clown Buster Keaton. While the quite different modalities of these figures and films demand considerable scrutiny, they together offer a vision of what it means to refuse the bid for dramatic realism in favor of relentless motility and outlandishly creative aesthetic play.

Adventurous Play: Kid Gangs and Oriental Thieves

The Hal Roach lot was hopping this year. I mean this quite literally, given the performance of such gloriously inept figures as Charlie Chase, who appeared in twenty-eight slapstick shorts during these twelve months alone, predominantly as the character "Jimmy Jump." The knobby-kneed Stan Laurel proved equally popular, whether as a plumpish jockey who races the wrong horse to victory (*Zeb vs. Paprika*), as the not-so-bonny lad of a feuding Scottish clan (*Short Kilts*), or simply as "Willie Worst," the dunce who barrels through a seemingly infinite system of mail chutes in the amazingly kinetic *Postage Due*. Less dunce-like, but equally frenetic, was Roach's youthful band of miscreants—Mary Korman, Jackie Condon, "Freckles" Daniels, "Fat" Joe Cobb, "Sunshine" Sammy, and, of course, Farina—known simply as "Our Gang."

Given the popular and critical approbation of child stars like Jackie Coogan (*A Boy of Flanders*) and Baby Peggy (*Captain January*) in the year's dramatic feature vehicles, the ongoing success of a children's comedy troupe may come as little surprise. What warrants attention is the degree to which the delinquents comprising "Our Gang" derange the ordinary world through inventive, physical play. The prototypical *Sun Down Limited*, for instance, locates the mischievous band on a railway track where they opt to "play engineer" by designing their own train. Comprising wrecked parts, rusty iron struts, and a fence-board-style decking, the locomotive initially lacks steam power. This is where the kids get creative: by placing a dog inside the engine on a treadmill belt, and by placing a caged cat in front of his nose, the dog races forward and, thus, the wheels spin. As with the majority of "Our Gang" comedies, however, the fun of playing grown-up games spirals out of control. In this case the cat escapes, the dog lurches in pursuit, and thus the locomotive runs wild, plunging off the rails and barreling through street traffic. Editing tempos accelerate as well, generating the nigh hysterical havoc intrinsic to slapstick's fast-paced style.

Whether or not you think this is funny depends on your perspective. In fact, from the contemporaneous perspective of *Photoplay* reporter Mary Winship, antics such as these generated something other than hilarity. They revealed instead the truth of childhood at its most strenuous, creative best. The reiterative mode of her rhetorical approach is telling: "The kids in 'Our Gang' aren't actors. They're just kids. They don't act" ("Our Gang" 40). The absence of acting styles, as well as scenarios and screenplays, engenders what she describes as a mode of production that forgoes labor of any sort. Offering a behind-the-scenes testimony of this allegedly naturalized process, Winship explains: "Bob McGowan [their director] simply suggests ideas for new and fascinating games and, while they play them, he turns on the camera" ("Our Gang" 41). With the exception of that whirring camera, here the fantasy of children's ability to "simply" play obviates the laborious demands and effects of a mechanized, industrial world.

Even a cursory glance at popular and scientific discourse on child rearing in the early twentieth century reveals the fantasy of subverting modern industrialization and its stultifying effects through physical, imaginative play. It is hardly surprising, for instance, that one entry in the June issue of *Outlook* magazine intoned that activities like camping prove dire necessity to children in an urbanized world:

> Give them no artificial amusements, but give them all the magnificent plays and games that can mean so much to boys and girls. . . . Let them make all kinds of things, from camp buildings to their own cots. . . . And you will build up the mental and moral stamina and resourcefulness that mean so much in counteracting the artificialities and necessary restrictions of city and school life. ("When Your Boy" 125)

The valorization of all things active (gaming, playing, making, building), rather than "artificial," is coequal with what the author refers to as a "close acquaintance with the primitive." The rhetoric typifies the period's embrace of physical play. Whether one thinks of Theodore Roosevelt's "rough-riding" rhetoric at the turn of the century, or the emergence of organizations like the Boy Scouts—and by the mid-1910s the Girl Scouts—of America, or even the body-building techniques of muscle men like Eugene Sandow, it is clear that the culture exalted physical play as an antidote to the effects of over-civilization, to the city's perceived erosion of Americans' mental, moral, and physical stamina. More to the point, as film historian Gaylyn Studlar writes, no one embodied the fantasy of eternal childhood, endless energy, and relentless physicality more than Douglas Fairbanks, popularly known as "Mr. Pep."

Fairbanks turned forty this year. But "he will never grow old," proclaimed the *New York Times* in January, quoting a Mr. Crockett who had recently toured the star's new studio, recalling:

> For more than an hour he [Fairbanks] devoted himself to showing us about, boyishly . . . pointing out the features of the big settings. . . . Just back of the office is a vaulting horse, together with a ring which hangs from a long rope. Fairbanks told us with great glee that this unromantic 'charger' he uses to try out all his feats of acrobatic horsemanship. Not until he has perfected himself in his twists, turns, jumps, somersaults, sword-thrusts and so on, does he mount a genuine steed and put them into practice. ("Producers Busy")

This is typical news. Always "boyishly" eager and full of "great glee," Fairbanks reportedly practiced his stunts religiously, the likes of which offered glorious spectacles of physical daring in the swashbuckling adventure stories that he began producing in the 1920s (shortly after forming the United Artists Company in 1919 with stars Mary Pickford, Charlie Chaplin, and director D. W. Griffith). Rather romantic "chargers" and "sword-thrusts" of various sorts dominate the action of films like *The Mark of Zorro* (1920), *The Three Musketeers* (1921), and *Robin Hood* (1922). Each of these costume dramas stage Fairbanks's antics in a historical setting; in each he plays a legendary hero of mythical proportions. This year, however, he played a thief, one whose antics take place not in a romanticized, historical past, but even more fantastically in the storyteller's realm of "once upon a time." And at least one of his exercise routines was new: he vigorously trained for weeks on trampolines to perfect the opening sequence in which the thief outwits his pursuers by leaping from one life-size earthenware jar to another, bouncing in the manner of a rubber ball. The trampolines were located inside the jars on the set. And the mise-en-scène invited viewers to play in a faraway world, in an opulent, oriental elsewhere.

Reportedly, Fairbanks had intended to follow his version of the legendary Robin Hood with a story involving pirates (an intention that ultimately culminated in 1926 with the release of *The Black Pirate*). But in 1922 he received an edition of the new translation of the *Arabian Nights* and, as legend has it, stayed up all night poring over the volume, and decided the next day to produce an *Arabian Nights*–themed production. Work on *The Thief of Bagdad* formally commenced the following March. It was released fourteen months later, at which time *Photoplay* described in exquisite detail the film's laborious production. A double-page spread reveals images and information from behind the scenes, lauding "Doug," for instance, for his investment in gathering "dancers from Java, China, Japan and other parts of the Orient; chemists from Europe and bookworms from universities for his research work." Another insert highlights the nameless cast of 4,000 extras, and the construction of a "ninety-foot boom, operated by a derrick and hoist" that formed a director's platform capable of swinging over any part of the set. Lavish visual effects, particularly the scene of the magic carpet "flying through the air at 1000 miles an hour," received due attention; readers learned that the feat was accomplished by a "specially built mechanism . . . suspended by piano wire" that was whisked over the set at a mere twenty-five miles an hour while "the camera and the projector create the illusion of infinitely greater speed" ("How Doug" 62–63). A lavish production by anyone's standards, the final tally of the $2 million budget was

Known as "Mr. Pep," Douglas Fairbanks plays up his boyish athleticism and trademark insouciance in *The Thief of Bagdad*.

money well spent, according to one reviewer, since "the great imaginative quality and beauty of the picture is something that cannot be measured in dollars and cents" ("Shadow Stage" 54).

The long, intensive production of *The Thief of Bagdad* neatly reinforces the film's central theme: "Happiness Must Be Earned." As Fairbanks described the character he wanted to portray: "Our hero must be every young man of this age who believes that happiness is a quantity that can be stolen, who is selfish, at odds with the world and rebellious toward conventions on which comfortable human relations are based" (qtd. in Fairbanks Jr., *Salad Days* 104). The point of the story is to reform such a young man, thus echoing character-builders' belief that a strenuous, vigorous life offered the only antidote to the negative effects of civilization, to the moral, mental, and physical degeneracy encouraged by "artificial" amusements and the "restrictions" of city life. His scenario staff found the film's theme in a quatrain from Sir Richard Francis Burton's English translation of *Arabian Nights*: "Seek not thy happiness to steal / 'Tis work alone will bring thee weal / Who seeketh bliss without toil and strife / The impossible seeketh and wasteth life." Fairbanks simplified this to the dictum "Happiness Must Be Earned." And if the story of a lowly thief who falls in love with a princess and must exert himself to ever greater, ever more fantastical heights in order to win her hand remains unclear, "Happiness Must Be Earned" scrolls boldly across the opening and closing frames. Thus the story begins, and thus it ends.

For a story to be a story it must begin somewhere and in some time, of course. But imperative differences between story types emerge when we ask where, exactly, and when? The "once upon a time" temporality intrinsic to fantastic tales of adventure like *The Thief of Bagdad* often nullifies specificity in favor of a more abstract sense of time. Literary critic Mikhail Bakhtin calls this, simply, "Adventure-Time," by which he means one divorced from social and historical as well as biographical patterns. The organization of adventure is different from the linear continuum of dramatic realism, for instance, because the adventure story's relentless motility—the anticipation of what is to come, the *ad-venir*, the what will happen next?—is determined neither by the evolution of the character nor tied to a narrative trajectory of growth, change, and synthesis. Adventure-time is ruled instead by the arbitrary irruption of the moment, immured in the repetitive use of phrases such as "Suddenly" or "At that Moment."

Although the emphatic stress on the character's transformation in *The Thief of Bagdad*—from thief to prince—might seem to contradict adventure's play with time, the structure of the film holds together primarily through Fairbanks's familiar insouciance and buoyant humor. The image of the star prevails: his physical performance style, as well as the exuberance characterizing the protagonist, changes little across the epic length of the film. The figure that registers in the opening scenes, for instance, when he nimbly thieves around the bazaar, bears close resemblance to the figure that jumps with glee after slaying the dragon or riding the Winged Horse in the sequence of ordeals that test his courage. Of course, the episodic structure of the ordeal sequences functions quite specifically as an example of "adventure-time," free from the dictates of social, historical, or biographical principles. If each episode hints loosely at causality—"The Valley of Fire" leads to "The Valley of the Monsters," and "The Cavern of Enchanted Trees" offers clues to reach "The Old Man of the Midnight Sea"—one could easily imagine a different order, an alternative temporal organization. The process of development and change and connection remains subordinate to the fantastic moment, the spectacle, and the delightful thrill of the adventurous moment.

The abstraction intrinsic to the time of adventure is also true of narrative space in *The Thief of Bagdad*. To ask "where" the story takes place is to acknowledge the fantasy of an unidentifiable elsewhere, a place at once untouchable, alien, and exotic. In the most general and obvious way, the episodic sequences of the thief's ordeals shimmer with the magical nowhere of a fantasy realm, of valleys and caverns and creatures that exist only in the imagination—or as tinted images on the silver screen. Then again, the broader space of the story, which the title nominally specifies as "Bagdad," presents a highly stylized, orientalized landscape. Eschewing the specific and unique characteristics of the "real" city of Bagdad, the cinematic city draws predominantly from stereotypes of the East as an exotic locale filled with bizarre traditions and costumes, all of which Western modernity sought to appropriate and reconfigure with little regard for specific differences among regions, peoples, and traditions.

Of the many traditions from which Fairbanks drew, we must also include German expressionism, especially *The Cabinet of Dr. Caligari* (1920). Although he considered the film a commercial impossibility, he found the highly stylized mise-en-scène of Robert Weine's film, in which objects, décor, and lighting effects are painted rather than placed on the set, aesthetically fascinating. As he explained his spatial design for *Thief* to readers of *Ladies' Home Companion* (albeit without mentioning the German influence):

> By using a somewhat weird design, by painting trees and branches black even where we had real ones, by the use of light backgrounds instead of the customary dark tones which are thought to bring out the figures more clearly, by confining our colors to gray, silver, black and white for everything except the actual costumes, we obtained an unusual effect; but sets built on the ground will look as if they were. . . . To get away from this solidity, we painted our building darker at the top than at the bottom. This seemed to make them less solid and heavy at the bottom. We also built upon a highly polished black floor that had reflections. The vertical line of a house meets the horizontal line of the ground and ends there. Our polished floor reflects the building lines and lifts our city. And this black floor caused considerable extra work. There was endless brushing and polishing week after week.
>
> (Fairbanks "Films for the Fifty Million")

Once again, the labor involved in the production heralds the dictum: "Happiness Must Be Earned." Or perhaps we should say that what is earned is what Seldes calls "the projection of emotion by means *not realistic,*" a return to a world in which "the camera was as legitimately an instrument of distortion as of reproduction" (339). If one steps back and squints a little, it may even seem that the distortion in *The Thief of Bagdad* closely borders animation's representational modes. As John C. Tibbetts and James M. Welsh note in their study of Fairbanks: "It is as if a set of mobile black-and-white, pen-and-ink drawings had come to life, creating an animated mise-en-scène. Some 50 years later it seems that one of the essential formulas for popular success that the Disney Studio was later to exploit is here given its most effective early rendering" (142).

Not everyone, to be sure, considers Fairbanks's world and the subsequent evolution of Disney's magical kingdom to be neatly commensurate. In 1939, Frank Nugent wrote a post-obituary reappraisal of the star in the *New York Times,* emphasizing the sheer physical delight brandished in Fairbanks's mode of play: "Doug Fairbanks was make-believe at its best, a game we youngsters never tired of playing, a game . . . our fathers secretly shared. He was complete fantasy, not like Disney's, which has an overlay of whimsy and sophistication, but unabashed and joyous. Balustrades were made to be vaulted, draperies to be a giant slide, chandeliers to swing from, citadels to be scaled" (qtd. in Carey 224).

Whether or not you believe that Disney cartoons of the 1930s suggest an "overlay of whimsy and sophistication" is hardly the point. What interests us is the phenomenal and various modes of play available this year, a time in which the technological rendering of an animated realm flaunted, at its best, the antics not of a mouse, but of a notoriously wily cat.

Plasmatic Play: Felix the Cat

If you are looking for signs of animated motility on the screen, it will not be long before you run into Felix the Cat. He's a ubiquitous feline, to be sure, and lucky to boot—hence his name, "Felix," derived from "felicity." Then again, Lady Luck occasionally demonstrates a penchant for deserting him (*Felix Out of Luck*), just as do the female felines in Felix's world. In *Felix Finds 'em Fickle,* for instance, the momentary object of his affection cattily requests a flower from the thin peak of a thousand-foot-high precipice. This bud alone, she cries, will prove he truly loves her. Felix thus ascends, like Fairbanks's lowly thief turned prince, encountering an array of phantasmagorical shapes that morph into battling bears, angry hawks, and hungry mountain lions. Plucking exclamation points from the air (which prove handy as swords), Felix punctuates his journey, fends off all foes, and triumphantly descends at last with the chosen petal. His petulant beloved, however, claims he chose the wrong one. Thus the reel ends, foreclosing the possibility of happiness-ever-after, one that might be earned, which is precisely the point: for Felix categorically belongs to the realm of series production. He will return again, cavorting through another installment, another misadventure, in the coming weeks.

The creation of animator Otto Messmer, Felix was hardly new to the screen. In 1919, at the suggestion of businessman Pat Sullivan, Messmer made *Feline Follies* for the newly formed Paramount Magazine, followed swiftly by *Musical Mews*. It was John King of Paramount who dubbed the cat "Felix," Sullivan who received screen credit, and Messmer who supplied the visionary talent. But it was the indefatigable cat himself who received the applause. Indeed, Felix's phenomenal rise to stardom ignited a wave of cinematic spin-offs and imitations, among them Frank Moser's "Scat the Cat" and Paul Terry's "Henry Cat." In March, Walt Disney drew "Julius the Cat," a primary character in his new "Alice" series, whose shape and *savoir faire* demeanor uncannily approximated the well-known Felix. Perhaps rightly, Sullivan was upset, not least because it was Margaret Winkler of Warner Bros. who picked up Disney's series; she also sold the Felix cartoons for Sullivan at the time. Sullivan need not have worried (at least not yet—it was not until the end of the decade that Felix would surrender his celebrity status to a musical mouse named Mickey). But for the moment Felix prevailed over his thinly disguised competitors. Indeed, the wily cat's public appeal encouraged the company to double the rate of production this year; a Felix cartoon was released approximately every two weeks (tallying a total of twenty-two), during which time the figure's head gradually turned rounder and his body more curvilinear and less angular.

The impetus for the cat's geometrical honing emerged, in part, from the pragmatics of production. As Don Crafton explains, "Circles were faster to draw, retrace, ink, and blacken," a process of particular importance in a year when Sullivan hired "guest" animator William Nolan to help Messmer keep pace with accelerating production rates (*Before Mickey* 313). A crew of inkers and blackeners forged an assembly line production system, passing cel sheets from one station to the next for tracing and filling. The mechanized efficiency of the process, however, also fragmented the labor, dividing its parts among diverse workers. The stability and consistency of the design thus depended on Messmer's capacity to oversee the drawings as they developed, a process that blackener Al Eugster, who joined the team this year, remembers with a touch of awe:

> A film would begin with an idea and a few sketches that he [Otto] would give to the head animator. Everyone would talk it over and start drawing. As he worked, Otto would continually think out loud of new ideas, for this film or for the next one, and when an animator would finish roughing out a scene, he would bring it to Otto who would look at it and OK it. He was animating and thinking at the same time. I don't know how he did it.
>
> (qtd. in Crafton, *Before Mickey* 313)

Notwithstanding Messmer's capacious talent, doing two things at once is never easy (unless you're Buster Keaton, as we will see shortly). This may

Felix the Cat's signature, detachable tail playfully morphs into a question mark as he faces yet another perilous foe in *Felix Finds 'em Fickle.*

be why Felix's transformation appears, at times, a bit uneven. In the opening and closing scenes of *Felix Dopes It Out,* for instance, the cat's paws bear a strong resemblance to rectangular blocks. In the film's central sequence, however (which takes place in "Bola Bola," a South Sea Island where Felix seeks a cure for his friend's red nose), he pads about on distinctively spherical shapes. The spherical, circular shapes ultimately attained stability, and the fully calibrated, ultra-modern cat emerged.

The overlap between modes of production and aesthetic modes is intriguing. Insofar as Felix exists solely as a manufactured object—a set of images made to move in a machine—then his flat, round black-and-white form, similar to the geometrical abstractions of cubism or the streamlined curvilinear forms of art deco, indicates a vogue for machine-based aesthetics. It is also true that his body functions *like* a machine, an object capable of endless assembly and reassembly; his signature, detachable tail forms any number of instruments—a cane, an umbrella, a clarinet, a sword—and quite often a question mark. The question mark in turn can become a ladder for scaling walls or a swing for relaxing play. Occasionally, as in *Felix Out of Luck,* he attaches a question mark to his tail, and the prosthesis answers the question at hand: how to access a milk bottle poised just out of reach?

The question ultimately posed by Felix's body, however, concerns the pleasures and effects of technology's capacity to alter material reality. At once irrational and recognizable, the world Felix inhabits plays wildly with physical logic. Gravity occasionally exerts its pull, as when the owner of the milk bottle in *Felix Out of Luck* launches a well-placed kick and Felix falls. When he flies, as he does during his precipitous climb in *Felix Finds 'em Fickle,* he plucks two wings from a defeated hawk and sails upward to the next ledge. It is precisely in the clever capacity to utilize and remake every element of his world where Felix's appeal lies. Consider, for instance, a scene from *Felix Dopes It Out,* shortly after he arrives in "Bola Bola." Chased by a chef with a sudden penchant for cat meat, Felix dashes over a stump that transforms, instantaneously, into the shape of a dog, the tail of which spring-loads Felix back to the ground. Cornered by the snarling canine, whose barks materialize as air bubbles on the screen, Felix plucks the drawn circles from the air and lassos the dog with his own bark. He then turns to throw another bark bubble at the chef, who hobbles away in a manner best described as "dog-tied."

It would be hard to find a better example of what Soviet filmmaker Sergei Eisenstein termed animation's "plasmaticness": "a rejection of once-and-forever allotted form, freedom from ossification, the ability to dynamically assume any form" (21). With properties surpassing elasticity, which only pushes the boundaries of physical reality, plasmaticness, in Eisenstein's view, offered animation a kind of god-like "omnipotence." The specific god he has in mind is Proteus, the god of the sea:

> A being of a definite form, a being which has attained a definite appearance and which behaves like the primal protoplasm, not yet possessing a 'stable' form, but capable of assuming any form. . . . One could call this the *protean element*, for the myth of Proteus (behind whom there seems to be some especially versatile actor)—or more precisely, the appeal of this myth—is based, of course, upon the omnipotence of plasma, which contains in 'liquid' form all possibilities of future species and forms. (21)

Here the hint of infinite possibility, of future worlds and endlessly metamorphosing forms, attains mythical proportions. To grasp Felix as an avatar of technology's plasmatic play is to understand why M. Paule wrote in the January 1927 edition of *Hollywood Life* that Felix had become "the symbol of our generation scrambling to realize its wild dreams" (qtd. in Canemaker 113).

Surreal Play: *Sherlock Jr.*

Felix is a figure of modernity par excellence, of technologically determined motility and pleasurable indeterminacy. There is simply nothing natural about him. Could the same be said of film more generally? Could it be said that "film's properties and man's properties are of contrary orders altogether"? The quoted phrase belongs to Walter Kerr, who posits a fundamental opposition: "Man's presence in the universe . . . is a sustained one, continuous in time and space; film is discontinuous. Man's presence on earth . . . is organic, all of a piece; film is all pieces, broken, fragmented. Man's knowledge of himself is in great part a logical knowledge, moving in a linear fashion from cause to effect; . . . film is arbitrary on all counts"

(227). These terms warrant further scrutiny. While it is technically true that film depends on constant, discontinuous change—twenty-four different frames a second (unless you're shooting a de Forest phonofilm, which records at 21.5 frames a second)—how often do we experience cinema as such? Even a Felix cartoon sustains a thin illusion of continuity, piecing together a causal sequence of events that motivate the cat's movement from, say, the bottom of a precipice to the top. One might imagine, then, that Kerr is really talking about a tradition of avant-garde cinema, such as Fernand Léger's *Ballet Mécanique* (1922), an abstract homage to mechanical movement that precludes continuity editing, causality, and storytelling altogether. But this is not the case. Rather, Kerr is referring to Buster Keaton's *Sherlock Jr.*, a forty-five-minute comic masterpiece he describes as "plainly and simply, a film about film." "It pretends," he continues, "to be about a boy who wants to be a detective while actually earning his living as a film projectionist, but it eludes its human outline early and turns into an almost abstract—though uninterruptedly funny—statement of shocking first principles" (227).

It is hard not to agree with Kerr that *Sherlock Jr.* is a "film about film." But the question remains: what is "film" really about? How does it captivate and sustain and delight our imagination? Since I believe that *Sherlock Jr.* offers one of cinema's most profound commentaries on the medium's capacity to toy with, and thus undermine (rather than reflect), the very logic of oppositions, let us begin by briefly considering the justly famous scene that Kerr uses to illuminate his point. The scene takes place in a movie theater, where Keaton's "boy" falls asleep and dreams his way into the film he is projecting, *Hearts and Pearls*. His double-exposed image leaves the projection booth, walks through the theater, and leaps into the frame. He is knocked back out on the stage, but a second leap (the double of the first?) lands him in front of the screen house. He leans on the door as if to wait when suddenly he tumbles, the door having disappeared, and he falls over a bench in a park. A graphic match montage sequence thus begins its marvelous rotation: he sits on the bench that is now a city street; he steps to avoid the traffic that is now the edge of a rocky cliff; he peers over the precipice and now faces a lion in the forest; he backs away from the jungle beast and into the path of an express train in the desert; he sits on a mound of sand that is now a reef in a vast ocean; he dives into the water and now finds his head stuck in a snow bank. As he extricates himself, he reaches for a tree for support and falls over that bench again. He is back in the garden, and now fully in the film.[4] It is certainly true that few sequences in the history of American narrative cinema so visibly flaunt editing's capacity to conjoin one widely disparate image or space with another, transforming the familiar to the unfamiliar, jettisoning the organic for the wholly artificial. But it is also true that discontinuity appears most visible here precisely because the movement of Keaton's body remains continuous. The effect of the scene depends on the merger of both principles, on their tense and interrelated doubling, on their taking place *at once*.

At once: the marvelous alchemy of *Sherlock Jr.*, the "shocking principle" it flaunts, lies in what it has to say regarding film's unique capacity to play with any discernible boundary. Indeed, rather than supplying the story of a boy who wants to be a detective as a foil that must be overcome, transcended, or eluded, *Sherlock Jr.* relies on a double nature. It puts into play those oppositions and binaries that we too often consider mutually exclusive, whether those be understood as distinctions between the human and the cinematic, between the arbitrary and the deterministic, between narrative and performance, between the natural and the magical, between the physical and the artificial or, ultimately, between the experience of reality and that of dreams.

The film's opening title cards rehearses the logic it playfully re-scripts. The first card warns: "There is an old proverb which says: *Don't try to do two things at once and expect to do justice to both.*" A second card explains: "This is the story of a boy who tried it. While employed as a moving picture operator in a small town theater he was also studying to be a detective." The initial shot of Keaton, wearing a fake mustache and studying a detective's instruction book, widens to reveal a dirty theater and an angry boss who orders the boy back to the "real job" at hand. Thus he sets to work sweeping the lobby, which effectively becomes something other than work—it becomes, more precisely, a classic vaudeville-style performance piece. The routine begins with a touch of coincidental surprise: amid the rubble he discovers a dollar that he happily pockets, at which point a young woman arrives to search for a dollar she lost, which he dubiously asks her to describe. The funny assumption—that one dollar might look different from the next; that "this" dollar might not be hers—supports a delightfully silly bit of pantomime (the young woman even mimes a flying eagle). Convinced, the boy hands over the cash, and resumes sweeping when a teary-eyed elderly woman arrives, also seeking a lost dollar. Seized by repetition's grind, the boy shortens the interrogation; he rapidly pantomimes the size and shape of the dollar for her, pulls a buck from his own pocket, and borrows her handkerchief to wipe a tear from his eye. By the time a scowling hulk of a man appears the boy surrenders entirely to automatization and immediately hands him a dollar. This is funny stuff; funnier still is the sudden reversal of terms: the man dismisses the dollar as "trash" and paws through the litter to retrieve a wallet flush with cash.

More crucial for our purposes is yet another reversal of terms. For this sequence does indeed do justice to "two things at once": it flaunts the gag, the performance, while also developing the boy's character and establishing the story's motivating premise—everything a vaudeville-set piece ordinarily does not. We know, for instance, that the boy only has two dollars at the outset of the routine; he wishes to buy a three-dollar box of candy for his sweetheart and, alas, cannot. The dollar he initially finds would have allowed him to make a better impression, while the ultimate diminishment of his funds through the course of the performance reduces his choice to a one-dollar gift box. The resulting deception, in which he disguises the one-dollar box as a more expensive offering, leaves him open to being framed by his rival, the Sheik, and sets the whole story in motion, which is to say it sets in motion a story inextricably, seamlessly tied to flamboyant spectacles of physical performance. While attempting to distract the Sheik from his sweetheart's attention, for instance, the boy throws a banana peel on the floor; he then stands to see if his trick has worked, slips on the peel himself, and performs a marvelous pratfall. More marvelous still is the boy's rather literal interpretation of his detective manual's advice: "shadow your man closely." Suspicious of the Sheik, who has slipped the pawn ticket for a stolen pocket watch in the boy's pocket, he follows his rival out of the house, down the street, and toward a railway track. This makes good narrative sense, but another sense equally prevails. Executed with unerring precision, Keaton performs an imitative "shadow" act. Mimicking the Sheik's movements with comic exactitude, he consistently remains a scant foot behind his quarry, perfectly mirroring each stop, start, hand gesture, dip of the hat, and jaunty skip.

The deft physical coordination required of such vaudeville-style routines was second nature to Keaton. Having joined his parent's stage act at the age of five, Buster rapidly became the star attraction of the "Three Keatons" in a series of skits primarily based on mimicry and physical knockabout. It is well known that his father, Joe Keaton, often hurled his young son into the stage backdrop for the show's climactic finale in earlier years; by the time he was eight, Buster's spectacular leaps and violent falls formed the centerpiece of the program. The extraordinary physical grace exhibited by the child undoubtedly astonished audiences; the child, in turn, was astounded by the sleight-of-hand physical feats performed by his family's friend, Harry Houdini. As he would later stress: "No one, by the way, ever worked harder than I did to figure out Houdini's tricks. I watched him like

"The boy" (Buster Keaton) gives candy to his youthful sweetheart, "the girl," in *Sherlock Jr.*

a hawk every chance I got. I studied his act from all parts of the theatre, from both wings of the stage, from the orchestra and both sides of the balcony and gallery. I even climbed high up in the flies so I could look straight down on him as he worked" (51). The confusion generated by Houdini's signature performance style, the question of whether a feat had been achieved through natural means or through trickery, crystallized through his innovative approach to the craft. Disposing of the magician's traditional capes, turbans, and elaborate, smoky sets, Houdini practiced the art of exposure. He exposed himself quite literally, one could say, insofar as he appeared most often in loincloths or bathing trunks. More perplexing, however, was the fact that Houdini exposed his every prop—the handcuffs, manacles, trunks, iron chests, tanks, and so on—and carefully revealed their foolproof functions. Then, bound and submersed, he miraculously escaped.

As *Sherlock Jr.* proceeds to what we will loosely call "part 2," magical feats of escape increasingly prevail. (Having dreamed himself into the film within the film, the boy is now "Sherlock," the "world's greatest detective." That he is also the world's greatest magician reiterates the film's capacity to "do two things at once," especially when those things are apparent oppositions. If a detective strives to reveal truth and solve mysteries, then a magician generates illusions that can be neither fully discerned nor logically deduced.) A particularly riveting escape scene occurs midway through the film within the film. Aided by his trusty assistant, Gillette (who played the boy's boss in part 1), Sherlock searches for stolen pearls (rather than a stolen pocket-watch) and follows the master crook (previously the Sheik) to the crooks' hideaway. Before Sherlock enters the thieves' lair, however, he and Gillette set the stage: the assistant brings his master a round, flat box that Sherlock opens to reveal a woman's dress. He then replaces the dress in the box and places the box in the window of the hideaway. Moments later, ostensibly trapped by the villain and his henchmen inside the shack, and having learned of the girl's captivity, he dives with unerring precision through the window, snatching the pearls as he leaps, and instantaneously lands on the other side dressed as an elderly woman. This trick neatly confuses the thugs who rush outside in pursuit and stare, bewildered, across the sidewalk where an old woman hobbles past.

The viewer's bewilderment belongs to a different realm altogether. Whereas the alliance between vision and knowledge is most often assumed—"I see," we often say, meaning: "I understand"—magic toys with perceptual and cognitive stability. The resultant temptation is to look closer, to stare harder, or to change the angle of perspective (one can attain many perspectives if one is a small, agile boy who knows his way around the stage). Insofar as the scene we are discussing offers viewers a remarkably stable perspective—a single take and a straight angle frames Keaton's leap through the window—it heightens the believability, the seeming naturalness, of the apparently incredulous act. But here's the trick: the scene also, simultaneously, *flaunts* an illusion on which the believability of the stunt inherently depends. Put simply, the wall of the hideaway *dissolves*. Indeed, only by dissolving the wall shortly before Keaton's leap through the window can the film offer viewers the capacity to see both inside and outside the building at once, hence heightening the apparent naturalness of the remarkable physical feat. More noteworthy still, the intensity of the performance distracts the viewer from noticing the magical trick, the fact that this is a world governed by movement and light in which all things solid—like walls—readily dissolve into air.

What is the difference, then, between technological trickery and physical prowess, between the magical and the natural? The interconnection of these elements, we begin to see, insinuates a rift into any one self-defined term, undoing the structure of oppositions that might first appear mutually exclusive.

And yet is the larger film not predicated on oppositions? Is it not driven by a plot that most commentators understand as a transition from the "real" world of the everyday to the "dream" world of the screen? It is certainly true that the *film-within-a-film* is meant to be the boy's dream reliving of his real-life events. This is the story we are told. It is also an effect achieved through a formal pattern that intimates difference through similarity. At the structural level alone repetition dominates: both parts begin in a movie theater, transition to the interior of a house where courtship and crime intermingle, and ultimately move to an exterior street setting as the boy/Sherlock follows his man. A set of visual and iconic rhymes heightens the comparison. The father announces the theft of the pearls standing in a doorway just as he did when he revealed the theft of his watch in the opening. Although the setting in *Hearts and Pearls* is more lavish, similar curtains frame the doorways in both parts, and the same characters (each a more lavish version of their former selves, such as the handyman turned butler, or the maidenly girl turned stylishly chic female) are gathered. Undoubtedly, the second part reveals a more polished, more capable, more powerful incarnation of the erstwhile adolescent boy, whose uncanny intelligence allows him to detect the explosive #13 billiard ball, for instance, and slip it in his pocket. Previously, the distracted and inattentive boy proved easy prey for the Sheik, who slipped a pawn ticket into his pocket. A particularly ingenuous parallel connects the mirrored street scenes when the boy/Sherlock "shadows his man." In part 2, he is trapped on the roof of a building and lowers himself on a crossing gate, effortlessly landing in the back seat of the villain's passing car. The camera tracks left, following the car in which Sherlock sits following his man, just as a leftward moving tracking shot followed the boy following the Sheik in the earlier scene. In the earlier scene, of course, he is trapped on the top of a moving train (rather than a building) and lowers himself to the ground with a railway water spout (rather than a crossing gate), at which point he loses track of his quarry, is "all wet as a detective," and returns to the theater where the dream sequence begins.

If, at first glance, these parallels imply an absolute distinction "between life on screen and life in nature," between fantasy and reality, as Walter Kerr claims, then a second look intimates a far richer entanglement. The fact that Sherlock is trapped on the roof of the building in the film's second part, for instance, stems from his clumsiness—he is spotted by the villain, bumps his nose on the wall, and is thus imprisoned, if only momentarily. Sherlock may not be so extraordinary after all. In turn, the awkward ineptitude of the boy as he shadows his man in part 1 is countermanded by the extraordinary physical prowess of Keaton's vaudeville-style performance.

Indeed, if we glance back to our discussion of the overt performances striating the opening sequences, we recognize its staged nature and thus the evacuation of anything we might comfortably call the "real." The entirety of the first part, in fact, insists on typology. Rather than character names, and hence the illusion of individuality and dramatic psychological realism, the film introduces us to types.

It more specifically introduces us to *cinematic* types, and hence to referential play. "The Sheik" obviously refers to Rudolph Valentino's famous role as the eponymous hero of *The Sheik* (1921), although the "real" star's image as an adulated "Latin Lover" surfaces in *Sherlock Jr.* in the shape of a middle-aged, slightly oily, self-important businessman. One might say, then, that the Sheik who prowls Keaton's film resembles more closely Stan Laurel's spoof of Valentino's role as the toreador, Juan Gallardo, in *Blood and Sand* (1922), which Laurel performed as the character "Rhubard Vaselino" in the comic short *Mud and Sand* (1922). In case one misses the reference, a poster of Laurel's film hangs on the wall of the theater lobby where "the boy" sweeps litter and dollars in the opening routine. A portrait of "Little Mary," that is, Mary Pickford, "America's Sweetheart," also hangs near the lobby door; it is hardly coincidental that her iconic golden curls resemble those of "the girl," the youthful sweetheart of "the boy." And speaking of "the boy," it is imperative to note that the poster most prominently displayed in the lobby (aside from the billing of *Hearts and Pearls*) is Rex Ingram's *Scaramouche* (1923), a film that tells the story of an ordinary law student and average young man, Quintin de Kercadiou, who becomes an outlaw French revolutionary. The motive for his heroic transformation is vengeance; his friend has been unjustly killed, and the plot of revenge thickens through the elaboration of a love triangle. While it is relatively easy to recognize in the character of de Kercadiou a foreshadowing of the story of "the boy," who exacts a certain vengeance for his unjust treatment at the hands of the Sheik, the referential play tenses further when we recognize that Ingram's film takes its title not from the main character's given name, Quintin de Kercadiou, but rather from his assumed identity, that of "Scaramouche." More to the point, Scaramouche is a clown, a member of a *commedia dell' arte* troupe, a tradition from which the marvelously playful antics of the whole of silent-era slapstick comedy derive.

Whichever way one turns, the derivative meanings, the representational alignments and realignments that shape the very premise of *Sherlock Jr.*, indisputably introduce us to a world fiercely inimical to any *a priori* "real." It might be more proper to say that the film's "dazzling workmanship," to quote surrealist Ado Kyrou, offers "one of the most beautiful dreams in the history of cinema" (qtd. in Knopf 120). We would say so, however, only by way of remembering that in the lexicon of surrealism a dream is never just a dream. As André Breton wrote in his first *Manifesto of Surrealism*, published this year: "I believe in the future resolution of these two states, dream and reality, which are seemingly so contradictory, into a kind of absolute reality, a *surreality*" (14). Thus, Keaton plays.

Coda: Room to Play

It would be relatively easy to conclude with a story of what happens next, a story in which the years to come witness the American film industry's wholesale transition to synchronized sound (albeit not by utilizing de Forest's Phonofilm technologies), a transition marked by the end of the decade (and by the end of this volume). But rather than cast our glance to the future, let us play with the very concept of an ending by looking back, by looking more precisely at one of the first critical attempts to grasp what cinema might, could—and at its very best—does mean.

Written in 1913, Georg Lukács's aptly titled "Thoughts on an Aesthetics of the Cinema" is dedicated to "describ[ing] and evaluat[ing]" an aesthetics germane to the art of film. Proceeding from the distressing premise that "something new and beautiful has arisen in our time, but instead of accepting it for what it is we try by whatever means we can to slot it into old and inappropriate categories," Lukács's argument proceeds by definition (2). The categorically inappropriate in the case of cinema is an aesthetic predicated on the other arts, especially the stage with its measured space and ordered flow of time. Rather, the key characteristic of cinema in his opinion (one prescient, we recall, of Gilbert Seldes) is "movement itself, eternal mutability, the never-resting change of things." Such fluidity means that "in the 'cinema' everything can be achieved . . . the total unhindered movement of the characters; the background, nature, interiors, plants and animals being completely alive, and with a life which is definitely not restricted to the content and confines of ordinary life" (3).

The far from ordinary life of which Lukács speaks is the life of the imagination at loud pitch, the life of which we sometimes dream, the life that hovers, mirage-like, on the vanishing horizon of our youth—or in our purview on the screen. Perhaps this is why we go to the movies, "a place of amusement," Lukács announces with decided pleasure, a place where "the *child*, which inhabits all of us, is released" (4). As the history of the cinema proceeds, may we always experience just such a release. May we always be blessed with room to play.

NOTES

1. Coolidge's commitment to economy meant he also opposed the Veterans Bonus Act; it nonetheless managed to pass into legislation, and thus awarded veterans of the Great War paid-up insurance policies that were redeemable in twenty years.

2. The most notorious of scandals include the drug-related deaths of Olive Thomas in 1920 and Wallace Reid in 1923, the Roscoe "Fatty" Arbuckle rape trial in 1921, and the William Desmond Taylor murder case of 1922.

3. Some might qualify such a claim, noting for instance that erratic experiments with color—the use of a two-strip Technicolor process in *Wanderers of the Wasteland*; a Prizmacolor sequence in Annette Kellerman's vehicle *Venus of the South Seas*—heralded new technological possibilities for the medium.

4. In this case Keaton made an exception—the likes of which Houdini never did—and offered a behind-the-scenes explanation to film historian Kevin Brownlow: "We built a stage with a big black cut-out screen. Then we built the front-row seats and orchestra pit. . . . We lit the stage so it looked like a motion picture being projected on to a screen." By measuring the distance between the camera and his physical position at the end of the shot, Keaton developed a system for perfectly matching his bodily action with a chimerical mise-en-scène. "As we did one shot, we'd throw it in the darkroom and develop it right there and then—and bring it back to the cameraman. He cut out a few frames and put them in the camera gate. When I come [*sic*] to change scenes, he could put me right square where I was" (Brownlow 487). To be exactly—"right square"—where he was previously positioned gets at the continuity within the discontinuity.

1925

Movies and a Year of Change

GWENDA YOUNG

Midway through the decade, America was coming to terms with its emerging identity as a sophisticated, cosmopolitan society. The clash between traditional values and a developing modernist sensibility was expressed in the major political event of the year, the Scopes trial, and in the texts produced by America's cultural scene. This year was something of a watershed for the American literary world. The *New Yorker* magazine was launched in February and quickly proved to be a showcase for sharp literary talents such as Dorothy Parker, Robert Benchley, Alexander Woollcott, and Ring Lardner. Also in New York, African American cultural voices found expression in the continuing Harlem Renaissance and in the March publication of a special edition of the literary magazine *Survey Graphic* devoted to Harlem. Later that year, Alain Locke anthologized the poems, short stories, and nonfiction of a number of established and emerging black writers such as Jean Toomer, Langston Hughes, Zora Neale Hurston, and Claude McKay in *The New Negro*. The new confidence of African Americans, particularly in urban areas, was also evident in the flourishing of black popular music in the decade and the ongoing success of filmmaker Oscar Micheaux, who released what was arguably his most complex film, *Body and Soul*, in November. Starring Paul Robeson as a corrupt minister, the film was controversial for its negative portrayal of the clergy at a time when Christian fundamentalism and evangelical preachers such as Aimee Semple McPherson were capturing audiences (and their money) across America.

The nation's prosperity under the presidency of Calvin Coolidge provided the backdrop for a series of novels exploring the ruthless materialism increasingly celebrated in a new, more cynical America. Sinclair Lewis followed his satirical portraits of Gopher Prairie in *Main Street* (1920) and Zenith in *Babbitt* (1922) with *Arrowsmith*, an account of the life of a young medic struggling to retain his idealism in the face of greed and corruption. Theodore Dreiser exposed the veniality of the American dream in *An American Tragedy*, a tale of ambition, abortion, and murder based on a real case from 1908, while Anita Loos created one of American literature's great comic characters, Lorelei Lee, in *Gentlemen Prefer Blondes.* Recounting the tale of a Jazz Age gold digger, intended as a "symbol of the lowest possible mentality of our nation" (13), Loos's novel follows Lorelei on her tour of Europe (to "get educated"), where encounters with a cash-strapped English gentleman and various roguish Frenchmen lead her to conclude, "I really think American gentlemen are the best after all, because kissing your hand may make you feel very, very good but a diamond and safire [*sic*] bracelet lasts forever" (80).

F. Scott Fitzgerald's *The Great Gatsby* was published in April and remains the seminal exploration of the corruption of the American dream and the ruthlessness of the rich. Despite Jay Gatsby's self-made wealth, he remains an outsider in a world where inherited wealth and power continue to dominate. The novel's other protagonists, Tom and Daisy, are "careless people . . . they smashed up things and creatures and then retreated back into their money or their vast carelessness, or whatever it was that kept them together, and let other people clean up the mess they had made" (186).

The Great Gatsby's elegiac, introspective style is indicative of a year that saw many Americans questioning the present and future of their nation and its moral values. The major controversy of the year was the passing of the Butler Act in Tennessee, which banned the teaching of evolution in schools. The new law was a divisive one, opposed by many moderates in the state and provoking outrage from liberals across America. Encouraged by the American Civil Liberties Union and by local civic leaders intent on boosting their town's profile and commerce, John Scopes, a teacher in Dayton, Tennessee, agreed to test the new ban by continuing to teach George William Hunter's *A Civic Biology,* a set text that had been used for many years in the public school system and that contained a section on Darwin's theories of evolution. As planned, Scopes was arrested and brought to trial on 10 July. Clarence Darrow, fresh from his defense of child killers Nathan Leopold and Richard Loeb, offered to serve as chief defense counsel, while William Jennings Bryan, Progressive Era reformer, temperance advocate, and committed Christian, led the prosecution. The Scopes trial (colloquially referred to as the "monkey trial") proves a useful barometer of the tensions, conflicting ideologies, belief systems, and values of a divided America.

To conservatives and fundamentalists in the South and throughout America, teaching its youth that humans and apes were descended from common ancestors seemed to be symptomatic of a nation that had lost its religious and moral compass. In many ways, the Scopes trial brought to prominence the debates that had been going on for years regarding the teaching of Darwinian theories and, more broadly, the association between

Darwin and the eugenics movement. Bryan opposed the teaching of Darwin's theories of evolution, not simply because his Christian beliefs led him to affirm that God had created man as a higher being, but because "the Darwinian theory represents man as reaching his present perfection by the operation of the law of hate—the merciless law by which the strong crowd out and kill off the weak" (Larson 39). In a decade that emphasized the importance of success, Bryan's moral qualms about the "survival of the fittest" may have seemed a throwback to the Progressive Era of a decade before, but the fact that Scopes was found guilty and fined (a nominal sum of $100) and, more important, the teaching of evolution continued to be banned in Tennessee (soon joined by Arkansas and Kentucky) for forty years, indicates that he was not alone in his concerns.

In his venomous obituary of Bryan, who died suddenly four days after the trial, H. L Mencken sneered at his subject's folksiness, seeing it as a ploy that helped him stoke up the narrow prejudices of the ignorant. Bryan, he said, felt right at home in Dayton, a "one-horse Tennessee village" whose people "sweated freely, and were not debauched by the refinements of the toilet," a place frequently visited by "gaping primates from the upland valleys of the Cumberland Range" (143–44). In Mencken's judgment, Bryan represented an older, more superstitious age where intellectualism was viewed with suspicion: "Bryan lived too long, and descended too deeply into the mud, to be taken seriously hereafter by fully literate men, even of the kind who write school-books. . . . He seemed only a poor clod like those around him, deluded by a childish theology, full of an almost pathological hatred of all learning, all human dignity, all beauty, all fine and noble things" (144–45). Although Mencken's obituary was deliberately provocative, it indicates how the Scopes trial polarized American opinion.

At its simplest level the trial reveals how seriously many Americans viewed religion; the rise of evangelicalism during the decade also reflects the desire to keep religious beliefs central to American society. In an era of mass advertising, consumerism, and apparent sexual and moral liberalism, many believed that core values were being forgotten. One of the most popular books of the year was Bruce Barton's *The Man Nobody Knows*, an attempt by the guru of modern advertising (he invented Betty Crocker) to make the life of Jesus relevant to the masses. In a frankly crass way, Barton "sells" Jesus to his readers. In place of a distant biblical figure, we are given a portrait of a 1920s-style go-getter, a modern leader who understood the "principle of executive management" in his recruiting of the twelve disciples (his "organization"); a charismatic who combined intelligence with physical ruggedness (he's an "Outdoor Man") (26). According to Barton, the parables are like the best advertisements (simple, direct, repetitious) and the miracles evidence of Jesus' showmanship. Without a hint of irony, Jesus (a Jew) is linked with other "great men" such as Henry Ford (a notorious antisemite)! While modern readers might struggle to take Barton's book seriously, the fact that it was a best seller indicates how readers were clinging to traditional beliefs, albeit ones couched in the language of modern advertising.

The films released during the year also give insights into the taste and attitudes that characterized America. MGM finally released its ambitious epic *Ben Hur*, but it was a smaller, more downbeat film that won out at the box office and among critics. King Vidor's *The Big Parade* gave John Gilbert the opportunity to move away from the light roles he had specialized in, and the film's mixture of realism and tear-jerking melodrama captured the imagination of the nation. Indeed, the film's box office success surprised many in Hollywood who had believed that a film about the Great War would be met with indifference by a Jazz Age audience.

The collaboration between European directors and the Hollywood studio system continued with Erich von Stroheim's *The Merry Widow*, his most commercially successful film, Maurice Tourneur's *Never the Twain Shall Meet*, and Ernst Lubitsch's adaptation of Oscar Wilde's *Lady Windermere's Fan*, which became a hit for Warner Bros. European directors not only contributed to the studios' output, they also had a significant influence on American-born filmmakers. Von Stroheim's attention to detail, his elaborate staging of events, and his interest in the psychology of his characters influenced Clarence Brown and King Vidor, while the films of Malcolm St. Clair (dubbed "The New Lubitsch") and Monta Bell paid homage to Lubitsch's brand of risqué social comedy. Both St. Clair and Bell released films during this year that transplanted Lubitsch-type sophisticates to American settings and explored the clashes between traditional America and a modern cosmopolitan world.

Hollywood's engagement with issues of sexuality, youth, and the body found expression in a number of films: as Douglas Fairbanks characteristically proved his physical dexterity in the lively *Don Q, Son of Zorro*, his wife, thirty-three-year-old Mary Pickford, bowed to public pressure and donned her girlish outfit once again in *Little Annie Rooney*. Buster Keaton poked fun at urban America's romanticization of the West in *Go West*, while *Seven Chances* saw his naive hero pursued by hundreds of would-be brides, intent on marrying him to secure his inheritance.

As the consolidation of the studio system coincided with the rise of mass advertising and the expansion of the cosmetics industry, the general cultural emphasis on the importance of youth and beauty came into focus. To capture what it saw as its target audience of youth and women, Hollywood released a number of films that appealed directly to these groups.

Youth, Beauty, and the Generation Clash: *The Plastic Age, Are Parents People?,* and *Smouldering Fires*

Hollywood's prolific production of youth films and flapper films continued with *We Moderns,* starring Colleen Moore, *Wings of Youth* with Madge Bellamy, and several Clara Bow films (including *Parisian Love* and *My Lady of Whims*). The emergence of a new genre, the college film, was signaled by Harold Lloyd's *The Freshman* and Wesley Ruggles's *The Plastic Age,* both of which offered a perfect opportunity for Hollywood to appeal to the important youth audience. The 1920s saw a significant rise in the number of men and women attending universities (Fass 126) and, of course, the celebration of youth and vitality was a defining feature of the Jazz Age. While *The Freshman* offers a witty, satirical insight into the peer pressure of college life, *The Plastic Age* gives it a more uncomplicated and positive endorsement. Dedicated to the "Youth of the World" and based on a popular novel published in 1924 by Brown University professor Percy Marks, the film follows the college education of Hugh Carver (Donald Keith), who leaves his doting parents to take up an athletics scholarship at "Prescott College." In a departure from Marks's idealistic novel, where Hugh's progression from boyhood to manhood is centered on his ability to open his mind to nonconformist thinking and intellectual debate, the film treads a more conventional path whereby success and happiness are linked to romance and sporting achievements. This changed focus is apparent from the first scene of the film: as Hugh leaves for college, his father reads about his athletics scholarship in the local newspaper, and the camera irises in on the section extolling his sporting success, cutting out a line concerning his academic abilities. As Paula Fass has noted, in a decade that produced some of America's greatest writers there was still a suspicion of intellectuals (evidenced in the conservative reaction to the teaching of Darwinian theories of evolution) and a devaluing of academic studies, even in universities (182). While Marks's novel is critical of the anti-intellectualism and conformism of college students of the 1920s—one of the film's co-writers, Frederica Sagor Maas, called it an "exposé of the emphasis put on sports in colleges and universities at the expense of learning" (43)—Ruggles's film barely makes reference to Hugh's scholastic activities. Instead, its emphasis on sporting success was designed to appeal to a nation obsessed with youth and vitality. The changed focus is succinctly illustrated by a scene significantly altered from the original. In the novel, Hugh's education only begins when he meets an inspirational English literature professor, Mr. Henley, who launches a tirade against the "horrible little conformers" (192) that make up his class: "The college is made up of men who worship mediocrity; that is their ideal except in athletics. The condition of the football field is a thousand times more important to the undergraduates and the alumni than the number of books in the library or the quality of the faculty" (194–95). The speech has a profound effect on Hugh and he begins to take his academic studies seriously. In contrast, the film gives the speech to 'Coach' Henley (David Butler), who delivers it to a locker room full of semi-naked teenagers. The shots of muscled torsos (including a young Clark Gable) and the celebration of the rituals of male bonding are in keeping with the film's emphasis on the importance of fraternal love and athletic prowess, but they are also indicative of broader interests in sports and physical culture that were emerging in the 1920s. As Heather Addison has noted, the decade was witness to various fitness and reducing crazes, promoted heavily through mass advertising, and linked to restoring an ideal of rugged masculinity and lithe femininity (42). The valorization of physical perfection and sporting achievement helped to "enshrine commercialized youth and vitality as central parts of the consumer culture" (Dumenil 78). Hollywood stars contributed to this "selling" of the body through endorsements of products promising youth, beauty, and fitness, and by developing star personae that seemed fixated on using the body as an expressive tool.

Gaylyn Studlar's analysis of Douglas Fairbanks explores American society's obsession with restoring traditional notions of masculinity, made manifest through the agile or bulked up male body, in response to fears that American men (and, by implication, America) were becoming weak and effeminate in a consumer world in which physical exertion was rarely required for survival. The irony was that the selfsame culture that had turned American men "soft" sold them products that promised to restore a more rugged masculinity.

If the products didn't produce the required results, sporting success was one tangible method of proving one's masculinity in a soft consumer society. In *The Plastic Age*, sporting achievement isn't merely a culmination of Hugh's college education; it is clearly a rite of passage from boyhood to manhood. Success as an athlete reaffirms his prestige amongst his (male) peers, ensures his father's approval, and proves him a worthy graduate of his father's alma mater. Winning the big game also wins him Cynthia (Clara

Models of 1920s masculinity: Carl (Gilbert Roland) and a teammate (Clark Gable, in an early role) strip off in *The Plastic Age*.

Bow), the symbol of Jazz Age vivacity and desirability. Having previously ended their relationship because she felt she was a corrupting influence on his adolescent purity, Cynthia distanced herself from Hugh, allowing him to channel his vigor into athletic training. Following his sporting victory, Hugh is presumably ready to renew (and consummate) his relationship with Cynthia, now changed into a "quieter," more respectable woman. The sexy Cynthia, first glimpsed in the film as a bare-shouldered pinup, has been transformed into a mature woman who attends the big game dressed in an understated outfit. The film also introduced a love triangle between Hugh's best friend, Carl (Gilbert Roland), Hugh, and Cynthia, not present in the novel. A probable concession to the demands of Hollywood, it is interesting in its playing out of themes of homoeroticism and male bonding. Having proven his masculinity, Hugh can reconcile with Carl, with whom he had fought for Cynthia's affection. In the post-game celebrations, Ruggles cuts between close-ups of Carl, looking hopeful and rather desperate, and Hugh, the hero of the game. The scene concludes as Hugh relents and embraces an ecstatic Carl. Yet any suggestion of homosexuality is (somewhat ambiguously) ruled out in the final scenes of the film as Hugh, leaving Prescott College, goes in search of "one more fellow," Cynthia. Interestingly, Ruggles downplays the sincerity of Hugh and Cynthia's reunion by ending the film with a comic shot of them falling off a bench that has been upturned by the passion of their kiss. This conclusion most obviously works to meet the expectations of the audiences who had paid to see a "college film" and, moreover, a Clara Bow vehicle, but it also disavows any suspicion of a homoerotic attraction that might have been evoked by the physical affection shown in the men's reconciliation scene.

The Plastic Age also addresses a central debate in American society: the clash between generations. This perceived tension was regarded as one of the defining features of the Jazz Age, and a number of commentators had written about the shortcomings of both generations. Writing in 1922, Charlotte Perkins Gilman, while welcoming the new independence of the young, and particularly of women, was critical of the ways in which this freedom was being exercised: "Youth, with its holy enthusiasm, its boundless courage, its passionate demands for a broader, higher, happier life, is the lifting force of the world, or, as was sadly said before, it should be. What hope is there for the world if youth itself becomes corrupt, turns traitor to its duty of leadership, and sinks to a level of behavior resembling senile decay" (351). *The Plastic Age* touches on the clash in the opening scene. In a middle-class home furnished with turn of the century décor, Mrs. Carver packs Hugh's bags for college, complete with long johns, a garment soon rejected by Hugh as old-fashioned, not the attire of a "college man." Later in the same scene the gap between the generations is further implied when Mrs. Carver suggests to her husband that he have a word with his son about the "things he should know." Following a vague and evasive talk by an embarrassed father (played by Henry B. Walthall, famed for his work with D. W. Griffith in the 1910s) to a bemused son, Hugh departs for college, but it can be assumed from his enthusiastic pursuit of Cynthia that he already knows all about the "things he should know." While some cultural commentators seemed genuinely repelled by the younger generation, *The Plastic Age* has a rather more benign attitude toward it, its central protagonist being an ideal representative youth. This imagined group was respectful of its parents (Hugh's greatest fear when running his big race is letting his parents down), wary of becoming too involved with "fast" women, and committed to the rules of good sportsmanship.

The generation divide is further evident in the contrasts drawn between Hugh's old-fashioned mother, played by Mary Alden, a veteran of D. W. Griffith films, and the vivacious Cynthia, introduced as a girl who wants her "own fraternity."As noted above, our first glimpse of Cynthia is a pinup shot, with bare shoulders, seductive eyes, and a head thrown back in youthful abandon. In the course of the film, Ruggles includes shots of her drinking and dancing frenetically to the music of a black jazz band in a speakeasy. However, as in many Hollywood films of the decade, the fast flapper is ultimately revealed to be a highly moral girl whose youthful vitality will presumably be tamed by a respectable marriage. While the containment of the flapper by marriage might seem a conventional Hollywood ending, it confirms the observations of one social commentator of the 1920s. In his book *The Revolt of Modern Youth*, published this year, Judge Ben Lindsey, well known for his work in the juvenile courts of Denver, Colorado, concluded that the troubled flappers and new women who appeared before him usually went on to become highly respected wives and mothers. Lindsey was a controversial personality in America: his advocacy of sex education, birth control, and modern methods of parenting won him the approval of liberals, but incurred the wrath of conservatives concerned about the apparent moral decline of America. Yet, despite his liberalism, Lindsey's observations about flappers carried with them a reassuring element and affirmed the notion that America's youth were simply "acting out," a natural and necessary step toward maturity.

Another film released this year, which explicitly tackles the issue of the clash between generations, was Malcolm St. Clair's *Are Parents People?*, a visually inventive comedy that clearly shows the Lubitsch influence. Praised upon its release for its "clever handling and sympathetically humourous characterisation" (Rev. 90), more recently the film has been commended by William Everson for its sophistication and its ability to effortlessly shift moods and tones. The story traces the effect that a wealthy couple's decision to divorce has on them and on their daughter. In the opening scenes, St. Clair establishes both the past affection and the current tension between the couple: a montage of close-ups shows a woman's hand tearing up (love) letters, a close-up of her disgusted face, a man cleaning out a closet full of women's shoes, and the woman reading an inscription of "undying love," dated 1908, in a book that she discards. All this is witnessed by a maid and a butler, both dismayed at their employers' pettiness. We are then introduced to Mr. and Mrs. Hazlitt (played by Adolphe Menjou and Florence Vidor), who have summoned their daughter, Lita (Betty Bronson), from her private school to break the news of their impending divorce because of "incompatibility." Distraught at the prospect of being a "grass orphan," Lita contrives to reunite her parents by acting upon the advice offered to her by a useful manual, *Divorce and Its Cure*. By pretending to be in love with a notorious "movie sheik," she worries her parents enough for them to come to their senses and realize they are still in love. The thin plot, given a light touch by St. Clair and his performers, was a topical one for an America witnessing rapid changes in attitudes toward family and marriage. Concern over rising divorce rates and loss of traditional family values led one commentator to put the blame on a new breed of parents who "pursue their own pleasures with little consideration of their duties to their children" (Hinckle 2). In a variation on the standard generation-clash plot, *Are Parents People?* posits the youth generation (perhaps the film's intended audience) as the mature and sensible force, while the older generation is petty, materialistic, and whimsical. The film's ending, which sees Lita reunite her parents with the help of a doctor/romantic interest whom we assume will be *her* future husband, endorses marriage, albeit a sophisticated, modern model of it.

Marriage, youth, and the generation clash were also themes in one of most interesting films of the year: Clarence Brown's *Smouldering Fires*, starring veteran actress Pauline Frederick and emerging starlet Laura La Plante. The story of a middle-aged business woman who falls in love with one of her young employees, the film sensitively portrays the taboos surrounding romance between an older woman and younger man. A deeply ambiguous text that divided critics upon its release and subsequently, the film also explores 1920s attitudes to working women, youth, beauty, femininity, and masculinity.

The film opens with a shot of a large factory, followed by a series of shots showing a figure, back to the camera, feet tapping impatiently, thumping a fist on a conference table around which a group of cowed men sit. As the action unfolds, it is revealed that this formidable president of the Vale Garment Company is a woman, dressed in masculine attire, her hair cut in a severe fashion that seems visual shorthand for the 1920s stereotype of the lesbian. In these early scenes, Brown indicates Jane's centrality and dominance by shooting Frederick in single close-ups, while her employees crowd into medium shots. This singling out of Frederick, while initially suggestive of her powerful position within the company (and film narrative), also implies her detachment and lack of human contact. The opening scenes explicitly suggest that Jane's assertiveness and attire are not qualities to be celebrated; instead, they are seen in negative terms as evidence of her mannish qualities. Frederick's performance in these scenes stresses her aggressiveness and her need to control every situation (underlined by comic scenes of her absent-mindedly pocketing her assistant's pencil every time she signs an employee dismissal notice). Frederick's rigid body and limited movements suggest a woman who is deeply repressed, inflexible, and unyielding, unattractive qualities in a culture that celebrated vigor, initiative, and expression of sexuality. In many ways, the character of Jane Vale seems to be a cliché version of the feared career woman who rejected men in favor of a profession and whose success and independence represented a challenge to traditional models of masculinity. The fact that Jane holds the power but is still subject to ridicule because of her gender is underlined by a scene in which she catches a male employee sketching a cartoon in which he has depicted her kicking a figure of Cupid: although she fires the offender, the humor of the cartoon (and its seeming accuracy) is emphasized. In a paradoxical way, the film suggests the continuing gender inequality of American society, while reassuring its audience that the overly self-assured woman can be brought down a peg or two by reference to her lack of romantic success.

The clash between different models of femininity, and indeed different generations of women, is emphasized in the film's first few minutes. Jane's mannishness is contrasted to some of the female employees at the factory who dress in the latest fashion and see the workplace as a potential dating arena that will help them to secure their ultimate goal: marriage and retirement out of the workforce. An exasperated Vale's question to one flirtatious secretary—"Do you girls ever think of anything except clothes and a man to lean on?"—is met with an impudent retort: "By the time I am forty I hope I'll have something better than a desk to lean on." The secretary (Helen Lynch) is fired, but Jane remembers this second slight of the day. Jane's independence and power are directly linked to the legacy of her father, who gave her two mottos to live by: "Be necessary to others" and "Let no man be necessary to you." However, Brown forces us to modify our assumption that Jane's success is solely attributed to the inheritance from her father: mention is made of how Jane has built up her father's relatively modest factory into a vast model of 1920s efficiency. The film comments on American business's stress on developing ever more effective systems of production, and it is through an interest in increasing efficiency that Jane meets Bobby (Malcolm McGregor). A boyish go-getter, he approaches her with ideas on how to improve production output, and although she initially dismisses him, she is impressed when he stands up to her overbearing personality. Like Jane, Bobby rejects an emotional life that will divert him from his career ambitions: in one scene, a saucy seamstress's attempts to distract him by flashing her gartered leg are met with indifference. Arguably, Jane's attraction to Bobby is partly narcissistic: she sees in him a reflection of her younger self, as well as a man strong enough to stand his ground when challenged by her. Her respect for him is implied by Brown's use of two shots showing them face to face, or side by side.

As news of the relationship between Bobby and Jane spreads along the production line (shown in a long tracking shot of workers gossiping), Bobby finds his masculinity in question. Assuming that this unusual May-December romance must have a maternal quality to it (and with it, an emasculation of Bobby), one seamstress (Wanda Hawley) changes the label on the baby romper suit she is working on from "Baby Romper" to "Her Baby's Romper" and deposits the article on Bobby's desk. The ensuing argument sees Bobby defending his relationship with Jane by vowing to marry her; more important, this promise, and the fistfight he engages in with a mocking male machinist, reasserts his sense of masculinity. By (reluctantly) proposing marriage, Bobby takes the lead in the relationship, and it is significant that after the engagement there are relatively few scenes of Jane and Bobby in the workplace.

An intertitle tells us that "the careless and cynical world saw only a middle-aged woman in love with a boy and they laughed . . . the woman only saw happiness." The romantic awakening of Jane is signaled by the more fashionable and feminine costumes worn by Frederick (who has had her "star glamour" restored) and by a change in how she is lit: while the early shots of the "mannish" Jane were flatly lit, the "feminine" Jane is afforded diffused close-ups. In addition to softer lighting, the increasingly sympathetic treatment of Jane facilitates a softening in the audience's attitude to her. Indeed, the film becomes more sensitive and complex in the scenes depicting Jane's love for Bobby, the tragic love triangle that develops when Jane's younger sister comes on the scene, and Jane's eventual renunciation of her love.

One of the film's major themes is the prevalence and valorization of youth in the culture that surrounds the characters, which is itself symptomatic of a wider national obsession. As Kathy Peiss explores in her study of the beauty business and advertising, the 1910s and 1920s witnessed a rapid expansion of the cosmetics industry in America (*Hope* 98). By now sales of cosmetics were estimated to be worth $141 million (Dumenil 141) and the American cosmetics industry spent more on advertising than any other industry (Banner 273). According to Lois Banner, there were now 25,000 beauty parlors in America (271). The emphasis on conforming to ideals of beauty and physical perfection was indicative of American society's attitudes to the body, the citizen as consumer, and the necessity to retain a youthful appearance.

The most problematic aspect of *Smouldering Fires* is the assumption that Jane finds her femininity only when she falls in love, but while this femininity may be seen to be more "natural" than her mannishness at the start of the film, it is clear that retrieving it requires much work and cosmetic aid. Soon after her engagement, Jane embarks on a regimen of beauty procedures and anti-aging treatments designed to prepare her for a marriage to this young man. A scene showing Jane immersed in a sauna looking frazzled and worn is played for comic effects, but it does offer an insight into the desperate measures taken by women in the 1920s to preserve their youth. While the scene suggests that the beauty treatment Jane endures has had a positive effect (she emerges looking more glamorous), the treatment requires her to cede control to the therapist and the technology, important in a film that has emphasized the link between her body and her authority. A later scene offers a much more ambiguous, pessimistic take on the same theme. The scene begins with a shot of Jane waking up at 5:30 A.M. to begin a rigorous beauty regime. Screened off from her sleeping husband, she opens a dressing table drawer to reveal an array of beauty products and anti-aging treatments, which she methodically applies. The shots of Frederick enthusiastically applying the creams are held for several minutes, enough time for audiences to register the comic elements but also to appreciate the underlying tragic and pathetic implications: rather than inspiring confidence in the viewer, the huge number of products suggests Jane's increasing desperation and susceptibility to the false promises of the cosmetics industry. Interestingly, this scene was cut from American release prints, although it was present in prints released in Europe. Immensely effective, it offers a subtle and thoughtful commentary on the beauty industry's exploitation of human vanity and vulnerability, and ultimately concludes that no one can ever fend off the inevitability of time and age.

Jane herself reaches this conclusion when she hosts a party for her sister Dorothy and her friends. As Jane reads "Youth," a poem in *India's Love Lyrics* (a collection by Laurence Hope that was popular in the 1920s), a miserable Bobby broods in the corner. The dreariness of the moment, underlined by Brown's use of flat, gloomy lighting and the antique décor of the room, is interrupted when Dorothy arrives home with some of her friends and an impromptu party ensues. The red filters used by cinematographer Jackson Rose introduce a new energy in the scene, suggesting the vitality of Dorothy's (and Bobby's) generation. A staid evening is soon transformed into a Jazz Age party as Dorothy's friends roll back the carpet and spontaneously dance around the room. While Jane does join in, she quickly feels out of place (one guest assumes she is Bobby's mother!) and becomes physically

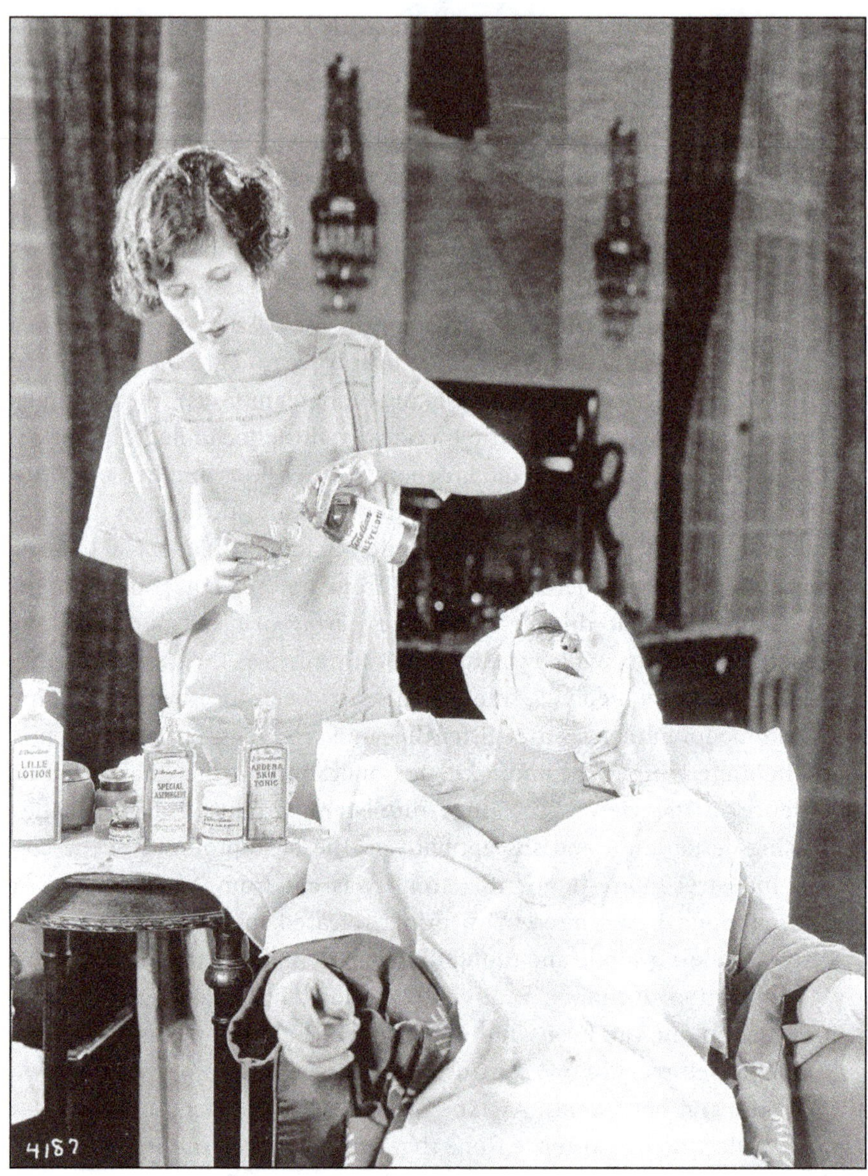

The price of beauty: Jane (Pauline Frederick) endures beauty treatments in *Smouldering Fires*.

exhausted. This reference to Jane's age and physical weakness is an echo of a previous scene in which her fatigue on a day out in the country results in her early retirement, leaving the path clear for Dorothy and Bobby to engage in some rock climbing, a brush with death, and even a passionate kiss. The party scene is a turning point in the narrative: not only does Jane realize that the age gap between her and Bobby cannot be overcome, she also becomes aware of Dorothy's love for Bobby. In a visually inventive shot, Jane calls out Bobby's name, only to see Dorothy's startled reaction, captured in her reflection on the window and revealing of her true feelings for her sister's husband. In the best tradition of melodrama and the self-sacrificing heroine, Jane resolves to allow Bobby his freedom. The film's final scene, where Bobby and Jane host a twenty-first birthday party for Dorothy (in which many jokes and comments are made about aging, much to Jane's mortification), is the culmination of Jane's journey toward self-sacrifice. Wearing a party hat that is, significantly, a clown's hat (shades of *Pagliacci*), she presides over a table that is divided along generation lines: while Bobby and Dorothy are visually aligned with each other, Jane is framed in shots with her assistant, Scotty (Tully Marshall). Contriving to distract them while she steels herself for her sacrifice, Jane sends Bobby and Dorothy upstairs on a search for a present that is supposedly hidden in her dressing table. There they come across her anti-aging treatments, a source of embarrassment and amazement to them and another reminder of the age difference between husband and wife. Jane stages a final scene that she intends them to overhear: she tells Scotty that her marriage was a "mistake" and that she "must have [her] freedom." The budding lovers are stopped in their tracks and the film concludes with a repetition of the emblematic three-shot that has been used throughout the film to suggest the ménage-à-trois theme: Jane strokes Bobby's hair, while Dorothy rests her head on her sister's shoulders in a succinct allusion to the trio's changed relationship. Jane, who has always been a big sister to Dorothy, is now a self-sacrificing mother figure, while the stroking of Bobby's hair underlines the maternal aspect of Jane and Bobby's relationship.

As noted, *Smouldering Fires* divided critics when it was released. Alma Whitaker attacked the film's portrayal of a woman over thirty, noting that the script's co-author, Sada Cowen, once remarked that she didn't like women. Whitaker was critical of the film's assumption that "a woman is a crocky old wrinkle-remover addict before she is 40," and found it implausible that the character of Bobby would choose Dorothy, a "fluffy headed little blondie" over Pauline Frederick's "infinitely more fascinating and attractive" Jane (yet Anita Loos's observations about clever men falling for dumb blondes over fascinating intellectuals would seem to contradict Whitaker's opinion). Florence Lawrence's review of the film for the *Los Angeles Examiner* was generally positive, especially praising Brown's direction and Frederick's acting, but she noted that the producers had "evidently decided that abiding love cannot come to a woman of forty." Kathleen Lipke's profile in the *Los Angeles Times* revealed that the denouement was imposed on Brown and that his original conclusion saw Jane back in her role as president of the Vale Garment Company "showing her again taking up the threads of business . . . ending the picture triumphantly." More recently, Sumiko Higashi has argued that Brown's production is a "deadly film," in which "Vale's success was mocked and her failure made glaringly evident" (*Virgins* 108–09), while in his study of American silent films Richard Koszarski offered a balanced assessment of a "courageous" film, which "showed a middle aged female business magnate marrying her boyish private secretary. . . . As was inevitable in the 1920[s], the film insists that 'May-December' romances are ill-starred . . . [but] what is interesting here is not just the admission of sexual longing in a woman over forty, but the fact that the character has the power to make all the decisions that impel the drama" (189).

A deeply ambiguous text, *Smouldering Fires* nevertheless remains one of the few films of the twenties that offered critical comment on the valorization of youth in America. Released through a studio system that colluded with the cosmetics/physical culture industry to sell the ideal of youth and beauty, it was an unusual production.

Women's Roles and Mothering: *The Home Maker, The Goose Woman,* and *Stella Dallas*

While *Smouldering Fires* exhibited a profound ambivalence toward women and their changing role in society, King Baggot's *The Home Maker*, released a few months later, endorses an unusual model of the modern, working woman. Based on the 1924 novel by Dorothy Canfield Fisher, the film tells the story of Eva and Lester Knapp, a couple struggling to make ends meet in the fast moving, efficiency-conscious America of the twenties. Although Fisher was primarily known as a novelist, she was also noted for popularizing the Montessori Method in a number of books written in the 1910s. In a letter to her publisher, she stressed that the novel "should be taken as a whoop not for 'women's rights' but for 'children's rights'" (Fisher viii); nevertheless, both novel and film offer striking insights into the broader cultural debates around child rearing, the roles of husband and wife within marriage, and the place of the family in a consumer society. Estelle Friedman has noted that a link was commonly made between the decline of the traditional model of the American family and the movement of women into the workplace in the teens and twenties (382). This cultural anxiety, in tandem with a burgeoning consumer culture that promoted advancements in household technology, led to a new consciousness and promotion of homemaking as a profession, complete with commodities as antidotes to natural familial tensions (Cohen 188). In her history of domestic work in the United States, Phyllis Palmer argues that "a housewife's role in consumer culture was not just buying. Rather, her choices and decisions in buying expressed her household's standard of living and defined its social connections" (22).

In a culture that stressed hard work, cleanliness, and perfection, homemaking (and the child rearing it sometimes entailed) was a high-pressure profession and, like the ideals of beauty and youth so heavily promoted in society, it was often difficult to live up to social (and gender) expectations. Fisher herself expressed concerns that the evolution of a fast-paced consumer society had led to a skewed emphasis on trivial things in the life of the American homemaker: "The little things of life, of no real importance, but which have to be 'seen to' by American homemakers, is like a blanket smothering out the fine and great potential qualities in every one of us" (xiv).

With an adaptation by Mary O'Hara (later famed for writing the children's novel *My Friend Flicka*), Baggot's film begins with an exterior shot, bathed in soft, natural light, of a wedding, followed by the deflationary intertitle, "but that was 13 years ago." A close-up of scrubbing hands opens to a medium shot of Eva Knapp (Alice Joyce) on her knees, scouring the floor with maniacal intensity. Her cleaning is interrupted by her troublesome son, Stevie (Billy Kent Schaefer), who is amusing himself by playing with Eva's precious sewing machine; punishment ensues and a defiant Stevie is confined to a rocking chair, which he rocks furiously. In a remarkably concise fashion, Baggot delineates the themes of the film and gives his audience a sense of character psychology: the Knapp home is a grim place, where work is an unending chore, where household technology is used only to produce tangible and material results, and where a rocking chair, traditionally associated with the nurturing, maternal impulse, is transformed into a means of punishment.

Baggot next introduces the audience to Eva's husband, the head of the household, Lester Knapp (Clive Brook). Working despondently in a bleak-looking office, Lester chews soda mints in a vain effort to alleviate the constant nervous tension brought on by his unhappiness in a job that he hates. Although he is one of the longest-serving employees in Willing's Department Store, he soon learns that he has been passed over for promotion, due to his lack of efficiency. In contrast, the early scenes of Eva at home and in her neighborhood stress her skill at managing her household: her friends at the Ladies Auxiliary go to her when they need advice on homemaking, fashion, and families. Much admired by her peers, she is also pitied for her choice of marital partner: "It's a pity to see such an efficient woman tied to a useless man." The stresses of struggling to maintain a decent standard of living and to fulfill society's expectations of her roles as wife and mother take their toll on Eva who, like Lester, suffers from illness brought on by her frustration at the "monotonous round of sewing, scrimping and scrubbing." Early scenes of family life are strikingly wretched as her husband and children live in fear of her temper and her impossible standards. Baggot intercuts shots of Eva furiously working in the kitchen and living room, with shots of Lester and the children, huddling upstairs in darkened rooms, lurking in doorways, afraid to venture into Eva's domain. A family meal is represented as an ordeal, marked by Eva's constant correcting of the children's table manners and her despair over a grease spot on the floor. The devastating impact of Lester's failure to secure promotion means a further reduction in Eva's respect for him, and his inability to meet his social role as chief breadwinner and strong patriarchal head of the household reinforces Eva's sense that she is married to a "useless" man.

A character that seems remarkably prescient of the women profiled in Betty Friedan's 1963 best seller, *The Feminine Mystique*, Eva is a woman trapped in a role of wife and mother that society has conditioned her to believe is normal, yet which the film suggests is deeply unnatural to Eva. It is only after an "unnatural" turn of events that a more natural and fulfilling way of life is awarded to each member of the family. In his despair, Lester attempts to kill himself but proves "a bungler even at dying" and becomes wheelchair bound. Traditional roles are reversed and Eva becomes the chief breadwinner when she takes a job as a saleswoman in Willing's Department Store. Happy in her job, Eva becomes a vital, sexy wife (Alice Joyce's costumes also follow a transformation from housecoats to slinky black satin), and a relaxed, fun-loving mother. In turn, Lester, the homemaker, presides over a happy home, where chores become adventures and expressions of parent-child bonding. In one delightful scene, Lester encourages the rebellious Stevie to explore the kitchen, allowing him to play with the domestic implements that had previously been mere utility items. The film's progressive attitude to child rearing places it within a wider cultural discourse in the 1920s, influenced by theories of child psychology, that stressed communication and nurturing between parents and child over more traditional methods of disciplining children by threats and coercion.

The Home Maker is a fascinating critique of traditional models of marriage and the social pressures placed on men and women. Koszarski has gone so far as calling it a "radical" film, "one of the few dramatic works of

An anxious Eva (Alice Joyce) looks on as her injured husband (Clive Brook) sleeps, in a scene from King Baggot's *The Home Maker.*

the 1920s to argue unequivocally for the abandonment of stereotyped sex roles and to criticize the structure that prescribes such behavior" (189). The film does indeed contain some very subversive (and very modern) elements, especially in its contention that homemaking and motherhood don't always come naturally to women. Similarly, the film's treatment of the couple's unhappiness with their prescribed roles, and the impact that this has on their children, is infused with a darkness rarely found in Hollywood portrayals of marriage in the 1920s. However, the film is rather more conventional in its attitude to Eva's career. While it is refreshing to see the connection made between a successful career and a woman's personal fulfillment, it is significant that Eva's career is as a saleswoman. Endorsing the common perception of the department store as a female domain, the film suggests that it is Eva's own experience of being a consumer, and her willingness to participate even more in the consumer society, that leads to her professional success. As Susan Porter Benson notes in her study of the evolution of the American department store, "selling skills valued women's culture, rewarding both typically female personality traits and expertise in matters of dress and domestic management" (289).

Eva's embrace of the consumer society is evident in her changed attire and in the important fact that she stops making her children's clothes (once the proof of her efficiency as a homemaker) and instead buys them in stores. Significantly, while the novel does contain Lester's barbed comments on the ruthless consumer society that is symbolized by the department store—"materialism fatly triumphant" (253)—the film contains no such critique. Indeed, it is only when Eva becomes fully immersed in the consumer world of selling, with its manipulation of human vanities and exploitation of insecurities, that we see the "real" Alice Joyce (glamorous, vital movie star) emerge. Ultimately, *The Home Maker* remains a perceptive insight into changing attitudes toward marriage and careers in the twenties, in spite of its rather naive endorsement of consumer society. Its refusal to support a notion that motherhood and the maternal impulse were "natural" and innate is interesting in light of two films released during the year: Clarence Brown's *The Goose Woman* and Henry King's *Stella Dallas*. Both offer portraits of unusual mothers who, in their attitude toward children, clash with society and the expectations built up around the mother-child bond.

Based on the notorious Halls-Mills murder case of 1922, *The Goose Woman* offered audiences a sophisticated handling of mise-en-scène, intricate editing, and a complex narrative structure that utilizes numerous flashbacks (not all reliable), while providing Louise Dresser with a career-defining role. Superficially a "whodunnit," it tells the story of Mary Holmes (Dresser), a former opera singer now reduced to living in filthy conditions in a shack, earning money for gin by tending a flock of geese. Following the murder of her wealthy neighbor, she reveals that she is the crime's only eyewitness. An eager state's attorney, who remembers her as the great Marie de Nardi, decides to groom her as his star witness for the prosecution and sets about transforming her from a dirty, bitter, foul-mouthed crone to a regal society matron. In a further commentary on *Smouldering Fires*'s themes of youth and beauty, Brown's follow-up film also features a scene of physical transformation as a team of therapists and manicurists set to work on changing Mary back into Marie. Relishing his chance to depict the transformation in as much realistic detail as possible, Brown uses close-ups of filthy fingernails, stained clothes, and a grime-ringed bathtub to convey the hard work that goes into being beautiful. The makeover not only restores "Marie," the confident and sophisticated woman of twenty years before, but also reiterates Dresser's star quality. More important, the scene suggests a new beginning for Marie: the physical cleansing of her dirty body will soon be followed by a moral cleansing that sees her reuniting with the son she has rejected since birth.

One of the most unusual aspects of *The Goose Woman* is its depiction of Mary's attitude to mothering and relationship with her son. At the beginning of the film, the drunken, reclusive, alcoholic mother expresses her contempt and hatred for her son, Gerard (Jack Pickford), whom she blames for losing her voice: "You've changed me from a nightingale to a frog. It's your fault and I hate you." Their every encounter is filled with reproach and bitterness, and Mary truly seems an "unnatural" mother. Intent on destroying his newfound happiness with his fiancée, Hazel (Constance Bennett), she reveals that he is illegitimate, prompting him to exclaim, "You've shown me something I didn't believe God ever made—a woman without mother love." As Mary is such a repellent character, one can only agree with his assessment. It is only when Mary is transformed into Marie and her son's very life is threatened (her eyewitness account of the murderer as a man in a white overcoat driving a car with a broken headlight implicates Gerard, who has both the coat and the faulty headlight) that she embraces her mothering role and confesses that her story is false. While the state's attorney expresses doubt about her change of story ("Madam, it is only natural for a mother to lie to save her son"), the audience knows that Mary has never been "natural" and that she indeed must be telling the truth. She admits, "I've been a bad mother, but he's my boy—he's fine and *clean* [emphasis mine]. He's mine, mine!" Following a convenient confession from the real killer, Gerard, Marie, and Hazel are framed in a trademark Brown three-shot of reconciliation and optimism.

Although *The Goose Woman* takes risks in having its star so convincingly play a repellent vision of motherhood, ultimately the film suggests that reintegration into society and immersion in the world of beauty and fashion will help restore the woman's natural instinct to be a nurturing and self-sacrificing mother. In Henry King's film of Olive Higgins Prouty's best-selling novel *Stella Dallas*, mothering is represented as an intense, natural, and innate instinct, its greatest expression lying in the mother's ability to sacrifice herself for her child's happiness. Belle Bennett plays Stella, a working-class girl who longs to escape from her grimy home (her own father, head of the household, even calls it "a dump"). When she meets the upper-class Stephen Dallas (Ronald Colman), who is in shock following his father's suicide and a broken engagement, Stella reels him in with her apparent simplicity, lack of pretensions, and romantic girlishness.

Soon after their marriage, Stephen realizes that he has made a mistake—Stella, whom he thought refined and old-fashioned, is actually an avid consumer, devoted to fashion, women's magazines, beauty treatments, and vulgar humor. Her choice of the crude Ed Munn (Jean Hersholt) as a friend offends Stephen's sensibilities and leads him to conclude that she is not a good mother to their daughter, Laurel. When he threatens to take Laurel away from her, Stella, who had seemed a rather lax mother when she leaves her baby in the care of a pipe-smoking old woman, becomes fiercely protective and hysterical, claiming that she would die if Laurel is taken away from her. Something of a turning point in the film, the scene helps to shift the audience away from disapproval of Stella toward a more compassionate understanding of her and the intensity of her maternal love. Although she is crude and common, she is the human center of the drama, an accessible, warm character who dismisses the highbrowed pretensions of the social set in favor of popular literature (her favorite author is Elinor Glynn, of *It* fame), burlesque shows, and friendship with the very human Ed Munn. Her down-to-earth quality doubtless appealed to a cinema audience that often viewed the upper class and intellectualism with some envy and suspicion. Stella's attempts at respectability and her efforts to fend off the signs of aging seem like endearing human frailties rather than unattractive vices. As with the novel and King Vidor's more famous 1937 version, the film effectively steers a course between "convincing sentimentality and lachrymose melodrama," in the words of its scriptwriter, Frances Marion (qtd. in Beauchamp 171).

The film ends as Stella, who believes she is an impediment, a "shackle" to Laurel's happiness and social advancement, facilitates her entry into the upper-class world of Stephen and his new wife, Helen (Alice Joyce). As she stands in the rain, watching her daughter's marriage through a window, Stella's vulnerability and her sacrifice are emphasized and the audience can't help but conclude that entry into the upper classes comes at too great a price. The popular success of the film, and the critical plaudits awarded to Belle Bennett, indicates that audiences wholeheartedly endorsed Bennett's affecting performance as a contemporary representation of the age-old stereotype of the self-sacrificing mother.

■ ■ ■

This was a profitable and productive year for the American film industry. While big budget productions such as *Ben Hur* and *The Phantom of the Opera* pulled in the audiences and now appear so emblematic of the big Hollywood studio production, it is the smaller melodramas and comedies that continue to offer fascinating insights into American society's ambivalent attitudes toward youth, gender roles, and sexuality.

1926

Movies and Divine Stars, Defining Gender

MAUREEN TURIM

Early in the year, technological advances stole the spotlight: U.S. inventors worked to address the development of television, spurred by competition with British inventor John Logie Baird. At the Royal Institution in London, Baird demonstrated a moving-object image with thirty lines of resolution on his mechanical television system. In the United States, Charles Jenkins transmitted a TV signal between cities, and Bell Telephone Labs transmitted a film. Pursuing advances in military technology, Robert Goddard launched the first liquid-fueled rocket on 16 March. Meanwhile, the technological change to sound film edged toward actualization as key industry alignments with sound systems took place over the summer. On 23 July, Fox Film bought the patents of the Movietone sound system for recording sound onto film. Then on 6 August in New York, the Warner Bros.' Vitaphone sound-on-disc system premiered with the short film *Don Juan*, starring John Barrymore. Kodak manufactured 16 mm film stock, and the first 16 mm movie was shot.

On 26 February, President Calvin Coolidge signed the Revenue Act into law, reducing income taxes as well as other fiscal duties. Historians see this act, long sought by the Republican Party and finally enacted despite the ongoing grand jury investigation of the Harding administration's corruption scandals, as weakening the economy and leading to the uncontrolled market speculation that would bring on the stock market crash three years later. On 9 April Coolidge declared that "non-interference" would be his foreign policy, calling the international political controversies "none of our affair." Nonetheless, in May the U.S. Marines invaded Nicaragua to quiet the uprising against Chamorra's coup d'état.

Labor issues were well covered in the communist and labor press; for example, the *Daily Worker* published a program for "A Fighting Union for the Needle Workers!" which was adopted at a conference of delegates on 12–14 September. It was, however, a relatively quiet year in terms of strikes, which led those in power to believe that prosperity had reached the working class, thus producing this effect. Perhaps it was for this reason that the press gave significant coverage over the year to the political and labor unrest in Great Britain. On 1 May the coal miner's strike began there, and two days later a general strike ensued in support. By 9 May the government imposed martial law, which ended the strike three days later. Martial law remained in effect until 2 December.

Events covered by the press but whose full significance would not be understood by U.S. citizens until the thirties included failed assassination attempts on Benito Mussolini in April and September; Michinomiya Hirohito being crowned as the 124th Emperor of Japan; Adolf Hitler publishing the second volume of *Mein Kampf*; and Gabriel D'Annunzio forming the league of fascist artists. The Geneva Disarmament Conference and the World Court occupied the U.S. efforts for transformation of international relations, while European allies still were dismayed about the U.S. failure to join the League of Nations, or to intervene more positively in debt and reparation negotiations in Europe. Lebanon, Iran, Portugal, Poland, and Mexico were among the smaller countries that had momentous, strife-ridden years, without garnering the attention they deserved in the United States; clearly the nation's southern neighbors were of concern, but primarily when revolutionaries became a threat to plantations and shipping.

On 18 September a strong hurricane devastated Miami, leaving over a hundred dead, causing several hundred million dollars in damage, and leading to a pall in Florida real estate speculation. Law enforcement's struggle with mob boss Al Capone in Chicago resulted in his first arrest, but he was released on insufficient evidence pertaining to the three murders for which he had been charged. On 20 September, twelve cars full of gangsters opened fire at Capone's headquarters at the Hawthorne Inn but largely missed their targets.

It was a banner year for blues music, as evidenced by Jelly Roll Morton's RCA Victor recordings with the Red Hot Peppers, "Smoke-House Blues," "Sidewalk Blues," and "Black Bottom Stomp," and Blind Lemon Jefferson's big hits, "Got the Blues," "Long Lonesome Blues," and "Black Home Blues" on Paramount (recordings that at the time were known as "race records"). Louis Armstrong and His Hot Five's "Heebie Jeebies" on Okeh Records included a famous chorus of scat singing that helped popularize the jazz style. While the Charleston remained the rage, the Black Bottom became increasingly popular. *The George White Scandals* featured the Black Bottom dance at the Apollo Theater in Harlem, and its new competitor in the neighborhood, the Savoy Theater, opened. Jazz infiltrated American high culture; Eric De Lamater's "After Walt Whitman" as performed by the Chicago Symphony Orchestra was composed of a collection of jazz pieces mixed with Kentucky folk melodies and popular ballads.

The Book-of-the-Month Club was founded this year, as were the publishing firms Simon & Schuster, Random House, and Viking. Ernest Hemingway published *The Sun Also Rises*, F. Scott Fitzgerald *All the Sad Young Men*, and Langston Hughes *The Weary Blues*. The Pulitzer Prize went to Sinclair Lewis for *Arrowsmith*, which he famously refused.

This was not a year of momentous events, perhaps, as German cultural historian Hans Ulrich Gumbrecht contends in his study of the zeitgeist, *In 1926: Living on the Edge of Time*, but rather an ordinary year in which one can gauge the ongoing cultural concerns of a world poised, fairly unconsciously, between two world wars. High fashion brought women's skirts up to their shortest length of the decade, though for the coming year the designers would begin to lower hemlines. The weight of the Great War was beginning to lift in the face of cultural exuberance, emblematized by such films as *The Jazz Girl*, *His Jazz Bride*, and *Dancing Mothers*. The crushing event of the year for many star-struck followers of popular culture was Rudolph Valentino's death on 23 August. His starring role in *Son of the Sheik* was among the year's most popular when it was released in September. Also released the same month was Buster Keaton's *Battling Butler*, a satire on received notions of masculinity that sent up outdoor sports and boxing as its two measures of manhood. *What Price Glory?*, directed by Raoul Walsh for Fox from the 1924 play by Maxwell Anderson and Laurence Stallings, presented a sharply drawn reaction to the Great War. *Battleship Potemkin*, *The Crazy Page*, and *Faust*, all reviewed in the *New York Times*, were among the groundbreaking foreign films.

A Tale of Two Actresses

My examination of this year focuses on two actresses whose careers overlap at MGM in a remarkable fashion: Lillian Gish and Greta Garbo. Each made two seminal films: Gish starred in *La Boheme* (released in May), then in *The Scarlet Letter* (August), while Garbo made her U.S. debut in two films adapted from the works of a Spanish writer, Vicente Blasco Ibañez, *The Torrent* (February) and *The Temptress* (October). All four films were among the year's biggest box office successes, and one can learn much about the transformations occurring in U.S. cinema and culture by comparing them. In contrast to these female-centered dramas, a nearly entirely male-centric film was also a huge success, *Beau Geste* (August). Of course, it would be a triumphal remake as a sound film starring Gary Cooper in 1939, but even this famous version does not overshadow the power of the earlier film, which already speaks to both the desire for male heroism and a mournful look at both this hero and, perhaps, at the larger colonial enterprise.

In many ways Gish and Garbo may be seen as polar opposites: the established actress who had been confined to roles of youthful, even childlike purity would be challenged by changing expectations for female leads, while the Swedish newcomer to Hollywood was courted by the studios for her worldly-wise allure and sexuality, everything that Gish was not. Yet one could imagine Garbo playing Gish's MGM roles, especially since her future triumphant role in *Camille* (1936) has much in common with *La Boheme*'s Mimi. Moreover, Gish plays Mimi opposite John Gilbert, who would become Garbo's favorite leading man. While Garbo may not strike one as the ideal Hester Prynne, she becomes more plausible once one considers that the Gish film also starred Lars Hanson and was directed by Victor Sjöström, so that her casting would have carried the Swedish-Puritan demeanor connection, already noted in the press, a step further. The inverse, Gish playing Garbo's role in *The Torrent* or *The Temptress,* on the other hand, seems unimaginable. This speculative exercise demonstrates that Gish, in choosing these vehicles, was trying to find bridge roles between her experience with D. W. Griffith and a new projection of a more adult role. Her MGM contract, signed in 1925, assured her $400,000 per film and gave her complete control over her productions, including her choice of co-stars and directors. She was trying, perhaps unconsciously, to meet the challenge that young actresses like Garbo presented to all that she had done in the past. Although the public responded very positively to these films, reviews of Gish's performance in *La Boheme* were mixed.

Gish Chooses Her Classics

While King Vidor's film version of *La Boheme* comes from the same source used for the libretto of Puccini's opera (Henri Murger's 1849 stage play and his 1851 novel, both entitled *Scènes de la vie de bohème*), copyright problems kept MGM from using Puccini's music or, apparently, scenes drawn too closely from the libretto. Instead, the film uses original music designed to create similar moods. Some reviewers regretted the absence of Puccini's music and certain favorite scenes in the opera. To place this in context, in January, the debut of soprano Mary Lewis thrilled Metropolitan Opera audiences in her rendition of Mimì, according to the *New York Times,* bringing a homegrown talent nurtured in the musical hall to the august and

European-influenced house. Other reviewers, perhaps less familiar with both the opera and Murger's works, seemed to enjoy the film more on its own terms.

Mimi in Vidor's *La Boheme* is a role that has much in common with those Gish played in such Griffith films as *True-Heart Susie* (1919), *Way Down East* (1920), and *Orphans of the Storm* (1921), drawing out of its sources a character changed to address an audience constructed by that filmic tradition. Mimì in Puccini's opera is flirtatious and seductive in the tradition of the Paris "Grisette," in a manner we don't associate with Gish, an independently employed young woman who lives alone and loves without concern for bourgeois morality. The theatrical and literary sources clearly have an even more salacious and mercurial Mimi in mind, one who partakes of much wine, schemes against her rivals, is alternately indifferent toward and amused by the poet who loves her, seeking instead a richer lover. Yet we should also note that the wry voice of narration in the novel keeps readers guessing as to which observations or assumptions are imagined by jealousy and misjudgment on the part of her poet lover, Rodolphe. What writers Fred De Gresac and Ray Doyle and intertitle writers William M. Conselman and Ruth Cummings derive from these sources is a Mimi who arrives in an 1830s artistic garret of Paris not as herself an artist or writer, nor as a prostitute, but as a single, orphaned working girl. They reconstruct Mimi as a very interesting transitional object for Gish and for this moment in U.S. film history.

The film follows the opera's lead in transforming Mimi into a poor seamstress who ultimately trusts in the goodness of her companion. Gish focuses on this aspect of Mimi, bringing her more in line with past pure-of-heart heroines of lowly social position who fight against exploitative men, and for the heart of the man they love, despite obstacles. The script of *La Boheme* contrives to make all of Mimi's encounters with other men, the landlord and the Count, innocent efforts to get by, unfortunately misunderstood by Rodolphe and his companions as the social-climbing schemes the play and novel depict. While in the opera Rodolphe sends Mimi away, it finally is not due to her capriciousness, though that seems at first to be his motive; ultimately, he wishes she might find a wealthy benefactor to cure her of her developing illness. In the film, Rodolphe and Mimi fight and separate as they do in Murger's novel, but not due to Mimi's unreliable nature; all arguments are based on Rodolphe's misunderstandings and his refusals to believe in Mimi's virtue.

A key scene has Rodolphe come to her garret window from the rooftop and flirt with her through the glass. This mise-en-scène thus inserts a glass barrier in between the lovers as substitute for the bedroom scenes that lace Murger's prose. Acting out desire across this barrier is a tour de force by both Gilbert and Gish, even as it serves as a measure of how the film thought it needed such contrivances to avoid the sources' more suggestive sexuality.

Cedric Gibbons's sets for *La Boheme* stunningly draw on German expressionism, particularly for the garret rooms in the first part of the film, with their angled broken floorboards and shadowed curved vaults, but for the street scenes in the Latin Quarter as well. An elaborate pawnshop scene, in which Mimi sells off her warm clothing for rent money, illustrates the title "All of Paris" by combining a large set, teeming extras, and sweeping camera movement by Hendrik Sartov. Gibbons designed the sets for all four Gish and Garbo films under discussion here. Camera work by Sartov on the Gish films and William H. Daniels on Garbo's represent collaborations between set designer and lead cameramen that advance both MGM style and film style in Hollywood in general.

Another scene from *La Boheme* that highlights Sartov's camera work involves a long, playful seduction between Rodolphe and Mimi that takes place when the bohemians join a working-class Sunday excursion to the country. Filming here prefigures aspects of Jean Renoir's *Une partie de compagne* (1936). Mimi runs from an endlessly pursuing Rudolph, virtually in a game of hide-and-seek, substituting this visual expression of Rodolphe's pursuit for the fickle departures of Mimi in Murger's novel. Vidor's country interlude culminates in the first erotic exchange displayed in the film, as Rodolphe covers his now docile and willing lover's face with kisses.

Rendered in a single take, Mimi's pantomime of Rodolphe's entire stage play that she is attempting to sell to the Vicomte when he visits her in her room, represents its own tour de force. From the vantage point of his adjoining garret window, Rodolphe misinterprets her closing gestures as an embrace of the Vicomte. Entering across the rooftops through her window, Rodolphe stages a powerful scene of violent male jealousy, abusively pulling Mimi's hair as he drags and batters her. Despite her protestations of innocence, he accuses her of being "a light woman," thus providing under reworked cover the violent passions of sexual promiscuity that Murger treats in his novel.

Cast out on her own, already weak from tuberculosis, Mimi appears alongside other women workers in a brief, brilliantly staged factory sequence. There Mimi battles huge looms in "the slums of Paris," the scene thus supplementing the earlier sequences of her staying up all night to embroider piecework in order to secretly support Rodolphe. Mimi's self-sacrificial

La Boheme: a two-shot of Mimi's last moments, with John Gilbert and Lillian Gish.

demonstrations include her staggering from her deathbed back to Rodoloph's garret, filmed as she crawls along a quay and then drags herself holding on to the back of a cart, only to fall off, resist the rescue of passersby, and hitch herself again behind another carriage. Rodolph, meanwhile, has seen his play performed, thanks to her earlier efforts, and has realized her self-sacrifice, shown by the superimposition of her face over his author's speech before a cheering audience. The final death scene, then, is largely rendered in a two-shot, visually evoking Puccini's famous love duet, Mimì and Rodolfo's "Sono andati?" (Have they gone?), and the duet's lyrical evocation of their happier days here takes the form of a flashback image of their embrace in the country.

Gish's next film, *The Scarlet Letter*, was another prestige showcase, though some critics assumed a somewhat faithful adaptation of Nathaniel Hawthorne's famous novel *The Scarlet Letter, a romance* (1850), as promised by the advance publicity by the studio. In significant ways, however, the script transforms Hawthorne's narrative, which in any case is often misread and misremembered by its large American public. Rarely is the novel fully understood as a product of the nineteenth century looking back at Puritan culture, nor do most readers follow the complications of voice in

Hawthorne's writing, turning instead to the memorable scenes of punishment and confrontation. Yet the film largely changes even the key scene of Hester Prynne's public humiliation.

Frances Marion's screen adaptation devotes its first half to the budding romance of Hester and the Reverend Dimmesdale, which has already occurred before the novel begins. Whereas Hawthorne's concern lies not with the affair but with the aftermath, as he traces its effect on Dimmesdale—"The only truth that continued to give Mr. Dimmesdale a real existence on this earth was the anguish in his inmost soul, and the undissembled expression of it in his aspect"—the film pointedly creates an innocence and charm defining the romance. This opening interlude becomes the film's argument against Puritan values, here depicted as an excuse for spying and gossiping about others' alleged misdeeds. So although a rose bush remains the first image, and the gathering of the settlement in their church the first major action portrayed through a magisterial crane shot that takes in the crossing of the town square in multiple directions, this sets up a scene of Hester primping in a new lace bonnet that she has chosen over a plainer one in front of a mirror normally disguised by a sampler bearing the ironic inscription, "Vanity is the root of evil." Some of the townspeople, passing her window, witness her actions with disapproval, while she then turns to play with her canary. As the bird suddenly flies away, she runs off chasing it. This sets up their indignant demand to the reverend that she be punished for running and playing on the Sabbath. Dimmesdale admonishes her from the pulpit, shown in a dramatic series of shot-reverse-shots of him as an angry father figure and the demure young woman standing meekly before him in the church aisle.

The next shot shows that she has been placed in the stocks, this humiliation substituting for Hawthorne's opening public disgrace; the film eventually reaches the point of the novel's opening by introducing a second public mortification. (In the novel her humiliation occurs in chapter 2 in response to her adulterous childbirth, taking the form of her standing alone in the public square bearing her embroidered "A" that she, ironically, has rendered too lavishly.) Hester's confinement to the stocks allows for a striking two-shot of Dimmesdale offering her water during her penance, which constitutes their first touch as he puts his hand on her arm to comfort her with the words, "I didn't think the committee would impose further punishment."

Max Rée, the Danish costume designer newly hired by MGM who would go on to design Garbo's costumes in *The Torrent* and *The Temptress*, relates how Gish's costumes in *The Scarlet Letter* were designed to make her appear more vulnerable:

The Scarlet Letter: Hester (Lillian Gish) in stocks, a mise-en-scène departure from Hawthorne.

> We wished to stress the pathos of Hester Prynne by making her small, almost immature. Miss Gish is of a good height. To give her the appearance of being shorter, I broke the lines wherever possible. Across her circular skirt I put several rows of broad tucks. On her short jacket were broad bands of black velvet edging the neck and the end. Her shoes and cap were round. All this tended to flatten her silhouette.

Knowing this was their design, the script's preoccupation with Hester's clothing becomes a way of highlighting the particular sensuality she exudes. Following the bonnet incident, the film pursues both narrative development of a Puritan law against women displaying underwear where a man might see it. Hester, having laundered her undergarments with the other women, is hanging them out to dry when Dimmesdale passes. She runs off, as he pursues the as-yet-unknown woman who has broken a rule. Still hiding an undergarment behind her back, she evades him as he chases her around a large bush. Once they are face to face and he asks what she is hiding, she retreats, only to have him advance and, in a two-shot, swing her around until a cut to her backside facing him displays her drawers dangling over her buttocks. Embarrassed, Dimmesdale heads off, reading his scriptures, only to be chased by Hester, who has by now tossed the drawers away. A shot is devoted to them dangling on a branch. A tracking shot of the two from behind follows their progress down a country lane, then inverts cleverly into a track back as Dimmesdale changes direction, now with the two walking briskly toward the camera. The product of this intriguing camera work will be Hester's comically perverse plea, "It would be pleasant, sir, to walk beside thee and hear thee condemn me for my sins." Dimmesdale reverses direction again, and again a track forward follows Hester's pursuit, until a bush obscures the couple momentarily, at which point they are seen holding hands to cross the meadow on the other side of the path. A pan left back to the bush reveals that the undergarment still dangles from the branch where Hester had tossed it earlier.

Through such visual means, an argument is made concerning the adolescent nature, even innocence, of their attraction and sexual encounter. When we fade in once more it is on their reflection inverted on a pond, as an introduction to two-shots of Hester questioning why her thoughts should be considered sins, resolving in Dimmesdale embracing her after saying that, while "I have fought against it, . . . I love thee." Comedy then ensues as the film cuts to the rules of Puritan courtships, including speaking tubes, illustrated by other characters; the male suitor grabs his fiancée to steal a kiss out of sight of her parents, only to have her denounce his "unbridled passions." This humorous display of regulation and hypocrisy occurs before returning to the serious scene of Hester at home confessing to the visiting Dimmesdale the circumstances of her previous marriage.

The scene of Hester's public humiliation occurs after Dimmesdale's return from a voyage to England, a full eight minutes into the film. The style shifts to a serious and deliberate playing out of Dimmesdale's guilt in the face of Hester's determination to avoid being his downfall, with mise-en-scène and editing prefiguring Dreyer's *Vredens dag* (Days of Wrath, 1943) and Robert Bresson's *Procès de Jeanne d'Arc* (Trial of Joan of Arc, 1962). By this I mean that Sjöström edits the scene focusing on shots of key characters looking silently at each other, deliberately exposing tensions and anguish through an impassive immobility that resonates with the viewer.

The film inserts a baptism scene in which Dimmesdale baptizes Hester's daughter, Pearl, in the name of the "Father, the Son, and the Holy Ghost." While the Massachusetts Bay colony practiced infant baptism, nowhere in Hawthorne does this occur. Instead we are pointedly told that Hester names Pearl in chapter 6, entitled "Pearl," in the context of our narrator's afterthought: "We have as yet hardly spoken of the infant; that little creature, whose innocent life had sprung, by the inscrutable decree of Providence, a lovely and immortal flower, out of the rank luxuriance of a guilty passion."

Pearl is above all a vehicle for Hawthorne's irony, as he juxtaposes her wild innocence to the guilt that surrounds her, including her mother's fear that her child will be corrupted, indeed damned, merely by her heritage. The film adopts an attitude more consonant with later American Protestantism in presenting this baptism by Dimmesdale, gracing him, Hester, and Pearl with a born-again goodness of spirit quite outside of Hawthorne's attitude toward his characters.

The denouement of the film begins with the appearance in the Colony of Chillingsworth, Hester's long-lost husband, ironically acting as physician to Pearl, as Hester fears she is dying. This illness of the child also necessitates the call to the minister, thus bringing the four principals together in a manner much different from Chillingsworth's long habitation with and slow torture of Dimmesdale in the novel. A further innovation involves Hester and Dimmesdale's plot to escape to England, interrupted by a dunking scene in which one of the townswomen receives punishment for gossip, played as comedy. Dimmesdale's sermon with Chillingsworth staring encapsulates the long passages of their interactions in the novel, as Chillingsworth's knowledge threatens the couple's escape plan. Absent the uncertain narrator who concludes Hawthorne's novel by suggesting possible elements of closure, while clearly marking them as ambiguous unknowns, the film ends with a passionate revelation of guilt by Dimmesdale as he burnishes his brand of infamy, a scarlet "A" seared into his chest. As Hester comforts him, her embroidered "A" falls from her bodice to rejoin the brand in his flesh. The *Washington Post*'s preview called this "one of the most tremendous emotional climaxes the silversheet has seen this season" ("Lillian Gish Opens").

Not all critics were so kind to the film, and James Metcalfe's column on "The Theatre" in the *Wall Street Journal* takes the occasion of this film to make a general case against "What the Movies Do to Classics," beginning with an imagined conversation attributed to "the movie-educated person of the future and perhaps the present":

> "Hawthorne! Hawthorne! Never heard of him."
>
> "Yes, you did, too. He was the bird who wrote that silly movie about the skirt what went wrong with a minister and had to wear a big A on her chest all the rest of her life. Don't you remember how her husband trailed her, and the minister cashed in his checks on the gallows?"

Metcalfe goes on to explain:

> The main inaccuracy with respect to the latest produced movie is the program announcement that "Miss Lillian Gish is appearing in Nathaniel Hawthorne's

> *The Scarlet Letter."* Not having lived in the early Colonial days we lay no claim to exact knowledge of the general correctness of the production but we have read Nathaniel Hawthorne's *The Scarlet Letter* and feel entirely competent to say that this movie drama is not Nathaniel Hawthorne's tragic and austere romance but more in the nature of a burlesque of it. The adapters of the tale to the screen have not been content with destroying the atmosphere created by the author but have man-handled the plot in a way to make it almost unrecognizable.

Certainly these adaptations of *La Boheme* and *The Scarlet Letter* not only set the standard for much of MGM's prestige productions, but also pumped new life into Gish's career, simultaneously reinforcing the best of her trademark earnest and intense vulnerability and fortitude, while offering her a shade of sensuality beyond that which colored her earlier characterizations. However, the contrast with the two films that introduced Garbo to American audiences remains pronounced.

Garbo's Debuts in Spanish Dramas

Garbo's introduction in what was at the time called *Ibáñez's Torrent* was met with immediate critical acclaim. "Miss Garbo makes her American screen debut in this picture, and proves to be the great 'find' that was rumored. . . . Her talent and beauty are very considerable, and she ranges through a varied role with the greatest ease" ("Great Garbo"). In the *New York Times* Mordaunt Hall offered a behind-the-scenes piece two days after the film opened, under the headline "Hollywood Surprises New Swedish Actress." Garbo speaks primarily of how much larger and more compartmentalized MGM is than any comparable Swedish studio.

Absent from the critical discussion is any revelation of the turmoil that marked the beginning of this production; Mauritz Stiller, having come to MGM with his protégé Garbo, had not been chosen to direct her first film there. Rather, the established director Monta Bell was Irving Thalberg's choice. Distraught, Garbo thought of returning with Stiller to Sweden, but he insisted they stay. He secretly rehearsed her scenes with her in the evenings before she would appear on the set without him.

Mordaunt Hall also noted the prevalence of adaptations of novels by Blasco Ibáñez: he remarked that *The Torrent* was by "the prolific Spanish writer . . . whose *Mare Nostrum* was presented last week in pictorial form" ("Another Ibáñez Story"). In the absence of an internationally distributed Spanish cinema, this writer was becoming a favorite Hollywood source, especially after his novel *Four Horsemen of the Apocalypse* (1921) had became a major success, launching the film career of Rudolph Valentino, as well as displaying the cost of the Great War in a melodramatic allegory.

In *The Torrent*, Garbo plays the diva risen from poverty who goes on to stardom as an opera singer under a stage name, La Brunna, becoming an international recording star with all of Paris at her feet. The film seems to draw on the diva tradition in Italian silent cinema and echoes aspects of Marcel L'Herbier's *L'Inhumaine* (1924), as MGM borrows selectively from this more avant-garde precedent. Max Rée was likely the creative force behind the four graphically daring fur coats that appear, seemingly indebted to Paul Poiret's designs for *L'Inhumaine* even if that film's astounding sets by Fernand Léger and Robert Mallet-Stevens have no parallel here.

Key moments in the film directly anticipate the arrival of sound, as they use singing and a record player not only as sound cues but as motives and jokes in a manner predating similar visual/audio riffs in films by René Clair and Jean Vigo. La Brunna tricks her former lover, who is in the town barbershop wondering if she had fallen into poverty; from the other room, she places what we presume to be an orchestral passage from an opera on the phonograph and sings along. He recognizes the voice as La Brunna and remarks on the barber having the record. Only when he walks into the other room and sees her singing does he realize that his former love is the famed La Brunna. Earlier La Brunna hears a banjo strumming and an African American performer in Paris singing "I'm a goin' home," as indicated by a title that gives us the lyrics and notes from the popular song written in 1922 by William Arms Fisher, who set words to a version of the melody of the Largo from Antonín Dvořák's Ninth Symphony, From the New World. She rises in the nightclub to salute him with a gift of money as a token of her esteem for his artistry, and as evidence of how his song touched her. This is the experience that compels her to return to her natal village in Spain; the staging presages the next year's Warner Bros. sound hit, *The Jazz Singer*, in which the blackface number "Mammy" is portrayed as speaking to audience members, such as Jack's mother, about a more general nostalgia for one's mother.

The film survives in its tinted print, with the opening rose section devoted to establishing the farmhouse and village in Valencia, as a house that for a hundred years has withstood storms and floods. Garbo appears here as the luminescent Leonora, an innocent in nature, singing alongside the birds in an orchard of orange trees. Yet in contrast to the roles written for Gish, she is given even from the outset and in the context of youthful innocence the more forward lines and gestures in her meeting in the orchard with her lover, Don Rafael Brull (Ricardo Cortez), the son of a powerful and ambitious widow of the town's major who also holds the deed to her parents' farmhouse.

Class disapproval and political ambition for her son leads Don Rafael's mother to evict Leonora's family, while retaining her mother as an employee. Don Rafael watches as his mother feeds Leonora's departure love letter to the hogs that signify wealth in the town, and the film dissolves to sequences in red tint that capture La Brunna's life in Paris after several years have passed, a life emblematized by a nightclub, the Café Americain. It is through the table gossip of others that we are told of La Brunna's many affairs, as performers dance the Charleston and the chicken walk, seemingly referencing Josephine Baker's revues. La Brunna stands out regally in her lamé opera coat trimmed with abstract pattern of black and white fur. That MGM showcased another star, Joan Crawford, in *Paris,* a film exploring the wild side of this city, indicates that already Paris had become the emblem of an extravagant and sexual culture, creating a variation on the flapper in U.S. films. In addition, this setting and these castings seem to point to Hollywood's pursuit of the European market.

"The great prima donna came home" is the title that introduces a luxurious chauffeured car speeding past donkey carts and horse-drawn rigs. At the threshold of her childhood home, La Brunna impatiently opens one of her trunks to display the fancy presents she has brought for her bewildered mother, including another stylized fur cape. With Don Rafael running for governor, Leonora's return takes on a certain ambiguity; she seems to be plotting to win his love and finally steal him from his mother's grasp, but alternatively, she is aiming at revenge that will make his life miserable should the victory in love not be hers.

Don Rafael goes boating with his mother and fiancée, Remedios, but he abandons this pair in search of orange blossoms, seemingly drawn to the sound of Leonora singing an aria from *Carmen,* translated in the titles as "If you love me, if you love me not, beware." When he finds La Brunna in a lace dress at the piano, she laughs at his indecision; he runs off, as a rain storm begins, to find Remedios, to whom he proposes in the same orchard where he once courted Leonora.

"A torrent as relentless as the passion" is the manner in which the film announces that the downpour is but the beginning of the deluge. The film documents with elegant special effects the bursting of a dam and the flooding of streets. Metaphors circulate, of course, for the passions Don Rafael was trying to confine and rechannel, and to no avail, as his thoughts subsequently are presented by the title "Leonora, is she safe, the dam is leaking—her house will be under water."

Don Rafael returns to rescue her, only to find her sanguine in her family farmhouse bedroom, laughingly offering him dry clothes. She dresses him in yet another opera cloak, this time a black fur with ermine striped trim at the collar. Still Don Rafael will not forgive her worldliness, saying, "You are not the same Leonora who went away."

This challenges her, and sets the scene for her most self-confidently aggressive seduction, riddled with revenge. "You came because you love me," she says, as in close-up she smiles with a wry allure. Then turning inward, her face revealing her sadness, she says, "I believed in love once and love failed me." She displays pointedly the "beautiful things" she has been given by others, showing him box after box of her jewels, then the figurine given her by a "sculptor who admired my figure." This daring, angry, yet self-assured and sexy presence, these moods that change rapidly, yet convincingly, will be the aspect of this film that future Garbo films will mine endlessly. Don Rafael is not up to this challenge, uttering, "Everything they say about you is true," and returning to marry Remedios.

In the next sepia section of the betrothal feast of Rafael and Remedios, Leonora makes yet another stand, appearing at the celebration attired in her most amazing costume, an abstracted jester design with a cloche hat that frames her beautiful face with great visual power and irony. Amongst the orange blossoms, she avows, "I love you." Then, rejected once more on the basis of propriety, she asks, "Why can't I just hate him?"

In its coda, the film returns to Paris, where a deco-styled poster for La Brunna in *Carmen* leads us into a dressing room where Leonora sports her Carmen costume as orange blossoms arrive from Don Rafael, begging for an audience: he appears quite aged, and admits under La Brunna's bemused questioning that his wife is a good woman, that he has five children, but that he longs for her. Last act all over.

On stage, La Brunna performs with great flourish, Garbo sweeping her hands wide in triumphant song. This is crosscut to the provincial husband and wife. La Brunna exits the theater to throngs, in another fur coat with large striped collar, then enters her waiting car. One of her female fans comments to a male companion, "She has everything she wants." As with so many Hollywood melodramas, the film gains its energy from the rise to fame of a woman who breaks with provincial roots and rules to pursue a career, often on the stage, but which must temper this success by emphasizing her lack of emotional fulfillment. Here, the alternative—the safe, traditional marriage—also receives negative treatment. *The Torrent* profits from an ability to frame a talented young star as seductive in an ironic and charged manner, using Garbo's ability to convey complex motivations underlying every turn of gesture, and coupling that display of passionate and decisive intimate action with a large-scale pathetic fallacy that draws a disaster sequence into the love story as consummate metaphor.

Repetition with slight variation becomes Thalberg's goal after the success of *The Torrent*, as the studio assigns Garbo to another Ibáñez adaptation, *The Temptress*. The concession made was to give the film to Stiller to direct. After two weeks of shooting, Thalberg dismissed Stiller, handing the film over to Fred Niblo, whose reputation had been secured by the success of *Ben Hur* (1925). For years it was thought that some scenes shot by Stiller, notably the opening scene and an elaborate dinner party sequence, survived in the finished film, but in fact any such sequences were in all likelihood reshot, retaining the Swedish director's daring ideas in the mise-en-scène and camera work.

One such scene is the opening grand costume ball in Paris. In the foreground on an interior balcony, we see Elena, the Russian emigrée played by Garbo, with her suitor, an older elegantly dressed man, her lover Fontenoy, as a crowd revels in the background behind them. She refuses his attentions. Upon running out into a garden Elena comes across a stranger, Robledo (Antonio Moreno). Elena requests that he remove his mask first; the subjective shot on his handsome face secedes to the reaction shot displaying Elena's pleasure. Elena's unmasking reveals her glowing, sculpted face captured through a lighting diffuser, and a reverse shot captures his smile in delight. He says, "You are—beautiful." She enjoys his approval. Commedia dell'arte figures cavorting in the background provide a frame hinting at a seduction and tryst in the garden, indicated by ellipses as the couple retreats to the woods.

The morning after, still in the garden in the previous evening's costumes, Elena tells Robledo that she belongs to no one else, but leaves him without revealing her identity. The next day her husband introduces Elena to his friend from Argentina, Robledo, which is how this visitor learns that she is married, and the vows of love proffered the previous night contained, at best, half-truths. Ambiguity cloaks her character: has she orchestrated this scenario to cover her own manipulative seductions of ever more powerful men? One answer awaits, as both her husband and the Argentine accompany her to a dinner invitation at Fontenoy's, a most memorably filmed sequence.

A crane shot pulls back from the host at one end to reveal an extremely long table filled with flappers and their dates in tuxes. Then shots on the flappers' and dates' legs under the table have the air of those typical of Busby Berkeley. Cuts to particular legs show flirtations, then display two

Greta Garbo's radiance is evident in *The Temptress*.

shots of pairs. The festive assembly has been brought together for a more sinister purpose, as Fontenoy empties poison into his glass, issuing a "Denunciation of the Temptress as a banker's ruin."

As a montage of newspapers shows this suicide echoing through Paris, Elena contemptuously empties her jewel box to pay her husband's debts, repeating the jewel box imagery from *The Torrent* to indicate sexual promiscuity. Elena, like Leonora, is defiant, as she argues that she was a victim of her husband's ambition, essentially pimped to the influential Fontenoy in return for financial gain. "May God forgive you for what you have done to me," she exclaims.

Here the film shifts to the Argentine, following Robledo who has returned home to pursue the building of a dam. It takes on the air of a western, though set in South America. A rivalry between the engineer Robledo and the bandito, Manos Duras (Roy D'Arcy), who would otherwise be the most powerful figure, dominates the territory. Into this macho confrontation, Elena arrives, ostensibly to join her husband.

"No country for a European woman," Robledo tells her husband, as we see her legs on the staircase from his point of view. Ironic line, as the film wants to isolate her in this land of men to present her urbane seduction as even more blatant and troublesome in the context in which she is surrounded by desperate males, including Italian laborers on the mine project who forget all else in their lives in her presence. The film highlights her smile at her reflection in the vanity mirror, and partakes of a second descent down the staircase, this time dressed as a Latin version of a deco goddess. As she dines surrounded by men, the editing emphasizes her captivation of all the male gazes.

A guitar announces that even the bandito, Duras, is drawn to her presence; fascinated, she meets him on the steps, offering a kiss. A violently erotic fight using Argentine whips ensues between Duras and Robledo as she watches from the balcony. As the men strip for the fight, the film cuts to show us her excitement, then reiterates this cut to show the violent spectacle. When Robledo vanquishes his opponent, she rushes to him and leads him inside, where she attempts to nurse his wounds. Her fascination with his naked bleeding body and his suffering is evident. Yet he rejects her, saying, "I didn't fight for you. I fought for mastery here."

Duras rides by shooting his weapon, presumably trying to kill the man who whipped him into submission, but he kills Elena's husband instead. Although ordered to leave, Elena stays for the Festival for the Marquis that will be held at the dam and causes further havoc as another fight between the men over her results in a murder.

Elena pleads her case to Robledo, insisting that the man may have died "because of me, but not through any fault of mine." She says her "husband sold me to Fontenoy," and that men are attracted to her "not for me, but for my body. Not for my happiness, but for theirs." Her feminist defense falls flat, as Robledo now sees her as a liar, and vows that she "shall not destroy me."

Yet the forces she has unleashed will be channeled by the melodrama to reach the kind of metaphoric expression found in *The Torrent,* as Duras blows up the dam and flooding ensues. She finds safety and is dressed in white lace when Robledo returns from the crushing onslaught of physical destruction. In expressionist lighting, Robledo damns her, then in a close-up soft-focus two-shot, he begins choking her: "I want to kill you but I can't." After one more plea for understanding, she leaves Argentina.

Two alternative codas were shot, one taking us six years into the future as Robledo returns to Paris with his Argentine fiancée to acclaim for having completed his dam. Elena is in the crowd, but poor and suffering. She retires to a café-bar where she sits in a posture recalling Manet's absinthe drinker. Robledo leaves his bride-to-be to follow her to the café-bar. He attempts to give her money, but she feigns indifference and lassitude. He leaves, sad at both her state and her refusal to acknowledge him. The imagery toys with her absinthe hallucination by superimposing Christ's face on another bar patron, to whom she gives her last remaining jewel before she heads up the street toward Notre Dame; such imagery also suggests religious redemption. Although drug hallucination and saving grace might seem hard to reconcile as equally plausible meanings, the film seems, even in this ending, to be hedging its bets.

An alternate ending was shown in more conservative rural markets, according to Mark A. Viera, and was actually shot much later than the rest of the film, after filming on *Flesh and the Devil*, Garbo's 1927 release, was completed. Here the dam completion is celebrated at the dam site in Argentina, with full Argentine military pomp. Elena attends in full sartorial splendor, including a fetching cloche hat, and Robledo credits her love with sustaining him through the rebuilding process. The film ends on a close-up of the couple's embrace.

The Temptress thus uses as its backdrop issues of development in Latin America. Although we never learn who is financing the dam, or what purpose this engineering project serves, one such famous large dam was built in 1915 at San Roque, Argentina, the construction of which the provincial Legislature of Cordoba authorized. For Ibañez to incorporate such a landmark into his fiction, and to propose that its architect later would be feted in Paris, was consonant with the life of the author, a native of Valencia who was a militant Republican pamphleteer against the king of Spain, and spent years in Argentina, the United States, and Paris. So if the politics of colonialization and its aftermath formed the backdrop of *The Temptress*, Blasco Ibáñez offered a melodramatic rendering of his experience to Hollywood adaptation. Only retrospectively may we read something of Argentina's history and a vision of neocolonial enterprise emerging from what was still commonplace to call "greater Spain," as Henry Longan Stuart did in a 1925 *New York Times* article, "Blasco Ibáñez in Tales of War and South America."

Founding the Myth of the Foreign Legion

Similarly, another of the major film successes of the year, Famous Players–Lasky's *Beau Geste*, distributed by Paramount, begs today to be read as a work that celebrates male bravado and mythologizes the colonial enterprise, as typified by the French Foreign Legion. In contrast to the Gish and Garbo films, *Beau Geste*, from a scenario by Paul Schofield, in turn based on the adaptation by John Russell and Herbert Brenon of the novel by Percival Christopher Wren, tells the story of men struggling with a military desert outpost. The desert scenes were filmed in Yuma, Arizona, location of many legionnaire melodramas to follow the success of this film. At the center are three British brothers who join the legion in the spirit of solidarity, as each believes the other to have stolen a precious sapphire.

Overshadowed in contemporary memory by its remake in 1939, director Brenon's original Hollywood rendering actually served as a nearly shot-by-shot model for William A. Wellman's sound film—so much so that a ploy at the later film's debut to run the silent film first as prelude to the new version almost backfired. Some critics were struck by the great accomplishments of the first version, as well as the similarities, rather than the progress in film technology Paramount had hoped to demonstrate.

A pair of high-angle long shots worthy of Eisenstein open the film; one shot depicts Legion troops winding into the distance, and the other from the opposing angle depicts the troops snaking across the sand dunes toward the camera.

They are preceded by an epigraph (credited as "An Arabian Proverb") citing brotherly fidelity as the highest good. Prelude, this, to a series of uncanny discoveries at Fort Zinderneuf following an attack by Algerian rebels; what appear to be legionnaires manning each embrasure turn out to be corpses frozen in their last actions, their immobility emphasized by a phantom bullet fired at the rescue party. Then a scout who scales the fort's walls discovers strange cues, as a French bayonet in the corpse of the captain indicates a murder by his own men, and a note found on the corpse confesses to the theft of the great sapphire known as "Blue Water" from Lady Patricia Brandon. Opening the fort's gate to the soldiers assembled beyond offers another striking shot, with a graphic contrast indicative of the care for image design throughout the film. The scene ends with the mysterious disappearance of the corpses of the captain and the soldier lying next to him, followed by the burning of the fort.

Several mysteries surround the military defeat of the Legion, mixing the personal with the political; explanation will entail a flashback to "Brandon Abbas, in country England" fifteen years earlier, as three young boys and a young girl play at performing a naval battle on a small pond, complete with full-dress admiral costumes, and with cannon fire on the others' ships. Their play includes a comical surgery for a splinter performed as if at an evacuation hospital, and a "Viking's funeral" in which a toy sailor stands in effigy for the sailor's corpse burned on board a ship at sea.

These childhood games, ending on a burning structure as did the frame-story opening, foreshadow the revelation of the mystery at the fort, as does the next scene, a visit of Legion Captain Henri de Beaujolais and the turbaned Rajah Ram Singh, for whose appraisal Lady Brandon's sapphire will be displayed. The children request the captain's war stories: "Tell us about the Legion—and fighting Arabs." The captain responds by calling the Legion the "Exile of the self condemned" and calling the veiled Tuaregs the fiercest of the Arab fighters. This inspires the children to play a game in which three of them don sheets to murder the other, whom they call the "Legionnaire," certainly a curious sequence that exposes the latent racism underlying the film that of course never met with critical comment at the time. That these sheets evoke the KKK more than the Tuaregs makes the sequence all the more unselfconsciously revealing of societal attitudes; although this reference makes no sense in the context of the acting out of violence against the European, it is a moment in which the representation revealingly exceeds its context.

The children, hiding behind an armor display, overhear their aunt receiving a check from the rajah; though this event is told cryptically, we understand that their divorced aunt is able to raise her orphan nephews in a proper English upper-class manner, due to outside benefactors.

The first appearance of the male stars doesn't come until many minutes into the film, as the narrative jumps forward to the young boys now grown into "splendid manhood." Here we return to the drawing room mystery as the aunt learns from her estranged husband that she must sell the Blue Water sapphire. There is a close-up of a hand on lights, and in the darkness the jewel disappears. Each of the young men, Digby (Neil Hamilton), Beau (Ronald Colman), and John (Ralph Forbes), claim responsibility for the theft, and each heads off to the French Foreign Legion, forgoing Oxford, to atone for the sins of one another.

Marseilles, the Legion Canteen, and the arrival at Sidi-bel-Abbes for training provide the film with some of its most intriguing moments, inserting its characters into a quasi-documentary bracket sequence of induction into the Legion. No sooner are they legionnaires than the jewel thief plot continues to be the structure on which all the action is hung: a ne'er-do-well thief, played convincingly by a young William Powell, overhears their mutual joking—"Enter the third robber!"—and corrupt Captain Lejaune will be the downfall of the brothers as they each plot to steal the famous jewel.

A barracks fight initiated by the first robbery attempt leads to dividing "a clique" comprising the brothers and their other English-speaking friends between Fort Zinderneuf under Lejaune and a unit under the command of Captain de Beaujolais. Under Lejaune, deserters, once caught, are punished by being whipped and driven into the desert, and the soldiers plan a mutiny in a secret meeting in the oasis, but a spy foresees the mutiny as a chance to plot to get the jewel.

An attack by mounted Arab rebels cuts short the mutiny, the jewel plot, and indeed the internal strife in the unit, as Captain Lejaune proves to be a clever and relentless commander of his troops, even posing them after their deaths to serve as decoy (thereby explaining the ghostly frozen poses of the opening sequence). Action sequences are cut dynamically, alternating shots from the interior and the exterior of the fort. Repetition of a track left along the embrasures serves as a motif for the fighting.

"They believe in God! We believe in France!" one of the titles that punctuates the battle screams, helping us situate this film as a key early example of filmic entry into colonial and post-colonial discourses; positing the Arabs as religiously motivated fanatics may well seem an uncanny prefiguration of Al-Qaeda, but here it is meant to rule out any legitimate nationalism seeking to end colonial rule. Nationalism is rather posited as the righteous cause of the colonizers, and the British brothers nobly pledge their loyalty to France. Yet the film seems to overlay a certain surrealist element on the nationalist assumptions, as it depicts the slaughter of the colonial forces in gruesome detail, without the redemptive moment of rescue, the cavalry charge. Instead, the mad laughter of a soldier killed at a guard tower serves to prefigure an ironic knowledge of the demise of the colonial enterprise.

The rest of the film serves to explain the remaining mysteries of the film's opening, giving us a complex denouement in which we learn of Beau's demise and John's bayonneting of Lajeune for mistreatment of his brother's corpse. The third brother figures as well, as Digby enters the fort before the rest of the relief troops and gives Beau the Viking's funeral ritual, prefigured in the childhood sequence. The two surviving brothers meet while escaping in the desert, but since only one camel remains alive for the two of them once they are helped by comrades, Digby sacrifices himself so that John can return to marry his fiancée.

Back in England, John Geste surrenders to Captain de Beaujolais, who dismisses the need for his gesture, as officially all at Fort Zinderneuf died as heroes. A note explains Beau knew from his childhood eavesdropping that their aunt sold the real Blue Water, so he stole the fake to protect her, a revelation that makes good on the pun in his name "Beau Geste," which translates as "Good Gesture."

Certainly all five of these films have in common their box office success, their adaptations from literature, and their prestige production values. If they may be taken as emblematizing the year in film, we might conclude that at the cusp of the development of sound, the silent American film had reached a technical apex, and a facility with large-scale storytelling, including elaborate special effects. The industry was clearly anticipating the introduction of sound, using narrative forms and visual sound motifs that would easily translate into sound productions in the ensuing years. It was reaching beyond the borders of the country for its settings as well as its audiences, often telling stories set in Europe, Latin America, and North Africa. It was attempting to define gender, struggling mightily with the definition of the heroine, as evidenced in the conflicts in the images projected by Gish and Garbo, and equally contrasting those heroines with films devoted to the nationalist male hero, even as comedies could question masculinity. So gender at this moment hangs between the traditional and nostalgic roles on one hand, and troubled, intriguing modernist variations on the other.

1927

Movies and the New Woman as Consumer

SUMIKO HIGASHI

Sensational events and personalities that made headlines this year were signs of an American culture deeply divided about the nature of consumer capitalism and modernization. Demographic change had resulted in more urban than rural dwellers, but ethnic and racialized people in cities represented the unassimilatable Other and were scapegoated. Nicola Sacco and Bartolomeo Vanzetti, for example, were electrocuted for murder after an unfair trial that accentuated ethnic, class, and ideological differences in Brahmin Massachusetts. Amid a power struggle involving several black leaders and organizations, Marcus Garvey, radical founder of the United Negro Improvement Association, was imprisoned for mail fraud. The Ku Klux Klan enjoyed a resurgence in the Midwest and South; its candidates triumphed in Alabama. Aimee Semple McPherson, the world's "most pulchritudinous evangelist" and a star of segregated urban pentecostalism in Los Angeles, was reportedly "kidnapped." Actually she had decamped with a lover. And in the industrial Northeast, Governor Alfred E. Smith, the New York sidewalk politician who personified urbanism, was gearing up to make an ultimately unsuccessful bid for the White House (Leuchtenberg 82, 211–16; Dumenil 180–85, 235–45).

Undoubtedly, the year's most publicized event was Charles Lindbergh's flight to Paris, a scene that exemplified America's fascination with such aspects of modernity as celebrity, media, and science. Fox Movietone newsreels showed Lindbergh taking off from Roosevelt Field and replicated the sight for awestruck moviegoers. Although H. L. Mencken claimed that popular writers seldom wrote about science "with any intelligence," publications bulged with articles. An ad in a movie fan magazine even claimed that "science has found the way to add inches to your height" ("Grow Taller"). Capitulating to demand, Henry Ford, who championed scientific management, ceased production of the black Model T in favor of a Model A in colors like Dawn Gray and Arabian Sand. Advertising influenced the public's perception of a new "smart and stylish car" for classier buyers. Postwar laissez-faire business practices spurred consolidation so that both bank and utilities mergers were unprecedented. Chain stores became ubiquitous and made record profits from grocery, drug, and clothing sales. Spending on personal goods, furnishings, appliances, cars, and recreation tripled during the second two decades of the century. But increased consumption and leisure were enjoyed mostly by skilled and middle-class workers (Leuchtenberg, 190–201, 270–71; Carter 72; Marchand 157; May 52; Dumesnil 77–85). The fabled prosperity of the Jazz Age, fueled by advertising and installment buying, was scarcely accessible to all. Class, race, and gender were still significant determinants of economic status.

A symbol of American ambivalence about modernity, the New Woman shopped, used cosmetics, bobbed her hair, wore short skirts, and smoked. According to F. Scott Fitzgerald, she was "lovely and expensive and about nineteen." She was also flirtatious and sexually precocious. Although contraception remained illegal and inaccessible to working-class, ethnic, and racialized women, it provoked discourse on female sexuality. During the Jazz Age, a younger generation of affluent women became accustomed to more personal freedom and expression. As the *Cornell Sun* pleaded, reformers should "let the world and morals alone." Dating became a new ritual on college campuses and spurred debate about the practice of petting (Leuchtenberg 173, 192; Fass 262–63, 356). Since personal appearance was an important sign of attractiveness, women learned to define themselves with consumer goods but, in turn, risked self-commodification and objectification. A vivacious star like Clara Bow, the "It Girl," became a role model by setting fashion trends in well-orchestrated campaigns. But in becoming the centerpiece of a modern consumer culture, was the New Woman really new?

Did modern women really change during the Jazz Age revolution in manners and morals, and, if so, how? Actually, Victorian women may have enjoyed more, not less, sexual expression due to strong kinship and friendship ties forming a homosocial culture in which "men made but a shadowy appearance" (Smith-Rosenberg 53). Diminished emotional commitment to conventional marriage, or same-sex relations in so-called Boston marriage, were displaced, however, by heterosexual romance in companionate marriage in the twenties. When Judge Ben Lindsey and Wainwright Evans published *Companionate Marriage* this year, they argued that it was a contract that could end in divorce. Since marital breakups increased in the second half of the decade, reforming marriage was an effort to preserve the traditional family (*Historical Statistics* 48). Surely a historic transformation, the change from a homosocial to heterosocial culture was not restricted to the middle class but also pervaded working-class amusements (Peiss *Cheap*). A significant basis for this social change was the transition in twentieth-century self-making from emphasis on character, based on morality, self-restraint, and civic duty, to personality defined by self-commodification (Susman). As attractive and vibrant modern personalities, women could now compete with men in defining the self, even though they lacked political and economic clout. Yet as spectacle based on consumption and objectified in romance, the New Woman was scarcely new in the sense of breaking boundaries and exploring new territory.

Silent Finale and Sound Experiments

Silent films of this year were among the last from a fabled era as studios experimented with sound in shorts and newsreels but continued to promote stars in genre films. Several period films, for example, attracted filmgoers accustomed to history as eye-popping spectacle. *Ben Hur* featured an exciting battle at sea, a thrilling chariot race, and a sexy harlot (Carmel Myers) wearing a sensational wig. Ramon Novarro led a cast of thousands. Cecil B. DeMille filmed his acclaimed version of the life of Christ in *The King of Kings*. Stealing the show was Mary Magdalene (Josephine Logan), wearing a jeweled bra and serpentine cape and riding a chariot drawn by zebras. The director had a penchant for equating excess with exotic Orientalism. As the *Beloved Rogue*, John Barrymore reenacted the adventures of poet François Villon in fifteenth-century France. Seventeenth-century Spain, teeming with gypsies and peasants, served as the backdrop for Ronald Colman and Vilma Banky in *Night of Love*. Ernst Lubitsch's *The Student Prince of Old Heidelberg*, starring Ramon Novarro and Norma Shearer, charmed audiences with a Viennese romance.

War films like William Wellman's *Wings*, featuring aerial dogfights, and Raoul Walsh's *What Price Glory*, reprising American combat in France, focused on male camaraderie. Pola Negri portrayed a French peasant woman in a town under military siege in *Barbed Wire*. A Zane Grey story titled *The Last Trail* featured Tom Mix, an enormous box office draw, with "the fastest horse, gun, and smile of any man in the Old West." Buster Keaton's latest comedy, *The General*, was a hilarious parody of the Civil War. A popular horror film, *The Cat and the Canary*, featured German expressionist sets. Pert Laura La Plante, who seemed to wander into the wrong genre, deflated the haunted house atmosphere. Josef von Sternberg used noir atmospherics in *Underworld*, a gangster film that showed seedy characters in saloons and tenements. Star Evelyn Brent played a prototypical Marlene Dietrich role opposite George Bancroft.

Among the year's best attractions were melodramas that showcased legendary silent screen actresses. Janet Gaynor, a newcomer in the best tradition of Mary Pickford, personified girlish innocence in Frank Borzage's *Seventh Heaven*. Joan Crawford held her own against Lon Chaney as a woman fearful of her sexuality in *The Unknown*. As a producer, Gloria Swanson remade *The Eyes of Youth*, a film that had cast Rudolph Valentino in a small part in 1919, as *Love of Sunya*. Styling her hair in a lacquered bob, she wore chiffon, velvet, and white fox to enhance her reputation as a fashion plate. Clara Bow became one of the year's biggest box office attractions by redefining sex appeal and working nonstop in *Wings, It, Rough House Rosie, Hula, Children of Divorce*, and *Get Your Man*. Stage star Jeanne Eagels, triumphant as Sadie Thompson, was an extravagant New Woman who drove an infatuated newsman back to his mother in *Man, Woman, and Sin*. Greta Garbo was typecast as a siren and displaced Lillian Gish, whose costume drama *Annie Laurie* had been a failure, in a version of *Anna Karenina* titled *Love*. As the silent era drew to a close, the studio system perfected a mode of expression that was both art and commerce.

Although *The Jazz Singer* is celebrated as the first talkie, revisionist historians argue that technology produced a continuum of products so that silent film already featured musical accompaniment and sound effects. Granted, there are bits of spoken dialogue in two scenes and synchronized vocals throughout, but the film is mostly silent, especially in its use of intertitles and acting style. Based on Samson Raphaelson's short story and play, the picture focuses on the split identity of Jake Rabinowitz (Al Jolson), renamed Jack Robin. An aspiring jazz singer, he breaks with his Orthodox Jewish father, a cantor (Warner Oland) who condemns profane music, and leaves his beloved mother (Eugenie Besserer) in a Lower East Side ghetto to tour with vaudeville. Years later, when Jack returns to scale Broadway heights, Cantor Rabinowitz, in a reverse trajectory, lies dying and says tearfully, "My heart is breaking—in my dreams . . . [Jake] sings Kol Nidre." Since a bitter quarrel triggered his father's illness, Jack bears some guilt for straddling two cultures. Acknowledging that "there's something in my heart—the cry of my race," he finally sings Kol Nidre on Yom Kippur but still attains Broadway stardom. Unable to reconcile generational and cultural conflict, Jack becomes a star not as himself, but as a blackface minstrel. Despite his romance with a classy blonde dancer (May McAvoy), he cannot escape his racial identity as a Jew and thus appropriates the mask and music of a more despised racialized group. Critics have interpreted this disguise, a bigoted tradition in American entertainment, as Jack's endeavor to assimilate in mainstream culture, but it remains racist and regressive. Aptly, the film ends as he sings "Mammy" to his cherished mother rather than a romantic song to his *shiksa* sweetheart.

When it premiered at the Warners' Theatre in New York on the eve of Yom Kippur, *The Jazz Singer* was not a noteworthy event. As Charles Wolfe argues, the film was "less a decisive break" in film history than a "bold" move "amid a cluster of related and ongoing experiments" (Wolfe 66–67). Indeed, Robert Carringer asserts that the sound era began in 1926 when Warner Bros. premiered *Don Juan* with Vitaphone's synchronized sound-on-disc, a byproduct of the phonograph record business that rivaled Fox Movietone's recording of synch sound-on-film (Carringer 15–16). A movie palace like the Roxy was equipped with projectors that ran both systems, but uncertainty in the industry loomed ahead. As for *The Jazz Singer, Exhibitor's Herald* claimed that it was not much of a picture and "should properly be labeled an enlarged Vitaphone record of Al Jolson in half a dozen songs" (Crafton, *Talkies* 110). Competing with the film in trade journals were reports of the untimely death of Sam Warner, who had worked on Vitaphone on new West Coast sound stages on the day before the premiere. During the first week, *Variety* noted that Warners' attraction was overshadowed by the Capitol Theatre's investment in a live jazz orchestra. An extended twenty-three-week run meant that *The Jazz Singer* had to compete against higher-grossing blockbusters like *Wings, Love, What Price Glory?,* and *Seventh Heaven*. Donald Crafton concluded that the film did not always fill seats to capacity and was slightly above average in grosses (Crafton, *Talkies* 516–31). Significantly, *Film Daily* reported that state admission taxes, an index of national ticket sales, declined more than 14 percent from the previous year ("1927 Amusement"). Audiences were not flocking to hear sound. Still, Warner Bros.' successful experiment with Vitaphone paved the way for its success in the 1930s.

From Vamping to Shopping: The New Woman in *Sunrise, Flesh and the Devil, My Best Girl,* and *It*

A focus on the New Woman as a sign of modernity in four films, *Sunrise, Flesh and the Devil, My Best Girl,* and *It,* shows how women and consumerism were linked in modern urban culture. Consumption initially meant to pillage, devour, and waste, as Raymond Williams argues. And it was also used to signify a dreaded disease, tuberculosis (Ewen and Ewen 31). Americans brought up to value thrift spent money and pursued pleasure with a bad conscience. A small-town banker who bought a used car, for example, titled an *Atlantic Monthly* essay "Confessions of an Automobilist." Also feeling guilty was the seller, as is evident in *Harper's* "Confessions of a Ford Dealer" (Mowry 47, 26). At the center of a historic transition from a culture of scarcity to abundance that showcased autos was the New Woman. She was descended from the vamp, in contrast to the sentimental heroine, as a figure signifying grim attitudes about women in relation to consumption. "Spending," it should be noted, was the term for orgasm in the scarce economics of Victorian sexuality. Classic films about seduction, such as Kalem's *The Vampire* (1913) and Fox's *A Fool There Was* (1915), starring Theda Bara, showed weak-willed men squandering their fortunes on selfish women craving luxuries. Such character types hardly represented a consumer life style construed as fun. The New Woman, on the other hand, transformed the department store into a playground. She personified modern urban trends that were becoming dominant in defining the self in relation to goods and leisure.

Undoubtedly, one of the most celebrated films of the silent period is F. W. Murnau's *Sunrise: A Song of Two Humans*. After luring the German director, famous for the mobile camera in *The Last Laugh* (1924), to the United States, Fox gave him carte blanche to make the picture. Cameraman Charles Rosher, who had visited UFA studios after working with Cecil B. DeMille and Mary Pickford, chose Karl Struss, a Photo Secessionist associated with Alfred Stieglitz, as second cameraman and thus shared the first Oscar for cinematography ("Channel 4"; Harwith). Adapted by Carl Mayer, whose credits included *The Cabinet of Dr. Caligari* (1920) and *The Last Laugh*, the film was based on Hermann Sudermann's story "A Trip to Tilsit." Aptly, it begins with an intertitle expressing the binarisms that delineate nature, plot, characterization, costumes, sets, lighting, tone, and morality:

> This song of the Man and his Wife
> is of no place
> and every place;
> you might hear it anywhere
> at anytime.
> For whenever the sun rises and sets . . .
> in the city's turmoil
> or
> under the open sky on the farm,
> life is much the same;
> sometimes bitter, sometimes sweet.

Murnau sets up an allegory with character types, The Man (George O'Brien), The Wife (Janet Gaynor), and The Woman from the City (Margaret

Livingston), who lack names and signify a moralizing discourse on modernity. Caught between an innocent blond wife and a voracious dark siren, The Man is tempted and seeks moneylenders. And he agrees, in a moment of frenzied passion, to The Woman's entreaty, "Leave all this behind . . . Come to the City!" A kinetic vision of bright lights, speeding vehicles, high-rise buildings, nightclubs, blaring jazz, and frenzied dancing entices. Although The Man agrees to drown his wife during an outing and sell his farm, he is seized with guilt as he is about to commit murder, becomes remorseful, and wins forgiveness. After an excursion in the city, where they reconcile, the couple sets across the lake to return to the farm. But strong winds and roiling waters upset their boat. Unable to locate his wife in the storm's wreckage, The Man attacks The Woman from the City, who literally falls out of the frame and is next seen retreating on a wagon. When The Wife is found alive after a desperate night of searching, rays of sunlight at the conclusion signify a more beneficent nature.

Integral to Murnau's vision of the metropolis as fragmented and disorienting, yet sensory and seductive is the representation of The Woman from the City. She is first seen wearing a kimono and lacy lingerie, lighting a cigarette, and combing her bobbed hair. A high-heeled shoe rests on a dresser that forms a strong diagonal in the midst of a disheveled room. A cut to a deep-focus shot shows a married couple dining in the foreground as she emerges from the hallway. Disrupting a domestic scene, The Woman from the City demands that her shoes be polished. As she walks to The Man's farmhouse, the camera tracks her movement through the village so that she is contrasted with elderly neighbors, a man leading his horse, aproned wives conversing, and a mother indoors with her child. Since tracking shots can be liberating and seductive, its use here to characterize The Woman from the City is brilliant. The timebound villagers, on the other hand, are locked in stasis. Aptly, a longer and more convoluted tracking shot is used to follow the Man in his rendezvous with The Woman beneath a full moon. During the seduction, intercut with scenes of the tearful Wife with her child, The Woman becomes a monstrous vampire who preys on men. She is aggressive and frenzied. And she is often on top as her fingers spread like claws to clutch her hapless lover. Both The Woman from the City and The Wife, in sum, are stereotypes familiar to filmgoers.

According to F. W. Murnau, *Sunrise* "can be defined as modern . . . but it doesn't conform with the standard modernity of any particular nation. Its sets are a mixture of every nation." Art director Rochus Gliese, who built sets in false perspective, recalled, "Fox . . . only asked one thing: that the city was not Tilsit, as in Sudermann's novel. We said: 'OK, as long as it's not an American city either'" ("Channel 4"). Constructing a fable to preach moral values, Murnau, unlike American realists who focused on gritty urban detail, renders the metropolis an abstraction. With the exception of some comic sequences in the city, where The Man and The Wife reconcile, the film has an air of unreality. Indeed, the farm scenes are populated by nineteenth-century peasants untouched by Sears catalogs and rural free delivery. Sheltering their enclosed world from the enticement of the city is a large body of water (California's Lake Arrowhead) so that two cultures that rarely intersect are spatially as well as temporally apart. Whatever exchange occurs does so in the lateral movement of the two female characters. The Woman from the City brings narcissism, greed, and evil to the farm so that, despite a full moon, she muddies the landscape. A famous tracking shot of a trolley conveys The Wife to the city, where a process shot evoking an Edenic paradise blots out hectic traffic. Such interpenetration of rural and urban scenes, however, represents but an interval. At the end, The Man, who wins forgiveness during a wedding ceremony witnessed in the city, reclaims his position as agrarian breadwinner. Still characterizing his wife is the minister's description of the bride as church bells toll: "She is young . . . and inexperienced. Guide her and love her—keep and protect her from all harm." The Wife is thus labeled in terms of her subordinate position and function, whereas The Woman from the City represents modernity as a threat to the heterosexual status quo.

Coincidentally, *Flesh and the Devil*, like *Sunrise*, was based on a work by Hermann Sudermann. Benjamin F. Glazer adapted the novel *The Undying Past* for MGM director Clarence Brown. But unlike *Sunrise*, the film is a more realistic indictment of modernity as represented by Felicitas (Greta Garbo), a selfish, hedonistic, and amoral woman. She intrudes between two inseparable German aristocrats, Leo (John Gilbert) and Ulrich (Lars Hanson). Also a part of this tight-knit family is Leo's mother (Eugenie Besserer) and Ulrich's sister, Hertha (Barbara Kent). After becoming obsessed with Felicitas, Leo abruptly discovers that she is married and kills her husband in a duel. The film cleverly depicts the outcome by dissolving a shot of silhouetted dueling figures to Felicitas trying on a black veil in an expensive boutique. Since he must serve a term in exile for the duel, Leo entrusts Felicitas's care to Ulrich. At first indifferent, Felicitas becomes attracted when she learns that Ulrich is very rich. When Leo returns, he is stunned to find that the woman he loves has married his best friend. Although he is warned that the devil "creates a woman beautiful enough to reach us through the flesh," Leo remains enamored and must duel with his cherished friend. Succumbing uncharacteristically to Hertha's emotional plea,

Felicitas rushes to stop the fighting but perishes in icy waters. Leo and Ulrich, however, have renounced dueling of their own accord and embrace at the end. An alternative ending shows Leo courting Hertha under his mother's approving gaze as he returns to family and community.

Although Felicitas reminded viewers and critics of Theda Bara as the vampire, *Flesh and the Devil* launched Garbo into stardom by creating a mystique that rendered the stereotype alluring. Particularly effective was the star's subtle and restrained acting because her character remained illegible. John Gilbert, by contrast, overacted so that one critic noted "his grimaces finally brought laughter from the audience" (McGowen). Also crucial was the way in which William Daniels, Garbo's favorite cameraman, used gauze, filters, Vaseline, panchromatic film, and portrait lighting to enhance repeated close-ups ("Cinema Club"). The first close-up in *Flesh and the Devil* is withheld but well orchestrated. Subject to point-of-view shots, Felicitas is sighted by Leo in long and medium shots as she descends from a train and enters a carriage. Already mesmerized by her beauty, he searches for her in a ballroom. She finally appears in an extreme long shot of guests, but the close-up follows a dissolve rather than a straight cut to dramatize her presence. A high-angle tracking shot then follows the circular movement of the couple, entranced with each other in medium close-up, during a seductive waltz. As they sit in a gazebo outdoors, dramatic lighting, especially when a cigarette is lit, sculpts Garbo's features against the darkness in extreme close-ups and two shots. Although repeated close-ups enhance Garbo's eroticism, she remains elusive. Conversation conveyed by intertitles heightens the mystery of her identity. "Who . . . are . . . you?" queries Leo. She responds, "What does it matter?" When he points out that blowing out the match is "an invitation to kiss," Felicitas seizes the opportunity to seduce her admirer.

Distinctly not the stereotype portrayed by Margaret Livingston in *Sunrise*, Felicitas is so sensual that she nevertheless represents consumption as evil. With scant regard for marriage and social convention, she is about to decamp with Leo when Ulrich returns from a trip with a dazzling emerald and diamond bracelet. She then confesses to Leo, "I'm not brave enough to leave all this." Desiring luxury, Felicitas is showcased in opulent surroundings with high ceilings, pilasters, chandeliers, paneled and coffered doors, arched windows, floor-to-ceiling drapery, rich upholstery, paintings, and statuary. Indeed, the *New York Evening Graphic* reported in January that sets by Cedric Gibbons and Frederick Hope were decorated with "antiques worth a fortune" (Garbo scrapbook, LMPA). Felicitas also has a costly wardrobe, including fur coats that drape her tall and statuesque figure. Although Garbo transcends caricature in her portrayal, she is unable to escape the

Greta Garbo won popular and critical acclaim for updating the vamp as a seductive woman addicted to luxury in *Flesh and the Devil.*

fate meted out to vamps who defy convention. As a critic notes, at the end she is "opportunely drowned." Agonizing about the duel, Felicitas "is permitted to become overwrought. . . . Miss Garbo clutches at her hair—pounds her forehead, and—worse yet—prowls in the manner of Felix the Cat." But "wicked ladies are . . . more popular with the censors and the box-office if they show signs of reforming . . . whether such an exhibition happens to be 'in character' or not" (Bow clips, MHL; Rawson; Waldorf).

An idealized sentimental heroine who was the antithesis of the vampire, America's Sweetheart Mary Pickford pinned up her famous corkscrew curls for her first onscreen kiss in *My Best Girl.* Adapted from a Kathleen Norris story by Hope Loring, the United Artist film was directed by Sam Taylor and photographed by Pickford's favorite cameraman, Charles Rosher (also credited with *Sunrise*). Although she takes on an adult role in her last silent, fans could still identify with "Little Mary" because she is a lower-middle-class character in a Cinderella scenario. Significantly, the site of her trajectory into the upper class is a five-and-ten-cent store. The film opens with a close-up of a cash register and pulls back for a montage showing dolls, jewelry, flatware, tools, and candy; it ends with an extreme long shot of the entire floor. The Merrill Store may not be a palatial emporium on Manhattan's Ladies Mile, where middle-class women shopped, but its customers, including a black woman, are well dressed. A lowly stock girl in a gingham apron, Maggie Johnson (Mary Pickford) is unaware that the new employee, Joe Merrill (Buddy Rogers), is the boss's son working incognito to prove himself. Joe is secretly engaged to socialite Millicent Rogers (Avonne Taylor), but is instantly attracted to Maggie's innocence, goodness, and homespun charm.

Although *My Best Girl* represents class difference through characterization, costumes, and set design, its light comedic tone and its star, who personified rags-to-riches in real life, defuse social issues. Certainly, the Merrills live in opulence. At the end of the sequence in the five-and-dime, the camera dollies in on the cash register, in a reverse of the opening shot, and the scene dissolves to an extreme long shot of the three-story Merrill mansion topped by a mansard roof. A foyer with crystal chandelier, paneled walls, framed circular painting, alcoves with statuary, demi-lune table, and diamond patterned tiles leads to a high-ceilinged living room with arched and draped windows, elaborately molded doorways, Oriental carpeting, antique furniture, brocaded upholstery, candelabra sconces, porcelain lamps, and flower-filled vases. The Johnsons live in a humbler two-story abode on Goat Hill, but they have indoor plumbing, a fireplace, lace curtained and draped windows, carpeting, tchotchkes, and a Victrola. What renders them lower as opposed to middle class is their representation as a comic family. The thin, balding father (Lucien Littlefield) cannot assert authority; the untidy, overweight mother (Sunshine Hart) sobs about funerals; and the rebellious sister (Carmelita Geraghty) acts like a New Woman but is a floozie with poor judgment.

Audiences expect Joe Merrill to marry into this dysfunctional family because he is smitten with America's Sweetheart. Asserting "Little Mary's" equivalence with a chain store heir, the film constructs symmetries through plot, editing, and camera movement. Sequences that involve transportation, dinner, and Joe's birthday are telling. After a truck ride, which is mostly shot as backtracking, Maggie invites Joe to supper, but family shenanigans frustrate her desire. When Joe tricks Maggie, still unaware of his identity, into having dinner at the mansion, her ignorance and lack of manners amuse tuxedoed servants. Anticipating Joe's birthday, Millicent, seated on a divan and wearing a fur-trimmed negligee, plans to give him a watch. A uniformed maid walks in with a silver tea service on a tray shown in close-up. A dissolve to a bottle of milk and sandwiches shows Joe and Maggie having lunch in the storeroom. She, too, remembers his birthday and gives him a watch. During an outing that evening, the Economy Furniture Company, whose plate glass window shows a contented family, becomes the site of scenes before and after the lovers' misunderstanding as

Attempting to modernize her image as America's Sweetheart, Mary Pickford is a stock girl romanced by the heir to a dry goods store in *My Best Girl.*

Joe's real identity is revealed. At the end, when Joe and Maggie climb aboard a car to catch an ocean liner to wed and honeymoon in Hawaii, the camera tracks forward, in a reverse of the earlier backtracking shot of the truck ride. Although the film emphasizes class difference, sequences that contrast are also symmetrical so that problematic social issues are elided. Also, the Cinderella ending precludes scenes of Maggie, who symbolically loses her luggage, perplexed in upper-class settings. Characteristically, when she and Joe celebrate his birthday, she scolds him for spending money. Pickford, in sum, was wedded to values of thrift in a Victorian sexual economy and could not translate her sentimental appeal as America's Sweetheart into a version of the New Woman.

A Cinderella story similar to *My Best Girl* but notably different, *It* was based on a popular *Cosmopolitan* piece by Elinor Glyn, a clever screenplay by Hope Loring and Louis D. Lighton, and snappy titles by George Marion Jr. Directed by Clarence Badger for Paramount, the film opens with a shot of a skyscraper sign, Waltham's Worlds Largest Store (*sic*), that pulls back, tilts down for a view of the street entrance, tracks in, and dissolves to an extreme long shot of the interior. Particularly eye-catching in the lower left-hand corner is the lingerie department. As observed by an elderly gentleman accompanying his crabby wife, the counter's best attraction is delectable salesgirl Betty Lou Spence (Clara Bow), shown in close-up. Betty Lou, in turn, eyes Cyrus Waltham (Antonio Moreno), the store's handsome owner, and exclaims, "Sweet Santa Claus, give me *him*!" She fails, however, to get him to notice her. But his effete pal Monty (William Austen) inspects salesgirls, lined behind a stocking counter with plastic legs and in front of filing cabinets, as reified objects in a consumer culture. When he spots Betty Lou, he pronounces that she has IT! As defined by grand dame Elinor Glyn during an appearance in the film, IT involves "magnetic 'sex appeal' which is irresistible." Accordingly, Betty Lou's vivacity represents madcap, high-spirited, irresistible fun. When she tricks Monty into dining at the Ritz, where Cyrus shares a table with Adela van Norman, she violates dress and behavioral codes but finally attracts the attention she craves.

Unlike Maggie in *My Best Girl*, Betty Lou is a working-class girl who lives in a cheap apartment in Gashouse Gables. She has no family and is supporting a roommate, Molly (Priscilla Bonner), who is ill and has a baby. Although she and Cyrus have fun together during a night at Coney Island, where amusement rides include the Social Mixer, a misunderstanding illuminates the nature of female bargaining power. Women set postwar shopping trends in apparel and home decor, but they, in turn, were reified and commodified in a consumer culture. Despite the pleasure of mixed-sex leisure, female exchange value on the marriage market was still defined by Victorian standards. Assuming that Betty Lou gave birth to Molly's baby and is thus spoiled goods, Cyrus will not propose but offers to buy "diamonds—clothes—everything you want." Angered by his "left-hand arrangement," Betty Lou quits her job and exacts revenge by sailing with Monty on Cyrus's yacht as an unexpected guest. Commanding seductive point-of-view shots calculated to break down a man's defenses, she ridicules Cyrus when, dressed in a maritime uniform, he finally proposes. But all ends well. An accident that throws the principals overboard ends with the drenched couple perched on top of the anchor. As the yacht is named *Itola*, Betty Lou and Cyrus frame the letters "It" before the final clinch.

A flirty New Woman whose physicality and energy are irresistible, Betty Lou represents consumption as fun. But working-class women seldom had enough disposable income to be carefree shoppers. During a scene when she is refashioning an outfit to dine at the Ritz, Betty Lou unwraps artificial flowers in old newspapers and stares at a Waltham's ad for $11 dresses ($125.74 today).[1] She has to shake herself out of a reverie about tantalizing goods and scheme to increase her purchasing power. Salesgirls were recruited from the working class and endured low pay, long hours, fines, discipline, and bad conditions in emporiums that, except for the base-

Clara Bow, the "It Girl," personifies the commodification of the Jazz Age new woman as a salesgirl at the lingerie counter of a department store.

ment, catered to middle- and upper-class women. Sensational stories about shopgirls selling luxuries stressed the reality of their being lured into prostitution. Complaints about their dress, language, and behavior led management to initiate training programs. A Cinderella story, *It* displaces class difference on and off the shoproom floor onto another inequality in consumer culture: those who have "It" and those who don't. Adept at self-making as personality and performance, Betty Lou has considerable capital. Adela, her blonde socialite rival, on the other hand, is, as Monty says, "It-less." Betty Lou need only acquire a wealthy male to pay for her goods. Despite emphasis on mixed-sex leisure and companionate marriage, Edward Filene perceived the truth in describing the department store as an "Adamless Eden" (Benson 76, 128–47). So when the New Woman shops, she is not feeling guilty but having fun without men.

Critical and Audience Reception: Facts and Figures

Flesh and the Devil, which opened in January at the Capitol Theatre in New York, was the most popular of these four films. Audiences who attended the first run enjoyed a prologue featuring the Capitol Grand

Orchestra; a soloist playing the first movement of a Tchaikovsky concerto; news of the week; and a stage production with a coloratura soprano, the Capitol Ballet Corps, and the Chester Hale Girls (Capitol Theatre Program). "During the first week . . . the amount of business was phenomenal. Most of the newspaper critics had given the film a wonderful send-off. . . . The news began to spread . . . [that] a picture with a full-measure dose of sex appeal was showing at the Capitol." When a crowd of 1,500 people clamored for tickets one evening, police were called to help with the lines. *Variety* reported that the film grossed $248,296 ($2,963,856 today) in a record-breaking four-week run.[2] During its eight years in business, the Capitol, one of Manhattan's great movie palaces, had not held a picture over for so many weeks. Screening of the film then continued at Loew's, where it was also held over ("Third Week for Film"; "Police Hold Back;" "$248,296"; "Flesh and the Devil" clip).

Accounting for the film's enormous attraction was Greta Garbo. Critics who praised the film's "poetic glimpses" but disliked the painted backdrops, weak story, and denouement agreed that Garbo "stole the show." *Variety* reported, "This girl has everything. Gilbert [who received top billing] has to keep moving to overshadow her, even though she has a most unsympathetic role." The *Evening Graphic* observed that "she has a peculiar type of beauty which sets her apart from the others who play her kind of roles. . . . Miss Garbo possesses charm, ability and that which Elinor Glyn is wont to call 'It.'" Dissenting from the chorus of praise, the *Morning Telegram* labeled her "pathological." *Motion Picture Classic* described her as an "oversexed temptress." *Motion Picture Magazine* dubbed her a "beautiful nymphomaniac (a Freudian word for a lady who pursues men and just can't help it)" (Rev. of *Flesh and the Devil*; Colfax; "Flesh and the Devil" clip; "Celluloid Critic"; "Picture Parade"). Several notices, including those in *Variety*, the *New York Herald Tribune*, and the *Los Angeles Sun Times*, commented on the likeness of her role to Theda Bara's vampire. A cartoon pictured her with a serpentine arm and a serpent. Critics agreed, in sum, that Garbo was descended from the vamp but represented an allure all her own (Watts; Schallert untitled).

Unlike *Flesh and the Devil*, *It* played a standard one-week run in February at the refurbished Paramount Theatre in Times Square. Yet the film was enormously popular, grossed $76,791 ($916,638 today), and elevated Clara Bow to new heights as a star. As she herself later said, "My life was changed by that title" (Irwin). A program shows that audiences enjoyed the Rollickers in "Song Syncopation," Wurtlizer renditions of Irving Berlin tunes, and a divertissement with singers, corps de ballet, and violin ensemble during the prologue (Paramount Theatre Program). Clearly, urban audiences were flocking to see movies in which the New Woman redefined sexuality in relation to consumption. A *Motion Picture News* ad declaring "IT's a hit" repeated close-ups of Clara Bow. Critics focused on the star as well. *Film Daily* described *It* as "a sprightly little yarn" but concluded that "Clara Bow is really the whole show." Similarly, Laurence Reid claimed in *Motion Picture News* that there is nothing to *It* but Clara Bow: "She is so dynamic . . . so abundantly vital—that she makes the film entertaining in spite of itself . . . [and] engulfs Antonio Moreno." *Variety* reported that she "can troupe . . . and the manner in which she puts it all over the supporting cast . . . is a joy to behold." As for her co-star Moreno, it declared him to be "just a little too old" (*It;* Reid; Revs. of *It*). Indeed, the same could be said about Garbo's lover, Gilbert, in *Flesh and the Devil.* Women could more easily steal the spotlight before the arrival of sound when authoritative masculine voices reinforced the arsenal of male stars.

Although *It* and *My Best Girl* were both Cinderella stories scripted by Hope Loring, the Pickford film was a bigger production befitting a legendary star. According to the pressbook, she herself selected co-star Buddy Rogers "among dozens of aspirants" (and later married him after divorcing Douglas Fairbanks). A two-block set representing a downtown business district with five-story buildings, streetcar tracks, and pavement cost $120,000 ($1,432,415 today). Twenty-two truckloads of merchandise were carted in for scenes in the five-and-dime. A rainy night sequence, tinted blue, required 100,000 gallons of water to drench the cast. Charles Rosher had a special portrait lens made in Germany so that he could photograph the star in short-focus yet produce a stereoscopic effect (*My Best Girl* pressbook). Critics and audiences however, were lukewarm when the film opened at the Rialto in November. *Variety* and *Motion Picture News* used the terms "hoke," "hokum," and "hokumish" in reviews. Although *Photoplay* dubbed the story "flimsy," it was "still the best picture Mary has made in several years." Disagreeing, Mordaunt Hall thought she should "employ her talent in a more intelligent . . . picture," but still found her delightful, sincere, and earnest. *Variety* declared that the star is "her usual sweet and likable self." Reid claimed that the "star's name is enough" to draw audiences (Rev. of *My Best Girl;* Reid; Schallert; "Shadow Stage"; Hall). During three weeks at the Rialto, however, the film grossed diminishing returns: $33,800 ($403,463 today), $24,800, and $22,400. *Variety* concluded that the "engagement played to but fair money" ("Increases"; "Ruth Elder"; "Sorrell's Sons").

A special, *Sunrise,* with Symphonic Movietone Accompaniment composed by Hugo Riesenfeld, opened in September for an extended run at the Times Square Theatre. According to a program note that explains Movietone, a process rivaling Vitaphone, sound (changed into light variations) and image "are photographed simultaneously with the same camera and on the same film." Audiences heard the Vatican Choir and saw both the Fox Movietone News and Benito Mussolini in "The Man of the Hour" "expressing . . . his sentiments toward the US and . . . Italian-Americans" (Times Square Theatre Program). Clearly, this program foreshadows the disappearance of musicians and stage performers in prologues before screenings. Critics praised the film's aesthetics but were divided about its story and conclusion. Robert Sherwood wrote in *Life* that *Sunrise* was "the most important film in the history of the movies." Laurence Reid claimed in *Motion Picture News* that the film "actually shows what motivates . . . characters." *Variety* labeled the film "a distinguished contribution" in "the best manner of the German school" and singled out Movietone music and sound effects. Mordaunt Hall noted that Murnau "shows himself to be an artist in camera studies bringing forth marvelous results from lights, shadows and settings." But Frederick James Smith observed in *Liberty* that the "camera work is the only absorbing interest" in a film "otherwise turgid, drab, and dull." The *Evening Sun* concurred. *Photoplay* echoed *Motion Picture Classic* and labeled the film "the sort of picture that fools high-brows into hollering 'Art!'" and complained about "no story interest and only stilted, mannered acting" (Channel 4; Reid; Hall; Rev. of *Sunrise*; "'Sunrise' Brings a New Day"; "Shadow Stage").

An expensive production that flopped at the box office, *Sunrise* failed to break even during an extended run to publicize it for nationwide release. After the first week *Variety* deemed the picture "over [the] heads of [the] type of audience Italian statesman will draw for early rush." Indeed, the trade journal claimed that Mussolini was the primary attraction for the first four weeks. During week five, it voiced uncertainty: "An artistic success but still doubtful if Murnau has turned out a box-office clicker." By then receipts, based on tickets costing $1 ($12 today), $2, and $2.65, had fallen from an initial $19,450 ($232,171 today) to $13,000 ($155,178 today). A further drop to $7,000 in the seventh week led the journal to comment, "Not enjoying much action and slipping into oblivion." *Sunrise* failed to draw during Thanksgiving week when its take declined on one day to less than $400 ($4,775 today). *Variety* noted early in December: "Way down in four figures; giving tickets away by the handful; one picture trade unanimously deemed great but public won't buy it with Mussolini attached." During week fourteen, at year's end, the trade journal reported: "Can blow any time without causing surprise." Despite hemorrhage at the box office, the film was screened for an additional nine weeks in 1928 ("New and Old Films"; "Capitol Down"; "P.D.C. Drops"; "Sorrell's Sons"; "Joe and Sam";

"Broadway Ushers"). Unfortunately, such an unprofitable run in New York did not bode well. A *Film Daily* report of state admission taxes collected by the Internal Revenue Service did not specify rates but showed that New York's take, $6,985,248 ($83,381,421 today), was far in excess of Illinois's $2,150,153 ($25,665,920 today), Pennsylvania's $1,431,964 ($17,091,856 today), and California's $1,404,008 ($16,759,345 today). North Dakota, Vermont, and Wyoming, by contrast, did not exceed $12,000 ($143,241 today). Manhattan filmgoing, in other words, constituted a disproportionate percentage of industry profits so that first-run showings in the city, essential for publicity, also filled coffers ("1927 Amusement").

Unfortunately, *Variety* did not compute yearly top-grossing charts, so comparative figures for silent films are not readily available. But *Exhibitor's Herald* conducted an annual national poll based on theater grosses during a twelve-month period ending in mid-November. A chart listing over one hundred titles shows that *It* ranked fifth and *Flesh and the Devil* twenty-fifth for the year, whereas *My Best Girl* and *Sunrise* did not register. Since Clara Bow had three pictures, *It*, *Hula*, and *Children of Divorce*, on the chart, she climbed to second place, after Colleen Moore, on the exhibitor's list of "The Big Names of 1927." Significantly, Mary Pickford still ranked eighth despite declining box office power, while Greta Garbo, the year's sensation, was rated fifteenth. Indeed, exhibitors commented that Garbo's previous film, *The Temptress*, "is not the type that draws and satisfies a small town." As for the fans themselves, *Photoplay*'s readers voted *Seventh Heaven*, a sentimental melodrama with Janet Gaynor, as the year's best film. Although the magazine recognized Gaynor, who would win the first Oscar, "among . . . noteworthy newcomers," it named Garbo to its Honor Roll for her work in *The Temptress*, *Flesh and the Devil*, and *Love*. Yet *Variety* listed Garbo as MGM's top featured player, not star, in its listings for the year ("Biggest Moneymakers"; "Big Names"; "Temptress"; "What Was"; "*Photoplay's* Honor Roll"; Leading Film Stars"). As for the critics, they disagreed, but not overwhelmingly, with popular reception. *Sunrise* ranked among the *New York Times* top ten, but it was excluded as a roadshow from *Film Daily*'s poll of 235 critics who rated *Flesh and the Devil* tenth and awarded *It* and *My Best Girl* honorable mention ("Best Pictures"; "286 Critics").

Stars as New Women: "How to Behave Like Greta Garbo, Clara Bow, and Company"

Among the institutions that constructed consumer capitalism, advertising became an efficient means of communication to facilitate the exchange of goods and services.[3] During the 1920s, advertisers began to construct desire by using subjective techniques in narratives about personal triumph. Fan magazines, for example, promoted stars like Clara Bow as role models for aspiring working- and lower-middle-class readers. A destitute Brooklyn blonde, she was only sixteen when she submitted two cheap photos and won *Motion Picture Magazine's* "Fame and Fortune Contest." Judges told her that she was "different" and had "a unique personality." As the magazine decreed, "A person may have perfect features and yet entirely lack . . . personality . . . without which they can never become stars." Fittingly, a sister publication, *Motion Picture Classic,* characterized Bow as an "alluring little 'flapper' type" who was "plastic, quick, alert, young, and lovely." Among the prizes she won was a shopping trip for a "brown Canton crepe dress, cleverly trimmed with fashionable monkey fur . . . a pair of . . . cute little 'Sally pumps' . . . and a brown velvet hat with the brim petalled like a flower" ("New Star"; "Contest"; "Dream Come True").

Success was not immediate but after she achieved stardom, F. Scott Fitzgerald singled her out while redefining the flapper in a fan magazine. Whereas he had once portrayed "a neat bit of femininity, collegiate age, who rolled her stockings, chain smoked . . . mixed and drank a mean highball," he now found that a generation of free spirits had freed themselves from "restraints and inhibitions." Bow had engaged in campus high jinks in *The Plastic Age* (1925), but Fitzgerald observed that she was now the quintessential modern woman—"pretty, impudent, superbly assured . . . worldly wise, briefly clad, and 'hard boiled.'" Although her claim sounds apocryphal, the star credited herself with inventing the character of the "superflapper" or "jazz-baby" to succeed in pictures. Whether or not she was, in fact, the product of her own imagination, she demonstrated that the flapper was an expensive form of commodity fetishism (Marchand 56; Bow "Life"; Reid "Flapper").

"What It Costs to Be a Well-Dressed Flapper" in *Motion Picture Classic* shows Clara Bow modeling a silk faille coat trimmed with ermine, doeskin gloves, beige shoes, and pearls amounting to a total of $346.50 ($4,136.10 today). According to the piece, "it costs about as much to dress a modern girl . . . as it does to equip . . . a . . . well-furnished three-room flat." Part of a continuing series featured in the magazine, this article was followed by calculations of the cost of being a well-dressed debutante, bride, vacationer, and bather (Pierce). Attesting to the importance of personality rather than character in self-making, Bow states that "few dowdily dressed women are the center of attraction, no matter how great their virtues." She believes that "men like chic, smartly gowned women." Claiming that men are "secretly grateful" for women's "new freedom," she asserts that "keeping both a job and a husband" is a modern prerogative. She herself would not give up her career (Bow "Life"; Manners). Unfortunately, most women workers, including white-collar employees, were low-paid, secondary wage earners in the labor force.[4] Cleverly, fan magazines also used Bow to reinforce feminine roles by promoting a recipe for Chicken Chartreuse and to peddle affordable commodities: Golden Peacock Bleach Crème, the Clara Bow Hat, and Ben Hur toilet articles (Van Wyck; Golden Peacock; Clara Bow Hat; Ben Hur).

As sister magazines with the middlebrow pretensions of founders J. Stuart Blackton and Eugene Brewster, *Motion Picture Magazine* and *Motion Picture Classic* promoted self-improvement dictating consumption. Unsurprisingly, the commodification of culture, a troubling development anticipated by highbrow critics, was utilized to sell goods. An ad in *Motion Picture Magazine*, for example, claimed that *The Development of Culture* was a work that would teach readers how to enrich their personalities and make the right impression (*Development*). But culture, redefined in materialistic terms, meant acquiring the stylish goods displayed in movies. As Terry Ramsaye wrote in *Photoplay*, the film industry accelerated consumption of beauty products, fashion, and home furnishings. *Motion Picture Magazine*, for example, published a series by First National set designer Stephen Goosson. His advice on dining rooms included details about wall color, floors, window treatments, tables, plates, pewter, silverware, and candles. Articles also stressed the proper living room, furniture, holiday decorations, wall hangings, and patios. Goosson even dictated architectural design for new homes, with a preference for colonial, mission, Spanish, and Italianate styles (Ramsaye; Goosson). As for social entertainment in these settings, *Motion Picture Magazine* taught etiquette lessons by referring to the movies ("Etiquette").

Photoplay, which lacked middlebrow pretensions, ran a monthly section titled "Buy on Fifth Avenue through *Photoplay's* Shopping Service." The March issue sold items ranging from a French smock for $2.95 ($35.21 today) to a crepe frock in Palmetto green, Queen blue, cocoa, or tan for $15.95 ($190.39 today) ("Buy on Fifth"). Since readers were mostly lower-class women, fan magazine advertisers practiced market segmentation and peddled affordable wares like a "110-Piece Dinner Set" for $2.70 a month. Ads for soap, toothpaste, mouthwash, eye drops, cosmetics, and feminine hygiene products promoted beauty. Women were enjoined to develop bustlines, "get rid of fat," treat pimples, reshape noses, and color hair. Pamphlets on self-improvement taught readers to become piano players, beauticians, cartoonists, commercial artists, and actors. Clever ad stripping resulted in printing the conclusion of stories about stars on the same page as ads. But products were not enough to effect a transformation. A manual titled *Fascinating Womanhood* promised that "any woman can multiply her attractiveness by using the simple laws of . . . psychology" and become a "radiant bride" (Advertisements).

Yet stars like Clara Bow who showcased consumption proved that upward mobility did not necessarily erase class lines. Unlike earlier success stories such as Mabel Normand, who refined herself in terms of middle-class culture, Bow remained distinctly working class. She "succeeded in being at one and the same time innocuous and trashy," as Anita Loos quipped. An interviewer found her makeup, flaming red hair, and long and sharp fingernails excessive. After a tour of her Beverly Hills home, Adela Rogers St. Johns described the "Chinese room" as "beautiful and . . . bizarre, . . . exquisite and . . . commonplace—mingled in hopeless fashion [so that] a gaudy doll . . . leans against a wonderful Ming lamp." Apparently, the star was not reading Gooson's advice literature. Another writer titled an article "Clara Bow: The 'It' Girl's Notorious House in Beverly Hills" (St. Johns; Stenn). Unfortunately, headlines focused on her numerous engagements and multiple romances. Also trumpeted were scandals like her father's divorce from a "wild harum scarum girl" who was about her age. An affair with a nightclub owner was shocking because he was being sued by a jeweler for alienation of his wife's affection, surely a sign that love had become a commodity. Ultimately, Clara Bow was unable to control her success story, image, or salary negotiations. Paramount bought her contract with Budd Schulberg for $100,000 ($1,193,679 today) when he rejoined the studio as associate producer and became general manager. Although she was a top moneymaker, she was then earning $1,500 a week. When the decade ended, her salary had climbed to $5,000 a week ($59,684 today), but Colleen Moore, the only star outpolling her in the *Exhibitor's Herald*, earned twice as much. At the end of her spectacular but brief career, she sadly concluded, "I feel as if I've been exploited—as if almost everyone I had trusted had used me" ("Marital Ties"; "Richman"; Behlmer; Irwin).

Unlike the It Girl, Greta Garbo (Greta Gustafsson), who was barely out of her teens and learning English, was narcissistic and determined enough to deal with studio magnates. According to *Photoplay*, before her arrival with mentor Mauritz Stiller, she had signed a contract restricting her pay to a scale not to exceed $1,000 a week ($11,937 today). She earned $450–$600 a week while she made her first three pictures. Wrangling over her contract, Louis B. Mayer reportedly threatened to give her minor roles and deport her. Another report claimed that after a "long, drawn out battle," the star agreed to film *Love* for $3,000 a week ($35,810 today) and then negotiate another contract. Garbo believed that she was worth $7,500 a week and should be earning $15,000 a week ($179,052 today) in five years. Aside from a bigger salary, she wanted a voice in the selection of the film's director and leading man. Edmund Goulding, who had a reputation for working with temperamental stars, assumed the helm. Ricardo Cortez, a minor Latin lover and co-star in *The Torrent* (1926), was dropped as the lead. According to *Motion Picture Magazine*, Garbo had been filming *Love* for two weeks "when she became ill and the cast was dismissed. Her indisposition lasted oddly enough until John Gilbert was through with his picture, 'Twelve Miles Out'" ("Greta Garbo Settles"; York; Hynd and Calhoun). But Gilbert's performance in *Love* was diffident, a fact that the late James Card attributed to a failed romance with the star. Although Louella Parsons reported their elopement as a scoop, Garbo disappointed Gilbert by changing her mind and expressed doubt about marriage: "I like to be alone; not always with some other person." Unsurprisingly, Garbo also had strong opinions about her costumes. Andre Ani, the designer for *Flesh and the Devil*, found her "difficult to dress" because she had "very set . . . and very foreign" ideas and "innumerable dislikes." "She will wear nothing with fur. . . . She will wear no laces, no velvets. She goes in for flaunting, bizarre collars and cuffs. She likes short skirts when she should wear long ones. She is very fond of tulle and crepe marocain." Aptly, a *Photoplay* portrait of Garbo was captioned "the girl who waits until she gets what she wants" (Card; Parsons; Biery; Reid "Heroines"; Photo caption).

Although stars promoted consumption and materialistic lifestyles, they, too, were commodities and did not always control their exchange value at the box office. Garbo intrigues because, unlike America's Sweetheart Mary Pickford, she used neither femininity nor middle-class politesse to disguise steely resolve.[5] She was, moreover, uninterested in fashionable wardrobes or glamorous events and rarely attended premieres. She refused to become a captive of her screen persona. Clara Bow, on the other hand, felt ruthlessly exploited. Sadly, she commented about the flapper she grew tired of playing: "She's much happier than I am." Adding a dark postscript, she provided insight about the extravagant character who became a symbol of the Jazz Age. The flapper transformed consumption into fun, but underneath all that gaiety was "a feeling of tragedy. . . . She's kind of unhappy and disillusioned" (Bow clips, MHL). Why was she depressed?[6] As movies and fan magazines showed, goods were essential to construct a personality and to signify status in an impersonal urban society. But consumption could prove elusive as the basis for self-making. An urge to buy the latest goods as a sign of personal identity meant narcissistic absorption and tireless compulsive shopping. Consequently, celebrities with whom anxious individuals could identify were essential to promote products as the basis of consumer capitalism. Within this context, Garbo was unique, if excessively secretive, because she guarded her private life and so redefined the prerogatives of the New Woman. Certainly, she was self-absorbed even as she resisted market forces that commodified movie stardom. But by capitalizing on scarcity in an attempt to elude her image, she gained the status of a goddess rather than a flapper. Since her elusiveness inflated her stature as an icon, she remained an unusual star in a modern celebrity culture designed to promote endless consumption.

NOTES

1. Although equivalent figures are based on the Consumer Price Index for 2007 and given in today's dollars, readers should consider differences in cost and standard of living. Thanks to Robert J. Smith for computations.

2. Grosses are approximate as they were not audited, could be inflated, and depended on seating capacity, ticket prices, promotions, and so forth.

3. The title of this section was borrowed from an unidentified magazine page in Clara Bow's clipping file at the Margaret Herrick Library, Academy of Motion Pictures Arts and Sciences, Beverly Hills. Accounts of Bow and Garbo are based on newspaper, fan magazine, and trade journal reports at the time, not subsequent biographies.

4. During the 1920s, the percentage of women in the labor force dipped slightly, even though white-collar jobs were more available. Significantly, more older, married women sought employment. Usually, middle-class women sought respectable clerical jobs as opposed to sales work.

5. Despite little girl roles, Pickford, advised by her mother, Charlotte, proved herself a New Woman by negotiating a two-year, million-dollar deal with Adolph Zukor. She defected to his rival First National in 1918 and helped form her own distributor, United Artists, in 1919.

6. After she had a nervous breakdown in the 1930s, Bow suffered from repeated mental problems.

1928

Movies, Social Conformity, and Imminent Traumas

ANGELA DALLE VACCHE

For the average American living and working in a big city, it must have felt, more or less, like the previous year. As we learn from the beginning of King Vidor's *The Crowd*, every achievement felt possible and ready to be plucked from the tree of prosperity for generations to come. The Empire State Building was under construction, Alexander Fleming had discovered penicillin, and the Harlem Renaissance of Zora Neale Hurston and Langston Hughes was in full bloom. "Grow up and do something big!" This is the message that John Sims's father projects on his baby boy as Vidor's camera tracks along a line of twelve-year-old children sitting on the fence with little John. With a medium close-up on each one, every kid states his own plans for the future: "My father says I will do something big," little John declares, still unable to express a personal opinion. On the contrary, while choosing a predictable route of action, the African American child states: "And I intend to become a preacher." At one point of this humorous yet stereotypical gallery of pillars of society, a bookish, blond kid, with a funny female headdress and glasses, underlines the gap between self-image and actual physiognomy in the most pompous language: "And I suppose my purpose will be to become a cowboy."

From the black preacher to the white cowboy, the country, as a whole, seems locked in the grip of social conformity and dominated by an imperative for homogeneity. Under three Republican administrations, xenophobic policies toward southern and eastern Europe prevail. Only 150,000 immigrants from northern Europe are allowed into the country each year. Put another way, domestic isolationism seems to be the right answer to boost the Anglo-Saxon component of American society. Likewise, Washington tightens its borders by allowing less foreign trade from Europe. The message is "Enjoy your prosperity at home." Regardless of Hollywood's soothing and perhaps escapist "democracy" onscreen, this is a period of heightened racial intolerance. On the domestic front, with approximately five million members, the

Ku Klux Klan enforces the segregation of schools and buses in the South (Cahiers 515). Chicago and Cleveland witness the arrival of many new African American residents from the Bible Belt looking for employment in the factories and willing to live in the expanding slums.

Before turning to a closer examination of more films representative of this year's psychological climate, a few events are worth mentioning, for they convey the texture of daily life. In the wake of two aviation heroes' successes, those of Charles Lindbergh and Amelia Earhart, airmail and next-day delivery are developed for the first time by the post office system. Struggling at the ground level, or mostly enclosed inside an office cubicle, anonymous office workers embrace the small pleasures of bubble gum, candy bars, and soft drinks sold by automatic vending machines. Millions of dollars begin to be generated by quick and fun food meant to relieve stress and cravings in the workplace. Meanwhile, another automatic wonder, the bread cutter, becomes the rage of the moment, so that meal preparation can be reduced to making quick sandwiches. At home, the workload for women also decreases thanks to the introduction of new household appliances, such as the vacuum cleaner and easier-to-operate stoves and ironing boards. Of course, newspapers and magazines relentlessly advertise these new gadgets as the ultimate reward of the happy American nuclear family.

Buying furniture on credit or even a record player in installments to listen to some dance music spreads as a common practice among many young couples. Domestic travel is also encouraged as a form of tourism and consumption. For those who cannot yet afford their own car, trains are a popular means of transportation, offering trips to Niagara Falls or outings in Coney Island. This second location looms large in the New York City imaginary of the period, because it is the least expensive and controlled space where young couples can be flirtatious with each other. It appears that the masses enjoy themselves on the weekend, while corporations and firms rent boat tours and picnic spaces to organize parties and anniversaries with group activities for their employees. The goal, of course, is to strengthen the company's social profile and its sense of leadership in the market.

Newly elected Republican president Herbert Hoover would soon replace Calvin Coolidge, who had followed another Republican, Warren G. Harding. By the day of Hoover's inauguration, the country has experienced three successive presidential mandates favoring big business (Cahiers 499). This also explains why banks throughout the twenties are perfectly happy to make deals with the nine major Hollywood production companies: First National, Warner Bros., Fox, RKO, Paramount, MGM-Loew's, Universal,

Columbia, and United Artists. With quotas about international export negotiated in the aftermath of the Great War, American producers have prevailed over all their European competitors, while financiers have no motivation to support any kind of independent filmmaking on American territory. The industry of studios and moguls rules undisturbed. Just like his predecessor, however, Hoover faced the period's social evils and transgressions: alcoholism and bootlegging, gangsters, speakeasies, flappers, and, by the end of the decade, the beginning of the Great Depression.

Consumerism and criminality are not the only two ingredients of this year: in fact, major events characterize the artistic and the sport scene. Within the context of the previously mentioned Harlem Renaissance, on 9 April, the wedding of African American poet Countee Cullen to Nina Jolande, daughter of W.E.B. Du Bois, is considered the social thrill of the decade. After hanging out in Paris with Ezra Pound, F. Scott Fitzgerald, Ernest Hemingway, and John Dos Passos, poet Archibald MacLeish decides to return to America this year and farm at Conway, Massachusetts. This is also when MacLeish produces some very patriotic poems. Finally for MacLeish the year involves a trip on foot or on mule to Mexico with the purpose of retracing the routes of Spanish conquistador Hernando Cortes. In art the year is marked by Charles Demuth's famous achievement *I Saw the Figure Five in Gold,* an oil painting about a red fire truck based on an imagist poem by William Carlos Williams about traffic and noise in the American city. While anticipating Pop Art, this work in red, orange, and yellow features the number "five," which is the logo of an engine company. By oscillating between technology and commodification, the red of fire and the gold of money, Demuth plays with the double meaning of "bill" as a short version of William and as banknote. In the midst of an explosion of interest in jazz, the Roaring Twenties concludes with lots of gold even in the area of sport. Held in Amsterdam, the Summer Olympics this year witnesses American athletes winning the largest number of medals (56) and the largest quantity of gold medals (22).

Within such a stimulating climate of success and transgression, only two controllable problems seem to affect Hollywood at this point: labor disputes with unions protecting workers and a negative public image fostered by many years of decadent parties, scandals, divorces, and alcoholism; all this vice is countered, of course, by excellent box office revenues at home and abroad. Between 1921 and 1929 Hollywood's receipts increased fourfold, and this year the average weekly attendance at the movies is 65 million people. Furthermore, the number of movie theaters rises to 20,500, five times more than a decade ago.

This year is also the last in which film dialogue can still challenge conventional norms because the repressive Hays censorship code was soon to be established. In addition, by the late twenties, before the Wall Street crash, Hollywood practiced a sort of "movie-theater democracy," in the sense that films did not present a monolithic view of class relations. According to Steven J. Ross, class identity was "rooted in the more alluring world of consumption than in the conflict-ridden world of production" (67). Furthermore, in comparison to gang wars and criminal shoot-outs, the class struggle was not the main topic of newspapers headlines.

One of the most traumatic events in American history was the Wall Street crash of 1929 (Black Thursday, 24 October). As a result, the year before invokes one basic image: a whole world leaning over a precipice without knowing or without seeing it. These questions of vision and knowledge are obviously central not only to the relations among characters within a film, but also to the spectators' happy or sad reactions to what happens onscreen. One might argue that such a state of unawareness about the immediate future is appropriate to a film industry in the midst of a transition from silent cinema to sound films. After all, the aesthetic and narrative consequences of this forward leap into new technology were still undefined. By this year, however, Hollywood had reached such a degree of intellectual maturity and international success that technological change was not perceived as threatening, but rather as a new opportunity for creative storytelling and profit making.

To begin with, the industry's own sense of adulthood coincides with films of this year receiving some of the first Academy Awards (actually granted in 1929). This benchmark was meant to recognize that the cinema was "the" quintessential American and twentieth-century art form. Retrospectively, the technological changes from this year onward appear to have been manageable, in contrast to the unexpected plunge into the imminent Depression era. In fact, the industry continued to flourish throughout the thirties thanks to the gangster film and the musical, two genres that, together, articulated the tension between violence and escape, social commentary and utopian yearnings. Put another way, the industry's ability to survive one of the worst financial catastrophes in American economic history confirms the power of cinema as a looking glass for the masses. The latter were eager to negotiate hope and desperation through competing fictions of daily life.

While keeping in mind the power of Hollywood to adjust and diversify, a particular group of themes seems to hover around the sociohistorical context of the year. This is why the isolation provoked by a sort of historical blindness and the communal dimension of laughter, the flexibility of comedy in contrast to the rigid reversals of irony, the selfish quest of modern individualism and the possibility for human compassion, are topics worth exploring in relation to this year. To this end, I pay a special degree of attention to a few films because of their depth, subtlety, and self-reflection in regard to a certain American sensibility: Buster Keaton's *Steamboat Bill Jr.*, Paul Leni's *The Man Who Laughs*, and Josef von Sternberg's *The Last Command*. More specifically, references to laughter in *The Crowd* punctuate my discussion of the comic in *The Man Who Laughs*, and the maddening side of history in *The Last Command* is set against a certain kinetic restlessness that seems to haunt the American frontier in Victor Sjöstrom's *The Wind* and domestic life in *The Crowd*. Despite their use of a musical track as a form of melodramatic accompaniment, all these films do not just belong to the silent period, but also retrospectively mark the end of an era in the film industry and in American life.

King Vidor is the only major American director from the films chosen, while Leni, von Sternberg, and Sjöstrom are all European-born émigrés in Hollywood. This American cinema of émigré directors is characterized by exceptional acting, especially in terms of the contributions of Conrad Veidt in *The Man Who Laughs* and Emil Jannings in *The Last Command*. Put another way, these are film performers who do justice to Jacques Aumont's remark that the expressive possibilities of the human face and the posturing of the body reached their peak during the silent period (Aumont 127–48). It was during this marvelous year of organization and experimentation that looks and glances, close-ups of objects, amazingly accurate studio sets and crowd scenes made it clear once and for all: melodrama was silent cinema's most important register. In true keeping with the etymology of the term melodrama itself, filmic images thrived on the choreography of bodies in motion and on the eloquence of mute expressions. This was the case because the implied but inaudible speech in silent cinema was still supposed to lose itself into the visual poignancy of pantomime ranging from gesture to looking.

Melodrama may seem too mild a word for a year leading into a collective economic tragedy. Thus it makes sense to distinguish between tragedy and melodrama in such a way as to understand why and how the latter prevailed in the cinema of this year. To be sure, in Leni's *The Man Who Laughs* and von Sternberg's *The Last Command*, there are a few twists that hark back at the tragic idea of a fate so blind that it either repeats or reverses situations outside all human reason. As we learn from Peter Brooks, blindness is the mode of tragedy because this form presupposes that the all-seeing gods have more power than helpless humans (56–82). Thus, common mortals, unaware of what lies ahead, must accept cruel and humiliating developments that are the opposite of what they had hoped for.

Besides motoring Greek tragedy, the condition of not seeing or knowing the dangers and the pain that someone will be facing is also typical of cartoons. To be sure, the cliff-hanging moment is a standard of many animated narratives, and usually this kind of cinema is profoundly linked to laughter. This is the case because the viewers of cartoons can count on a happy ending for their hero. Most important, the link between blindness and ignorance and the cliff-hanger moment is only a temporary and sensational aspect of an overall narrative. Instead of amounting to a permanent condition based on a state of affairs that cannot be changed (the way it happens in tragedy), the cliff-hanger is the veritable extreme of the otherwise roller-coaster melodramatic structure of storytelling. Within this paradigm of motion and action, timing and speed, the last-minute rescue is the necessary corollary issued by the cliff-hanger situation. As soon as the viewer is willing to believe in the protagonist's survival from falling off the edge of a precipice, it becomes imperative to feel anxious about a co-protagonist charged with the duty of saving the day for all involved on-screen and off.

Even when cartoon characters know or see the dangers ahead, they go on as if an inexplicable or uncontrollable imperative of motion was much stronger than the one of safety. In film animation, the hero and the antagonist fall and resurface with an amazing degree of corporeal plasticity. After all, they are not human: on the contrary, they are simply made of moving lines, speed, and contours. Put another way, the bodies of animated figures are always indestructible, so that motion and transformation triumph over the finite experiences of life and death. This means that in cartoons constant spatial relocations win over the boundaries of time. How much a cartoon character does see or does know is hardly meaningful, because it is the behind-the-scenes human animator who occupies, at all times, a God-like position with access to maximum knowledge and vision.

New York, New York

Whereas the locations of cartoon characters can range from the Grand Canyon to the Arizona desert, a discussion of this year in American film must acknowledge the melodramatic lure of New York as the city of opportunities and dangers. Imagine a smoky pub, The Sandman, with cynical flappers and lots of drunks. Lonely and disillusioned, one of these women, the platinum blond (Betty Compson), attempts suicide but is fished out of the water by a tough stoker, Bill (George Bancroft), on leave for one night from his ship. Despite the seediness of the environment, the film ends with flapper and stoker committing to each other not just as husband and wife through a quick but official ceremony, but as two human beings in search of true love and mutual respect. Arrested because her clothes are stolen merchandise, at the last minute the stoker rescues his dame from jail. In the aftermath of the flapper's jump in the water, he felt compelled to come up with some wearable and dry outfits, but since nobody was in the store, he defiantly helped himself. Josef von Sternberg's *The Docks of New York* provides a glimpse of hope and sharing in a reckless, lonely, and nomadic world halfway between the criminal and the destitute.

Developed inside a Hollywood studio, The Sandman's set is competitive with von Sternberg's memorable tavern for *The Blue Angel* (1930). On the other hand, the quasi-documentary style at the beginning of von Sternberg's film is remarkable, with a highly mobile and independent camera surveying the gray waters of New York Harbor and documenting how timid the lineup of skyscrapers still looked at the end of the decade. Von Sternberg's emphasis on trading by ship strikes a note of nostalgia for the decades marked by long sea voyages preceding the airplane fad. The waves lapping against the docks and von Sternberg's camera capturing the Statue of Liberty remind the viewer that America can become everybody's country of adoption for a better life. The statue's silhouette, however, is far less memorable than the upside-down reflection of the flapper's image dancing around in the murky waters. Her trembling figure makes the viewer wonder what it takes for love to shift from a vague reflection into a much more delineated companionship. Put another way, von Sternberg's layered composition of the frame becomes introspective. Ironically, *The Docks of New York* starts with a descent into death, while it ends with no clear future. One could say that the film's surprising twists and unpredictable developments have little to do with superficial melodrama, and much more with what remains powerfully unsaid and existentially profound among the two main characters.

The City and the Masses

Interestingly, in *The Docks of New York*, the scenes involving groups of people are as frequent as the episodes devoted to the couple in private, so that it slowly becomes clear that the film is also a narrative about a community in search of itself. The rain, the fog, the mists—all these contribute to a dream-like atmosphere, and this is the reason why the film is one of the most poetic of von Sternberg's career. Besides *The Docks of New*

York, King Vidor's *The Crowd* is the most representative of Manhattan this year, while the plot is an ideal red thread to weave through this essay. *The Crowd* is also the film most in touch with the dilemmas of the lower-middle class struggling to move up in the world of bourgeois, comfortable living. Vidor's film specifies that optimistic John (James Murray) moves to New York as a twenty-one-year-old adult. Thus, the director informs us that his protagonist was born in 1900, on the Fourth of July, so it becomes clear that *The Crowd*'s narrative begins in 1921. Hence, its purpose is to chart a few years in a young man's life. The trajectory from 1921 to the present year should not be read in a futuristic, goal-oriented key, but rather as a reminder of John's smallness in comparison to a city with seven million people at this point in time. In fact, John's eventful arrival by boat does not prevent the director from dropping his protagonist out of the narrative for a while. To the contrary, Vidor turns his attention to Manhattan so that the city becomes a full character in its own right.

By mixing a rainy day of people carrying umbrellas with sunny days and the masses pouring out of the trains, Vidor alternates between superimposition and dissolves, bird's-eye views of roofs and rail tracks, in addition to even more comprehensive aerial shots of big and small boats sailing in the harbor. The general result of this montage sequence about the multiple faces of New York is a balance between documentary and avant-garde techniques, the realism of shooting on location and the precision of urban sets reconstructed in the studio.[1] To be sure, the documentary impulse is not alien to Vidor. In fact, the director is famous for having kept two chunks of quasi-improvisational footage in *The Crowd*, thus grounding his expressionist style in a real historical plight. The first insert from daily life involves a real-life cop telling traffic to move on. The second splicing of the New York landscape into *The Crowd* shows a desolate industrial location toward the end of the film.

Along with the documentary vein, Vidor stands out for his inclination toward social criticism. In *The Crowd*, the architecture of New York City is huge in comparison to the little employees who walk in and out of their dull offices on the equally impersonal floors of skyscrapers. Despite the financial power projected by these massive buildings, the values attached to human control are in a state of crisis. All individuals look like disposable commodities within the gaze of corporate power. Mass culture, in turn, seems to be made of little and subservient automatons crunching numbers and lining up. Hence, one's own sense of worthiness stems more from the approval of the others, while it depends a lot less on an authentic feeling of self-confidence.

At the end of *The Crowd,* Vidor's protagonist recuperates a sense of self-worth by laughing at a clown. The latter looks just like the clown John Sims had to become in order to survive economically, but he remains unable to recognize in this figure his own living double and self-image of alienation. Ironically, the more Vidor's everyday man behaves like a human being in pain, the more he steps outside the rhythm of his competitive colleagues. In the end, one wonders about some isomorphic relation between the indifferent, mechanical glass eye of the camera and the collective, dehumanizing image of mass culture. In fact, *The Crowd* deals with appearing or looking like everybody else, because its narrative concerns how human greed for material goods transforms our own sense of individuality into a nonhuman source of identity.

The Crowd demonstrates that in order to belong to the mass, the individual must give up a certain degree of introspection to the point of simplifying one's own self-image. Finally, since laughter is so ambiguously placed between joy and pain, while comedy can range from the superficial to the profound, the ending of Vidor's *The Crowd* is both self-conscious and inexhaustible. In other words, the American director manages to celebrate and question at the same time the mass culture to which he belongs. In *The Crowd,* John Sims finds work in an accounting firm, marries a lovely woman, Mary (Eleanor Boardman), and has two children, one boy and one girl. Money is tight, but the family budget improves when John draws an ad for a product called Sleight-o-Hand and receives a reward of $500. In order to visualize the theme of manual dexterity, John draws the image of a clown juggling balls. The choice of such a spectacular skill is not surprising, because in his happy moments John, too, juggles balls for his children on the beach. Likewise, in the tiny flat he shares with Mary, he plays the ukulele, speaks in rhymes, and loves to sing.

In the aftermath of the Sleight-o-Hand award, Mary and her husband lean out of their window to call their children back home and away from the busy street that is being used as a playground. Both parents are eager to show the kids their new toys. Framed in long shot by Vidor's camera, the apartment window cannot but echo the window shopping and actual purchasing that has just taken place. For a moment, domestic bliss seems to be measurable according to rates of consumption, but tragedy soon strikes. John and Mary's little girl is run over by a vehicle; the wheel of fate plunges downward, and John proceeds to lose one job after another, including one where he sells vacuum cleaners door to door; he starts drinking and even contemplates suicide in the middle of a rail yard.

James Murray and Eleanor Boardman in King Vidor's *The Crowd.*

Two events save John from total self-destruction and return him to his place inside an anonymous crowd of productive and quiet citizens. First, his own boy reminds him of his fatherly role as companion of games and fun; second, John, who, upon his first arrival in New York, had mocked a street clown juggling balls, takes on a street job. In a word, he becomes the clown he had previously drawn. Vidor's film ends with John reunited with his wife and his young boy, all of them happily laughing during a vaudeville show in a movie theater. The spectacle includes a reference to the Sleight-o-Hand ad. Hence, John can proudly tell his neighbor that he was the successful author of that image so ambiguously split between money and success, death and ridicule. Like the rest of American society hanging on the precipice of disaster, John is blind about the fatal consequences of his own skills.

Instead of showing viewers what his fictional audience is looking at, Vidor's camera often dwells on their faces distorted by the convulsions of laughter. It is as if happiness is contagious and group-building. Meanwhile, the negative side of the otherwise soothing power of the comic is that everybody is distorted or dehumanized into looking like everybody else. Nobody seems to be able to look at himself or herself through the help of a companion or a neighbor. Facial features lose their distinctive qualities and laughter becomes a way of leveling everybody's expression. No longer a visceral and liberating physical response that originates in the belly (Bakhtin), laughing here is mindless and devoid of any understanding of one's own place in the world in relation to others. Besides reversing power relations during the carnival, laughter can open human beings up to a sense of bonding with others, and even offer the glimpse of fulfillment reserved only to the gods. But in *The Crowd,* all the liberating and spiritual meanings of laughter have been reduced to empty entertainment.

This bitter sense of comedic homogeneity finds its telling anticipation in a previous scene from *The Crowd* set in the company's washroom at the end of a busy week. While John, with his back turned toward the camera, gets ready to leave the office for his double date with Bert, his colleagues go by and one after the other crack the same joke again and again. Humor, language, friendship, all seem to be in a state of redundancy under the heavy load of long rows of identical desks occupied by microscopic employees. This haunting image of industrial regimentation and human smallness is indeed what Vidor's unfastened and voyeuristic camera finds through the window of an immense skyscraper. At first, framed in an overpowering low angle, the skyscraper's vertical and smooth surface shows the vertigo of an impending downfall. But Vidor surprises us by climbing up to the top of corporate power, as if he were looking for an acrobatic performance through the cinema. Once again the cinematic apparatus explores the dangers of cliff-hanging, perhaps because cinema's origin is the result of a shift from the steady horizontal lines of pictorial perspective to a vertiginous engagement with unknown extremes placed either at the top or at the bottom. Finally, the contrast between the monumental architecture and the dull rows of accountants repeats itself in the hospital sequence. There

Mary's bed is lost in a crowd of other expecting and faceless women, to the point that one realizes how only identification numbers can guarantee the return of the right baby to the right mother.

Early on in *The Crowd,* Vidor shows his protagonist in high angle, halfway up the staircase leading to the room where his own father has just died. The frontal framing of Vidor's camera turns the space below into a claustrophobic tunnel. This corridor-like space has no exit, because it contains a crowd of observers at its bottom. The visual analogy between the crowd and a coffin could not be more complete. It is as if Vidor wanted to anticipate the link between public space, family, and death that will be explored later on in the film. More to the point, John climbing the stairs matches the high and low roller-coaster trajectory typical of melodramatic narrative. Furthermore, by not showing the father's room and by holding the shot steadily on John, Vidor underlines the idea that losing someone is comparable to standing on the edge of a psychological precipice. Put another way, the trope of the cliff-hanger not only belongs to action-packed films, but also to melodramas veering toward a tragic extreme.

John's and his father's dreams of greatness, of making it all the way to the top, retrospectively, look ironic if not self-destructive. Vidor manages to undermine the well-known Puritanical ethos about hard work and God's reward by using just a minimum number of elements: a stairwell, a face, and a group of people, all of it shot through a high angle. On the other hand, a strictly economic application of the American dream in the films of this particular year might be misleading. In fact, historians have noted that, by moving beyond an exploration of class identity, many films released this year underline over and over again the importance of romance and inner happiness (Ross 85). In *The Crowd,* love and marriage are central elements of the narrative because they document the switch from old Victorian morals, favoring arranged marriages to personal choices. Most important, the ups and downs between Mary and John are delineated with great attention to the constraints of their social class. In line with the fact that they live in an incredibly small flat, with a Murphy bed and a Murphy kitchen, they manage to share the usual mix of happy and not-so-happy moments experienced by most couples. As the narrative develops, Mary's identity as a modern woman stands out with particular force: on one hand, she does not hesitate to leave John several times when conflict is too unbearable; on the other, she is also protective of him and quite forgiving when it comes to his well-meaning but somewhat childish personality.

Divorce had been legal for some time in the United States, and women were further empowered this year by the development of the home pregnancy test. Just as in *The Docks of New York,* pre-Code Hollywood cinema does not hesitate to portray women who have the right through divorce to change their life's direction. Modern life also means a world where men and women are free to remain single and independent without having to bear any social stigma. This happens to John's friend, Bert, who drinks and dances the night away in the company of a few flappers.

While exploring a range of lifestyles, from John's nuclear family to Bert's fun-loving bachelorhood, Vidor suggests that Bert is more selfish and shrewd than John. The latter's inclinations involve the creative and imaginative side, since John can play music, draw, and sing. But art making is of no use in a greedy capitalist environment. By the end of *The Crowd,* it becomes clear that Bert has moved up the ladder of his company much more effectively than John, whose over-the-top fantasies doom him within the world of office politics. By setting up the career success of a pragmatic personality against a dreamer's survival, Vidor spells out that life is made of victories and losses. But even the twenties' economic imperative of quick success was coming to an end, so that Vidor's movie is the threshold film that marks the conclusion of prosperity and the beginning of the Depression. In contrast to Coney Island's roller coasters for young couples on an inexpensive date, the year and the portrayal of desperation in *The Crowd* are closer to the trope of the cliff-hanger. It is precisely because of this liminal and irreversible situation that the downward pull of gravity finds no counterpart in any curvy loop toward profound psychological recovery.

The Mystery of Keaton's Face

Notwithstanding the basic difference between tragic and melodramatic lack of foresight, similarities exist between Buster Keaton's feats in his films and the hoops cartoon characters go through. Everything is possible in comic strips, but what are the physical laws that regulate Keaton's balletic performance? His acting style seems to defy all basic relations of cause and effect so that the surreal elements of eccentric and unpredictable behavior are much stronger in a Keaton film than in a cartoon. In fact, a certain aura of loneliness and patient resilience makes this comedian unique in comparison to his much more readable contemporaries, the sentimental Charlie Chaplin and the conformist Harold Lloyd. A human being with no context in the world, Keaton seems to go through life as the eternal misfit who solves everybody's problems and fulfills all narrative expectations. At the same time, he is never a mere victim. To be sure, his inner formula is impenetrable. As Jay Telotte remarks, Keaton never smiles, so that "his films seem to show the individual deprived of all external supports and forced to constitute or give meaning to himself; he has typically been viewed—and valued—as a kind of proto-existentialist, an odd-ball creature who would, in turn, be embraced by Beckett and Sartre" (97).

When in *Steamboat Willie* (released on 18 May), Mickey Mouse prevails over a mean black cat according to an unbelievable chain of events, the monolithic and heroic mouse is easy to understand. But in *Steamboat Bill Jr.* (released on 20 May), Keaton is a living puzzle of incompatible features, despite the fact that his very human persona is never in question. William Canfield Jr. (Keaton) arrives in River Junction from Boston to meet his father, whose boating business is dwindling as a result of a much wealthier competitor, Mr. King (Tom McGuire). Short and thin in comparison to his towering and brutish parent, Keaton does not fit any code of strong and confident male identity. No matter which hat ends up on his head, something always seems ridiculous, aristocratic, or effeminate about the young man. When he walks out of the town's hat shop, the wind blows away a manly headdress chosen by his father, confirming that Bill is an unmanageable, unique creature no authority can control. Yet while he is inept in a traditional athletic sense, he slips in and out of water like a plastic fish. Though neither his appearance nor his behavior will ever be aligned with any kind of expectation about romance or physical strength, Keaton's unforeseeable terms of engagement prevail over every single situation he encounters, while his sheer presence makes the world appear to be on the edge of total collapse.

By the end of *Steamboat Bill Jr.*, Keaton does rescue a damsel in distress, Kitty King (Marion Byron), the daughter of his father's business rival and his own female friend from Boston. Mostly framed in long and medium shots, Keaton's silhouette wiggles itself out of any trap. Yet he is always at odds with machines, tools, and objects supposed to be used in a practical way. He is the ultimate hero of all kinds of last-minute rescues, because he fits nowhere and everywhere simultaneously. He can use all sorts of devices to help others, while he can barely survive himself, but he always does. Both heroic and off-centered in relation to the rest of the characters, Keaton's presence in the shot works like a destabilizing factor to further the action. At the same time, he appears to have no real agency in a world of floods, storms, and collapsing houses.

In short, Steamboat Bill Jr. does perform impossible feats just like Mickey Mouse, yet the hand-drawn cartoon animal is more conventional in an anthropomorphic sense than the famous, all-too-human comedian. Keaton keeps going like some kind of indestructible, extraterrestrial creature. Thus Keaton's performance is double-edged because it unfolds between the mechanical puppet and the shy romantic suitor. In the end, to understand the difference between Mickey and Bill, the key point is that cartoons have no mystery to be solved when it comes to their construction of character. On the contrary, it is through Keaton's transformation of his face into a blank mask that we renounce all psychological explanations and turn to the deepest mysteries of the human soul. So simultaneously profound and superficial can Keaton's countenance be that either laughter or tears seems always inappropriate as attributes. Still sad-looking at the peak of triumph, the comedian's expression can be so indifferent to the rest of the world that the viewer cannot help but imagine an unexplored and forever elusive continent behind his long mouth, thin nose, and slightly drooping eyes. Even when he is trying on different hats, for example, it is impossible to tell if he approves or disapproves of his reflection in the mirror. In the end, the viewer becomes aware that Keaton's refusal to reveal his private thoughts through his face enhances the plasticity of his external transformations to the point that he changes all the time, with every single hat.

Laughing or Crying?

Although the comparison between ancient tragedy and modern melodrama is useful in analyzing construction of characters and mass cultural responses, the blurry terrain between laughter and tears can be also studied in relation to the contrast between the hand-drawn cartoon and the photographic film, the artificial and the human. Philosophers and writers, such as Henri Bergson (1893) and Luigi Pirandello (1908), have defined the comic as a reaction induced by stress within an overly technological culture. Instead of being a kind of psychological relief and a form of joyous relaxation, laughter is an ironic, psychosomatic acknowledgment of someone's awareness but also inability to accept one's own pain.

In order to pursue this theory of laughter, one much more complicated than that usually associated with Disney's charming Mickey Mouse, I now dwell on Paul Leni's *The Man Who Laughs.* Like Vidor's *The Crowd,* Leni's melodrama intertwines laughter and suffering, the individual with the mass. As such, it challenges the difference between melodrama and tragedy on the one hand and comedy and melodrama on the other. But unlike Vidor's protagonist, Leni's "the man who laughs" stands for a quasi-divine gift to generate human introspection, even when the mass appears to be artificial, flat, monstrous, or dehumanized. The result leads to a series of interesting questions about modern conformity, human relations, the power of mass media, and the amorphous nature of the group.

In *The Man Who Laughs,* laughter is mostly linked to issues of either social superiority or class inferiority. Briefly the story: King James II (Sam De Grasse) orders the murder of his political rival Lord Clancharlie (Edgar Norton). Meanwhile the victim's little boy, Gwynplaine (Julius Molnar Jr.), is sold to a gang of Spanish mountebanks called "comprachicos" or child smugglers. In fact, they are notorious for kidnapping kids and subjecting them to a surgery that deforms their faces into a permanent laughing mask. After various reversals of fortune, the successor of James II, Queen Anne (Josephine Crowell), acknowledges the now-grown Gwynplaine's (Conrad Veidt) aristocratic lineage, brings him back to his rightful position in the House of Lords, and asks him to marry the sensual and decadent Duchess Josiane (Olga Baclanova). Social justice has triumphed, but personal happiness is still at stake.

Raised as an orphan by the philosopher Ursus (Cesare Gravina), Gwynplaine grows up and eventually falls in love with an angelic-looking blind girl, Dea (Mary Philbin). Her name means "goddess," whereas Gwynplaine's name evokes the idea of the plain face he will never have. Found in the middle of a snowstorm and in the arms of a dead mother, Dea is rescued by the little boy who recognizes in her another creature abandoned by God and humankind. The two children's savior, Ursus, bears the name of a strong man, even though he is an intellectual. Indeed, Gwynplaine and Dea are two survivors of the historical process, and their ability to live through the evils of power can only find an adequate explanation through the strength of philosophy of ideas about being and the nature of the world itself. To the contrary, history seems to belong much more to the Court of England and to the easily duped masses attending the staged events and the freak shows at the fairgrounds.

Based on an 1869 novel by Victor Hugo, set in seventeenth-century England, and produced by the German expatriate Carl Laemmle for Universal Studios, *The Man Who Laughs* exhibits many stylistic features harking back to the legacy of German Expressionism. Most expressionistic is the laughing grin literally "cut" into Gwynplaine's face: a frozen and grotesque combination of pain and joy whose indelible and unchanging physiognomy has all the intentional qualities of a cruel artist's signature—a tragic and ironic residue of an old-fashioned manual skill before the modern serialization of images. Twisted by the surgeon's knife, the angles of Gwynplaine's mouth never move out of their extreme angles, and, as such, they echo the bright red lips of a clown. But Leni's clown is very different from Vidor's in

Conrad Veidt in Paul Leni's *The Man Who Laughs.*

The Crowd. Most remarkable is Veidt's acting style, a marvel of the silent period: his eyes and postures speak volumes about love and rebellion, empathy and revenge, shyness and desire. In the end, this amazingly talented actor conveys levels of human emotion and nuances of inner thought, regardless of the fact that he works behind the most rigid and humiliating of masks. This is because of the way Veidt angles his face in relation to his torso: he slightly bends forward, while his hands are as expressive as the movements of his neck. Frail and strong at the same time, Veidt's thin and tall body imposes itself on the framed space with an aristocratic and innate sense of authority, so that the viewers are urged to guess a reservoir of knowledge and compassion hidden behind his stupid, if not cruel, grin.

The Man Who Laughs includes a long episode set at the Southwark Fair where many different kinds of stage performances spell out the popular, fantastic, and humble origins of the cinema, a medium that found its first audiences in the midst of all sorts of grotesque theatrical acts. Some of these spectacles include strange animals and bearded women, Siamese twins and odd acrobats. Every stand has a colorful sign or a loud barker to encourage the crowd to witness either the most horrific or the most sensational display. This whole sequence was carefully reconstructed in the studios of Universal, and its amazing level of historical accuracy was invoked during the distribution of the film as an art object for selected screenings in carefully chosen cities. As soon as we attend the show of "The Man Who Laughs" during the Southwark Fair, it becomes clear that the ridiculous and the grotesque registers are not what Leni's protagonist is all about.

Significantly, Gwynplaine belongs neither to the stage nor to the audience. In fact, during his performance, he stands on the edge of the theater beyond the curtain, but above the sitting area. From this interstitial locale, he slowly moves. Meanwhile, Veidt looks at his audience with his soft and lively eyes set against the same expression of stupid and motionless laughing cut into his face. This is why, when the masses react contemptuously, Leni's camera instead sees something that no fictional spectator can grasp. Whereas Keaton's unchanging mask absorbs our own ever-shifting expectations in front of different hats, The Man Who Laugh's face wears a special kind of mysterious smile. It is not an exaggeration to say that *The Man Who Laughs* tackles the power of an enigmatically smiling face as much as Leonardo did with his Mona Lisa, the famous painting where the natural landscape is historically recognizable, but the human element remains a puzzle of speculation open to something uncanny.

In other words, Gwynplaine has the smile of an ancient god fallen in the midst of human history. He benevolently looks down, making us realize the frail vantage point we occupy and from which we consider ourselves to be at the center of the universe. It is this confusion between small and big that the eye of the cinema—the medium of the close-up as the quintessential locus of confusion between the microscopic and the gigantic—can capture better than the human eye. It is not surprising, therefore, that by the end of the narrative, unable to fit into the petty rivalries of human history, the philosopher Ursus, the blind goddess of tragedy Dea, and the smiling god Gwynplaine run away by ship for an exile that may last well beyond time.

Hollywood Looks at Itself

One more reason exists why these three films, *Steamboat Willie Jr., The Crowd,* and *The Man Who Laughs,* fit so well together in this essay. It is as if Vidor's clown, Keaton's man who never smiles, and Leni's laughing god are all masks about self-knowledge on the threshold of disaster. Within this threesome of films about the human face as source of knowledge and vision, the presence of Leni's is paradigmatic of Hollywood's expatriate population seeking success abroad. This new contingent of creative talent, in fact, competed with American-born directors, like Vidor, who before the installment of the Hays Code were still free to question the American Tayloristic system from within the Hollywood industry.[2] On the other hand, taken together, Leni and Vidor demonstrate the close links between the United States and northern Europe. This American–northern European axis not only concerned Hollywood, but, as we have seen, the management of American immigration according to Washington's policies. In his recent book *America by Design*, Aristide Zolberg demonstrates how northern Europeans were much more welcome into the country than southern immigrants. Thus, thanks to the combined efforts of recent arrivals from abroad and longstanding citizens with an eye for social criticism, one could argue that, during the twenties, the previously used metaphor of the invisible precipice should alternate with that of the looking glass. But this heightened sense of social awareness belongs to Vidor's personal signature more than to Hollywood in general. After dealing with issues of unemployment and social consensus in *The Crowd*, that very same year King Vidor went on to shoot *Show People*, a film about the Hollywood industry as a site of labor. Always on the side of Mickey Mouse or the little guy who can make it against all odds, Vidor criticizes egomaniac directors involved in pretentious Europhile costume dramas. Thus, he aligns himself with lighthearted and lowbrow comedies punctuated by pies flying from one face to the next. Laughter, here, is not about stupidity, but rather about a new culture of action and entertainment and pokes fun at Hollywood's clumsiness with highbrow foreign models and failing imitations.

A much darker example of ironic commentary on the industry comes from the Viennese Josef von Sternberg's *The Last Command*, starring the German-born Emil Jannings (1884–1950). A melodrama about an old Russian general who becomes a humble extra performing under the directorial eye of his former Bolshevik antagonist, *The Last Command* invokes the image of a precipice-like space waiting for its next victim. Jannings, however, reached one of the peaks of his long career through this film, since he received the first Academy Award for acting. There is no question that such professional recognition was well deserved. In *The Last Command*, the proud general manages to soften his gait and lighten up his performance to play the role of seducer as soon as he meets a beautiful Bolshevik revolutionary. It is hard to tell how Jannings, with his rather heavy-set figure and undeniable age, can switch—in a fraction of a second—from a military but also humane posture to a clearly erotic yet formal inquiry about his lady's intentions.

As the title of the film suggests, this is the story of a last command held by an old general. Under the shadow of death, he turns into a resilient fighter who commands his former rival's admiration on the set. Yet life and death intermix during the performance, so that a compelling psychoanalytic dimension hovers over the emotions of the past coming back to life. While a Hollywood rehearsal happens to function like the talking cure, General Alexander Sergius utters his last words: "I won." Thus, he dies on a studio-made barricade. On the one hand, the low angle used by von Sternberg lends a monumental, heroic quality to Emil Jannings's corpse lying on the ground of the set. On the other, the cardboard setting and the electrical fan used by the director to simulate an artificial wind spell out Hollywood's crass sense of the historical European past. Although the gap between the Old and the New World is too deep to bridge, it is the former Bolshevik antagonist (William Powell), now Hollywood director and alter ego for von Sternberg himself, who offers a concluding and respectful epitaph about a man who took his job as a general of the czar most seriously.

Much more to the point for the historical context of the year, in *The Last Command* the expatriate von Sternberg is able to include an uncanny sequence that functions with an economic foresight about the American domestic situation. After showing an endless line of jobless individuals seeking some employment in Hollywood, von Sternberg uses a long tracking shot to illustrate the clothing of an extra on the set. As if he were going through the unfriendly windows of a pawnshop specializing in many kinds of items, Alexander Sergius manages to get by the assembly line of a Hollywood wardrobe: fur coat, boots, and military decorations land on his body, thus reconstituting his old self from a few years earlier. During the film, it also becomes apparent that it would be impossible for any viewer after this year to look at the breadline of hundreds of recent immigrants in Hollywood without flashing forward toward equivalent images of the unemployed during the Great Depression.

Winds of Change

The ghost of the assembly line—straight and repetitive—haunts Vidor's *The Crowd* as well as von Sternberg's *The Last Command*. For Alexander Sergius sitting in the studio makeup room, Hollywood is a Ford-like factory of generals, soldiers, peasants, and revolutionaries. In the makeup room, his neighbor, another extra struggling to make some money, complains that the old general's face twitches out of control as he looks at himself in the mirror, at the beginning of a long explanatory flashback about his vicissitudes in love and war. "I had a shock," Alexander answers while his own expression is incredulous about his present predicament. The dimension of the surreal grotesque so often explored by Luigi Pirandello

Emil Jannings in Joseph von Sternberg's *The Last Command.*

truly applies to this moment of incredulity or self-estrangement in front of a mirror that yields back the face of a stranger to its user.

At first sight it would seem that the films examined here are about conformist and orderly lives because of the emphasis on organization in the workplace. The question many have asked boils down to this: Were the twenties roaring or boring? But the fact is that *The Crowd* and *The Last Command* alike are filled with anxiety about not only the uncontrollable changes of history, but also the dangers of new choices, unfamiliar environments. This anguish about the winds of change travels from the electric fan used on the set of *The Last Command* to Victor Sjöström's *The Wind,* starring Lillian Gish in a Liliana story set on the frontier and suffused with an introspective and nightmarish use of landscape. Famous for his emphasis on open and natural landscapes, Sjöström's camera hardly goes outdoors in *The Wind.* Just like his female protagonist, Sjöström's camera is not only afraid of natural elements, but of change altogether. Letty (Gish), a young woman from the city, travels alone for the very first time to visit her beloved married cousin in California, while also hoping to build a new life for herself. Despite its frontier theme and cowboy characters, *The Wind* is not a western but a melodrama about an anxious female mind inside the most claustrophobic of spaces and under the highest pressure for movement. Over and over again, Sjöstrom shows us Gish's frail body being swept away and shaken up by the winds blasting the prairies outside the door.

Replete with references to animal flesh, butchery, and brutal sexuality, it is hard to tell if *The Wind*'s outdoor scenes of sandstorms are in any way exaggerated by the protagonist's stress in relation to a series of circumstances: traveling to an unknown land, surviving with no money, female rivalry in the family space, and rape in an environment so desolate that no legal defense can be found. Envious of the affectionate bond between Letty and her husband (Edward Earle), the cousin's jealous wife (Dorothy Cumming) does not hesitate to suggest violence and revenge. The blood on her knife speaks volumes of anger against Letty's quiet and clean use of the ironing board. Stalked by a rough cowboy (Montagu Love) she had met on the train, Letty decides to marry a local man (Lars Hanson) she does not love in such a way as to acquire some protection. This ruse, however, is not sufficient to prevent her persecutor from trying to rape her. In self-defense she not only kills him, but takes his corpse out in the middle of a storm to bury him under the sand. By this point in the narrative, however, Letty's fears of the incessant wind is so exasperated that it is hard to tell if the rape and the killing are figments of her out-of-control imagination or actual events.

With an uncanny feeling for the ways in which the supernatural can originate out of nature and weave itself with a sexual dimension, Sjöstrom sets up an intriguing analogy between the fantastic images of a white Indian horse born out of leaping flames and Letty's physical frame twisted by the wind as she tries to join the men outdoors. Eventually, love and trust grow between Letty and her husband. By then, however, Sjöstrom's narrative has made two points: the power of financial independence in soothing a woman's anxiety and the ways in which her experience teaches Letty about people and feelings. In contrast to Emil Jannings's extremely fast twitching imposed on his face by public history, the pronounced undulations and curvilinear reshaping of Gish's body is a reaction to the natural elements. Her acting style can be read as a series of emotional responses externalized for the sake of a film with an epic breath. Yet this melodrama of feminine autonomy and the discovery of sexual emotions is more in line with the tradition of German Kammerspiel than with the outdoor locations and natural lighting typical of Sjöstrom's Swedish films. In *The Wind*, the weakest level of privacy is endangered by the sand's penetration on the floor, the dishes, and, of course, the protagonist's consciousness.

Urban dwellers and tough pioneers come together during this year of meaningful changes, but the contemporary cinema was especially adept at telling stories about human finitude and internal transformation, as if the moving image itself could override the producers' instructions and the public's blind optimism. It is amazing how, through their insightful artistic temperaments, Vidor, Keaton, and various expatriate directors such as von Sternberg and Sjöstrom captured the hidden or invisible side of imminent traumas standing up against an imaginary future of unstoppable growth and impossible plenitude.

NOTES

1. I am referring here to two famous city films: Alberto Cavalcanti's *Rien que les heures* (1927) and Walter Ruttmann's *Berlin, Symphony of a City* (1928).

2. Named after its founder, Frederick Taylor, Taylorism originated in the United States in the late nineteenth century as the scientific management of labor, in which factory work was to be made more efficient by giving control to foremen. Workers were instructed in how to most efficiently fulfill their tasks and were paid when they met the factory's norms or quotas (Blackford 76).

1929

Movies, Crashes, and Finales

LUCY FISCHER

Wide Angle: The American Scene

During the 1920s there had been an extended boom in stock prices, with values quadrupling over a nine-year period. Investors, convinced that this trend was endless, continued to borrow funds to plow back into the market. When Herbert Hoover was inaugurated on 4 March, displacing Calvin Coolidge, he had predicted: "We shall soon, with the help of God, be in sight of the day when poverty will be banished from this nation." Yet this year would bring the stock market crash and would always be associated with it in American history. On 25 March a mini-crash had ensued with the *New York Daily News* reporting a "selling avalanche." During the spring and summer, the market rebounded, although various sectors of the economy showed signs of trouble (steel production, construction, car sales, and consumer debt). On 3 September, the market reached its apex, with the Dow Jones Industrial Average closing at 381.17. Sounding an ominous note, however, economist Roger Babson predicted that "a crash is coming." During September and early October, the market fluctuated madly, then on 18 October began to fall precipitously. On 24 October "Black Thursday" occurred, with stock prices plunging steeply and some 12,894,650 shares being traded—a paper loss of $5 billion. Just four days later, on "Black Monday," the stock market plummeted another 22.6 percent, the largest one-day loss in U.S. history. Markets around the globe responded in kind. Finally on 29 October ("Black Tuesday"), total alarm set in and over 16 million shares of stock were liquidated, with a $14 billion paper loss. On 23 November, the market hit its nadir, then stabilized. The causes of "The Great Crash" were numerous but included widespread speculation, the expansion of holding companies and investment trusts, and the proliferation of large bank loans.

While the stock market crash was the most sensational news item of the year, other national events garnered headlines. On 14 February, the St.

Valentine's Day Massacre (attributed to Al Capone) took place in Chicago, ending in the deaths of six members of the George "Bugs" Moran gang. On 1 July, the Immigration Act of 1924 was finally enforced, fixing an annual quota at 150,000 foreign individuals. On the agricultural front, a Mediterranean fruit fly invasion ravaged the nation's citrus crop (Allen 244).

As for America's broader social life: 70 percent of the nation's industries were electrified (Dumenil 58); most laborers worked a 44.2 hour week (Dumenil 79); Ku Klux Klan membership declined (Goldberg, *America* 106); and "only" nine lynchings took place (Miller 292). Divorces topped 205,000 (Miller 271) as some proclaimed the existence of "nervous housewife syndrome" (Dumenil 123). A family of four required an annual income of $2,500 to survive, but nearly 27 million families fell below the poverty line (Miller 282). Conversely, the *Wall Street Journal* touted the existence of many citizens worth more than $50 million (Miller 282). Union membership declined to 3.4 million in nonagricultural areas (Miller 282), and numerous coal miners lost their jobs as some 550,000 houses chose oil heat (Miller 287).

Culturally, the year saw the release of several influential literary works (many of which would eventually be adapted for the screen). Ernest Hemingway published *A Farewell to Arms,* which drew upon the author's experience as a young soldier in Italy during the Great War; William Faulkner's *The Sound and the Fury* appeared, an experimental novel that used interlocking monologues from different decades to tell the story of three southern brothers; and Sinclair Lewis published *Dodsworth,* which recounted the experiences of an American businessman and his wife on a grand European tour. In addition, two short stories by Katherine Ann Porter appeared: "Theft" and "The Jilting of Granny Weatherall."

As part of the Harlem Renaissance, Nella Larsen published *Passing,* her second novel, about the romantic fates of two light-skinned black women. Poet Countee Cullen released *Black Christ & Other Poems,* a work that sometimes took a political slant. Referencing the KKK in "To Certain Critics," Cullen asserted that "never shall the clan confine my singing to its ways beyond the ways of man" (63). Similarly, in "Black Majesty," Cullen considered his African ancestors and states: "These men were black, I say, but they were crowned and purple-clad, however brief their time" (64).

As for public commentary, Walter Lippmann published *A Preface to Morals,* a meditation on modernity and the "dissolution of the ancestral order." While many writers were exhilarated with contemporaneity, Lippmann highlighted the "vacancy in [peoples'] lives" (1, 3). Joseph Wood Krutch's *The Modern Temper* dealt with such topics as "The Disillusion with the Laboratory," "Love—or the Life and Death of a Value," or "The Phantom of Certitude," portraying the modern universe as "one in which the human spirit [could not] find a comfortable home" (xi). And sociologists Robert S. and Helen Merrell Lynd released *Middletown: A Study in Modern American Culture,* based on their observation of the small city of Muncie, Indiana. The novelty of their work was to treat middle-class America as comparable to the kind of "tribe" usually examined by anthropologists. Sections of the tome investigated such topics as "Getting a Living," "Making a Home," "Training the Young," "Using Leisure," "Engaging in Religious Practices," and "Engaging in Community Activities."

In American art, the momentous event of the year was the 7 November opening in New York City of the Museum of Modern Art, on Fifth Avenue and Fifty-seventh Street. (About a decade later, MoMA would become the first American museum to open a department of film.) The first exhibit was composed entirely of loans and entitled "Cézanne, Gauguin, Seurat, van Gogh." Indeed, at the time of the institution's historic opening, many American modernist artists were living in Paris, the center of cutting-edge aesthetic movements. Thus, from their European quarters, Alexander Calder produced wire pieces (*Circus Scene, Self-Portrait,* and *Kiki de Montparnasse*); Man Ray created photographs (*Lee Miller*) and oils (*Tableau ton goût* and *Gens du monde*); and Stuart Davis fashioned lithographs (*Places des Vosges, Hôtel de France*) and oils (*Arch Hotel*). On the American front, John Marin worked in New Mexico, painting watercolors (*The Mountain, Taos, New Mexico,* and *On the Road to Santa Fe, New Mexico*), while Arthur Dove produced paintings (*Alfie, Colored Barge Man, Distraction,* and *Colored Drawing*). In New York, Georgia O'Keeffe painted *The American Radiator Building,* portraying an edifice constructed in 1924. Likewise, her partner Alfred Stieglitz opened his gallery (called An American Place) on Madison Avenue (Schmied 49).

As for popular culture, the year saw the premiere of Popeye, drawn by E. C. Segar, in the comic strip *Thimble Theatre*. The earliest adventure strip, *Tarzan,* also debuted, created by Harold Foster. Finally, the year saw the production of the first four-color comic publication (not yet a true comic book). Sales of radios reached $412 million, up from $11 million eight years earlier (Goldberg 13). Guy Lombardo (who had recently begun a long booking at the Roosevelt Grill in New York City) began broadcasting from there over WABC, and Rudy Vallee (who appeared in the film *Vagabond Lover*) started performing on the Fleischmann's Yeast Hour. In August, "Amos & Andy" debuted on NBC radio. Connections between the radio and cinema proliferated. New York's Roxy (Movie) Theatre began broadcasting a Sunday afternoon concert over WJZ (Melnick 228); MGM collaborated with toaster maker Auto-Grill to launch a series of programs; Paramount and CBS merged; and Fox Studio received its own radio frequency (Hilmes 53).

Important advances were also made in the development of television. Electronic engineer Vladimir Kosma Zworykin, who had been working at Westinghouse in Pittsburgh since 1920, demonstrated the "camera tube" or "Kinescope" on 18 November, a device that had "all the essential properties of a modern television viewing tube" (Zworykin, qtd. in Hilmes 55).

Panorama: The Film Industry

On a corporate level in the film industry, two significant events took place. The Radio Corporation of America (RCA) established RKO studios, an "instant major" (Hilmes 54), and Walt Disney Productions, Ltd. was formed by incorporating Walt Disney Studios, Disney Film Recording, and Walt Disney Enterprises. Equally dramatic was the first awards ceremony held by the Academy of Motion Picture Arts and Sciences, on 16 May at Hollywood's Roosevelt Hotel.[1]

The era of the movie palace was still in full swing. Among such buildings that opened this year: the Fox Theatre (28 June) in San Francisco; Loew's Paradise (September) in New York City; and the Fox Theatre (25 December) in Atlanta. The Embassy in New York City (which had opened four years earlier) became the first "all news house" as well.

Technical achievements were also made. Irving Cummings and Raoul Walsh's *In Old Arizona* was the first full-length talking film to be shot outdoors (rather than in a studio), and King Vidor's *Hallelujah!* pioneered post-synchronization of sound. Harry Beaumont's *The Broadway Melody* was the first original musical and earned some $3 million for MGM. George Eastman demonstrated his first Technicolor movie in Rochester, New York, and the first full-length sound film produced entirely in two-strip Technicolor (Alan Crosland's *On with the Show!*) was exhibited in New York. Finally, twenty-four frames per second was established as the standard camera speed for sound motion pictures.

As for cinema production, the year was fairly schizophrenic, with filmmaking split between silent, sound, and hybrid movies. While sound projection speed had been standardized, the language for referring to such films was not. A perusal of *Variety* reviews discloses a dizzying surfeit of terminology to categorize them, including "dialog," "sound," "half dialog," "all dialog," "10 percent dialog with song," "100 percent talking," "dialog and songs," "all dialog with songs," "10 percent dialog," "songs only," "no dialog," "25 percent dialog," "1/4 dialog," and "Sound." Among the year's silent pictures (those shot without sound even if outfitted with a synchronized score), we find such works as Edward Sedgwick's *Spite Marriage*, W. S. Van Dyke's *The Pagan*, Frank Lloyd's *The Divine Lady*, and Erich von Stroheim's *Queen Kelly*. In the talking category, we note such films as Lionel Barrymore's *The Unholy Night*, Hobart Henley's *The Lady Lies*, and F. Richard Jones's *Bulldog Drummond*. To confuse things more, some movies were released in both silent and sound versions (since some theaters were not yet adequately wired), among them Clyde Bruckman and Malcolm St. Clair's *Welcome Danger* (with Harold Lloyd) and Lewis R. Foster and Hal Roach's *Unaccustomed as We Are* (with Laurel and Hardy). As Robert Allen has noted, the response of moviegoers to audio technology was still mixed: "As late as January 1929, for example, a survey of movie-goers in Syracuse, New York, found that only 50 percent preferred talkies to silents, and only 7 percent favored elimination of silent film" (14).

Interestingly, a few works of the year involved a plot point of ventriloquism (a resonant theme for the coming of sound). In James Cruze's *The Great Gabbo*, Erich von Stroheim plays a deranged and abusive ventriloquist who is cruel to his female assistant and treats his dummy as though he were real. And in Frank Tuttle's *The Studio Murder Mystery Tour*, the culprit is a film director who hides the fact that he has killed people by throwing voices from his victims' dead bodies, making others think that they are still alive. Clearly, the latter film (with its murderous cineaste) also tapped into film colony scandals of the 1920s.

Sound had already begun to have a transformative effect on the careers of stars. Many made their last silent appearances this year: Ramon Novarro in *The Pagan*, Janet Gaynor in William K. Howard's *Christina*, Laurel and Hardy in Lewis R. Foster's *Angora Love*, Joan Crawford in Jack Conway's *Our Modern Maidens*, John Gilbert in William Nigh's *Desert Nights*, and Gloria Swanson in *Queen Kelly*. Some also uttered their first onscreen words: Gaynor in Frank Borzage's *Lucky Star* and David Butler's *Sunny Side Up*, Douglas Fairbanks in Allan Dwan's *The Iron Mask* and Sam Taylor's *The Taming of the Shrew*, Novarro in Sidney Franklin's *Devil-May-Care*, Crawford in Jack Conway's *Untamed*, Harry Langdon in Lewis R. Foster's *Hotter Than Hot*, Swanson in Edmund Goulding's *The Trespasser*, Gilbert in Lionel Barrymore's *His Glorious Night*, Mary Pickford in *Coquette*, the "Our Gang" players in Robert F. McGowan's *Small Talk*, and Clara Bow in Dorothy Arzner's *The Wild Party* (the only film mentioned thus far directed by a woman). Another star could be said to have uttered his first words this year, period: Mickey Mouse, in *Karnival Kid*.

With such radical change in production methods, some careers were bound to decline. The most famous is John Gilbert's; reportedly his voice was ridiculed at a screening of *His Glorious Night*—an ironic title, in retrospect (Corey and Ochoa 46). Keaton, Bow, Pickford, and Swanson fared not much better, though their loss of favor was also due to a shift in popular screen types. Other stars like Crawford, Greta Garbo, and von Stroheim made the transition successfully—despite the fact that the latter two could have been hampered by their foreign accents. Another European, Maurice Chevalier (whose French pronunciation was considered "charming"), made his first Hollywood film: Richard Wallace's *Innocents of Paris*. While von Stroheim, the performer, finessed the shift to sound, his directorial career floundered with the production of *Queen Kelly*, from which he was fired for going over budget. Sound continued to impel Hollywood to import talent from the Broadway stage (as both performers and writers). Among such celebrities were the Marx Brothers and Paul Muni and screenwriters S. J. Perelman, George S. Kaufman, S. N. Behrman, Donald Ogden Stewart, George Abbott, and Robert Benchley.

A survey of films reveals that all established genres are present. The exotic adventure film is represented in *The Pagan*; the social problem film in Dorothy Davenport's *Linda*; the courtroom drama in Albert S. Rogell's *Painted Faces*; the literary adaptation in Edward Carewe's *Evangeline* (based on a Longfellow poem) or *The Iron Mask* (based on Dumas's *The Three Musketeers*); the classical theatrical adaptation in *The Taming of the Shrew*; the ethnic ghetto film in Frank Capra's *The Younger Generation*; the combat film in Henry King's *She Goes to War*; the thriller in *Bulldog Drummond*; the murder mystery in Tod Browning's *The Thirteenth Chair*, George Melford's *The Charlatan* and *The Unholy Night*, and Edward Laemmle's *The Drake Case*; the historical drama in Alfred F. Green's *Disraeli*; the western in Victor Fleming's *The Virginian*, Spencer Gordon Bennet's *Hawk of the Hills* and *In Old Arizona;* the gangster film in Howard Higgin's *The Racketeer*; the melodrama in *Coquette*, Lothar Mendes's *Dangerous Curves*, and William Wyler's *The Love Trap*; the comedy in James W. Horne and Leo McCarey's *Big Business* (with Laurel and Hardy), *Welcome Danger* (Harold Lloyd), Charles H. Rogers's *Skirt Shy* (Harry Langdon), and Robert F. McGowan's *Noisy Noises* (Our Gang).

The high-grossing films of the year reflect these myriad genres: *The Broadway Melody* ($4.4 million), *Bulldog Drummond* ($1.6 million), *Coquette* ($1.4 million), *The Taming of the Shrew* ($1.1 million), as well as Charles Brabin's *The Bridge of San Luis Rey*, *Disraeli*, *The Divine Lady*, *In Old Arizona*, *Innocents of Paris*, Lucien Hubbard's *The Mysterious Island*, *The Iron Mask*, *Lucky*

Star, The Pagan, S. Sylvan Simon's *Rio Rita,* Frank Borzage's *The River, Small Talk, Spite Marriage,* and *The Virginian.*

Outside of the Hollywood system, however, the year saw developments in the avant-garde cinema, though few filmgoers of the era would have seen such works. Ralph Steiner made *H_2O,* a poetic, abstract treatise on water that shows it flowing, cascading, raining, and forming ocean waves as well as constituting a surface for a modernist light and shadow play. Robert Florey shot *Skyscraper Symphony,* a city symphony and tribute to New York's high-rise buildings (through split screen imagery, low-angle framing, and rotating shots). Charles Vidor made *The Bridge* (an adaptation of Ambrose Bierce's "Occurrence at Owl Creek Bridge"), a work that presents the protagonist's imagined visions as he dies.

Finally, beyond sound technology, another major development involved the expansion of color film production using either the two-strip Technicolor or the Multicolor process. Films with color sequences included *The Mysterious Island, The Great Gabbo, Sunny Side Up,* and Victor Schertzinger's *Redskin.*

Genre, Race, and the Musical

Invoking the title of this chapter, there are two senses of the word *finale* that might be referenced. First is its definition as the last and often climactic event in a sequence; second, its designation as the last section of an instrumental musical composition. Both meanings will be cited because the dual implications of the term simultaneously summon up the realms of social history (climactic events) and of art (compositions). This diptych seems a particularly fitting framework in which to examine the trajectory of the year, simultaneously the last one of the twenties, the year the Depression begins, and an important year in film history. Aside from "finale," there are other terms to be employed that have dual connotations, among them *crash.* On the one hand it signifies a sudden decline or failure, as of a business—and, clearly, this pertains to the infamous stock exchange collapse of the year. But, on the other, it means a loud sound—which potentially returns us to the realm of music and art.

Here, the focus concerns the year's import in the development of the film musical—because, while 1927 may have ushered in *The Jazz Singer,* this was the year in which the genre proliferated and came of age. One film, in particular, contains a sequence that is almost self-reflexive in this regard. At one point in *Sunny Side Up,* Jack Cromwell (Charles Farrell) pledges his love to Molly Carr (Janet Gaynor) by addressing her photograph on his bureau. Suddenly, her picture becomes animated and sings to him a verse from the song "You've Got Me Pickin' Petals Off o' Daisies" (written by Ray Henderson, with lyrics by Buddy G. DeSylva and Lew Brown). As if this were not an adequate metaphor for the sound musical, the film also contains a song by the same authors entitled "If I Had a Talking Picture of You," which Farrell croons to Gaynor's photo. Its lyrics include the following lines:

> On the screen the moment you came in view
> We would talk the whole thing over, we two.
> I would give ten shows a day,
> and a midnight matinee,
> If I had a talking picture of you.

While many silent films were accompanied by piano players, live bands, or orchestras, it was, of course, the coming of sound that allowed the musical genre to develop and flourish. Clearly, the mode brought a new breed of stars from Broadway, vaudeville, the recording industry, and radio, including Al Jolson, Jeanette MacDonald, Marion Harris, Rudy Vallee, and Eddie Cantor. It also forced several silent screen players to try their hand (or voice) at singing, not always with sanguine results, as was the case with Gaynor and Farrell in *Sunny Side Up*. As evidence of the popularity of the musical, some of the highest grossing films of the year fell in that category: *Broadway Melody*, Alan Crosland's *On with the Show!*, *Broadway*, and Leo McCarey's *Red Hot Rhythm*.

The Sounds of Silence

In fact, the year saw a plethora of varied musical formats that have not been equaled in diversity since. On one level, we might even consider certain late silent films "proto-musicals." We can make this argument about *Our Modern Maidens* (released 24 August), the second part of an MGM trilogy that included *Our Dancing Daughters* (1928) and *Our Blushing Brides* (1930). All starred Joan Crawford (and featured Anita Page) as beautiful single women of the Jazz Age dealing with romance, and, in the final film, with work. The first two installments (released before the stock market crash) place the girls in settings of luxury and wealth that allowed MGM to flaunt its gorgeous Art Deco set designs and costumes. Specifically, *Our Modern Maidens* depicts a group of young people who have just graduated from school. The very first sequence shows them celebrating after the prom by hot-rodding and dancing outdoors to the tunes of a radio show that broadcasts music from a hotel in Washington, D.C. As a film that includes a synchronized score, the sound track conjoins the popular song "Should I?" to the images of the youngsters dancing. Similarly, a shot of a guy lying

A poster for *The Broadway Melody* designed with Art Deco graphics.

in a car's rumble seat playing the flute is matched on the sound track with a selection from *The Barber of Seville*. Almost immediately, the narrative concentrates on the glamorous Billie Brown (Crawford)—dressed in a spangled, elegant gown (with a transparent bodice), and her relationship with beau Gil Jordan (Douglas Fairbanks Jr.) and best friend Kentucky Strafford (Page), who, unbeknownst to her pal, is also smitten with Gil. Viewers would have known the (unsung) lyrics to "Should I?" which, significantly, ask: "Should I reveal exactly how I feel? Should I confess I love you?"

As evidence of the liberated spirit of the time, these youngsters are staying out all night and must catch a 7 A.M. train home. On board, they frolic, shoot dice, and pour themselves lunch. Gil plans to be a diplomat and Billie (the daughter of a rich motor car magnate) has high ambitions for him, wanting his first post to be Paris. When she recognizes the influential politician Glenn Abbott (Rod La Rocque) boarding the train, she "accidentally" walks into his car, flirts with him, and invites him to her upcoming Fourth of July bash, hoping to use him to secure an international assignment for Gil. The film next cuts to the party, which is set in the chic, lavish home of the Browns—replete with such Art Deco design and architectural touches as geometric wall sconces, accordion-pleated molding, abstractly decorated door panels, *moderne* pedestals topped by sleek statuary, and so on. The first shot of Billie shows her playing the drums. Almost immediately there begins a montage sequence (involving superimposition) that, while created from visual images, invokes sound in the manner of synesthesia. Thus, the film cuts between close-ups of hands playing the piano, violin, drum, saxophone, and xylophone; images of couples dancing, and a circular spiraling vortex that seems to signify giddiness or intoxication—all accompanied by jazz music on the sound track. Later Gil plays the piano and Kentucky the ukulele as couples continue to spin around the floor. Finally, we find Billie posed on the balcony of her two-story great room, clothed in a cutting-edge black-and-white cape and skirt. She removes the top as she begins to move, revealing a skimpy halter and bare midriff. She dances down the stairs and performs (to music on the sound track) a dramatic and graceful mime for her guests—a virtual production number. Billie's gala and dramatic entrance are imbued with a sense of erotic hedonism emblematic of the time. Tellingly, in a wry glossary at the back of James Thurber and E. B. White's satirical volume *Is Sex Necessary?* (published this year), the authors define the "amatory instinct" as "an interest in sex" and "passion" as the "expression of the sex principle without so much fuss" (189, 193).

Eventually, Billie weds Gil without realizing that, while she was toying with Abbott at her party, Gil and Kentucky have had sexual relations. Her nuptials are another instance of a musical "number" in the film, with the lavish bridal procession accompanied by "The Wedding March" on the sound track. After the ceremony, entirely through innuendo, Billie learns that Kentucky is pregnant with Gil's child and decides that her marriage must be annulled. She boldly announces to friends and the press that she will go on a "groomless" honeymoon. As she quips: "Modern, isn't it? I'm just starting the fashion," to which her vicious friend Ginger (Josephine Dunn) responds: "Do tell us . . . is this a modern moral . . . or just another immoral modern?" Billie exiles herself to Paris where Abbott (who has loved her from the start) finds her and the film ends with their happy reunion.

The Musical Revue

As for literal sound films, the most disjunctive sub-genre was the so-called revue. Some were short films, like MGM's Movietone featurettes that presented a few discrete stage acts with titles to introduce them. Marion Harris (billed as the "Song Bird of Jazz") performed work of this kind and is touted as having starred in such Broadway plays as *Artists and Models* and *A Night in Spain*. Another short film stars the orchestra from New York City's Capitol Theatre ("The Capitolians" led by Walt Roesner), reminding us that a night at a picture palace included a live stage extravaganza. The orchestra's selections range from quasi-classical to jazz pieces, evincing Hollywood's attempt to bridge the gap between high and low culture.

Some revues, however, were ambitious feature-length productions. MGM's variety film *The Hollywood Revue* (moderated by Jack Benny and Conrad Nagel directly addressing an absent audience) is one of the more interesting such vehicles. On one level, the film (which premiered on 14 August and was released on 23 November) presents a "galaxy" of studio stars: Joan Crawford, Buster Keaton, John Gilbert, Lon Chaney, Marie Dressler, John Barrymore, Norma Shearer, Laurel and Hardy, among others. But it also boasts numerous gorgeous stage sets created by Cedric Gibbons and Richard Day, masters of the Art Deco style. One modish "curtain," for instance, takes the form of three rigid semi-circles in a sunburst motif that are sequentially lowered or raised to frame the players. Another is more geometric in style, with V- and inverted V-shaped motifs. Finally, another sports a musical theme—with images of instruments, treble clefs, and notes. Moreover, several production numbers involve cinematic experimentation. In one tap routine ("Bones and Tambourines"), shadows of the performers are used to great effect, as is superimposition and the switch from positive to negative photography—all executed before a huge image of an abstract tambourine. In another sequence, a tiny Bessie Love is introduced as emerging from Jack Benny's jacket pocket. He puts her on his hand, then places her on the floor where she grows to full size before our eyes. The same minimizing technique is used on singer Charlie King at another point in the show, as well as on dancer Marion Davies (accompanied by accelerated motion) in "Tommy Atkins on Parade." On several occasions, as chorus girls dance, we get the kind of high-angle, overhead shots we later associate with Busby Berkeley—which reduce the women to circular patterns. Throughout the film, the sound of tapping feet is used as another percussive instrument.

One number that features elegant sets is "Lon Chaney's Gonna Get You If You Don't Watch Out," a piece in which chorines, asleep in an Art Deco bedroom (which seems borrowed from *Our Modern Maidens*), are scared by monsters. Geometric columns and screens adorn the walls as statues of Siamese cats rest on pillars, and a triangular *moderne* chandelier hangs from the ceiling. But perhaps the most modish number of all is "The Tableau of Jewels," conceived by French illustrator Romain de Tirtoff (or Erté), briefly under contract to the studio. As a tenor intones a love song, we view a two-tiered set composed of white sinuous lines. As it rotates against a black background, we find statically posed women in elaborate, exotic white costumes (making their bodies into silhouettes). Each is placed (like an ornamental sculpture) in a kind of illuminated niche, a common Art Deco architectural detail.

Some sequences are simply concert pieces. In one, Joan Crawford (known for her "musical" performances in silent films) finally gets to be heard. Introduced by Nagel as the "personification of youth and beauty and joy and happiness," she sings the upbeat tune "Got a Feelin' for You," then dances the Charleston. Other entertainers (like Cliff Edwards) are given the same solo treatment. A joke on sound technology is made when Charlie King complains that movie stars "can't sing" and Conrad Nagel renders a tune made famous by King in *The Broadway Melody* ("You Were Meant for Me"). The gag is that Nagel is only lip-synching King's voice as the latter looks on, dismayed. Another number raises similar issues. After Bessie Love appears from Benny's pocket, she sings the song "I Never Knew I Could Do a Thing Like That," which is all about silent players having to cope with the sound cinema. The lyrics talk about how "sound effects have made a wreck of [her]," about how "her vocalizing is weak" and has "a certain squeak," and about her need for singing lessons. In truth, Love is fabulous and has no problem with the musical format. Other witticisms attend to the uneasy relationship between stage and screen actors (with the former now numerous in Hollywood). While Nagel refers to the MGM stable as "one big happy family," screen star William Haines is openly hostile to radio personality Jack Benny and tears apart the latter's tuxedo.

The Backstage Musical

Somewhat less disjointed than the revue is the traditional "backstage" musical that concerns the lives of performers and generally alternates (none too fluidly) between quotidian events, rehearsals, and stage shows. Frequently, as in *The Broadway Melody*, these films are thinly veiled Horatio Alger narratives about ingénues who achieve the American Dream. Already this year, however, a more naturalistic musical began to develop that seamlessly merged dramatic and performance sequences. Here, the exemplary film is Rouben Mamoulian's *Applause* (premiering on 7 October), one of the highest grossing films of the year. It was produced by Paramount and stars Helen Morgan, a noted "torch" singer who had come to Broadway fame as Julie LaVerne in *Show Boat* (1927). Based on a 1928 novel, it concerns Kitty Darling (Morgan), a pregnant burlesque queen who delivers her child backstage and sends her away to a convent to be educated. As her daughter, April (Joan Peers), grows up, Kitty's career becomes more tawdry and she comes under the influence of Hitch (Fuller Mellish Jr.), a lover and fellow performer who exploits her. He convinces her that, in order to save money, she should remove April from private school and have her live with them. April comes home and is appalled by the sleazy life her mother lives. Hitch sexually harasses April and urges her to join the chorus in order to help out her mother. Distraught, Kitty takes poison and expires. Ultimately, April is saved by her romance with a wholesome young sailor whom she has met in New York. While *Applause* was approved by the National Board of Review, its invocation of suicide troubled the Motion Picture Producers and Distributors Association, which in December asked for a report on the film from psychologist Charleton Simon. His response mentioned that the film "may react disastrously upon morbid or depressed individuals of unstable or emotional instabilities" (*Applause* DVD).

Several elements separate *Applause* from other musicals of the year. Clearly, rather than portray the stage world as an attractive venue where young women merrily pursue wealth and fame, it is represented as a squalid place where burlesque trumps vaudeville. Thus, Mamoulian shows us portly, homely, matronly chorus girls rather than nubile nymphettes; and he makes reference to stripping, grinding, prostitution, "specialty numbers," and drinking. Beyond that, in a montage sequence that anticipates Laura Mulvey's focus on scopophilia, Mamoulian presents the male audience as voyeuristic, lascivious, and grotesque. Finally, the musical numbers hold little appeal; they are off-hand, pro forma, and executed by clumsy, repellent women. When Morgan sings, it is often in a real-life situation, unaccompanied by a nondiegetic orchestra. Thus, she casually rehearses a song in her apartment ("What Wouldn't I Do for That Man?") and sings another as April sleeps. Neither is she the ideal female star of the period; though only twenty-six, she looks much older (probably due to her chronic alcoholism), and Hitch calls her a "gin-soaked," "fat old woman." Moreover, Morgan's body type (stocky and buxom) did not conform to the popular flapper physiognomy, which was slim and androgynous.

In addition to its status as a musical, *Applause* was a pioneering sound film, marked by its fluid camera movements and inventive shooting angles (despite the "iceboxed" camera),[2] its utilization of offscreen sound, its employment of location shooting (the New York City subway system and the Brooklyn Bridge), and its choreography of multiple simultaneously recorded dialogue tracks (as when Kitty sings a lullaby to April while the latter prays). Mamoulian believed that sound motion pictures should utilize techniques honed in the silent era. He felt that the further the talking picture developed, the less it would draw upon theatrical methods (Tazelaar). *Applause* was also celebrated for its inclusion of expressionistic touches (shadow play and dream montage passages) usually associated with the silent era, as when April has a nightmare about her transition from the convent world to Broadway (that on an acoustic level intermixes "Ave Maria" and honky-tonk tunes). Significantly, the film was one of many shot in this period in Astoria, Queens (at the Paramount studios), in order to accommodate entertainers who worked on the East Coast.

The Screen Operetta

The year also saw the introduction of the so-called operetta film—works like *The Desert Song* (directed by Roy Del Ruth, with music by Sigmund Romberg) and *The Love Parade* (directed by Ernst Lubitsch, with music by Victor Schertzinger). The latter (based on the play *The Prince Consort* by Leon Xanof and Jules Chancel), like many such works, takes place in a fictional kingdom and involves the lives of royalty—giving studios a chance to show off palatial sets and lavish costumes. Specifically, it focuses on Queen Louise of Sylvania (Jeanette MacDonald), who has failed to marry, raising the concern of her ministers and countrymen. Into her life comes Count Alfred Renard (Maurice Chevalier), who has been called back from his post as Sylvanian military attaché in Paris due to scandals surrounding his sexual escapades. The two fall in love and marry, but their relationship faces obstacles when the queen treats her husband like a subject. Alfred also rebels against the fact that he is merely a prince consort (rather than a king) and has no official assignment save to please the queen. Eventually, the queen is put in her place; she learns to be a "proper" woman and be subservient to her husband, her royal title notwithstanding. Clearly, on the level of gender, the film conveys a conservative message that married women can never be powerful professionals but must defer to their partners—a theme that runs counter to so many more liberated films of the twenties. On the other hand, when Alfred complains of being a "mere plaything," we hear inverse reverberations of the usual feminist anthem. Regardless of ideology, the film bears the famed "Lubitsch touch," and is a charming, ironic, and innovative sound musical.

Unlike the backstage variety, there is no theater setting that motivates the music. In the opening moments of the film, the first lines we hear (part of the song "Champagne") are sung by the servant Jacques (Lupino Lane) as he sets a late-night table for Alfred and his date. Rather than arise from the scene, the number seems to substitute for exposition and dialogue. A similar tactic is used in a later sequence in the Sylvanian palace, when the servants gossip in the kitchen about the queen's marital difficulties (as Lulu [Lillian Roth] sings "The Queen Is Always Right"). At other times, the musical numbers arise from conventional dialogue sequences, as when the queen's ladies in waiting awaken her and she tells them about her oneiric fantasy by singing "Dream Lover" or, when at an intimate dinner party, Louise and Alfred erupt into "Love Parade." Furthermore, as the term operetta would imply, some of the music has a more classical feel to it—especially the pieces sung by MacDonald (such as "March of the Grenadiers"). Significantly, the queen and her prince attend a performance of the Sylvanian Royal Opera. On the other hand, the numbers rendered by Chevalier alone ("Paris, Stay the Same," "Nobody's Using It Now") take advantage of his more popular, cabaret background.

Beyond its status as a musical, there are other aspects of the film that are inventive in terms of sound practice. Frequently, rather than picturing the event from which a sound issues, Lubitsch allows the source to remain offscreen—as when Alfred and his Parisian date (a married woman) argue behind a closed door. During the queen's supper with Alfred we, at first, see nothing; instead we watch and listen as voyeuristic ladies-in-waiting, ministers, and servants (who see the event) narrate the scene that they observe.

On other occasions, Lubitsch reverses the arrangement: we see a scene but do not hear the words spoken—as when Alfred ostensibly tells an official a dirty joke, an act we witness through a closed window that blocks the sound of his voice. Finally, in the sequence in which Alfred sings goodbye to Paris, the song is first echoed by Jacques (saying farewell to the female servants he has known) and then by Alfred's pet, who barks his goodbyes to the female dogs whose company he has enjoyed. Interestingly, the next year saw another "canine musical," *The Dogway Melody* (a parody of *The Broadway Melody*). In *The Love Parade*, there are even jokes about Chevalier's French accent (which seems at odds with his ostensible status as a Sylvanian). Playing on notions of Gallic nasality, he claims to have had a cold in Paris that morphed into a permanent mode of speaking. Similarly, there are gags in the movie in which noise is a factor, as when volleys of cannon fire interrupt the royal couple's wedding night. Finally, as in many sound films of the era, there are jabs at radio, when an official makes an announcement on the air that is sponsored by the Sylvania Hardware Corporation.

The Musical Comedy

The Cocoanuts (based on a 1925 stage play by George S. Kaufman and directed by Robert Florey and Joseph Santley) is another film that was shot at Paramount's Astoria Studios, and it was one of the highest grossing movies of the year. With its premiere on 3 May and its release on 3 August, it presents yet another subset of the genre—a musical comedy (split equally between the two modes). Set in Florida, its narrative taps into the infamous land rush the state experienced in the decade. Starring the Marx Brothers, it concerns Mr. Hammer (Groucho), a shady resort owner whose hotel is on the skids. He woos the matronly but wealthy Mrs. Potter (Margaret Dumont) in order to have her bail him out. (At one point he calls her "well-preserved and partially pickled.") Meanwhile, a romance develops between Potter's daughter, Polly (Mary Eaton), and Bob Adams (Oscar Shaw), an architect (now working as a hotel clerk) who has hopes of developing a particular parcel of land. In the song "When My Dreams Come True," he confesses his hopes to Polly. Meanwhile, Mrs. Potter opposes the liaison and wants her daughter to marry Harvey Yates (Cyril Ring), an upper-class man who is actually a ne'er-do-well with plans to steal Mrs. Potter's diamond necklace and who is secretly involved with another woman, Penelope (Kay Francis). Zeppo Marx plays Jamison, a desk clerk at the Hotel de Cocoanut, and Harpo and Chico (playing characters with those names) arrive as two déclassé guests (but really small-time thieves). By the

The four Marx Brothers (Zeppo, Groucho, Chico, and Harpo) wreak havoc at a Florida hotel in *The Cocoanuts.*

end of the drama, of course, the proper young couple is united, Hammer's hotel is saved, and the valuable real estate ends up in the right hands.

Harpo remains essentially a silent comic whose lack of aural expression becomes especially funny in a sound film where no noise emerges when he laughs. Alternately, the acoustic medium is necessary for both Groucho's and Chico's brand of humor. For the former, the sound track allows the viewer to experience the fast-paced, nonsensical repartee for which he is known. Here, for example, is some dialogue from a sequence in which Hammer romances Mrs. Potter:

> *Hammer:* Your eyes, they shine like the pants of a blue serge suit.
> *Potter:* What? The very idea. That's an insult.
> *Hammer:* That's not a reflection on you—it's on the pants.
>
> ——
>
> *Hammer:* Why don't you grab me until you can make other arrangements?
> *Potter:* My dear Mr. Hammer, I shall never get married before my daughter.
> *Hammer:* You did once!
>
> ——

Potter: I don't think you'd love me if I were poor.
Hammer: I might but I'd keep my mouth shut.
Potter: I'll not stay here any longer and be insulted this way!
Hammer: No—don't go away and leave me here alone. You stay here and I'll go.

There are ethnic issues in the Marx Brothers' humor as well. Clearly, Chico's faux Italian dialect is only possible in the sound medium (as are his failures of understanding and malapropisms). At one point, Hammer tells him about the "big boom in Florida," to which Chico responds that he and Harpo are "two big booms too." Similarly, some of the lines smack of Jewish humor. When Hammer tells Chico about "the levees," the latter (hearing "the Levys") asks if "that's the Jewish neighborhood," to which Hammer responds that he'll "pass over" that remark. At another moment, Hammer inexplicably begins speaking with an Irish brogue.

In addition to comedy, the Marx Brothers were also known for the musical interludes that punctuate their films. At one point, when Penelope lures Chico to her room (in order to blame the necklace's theft on him), he plays the clarinet. Later, Harpo plays the instrument that gives him his name—with close-ups of his hands to show the intricacies of his fingering. In both cases, the brothers reprise the film's musical theme, "Till My Dreams Come True," lending the work a unified structure. Furthermore, as part of the depiction of a fancy reception at Mrs. Potter's home, there is a musical "production number" with a Spanish theme that includes a mock-operatic version of the Toreador theme from *Carmen.*

Black Jazz and Negro Spirituals

Above it was noted that Helen Morgan had appeared in the signal role of Julie in the 1927 stage version of *Show Boat.* What seems significant is that Morgan, a white artist known for singing the blues, plays a mulatto woman in that drama—rendering poignant ballads like "Can't Stop Lovin' Dat Man" (P. G. Wodehouse and Oscar Hammerstein). The dialect of the song's title in itself alerts us to the fact that the character who renders it may be black, but one of the consequences of the coming of sound was to institutionalize racial, class, and regional stereotyping of cinematic dialogue. Thus, Morgan's association with the blues underscores the early sound cinema's simultaneous avowal and disavowal, exploitation and suppression, of the connection between popular music and African American culture. Hence, while the notion of the "integrated" musical is often used to reference a work with smooth continuity between drama and song, its second sense might be associated with race.

Already in *The Hollywood Revue* (an all-white film) we had intimations of the importance of black music in American culture. One of the numbers was entitled "Palace and Minstrel," and another, "Low Down Rhythm," mentioned "Swanee River" and "Old Black Joe." But in the same year, Hollywood began to deploy African American artists, just one aspect of the film industry's importation of musical talent from other fields. While, on the one hand, entertainers like Al Jolson mimicked black jazz and sang minstrel songs like "Mammy," on the other, important black artists were enlisted for musical productions. Several of MGM's Movietone shorts of the year, for instance, feature George Dewey Washington, a famous baritone. In one, he sings the British imperialist ballad "On the Road to Mandalay," but, in another, dressed like a tramp, he croons a tune with Negro spiritual roots: "I'm Ready for the River."

Other more sophisticated short films of the year exploited the popularity of jazz and the association of black musicians with the form. A rather pedestrian effort starred Bessie Smith in a dramatization of "St. Louis Woman." Far more original is *Black and Tan* (directed by Dudley Murphy, who had worked with Fernand Léger on *Ballet Mécanique* [1924]). It stars Duke Ellington and Fredi Washington playing themselves. The story begins as two furniture movers (one of them stereotypically named Eczaema) arrive at the apartment of a financially strapped Duke Ellington, ready to repossess his piano. Regrettably, the workers are portrayed in a racist fashion as servile, ignorant fools (much like Stepin Fetchit) who ultimately accept a bribe of liquor to leave the piano there. This is fortunate because Ellington is composing an exciting new piece and Fredi has secured him a gig to play it at the club where she dances. Brief reference is made to her having a heart condition and to Ellington's concern about it. The film then abruptly switches from this mini-drama to the cafe itself, and the rest of the work is an extended performance vehicle featuring Ellington's band and the night spot's other entertainers. At first, we see a group of suave male tap dancers perform on an Art Deco stage against a *moderne* curtain, their bodies reflected in a black polished floor. We then find a gorgeously costumed Fredi backstage feeling faint. When the camera returns to the dancers, it depicts them in prismatic, cubistic, and kaleidoscopic shots, as though viewed through Fredi's failing eyes. Despite her illness, she goes on stage and does an "Apache" number. Images rotate dizzily and, at one point, we view her from below (through a glass floor). Eventually, she collapses and is taken away. Scores of her friends crowd around her bed as the music shifts to a

Negro spiritual. Abstract shadows fill the walls showing trombones sliding and hands raised in grief. Clearly, *Black and Tan* has complex and multifarious roots in jazz, the pictorial avant-garde, the blues, black gospel.

But most extraordinary of all, from a racial perspective, is the production of King Vidor's *Hallelujah!* (released 20 August). Billed as "All singing, all talking, all colored," it was one of the first all-black films produced by a major studio, the other one that year being Paul Sloane's *Hearts in Dixie* (these are in contrast to those authored by independents like Oscar Micheaux). Interestingly, writing in an African American publication, *Opportunity*, Robert Benchley opined (in a problematically essentialist and stereotypical way) that the "Negro voice" was the only type that could overcome the limitations of the talking picture. As he noted:

> One of the chief obstacles in the advance of the "talkies" has been the voice of actors. . . . They have either sounded like the announcer in a railway station or some lisping dancing master. . . . With the opening of *Hearts in Dixie*, however, the future of the talking-movie has taken on a rosier hue. . . . It may be that the talking-movies must be participated in exclusively by Negroes. . . . There is a quality in the Negro voice . . . which makes it the ideal medium for the talking-pictures. (122)

Shot on location in Tennessee and Arkansas, *Hallelujah!* tells the story of Zeke Johnson (Daniel L. Haynes), a poor black sharecropper who is led astray by his association with Chick, a honky-tonk woman (Nina Mae McKinney) whom he meets while taking his family's cotton crop to market. Though flirtatious with Zeke, Chick is really in cahoots with Hot Shot (William Fountaine), a crooked gambler. She encourages Zeke to risk his family's earnings on a wager and, of course, he loses. To make matters worse, in a fight that ensues, his brother Spunk (Everett McGarrity) is killed. Repentant, Zeke returns home and becomes a preacher and gets engaged to the wholesome Missy Rose (Victoria Spivey). While on the road with his revival troupe, he reencounters Chick, who again poses an erotic threat. She attends one of his sermons and, through shot/countershot editing, we perceive that Zeke looks at her lasciviously while preaching. She asks to be saved and, after Zeke baptizes her, they begin living together. One day, however, returning home from work, he finds her alone with Hot Shot. When confronted, she leaves, her lover in tow. Zeke chases the couple through the woods, killing them both. An image of Zeke toiling on a prison work crew informs us that he has been incarcerated. Shortly thereafter, the title "Probation" alerts us that he has been released. At the end of the narrative, we see Zeke wending his way back to the countryside, singing "At the End of the Road."

Zeke Johnson (Daniel Haynes) gambles with Hot Shot (William Fountaine) as alluring Chick (Nina Mae McKinney) looks on in *Hallelujah!*

Throughout the drama, the film incorporates songs and dances rendered by its African American players, whom Vidor located through a national talent search. Though some (like McKinney and Haynes) had theatrical experience, all were newcomers to the screen. Specifically, Haynes had been an understudy for the Broadway production of *Show Boat*, McKinney had appeared in New York in *Blackbirds of 1928*, and Spivey was a blues singer recorded on "race" labels. Much of the film's music draws on Negro spirituals ("Sometimes I Feel Like a Motherless Child," "Go Down Moses") and employs the Dixie Jubilee Singers (from Fisk University) as a chorus. Other pieces build on traditional tunes ("Old Folks at Home" by Stephen Foster), work songs ("Oh Cotton," "Roll the Cotton), and jazz ("St. Louis Blues" by W. C. Handy). A few contemporary pieces also appear in the film, Irving Berlin's "The Swanee Shuffle" and "Waiting at the End of the Road," specifically requested by Irving Thalberg (who wanted to ensure the work's popular appeal). With its nonfiction feel (including footage of saw mills, cotton gins, and so on), *Hallelujah!* portrays an entirely black world, and has, consequently, been criticized for omitting any representation of white oppression. Though documentary in tone, the film tends to portray the southern rural landscape as an idealized pastoral—one that (in typical twenties fashion) is contrasted to the evils of the more urban market town. Though poignant and sympathetic, the film is also rife with stereotypes of the era, most notably blacks' alleged hyper-spiritualism (they chant "Gimme That Old Time Religion"), propensity for singing and dancing (even after a hard day's work), lustfulness (Zeke not only craves Chick but pounces on Missy Rose), low moral standards (a couple with eleven children decide to get married), and proclivity for gambling (Chick even has dice embroidered on her blouse). While the sound track allows for a certain realism of speech in portraying the southern dialect, it also presents a cliché vision of blacks as quasi-illiterate (as when Zeke says to Chick: "You is just what I has on my mind"). In order to shoot on location and retain the fluidity of earlier cinema, Vidor shot the film as a silent and post-synchronized it with sound. Though not a huge success, *Hallelujah!* did reasonably well at the box office, appealing to both black and white audiences.

There is a final double entendre to explore—the so-called "color line" or "color bar." While in common parlance, both terms mean a barrier, created by custom, law, or economic differences, separating nonwhite persons from whites, within the context of the year we can think of each as applying equally to cinematic experiments with hue—a popular feature of the musical as exemplar of screen spectacle. In *The Hollywood Revue*, for instance, there are numerous color musical sequences: "Orange Blossom Time" and "Singing in the Rain," both filmed in Technicolor. Likewise, *Sunny Side Up* had sequences shot in Multicolor. In particular, however, *On with the Show!* brings the issues of race and tone together—this time over the bodies of African American players. Touted as "the first 100%, Natural Color, All-Singing Production," it includes several black performers shot in Technicolor—thereby linking the binary senses of the term. Thus, Ethel Waters sings two songs backed by the Harmony Four singers ("Am I Blue" and "Birmingham Berta"),[3] while a black group called The Four Covans executes a tap dance. Other musicals featuring color sequences with white performers include Sidney Franklin's *Devil-May-Care*, John W. Harkrider and Millard Webb's *Glorifying the American Girl*, *Red Hot Rhythm*, Del Ruth's *The Desert Song* and *Gold Diggers of Broadway*, and *Broadway*.

■ ■ ■

To close, let us return to the multiple denotations of the word *crash*—which, as noted, within the context of the year suggests both the stock market debacle and a brash noise (as in jazz music). To these, add a third meaning—to attend a party uninvited. While, on a literal level, black performers were invited to participate in Hollywood's coming of sound (and did not "crash" the cinematic festivities), in truth, their presence was highly equivocal. Hence, it was possible for Paul Whiteman (a white man, after all) to be named the era's "King of Jazz," and for his 1930 musical (of the same name) to have as its finale a production number on jazz history that proceeds without a single reference to African Americans. Regrettably, their onscreen absence in this work would be a harbinger of things to come.

NOTES

1. The winners' trophies would not be called "Oscars" until 1931.

2. According to Miles Krueger, in "Some Words about Applause" in the Kino DVD release of the film, cameraman George Folsey mounted the camera on a carriage with pneumatic tires in order to get the moving camera shots. It was ironically called "icebox" because the camera was enclosed in a box to soundproof it and the camera motor made it quite hot inside.

3. Robert H. Hill sang with William and Charles Campbell and Sunn Jackson in the Harmony Four Quartet. In 1935 it became the first all-black vocal group to sing on radio.

1927–1929

Select Academy Awards

The first Academy Awards were given on 16 May 1929, at 8:00 P.M. in the Blossom Room of the Roosevelt Hotel in Hollywood. The hosts were Douglas Fairbanks and William C. de Mille. The awards were for films of 1927 and part of 1928. Categories were different than they are today: awards were presented in the name of the individual only and could honor work on one or more films. Furthermore, two individuals who worked on the same film could be submitted as a single nomination.

1927–1928

Outstanding Picture: *Wings* (1927), Paramount Famous Players–Lasky

Unique and Artistic Picture: *Sunrise* (1927), Fox

Best Actor: Emil Jannings in *The Way of All Flesh* (1927), Paramount, and *The Last Command* (1928), Paramount

Best Actress: Janet Gaynor in *Seventh Heaven* (1927), Fox; *Sunrise* (1927), Fox; and *Street Angel* (1928), Fox

Best Art Direction: William Cameron Menzies, *The Dove* (1927), Norma Talmadge Film and United Artists, and *Tempest* (1928), Joseph M. Schenck Productions

Best Cinematography: Charles Rosher and Karl Struss, *Sunrise* (1927), Fox

Best Director (Comedy Picture): Lewis Milestone, *Two Arabian Knights* (1927), Caddo Co. and United Artists

Best Director (Dramatic Picture): Frank Borzage, *Seventh Heaven* (1927), Fox

Best Engineering Effects: Roy Pomero, *Wings* (1927), Fox

Best Writing (Original Story): Ben Hecht, *Underworld* (1927), Paramount

Best Writing (Title Writing): Joseph Farnham (not associated with any specific film)

Special Award: Warner Bros., for producing *The Jazz Singer* (1927), "the pioneer outstanding talking picture, which has revolutionized the industry"

Special Award: Charles Chaplin, for acting, writing, directing, and producing *The Circus* (1928)

1928–1929

Outstanding Picture: *The Broadway Melody* (1929), MGM

Best Actor: Warner Baxter in *In Old Arizona* (1928), Fox

Best Actress: Mary Pickford in *Coquette* (1929), Pickford Corp./United Artists

Best Art Direction: Cedric Gibbons, *The Bridge of San Luis Rey* (1929), MGM

Best Cinematography: Clyde De Vinna, *White Shadows in the South Seas* (1928), MGM

Best Director: Frank Lloyd, *The Divine Lady* (1929), First National, Warner Bros.

Best Writing: Hans Kraly, *The Patriot* (1928), Paramount

1929–1930

Best Actor: George Arliss in *Disraeli* (1929), Warner Bros.

All other awards given at this year's ceremony pertained to films of 1930.

SOURCES FOR FILMS

Many films from this decade are difficult to find. Some titles are only available in film archives. Some may be acquired for personal use, but only from small companies that distribute "collector's copies" on VHS or DVD-R. Typically mastered from video copies of battered and "dupey" 8 mm or 16 mm prints, these copies are often well below normal commercial standards. Quite a few silent films have been released by commercial distributors, but individual titles, particularly short films, can be difficult to locate when they appear on multi-title DVDs that vendors or libraries might catalog using only the overall title.

This guide will aid readers in locating sources for the films that are examined in detail in this volume. DVDs, like books, may go out of print over time, but the information below will nevertheless assist in the placement of Interlibrary Loan requests should a title become otherwise unavailable. A good source of information about the availability and quality of silent films on DVD and VHS is www.silentera.com.

All the companies and organizations indicated below have web sites that can be located easily by typing their full names into any Internet search engine. For companies whose titles appear multiple times within the following list, we have abbreviated the full names as follows:

Criterion = Criterion Collection
Grapevine = Grapevine Video
Image = Image Entertainment
Kino = Kino International
MGM = Metro-Goldwyn-Mayer
Milestone = Milestone Films
Paramount = Paramount Pictures
Unknown = Unknown Video
Warner = Warner Home Video

For titles discussed in this volume that do not appear in the list below, the reader may assume that the film has survived (unless the discussion indicates otherwise) but is available only in a film archive. Specific information about the location and preservation status of virtually all surviving films from this era may be found in the FIAF International Film Archive Database, an online database available from Ovid (www.ovid.com) via library subscription.

FILM AND SOURCES

The Ace of Hearts (1921) is on DVD on *TCM Archives—The Lon Chaney Collection* (Warner).

The Affairs of Anatol (1921) is on DVD from Image and is also on *The Cecil B. Demille Classics Collection* (Passport) and *The Gloria Swanson Collection* (Passport).

Applause (1929) is on DVD from Kino.

Are Parents People? (1925) is on DVD-R from Grapevine.

Black and Tan Fantasy (1929) is on DVD on *Hollywood Rhythm Vol. 1—The Best of Jazz & Blues* (Kino).

The Blot (1921) is on DVD from Milestone.

The Broadway Melody (1929) is on DVD on *The Broadway Melody (Special Edition)* (Warner), *Best Picture Oscar Collection (18-pack)* (Warner), *The Broadway Melody of 1929* (Warner), and *Best Picture Oscar Collection—Musicals* (Warner).

A Chapter in Her Life (1924) is on VHS from Nostalgia Family Video.

The Cocoanuts (1929) is on DVD on *The Marx Brothers Silver Screen Collection* (Universal Studios) and *The Cocoanuts* (Image).

The Covered Wagon (1924) is on VHS from Paramount.

The Crowd (1928) is on VHS from Warner.

The Docks of New York (1928) is on VHS from Paramount.

Down to the Sea in Ships (1922) is on DVD from Kino on *Parisian Love/Down to the Sea in Ships.*

The Electric House (1922) is on DVD on *The Art of Buster Keaton* (Kino), *College* (Kino), and *Electric House* (Synergy Entertainment).

Felix Dopes It Out (1925) is on DVD on *Felix! 1919–1930* from Lumivision Corporation.

Felix Finds 'em Fickle (1925) is on DVD on *Presenting Felix the Cat: The Otto Messmer Classics 1919–1924* (Bosko Video).

Felix Out of Luck (1925) is on DVD on *Presenting Felix the Cat: The Otto Messmer Classics 1919–1924* (Bosko Video).

Flesh and The Devil (1927) is on DVD on *TCM Archives—The Garbo Silents Collection (The Temptress/Flesh and the Devil/The Mysterious Lady)* (Warner) and on *Garbo—The Signature Collection* (Warner).

The Goose Woman (1925) is on DVD from Televista.

Hallelujah! (1929) is on DVD from Warner.

The Hunchback of Notre Dame (1924) is on DVD from Image.

It (1927) is on DVD from Milestone. It is also on *It Plus Clara Bow: Discovering the "It" Girl* (Kino).

The Jazz Singer (1927) is on DVD on a Three-Disc Deluxe Edition (Warner).

The Last Command (1928) is on VHS from Paramount.

The Love Parade (1929) is on DVD on *Eclipse Series 8—Lubitsch Musicals* (Criterion).

The Man Who Laughs (1928) is on DVD from Kino.

Manslaughter (1922) is on DVD on a double-feature edition called *Manslaughter and The Cheat* (Kino) and on *The Cecil B. Demille Classics Collection* (Passport).

The Mark of Zorro (1920) is on DVD on *The Mark of Zorro/Don Q: Son of Zorro* (Kino). It is also on *The Douglas Fairbanks Collection* (Kino).

Our Modern Maidens (1929) is on VHS from Warner.

My Best Girl (1927) is on DVD from Milestone.

Nanook of the North (1922) is on DVD from Criterion.

The Plastic Age (1925) is on DVD on *Show Off/The Plastic Age* (Image).

Pollyanna (1920) is on VHS on *The Golden Age of Silent Films- 2 Disc 7 Piece Set* (Edi Video) and on VHS (Nostalgia Family Video).

Salome (1924) is on DVD on *Salome/Lot in Sodom* (Image).

The Saphead (1920) is on DVD on *The Art of Buster Keaton* (Kino) and *The Saphead* (Kino).

Sex (1920) is on DVD-R from Unknown.

The Sheik (1921) is on DVD from Image and on *The Sheik/The Son of the Sheik (Special Edition)* (Image).

Sherlock Jr. (1925) is on *The Art of Buster Keaton* (Kino) and *Our Hospitality/Sherlock, Jr.* (Kino).

Smoldering Fires (1925) is on DVD from Sunrise Silents.

The Spanish Dancer (1924) is on VHS from Nostalgia Family Video.

Steamboat Bill Jr. (1928) is on DVD from Kino. It is also available on DVD from Image, which features new musical accompaniment by The Alloy Orchestra.

Steamboat Willie (1928) is on DVD on *Walt Disney Treasures—The Adventures of Oswald the Lucky Rabbit* (Walt Disney Video), *Walt Disney Treasures—Mickey Mouse in Black and White* (Walt Disney Video), and *Vintage Mickey* (Buena Vista Home Entertainment/Disney).

Stella Dallas (1925) is on DVD-R from Sunrise Silents.

Suds (1920) is on DVD from Milestone.

The Sun Down Limited (1925) is on DVD on *The Little Rascals Collection* (Movies Unlimited).

Sunrise (1927) is on DVD on *Studio Classics—Best Picture Collection (Sunrise/How Green Was My Valley/Gentleman's Agreement/All About Eve)* (Fox Home Entertainment).

The Temptress (1926) is on DVD on *TCM Archives—The Garbo Silents Collection (The Temptress/ Flesh and the Devil/The Mysterious Lady)* (Warner) and on *Garbo—The Signature Collection* (Warner).

The Ten Commandments (1924) is on DVD on *The Ten Commandments (50th Anniversary Collection)* (Paramount).

The Thief of Bagdad (1925) is on DVD on *The Thief of Bagdad Deluxe Edition* (Kino) and on *The Thief of Bagdad* (Image). It is also available on DVD on *The Douglas Fairbanks Collection* (Kino).

The Wind (1928) is on VHS from Warner.

A Woman of Paris (1924) is on DVD on *A King in New York/A Woman of Paris (2 Disc Special Edition)* (Warner).

WORKS CITED AND CONSULTED

ABBREVIATIONS

MHL = Margaret Herrick Library, Academy of Motion Pictures Arts and Sciences, Beverly Hills

LMPA = Library and Museum for the Performing Arts, Lincoln Center, New York

NA = Newspaper Archive, www.newspaperarchive.com

BOOKS AND ARTICLES

Abel, Richard, ed. *Silent Film*. New Brunswick: Rutgers UP, 1996.

"Actors to Go to Marion." *New York Times* 24 Aug. 1920: 3.

Addison, Heather. *Hollywood and the Rise of Physical Culture*. New York: Routledge, 2003.

Advertisements. *Motion Picture Classic* Mar. 1927: 83, 85, 123.

Affron, Charles. *Lillian Gish*. Berkeley: U of California P, 2002.

——. *Lillian Gish: Her Legend, Her Life*. New York: Scribner, 2001.

"Al Jolson Speaking during Warren G. Harding's Front Porch Campaign." Ohio Historical Society. 27 May 2007 <http://www.ohiohistory.org>.

Allen, Frederick Lewis. *Only Yesterday: An Informal History of the Nineteen-Twenties*. New York: Harper & Row, 1957.

Allen, Robert C. "From Exhibition to Reception: Reflections on the Audience in Film History." *Screen Histories: A Screen Reader*. Ed. Annette Kuhn and Jackie Stacey. Oxford: Clarendon, 1998.

"America First, Gompers' Word." *Van Wert Daily Bulletin* 1 Jan. 1920: 1. NA, accessed 12 Mar. 2006.

Anderson, Robert G. *Faces, Forms, Films: The Artistry of Lon Chaney*. New York: A. S. Barnes and Company, 1971.

Anger, Kenneth. *Hollywood Babylon*. New York: Dell, 1975.

Applause, dir. Rouben Mamoulian. 1929; DVD, New York: Kino on Video, 2003.

Rev. of *Are Parents People? Kinematograph Weekly* 17 Sept. 1925: 90.

Aronson, Michael. "1920, What of Prohibition?" Weblog Entry. *Daily Wid's Project*. 12 Aug. 2006. <http://widsproject.blogspot.com/2006/08/index.html>, accessed 1 Apr. 2007.

"Around Chicago Picture Theatres: Clermont has Clean Policy; Bookings Please the Mothers." *Moving Picture World* 17 Apr. 1922: 427.

"Arrest Insane Man in Gotham Bomb Mystery." *Waukesha Daily Freeman* 17 Sept. 1920: 1. NA, accessed 23 Apr. 2007.

Aumont, Jacques. "The Face in Close-Up." *The Visual Turn: Classical Film Theory and Art History*. Ed. Angela Dalle Vacche. New Brunswick: Rutgers UP, 2002. 127–48.

Bahktin, Mikhail. "Forms of Time and of the Chronotope in the Novel." *The Dialogic Imagination: Four Essays*. Ed. Michael Holquist. Austin: U of Texas P, 1981. 86–110.

——. *Rabelais and His World*. 1940. Trans. Helene Iswolsky. Bloomington: Indiana UP, 1984.

Banner, Lois. *American Beauty*. Chicago: U of Chicago P, 1983.

Barton, Bruce. *The Man Nobody Knows*. London: Constable, 1925.

Bazin, André. *What Is Cinema?* Vol. 1. Berkeley: U of California P, 1971.

"Be My Eskimo Baby." *Los Angeles Times* 10 Jan. 1922.

Beauchamp, Cari. *Without Lying Down: Frances Marion and the Powerful Women of Early Hollywood.* New York: Scribner's, 1997. Rpt., Berkeley: U of California P, 1998.

"The Beautiful and Damned." *Moving Picture World* 23 Dec. 1922: 609.

Behlmer, Rudy. "Clara Bow." *Take One* Mar. 1977: 453, 457.

Ben Hur Toilet Articles. Advertisement. *Photoplay* Oct. 1927: 149.

Benchley, Robert. "*Hearts in Dixie*: The First Real Talking Picture." *Opportunity* Apr. 1929: 122–23.

Benson, Susan Porter. *Counter Cultures: Saleswomen, Managers, and Customers in American Department Stores, 1890–1940.* Urbana: U of Illinois P, 1996.

Bergson, Henri. *Le Rire: Essai sur La Signification du Comique.* 1893. Paris: Presses Universitaires de France, 1940.

"Best Pictures of the Past Year." *New York Times Film Reviews 1913–1968.* New York: New York Times and Arno Press, 1970. 411.

Biery, Ruth. "The Story of Greta Garbo." *Photoplay* May 1928.

"Big Names of 1927." *Exhibitor's Herald* 24 Dec. 1927: 22–23.

"Biggest Money Makers of 1927." *Exhibitor's Herald* 24 Dec. 1927: 36–37.

Adv. for *Billions. Waukesha Daily Freeman* 18 Jan. 1921: 6. NA, accessed 3 May 2007.

Birchard, Robert S. "DeMille and *The Ten Commandments* (1923): A Match Made in Heaven." *American Cinematographer* 73.9 (Sept. 1992): 77–81.

Blackford, Mansel G. *The Rise of Modern Business: Great Britain, the United States, Germany, Japan, and China.* 3rd ed. Chapel Hill: U of North Carolina P, 2008.

Blake, Michael. *Lon Chaney: The Man Behind the Thousand Faces.* New York: Vestal, 1993.

Rev. of *The Blot. Variety* 19 Aug. 1921: 35.

Boardman, Fon Wyman. *America and the Jazz Age: A History of the 1920's.* New York: H. Z. Walck, 1968.

"Bobbed Hair." Exhibitors' Pressbook. Famous Players–Lasky Corporation, Title File. Rochester, N.Y.: George Eastman House, 1922.

Bodeen, De Witt. "How a Film Career Was a Pale Reflection of Her Genius as an Actress." *Films in Review* 23.10 (Dec. 1972): 577–604.

——. "Rex Ingram and Alice Terry, Part One." *Films in Review* 26.2 (Feb. 1975): 73–89.

——. "Rex Ingram and Alice Terry, Part Two." *Films in Review* 26.3 (Mar. 1975): 129–42.

Bordwell, David, and Kristin Thompson. *Film Art: An Introduction.* New York: McGraw-Hill, 1990.

Bow, Clara. "How to Behave Like Greta Garbo, Clara Bow, and Company." Unidentified clip, Clara Bow clips, MHL.

——, as told to Adela Rogers St. Johns. "My Life Story." *Photoplay* Feb. 1928: 106; Mar. 1928: 117; Apr. 1928: 57, 108.

Bowser, Eileen. "*The Docks of New York*: Program Notes." Typescript. New York: Museum of Modern Art, Film Study Center Archive, 1978.

Breton, André. *Manifestoes of Surrealism.* Trans. Richard Seaver and Helen R. Lane. Ann Arbor: U of Michigan P, 1969.

Brice, Fanny. "Second Hand Rose." Music by James F. Hanley. Lyrics by Grant Clarke. 78 rpm recording. Victor 27751-A, 1921.

"A Brief History." *International Fabricare Institute.* 12 Feb. 2006. *http://www.ifi.org/consumer/whatis-drycleaning.html.*

"Broadway Ushers Loafing Spell Week." *Variety* 28 Dec. 1927: 7.

Brooks, Peter. "The Text of Muteness." *The Melodramatic Imagination: Balzac, Henry James, and the Mode of Excess*. New Haven: Yale UP, 1995. 56–82.

Brown, Karl. "On James Cruze." *Films in Review* 37.4 (Apr. 1986): 224–36.

Brownlow, Kevin. *The Parade's Gone By*. Berkeley: U of California P, 1968.

"Building Sales before Publication Date." *Publisher's Weekly* 6 Jan. 1923: 21.

"Buy on Fifth Avenue through *Photoplay's* Shopping Service." *Photoplay* Mar. 1927: 69.

Cahiers du Cinema, eds. "John Ford's *Young Mr. Lincoln* (1939)." *Movies and Method: An Anthology*. Ed. Bill Nichols. Berkeley: U of California P, 1976. 493–528.

"*The Cameraman*." *Focus on Film* no. 26 (1977): 44, 46.

Canemaker, John. *Felix: The Twisted Tale of the World's Most Famous Cat*. New York: Pantheon, 1991.

"Capitol Down $26,000 to $79,000." *Variety* 26 Oct. 1927: 7.

Capitol Theatre Program. *Flesh and the Devil* clips, LMPA.

Card, James. *Seductive Cinema: The Art of Silent Film*. New York: Knopf, 1994.

Carey, Gary. *Doug and Mary*. New York: Dutton, 1977.

Carr, Harry. "Charlie Again Is Champion." *Los Angeles Times* 13 Feb. 1921: III 1.

——. "Harry Carr's Page: The Folks Who Name Movie Plays." *Los Angeles Times* 30 July 1924: C2.

——. "Harry Carr's Page: The Junkman's Story." *Los Angeles Times* 7 Jan. 1925: C2.

——. "Harry Carr's Page: Looking at 'Greed.'" *Los Angeles Times* 30 July 1924: C2.

Carringer, Robert L., ed. *The Jazz Singer*. Madison: U of Wisconsin P, 1979.

Carter, Paul A. *Another Part of the Twenties*. New York: Columbia UP, 1977.

Cather, Willa. *Not Under Forty*. Lincoln: U of Nebraska P, 1988.

"Celluloid Critic." Rev. of *Flesh and the Devil*. *Motion Picture Classic* Mar. 1927: 82.

"Channel 4 Silents Presents Live Cinema." *Sunrise* clips, MHL.

Cheatum, Maude S. "Bebe, the Oriental." *Motion Picture Magazine* Nov. 1919: 32–33, 123.

Cherchi Usai, Paolo. "The Color of Nitrate: Some Factual Observations on Tinting and Toning Manuals for Silent Films." *Silent Film*. Ed. Richard Abel. New Brunswick: Rutgers UP, 1996. 21–31.

Cherchi Usai, Paolo, and Lorenzo Codelli. *L'eredità De Mille*. Pordenone: Edizioni Biblioteca dell'imagine, 1991.

"Chicago to Probe 'Red' Situation." *Ironwood Daily Globe* 1 Jan. 1920: 1. NA, accessed 12 May 2007.

"Choose the Opening Program." Advertisement for Saxe Park Theatre, Waukesha, Wisc. *Waukesha Daily Freeman* 13 Dec. 1921: 3. NA, accessed 21 May 2007.

"Cinema Club 9 Program Notes." *Flesh and the Devil* clips, MHL.

Clara Bow Hat. Advertisement. *Photoplay* Oct. 1927: 149.

Cohen, Ruth Schwartz. *More Work for Mother: The Ironies of Household Technology from Open Hearth to the Microwave*. Scranton: Basic Books, 1983.

Colfax, Betty. "Flesh Does Well by Herr Sudermann." Rev. of *Flesh and the Devil*. *Evening Graphic* 10 Jan. 1927. *Flesh and the Devil* scrapbook, LMPA.

"Contest Brings Deluge of Beauty." *Motion Picture Magazine* Mar. 1921: 41.

"Coolidge Declares Non-interference His Foreign Policy." *New York Times* 9 Apr. 1926.

Corey, Melinda, and Ochoa, George, eds. *The American Film Institute Desk Reference*. New York: Stonesong, 2002.

The Covered Wagon: A James Cruze Production, Publicity Booklet. Hollywood: Paramount Pictures, 1923.

Crafton, Donald. *Before Mickey: The Animated Film, 1898–1928.* Chicago: U of Chicago P, 1982.

——. *The Talkies: American Cinema's Transition to Sound 1926–1931.* Berkeley: U of California P, 1999.

Cullen, Countee. *The Black Christ & Other Poems.* New York and London: Harper & Brothers, 1929.

Dannenberg, Joseph, ed. *The Film Yearbook 1925*: 43. <http:/books.google.com>

Davis, Murray S. "What's So Funny?" *The Comic Conception of Culture and Society.* Chicago: U of Chicago P, 1993.

Development of Culture. Advertisement. *Motion Picture Magazine* Feb. 1927: 85.

Doane, Adelaide. Letter to New York State Governor Nathan Miller. 20 May 1921. NYS Archives. Central Subject and Correspondence Files, Gov. Nathan Miller 1921–1922. 13682–78. Box 9. File 150–299 (part 4).

"Douglas Fairbanks Sr. Bio." *The Douglas Fairbanks Museum.* 31 Dec. 2005. <http://www.douglasfairbanks.org>, accessed 26 Apr. 2007.

"A Dream Come True." *Motion Picture Classic* Jan. 1922: 63, 94.

Druesne, Maeve. "Nazimova: Her Silent Films." *Films in Review* 36.6–7 (June/July 1985): 322–30.

——. "Nazimova: Her Silent Films." *Films in Review* 36.8–9 (Aug./Sept. 1985): 405–12.

Dumenil, Lynn, ed. *The Modern Temper: American Culture and Society in the 1920s.* New York: Hill and Wang, 1995.

"Edith May, The Cynosure of All Admiring Eyes." *Waukesha Daily Freeman* 18 Jan. 1921: 3. NA, accessed 27 Apr. 2007

Eisenstein, Sergei. *Eisenstein on Disney.* Ed. Jay Leyda. Trans. Alan Upchurch. London: Methuen, 1988.

"Eskimo Babies in New Burbank Review." *Los Angeles Times* 13 June 1922: III 3.

"Eskimo Opera in Denmark." *Los Angeles Times* 12 June 1921: III 48.

"Estimates for Last Week." *Moving Picture World* 27 Oct. 1922: 45.

"Etiquette as Taught by the Movies." *Motion Picture Magazine* Mar. 1927: 4.

Eugenics, Genetics and the Family. Vol. 1. Scientific Papers of the Second International Congress of Eugenics. Baltimore: Williams and Wilkins, 1923.

Everson, William K. *American Silent Film.* New York: Oxford UP, 1978.

Ewen, Stuart, and Elizabeth Ewen. *Channels of Desire: Mass Images and the Shaping of American Consciousness.* Minneapolis: U of Minnesota P, 1992.

Fairbanks, Douglas. "Films for the Fifty Million." *Ladies' Home Journal* Apr. 1924.

Fairbanks, Douglas Jr. *The Salad Days.* New York: Doubleday, 1988.

Fass, Paula S. *The Damned and the Beautiful: American Youth in the 1920s.* New York: Oxford UP, 1977.

Faulkner, William. *The Sound and the Fury.* 1929. Rpt., New York: Random House, 1984.

Fenin, George N., and William K. Everson, *The Western: From Silents to Cinerama.* New York Bonanza Books, 1962.

"Few Shed Tears at J. Barleycorn Bier." *Appleton Daily Post* 16 Jan. 1920: 6. NA, accessed 9 May 2007.

Fine, Ruth E. *John Marin.* New York: Abbeville, 1990.

Fisher, Dorothy Canfield. *The Home Maker.* 1924. Rpt., London: Persephone Books, 1999.

Fitzgerald, F. Scott. *The Crack Up*. Ed. Edmund Wilson. New York: Scribner, 1931. Rpt., New York: New Directions, 1959.

——. *The Great Gatsby*. 1925. Rpt., London: Penguin, 1979.

"Flesh and the Devil." *Morning Telegram* 12 Jan. 1927. *Flesh and the Devil* scrapbook, LMPA.

"Flesh and the Devil." Unidentified clip. *Flesh and the Devil* clips, LMPA.

Rev. of *Flesh and the Devil. New York Sun* 10 Jan. 1927. *Flesh and the Devil* scrapbook, LMPA.

Rev. of *Flesh and the Devil. Variety* 12 Jan. 1927. *Flesh and the Devil* clips, MHL.

Fox, Charles Donald, and Milton L. Silver. *Who's Who on the Screen*. New York: Ross Publishing, 1920. 301.

Friedman, Estelle. "The New Woman: Changing Views of Women in the 1920s." *Journal of American History* 61.2 (Sept. 1974): 372–93.

"Garfield Theater, Milwaukee." *Cinema Treasures*. 23 Apr. 2007 <http://www.cinematreasures.org/theater/4261>.

Gilman, Charlotte Perkins. "Vanguard, Rear-Guard, and Mud-Guard." *Century Magazine* 104 (July 1922): 348–53.

Goldberg, David J. *Discontented America: The United States in the 1920s*. Baltimore: Johns Hopkins UP, 1999.

Goldberg, Ronald Allen. *America in the Twenties*. Syracuse: Syracuse UP, 2003.

Golden Peacock Bleach Crème. Advertisement. *Motion Picture Magazine* Feb. 1927: 86.

Gomery, Douglas. *The Hollywood Studio System: A History*. London: BFI, 2005.

Goosson, Stephen. "Where Do We Eat?" *Motion Picture Magazine* Feb. 1927: 39–40, 117–18.

Gorgan, Ann Lee. *Arthur Dove: Life and Work with a Catalogue Raisonné*. Newark: U of Delaware P, 1984.

"Gorgeous Picture Coming to Star." *Monessen Daily Independent* 12 Nov. 1920: 3. NA, accessed 12 May 2007.

Grandinetti, Fred M. *Popeye: An Illustrated History of E. C. Segar's Character in Print, Radio, Television, and Film Appearances, 1929–1933*. Jefferson, N.C.: McFarland, 1994.

"Greta Garbo in Ibanez' *Torrent*." *Christian Science Monitor* 26 Feb. 1926: 8.

"Greta Garbo Settles for $3,000 Weekly." Unidentified clip, Greta Garbo clips, MHL.

Grieveson, Lee, and Peter Krämer, eds. *The Silent Cinema Reader*. London: Routledge, 2004.

"Grow Taller." Advertisement. *Motion Picture Magazine* Feb. 1927: 111.

Gumbrecht, Hans Ulrich. *In 1926: Living at the Edge of Time*. Cambridge, Mass.: Harvard UP, 1997.

Gunning, Tom. "Crazy Mischief in the Garden of Forking Paths: Mischief Gags and the Origins of American Film Comedy." *Classical Hollywood Comedy*. Ed. Kristine Brunovska Karnick and Henry Jenkins. New York: Routledge, 1995. 87–105.

Hall, Mordaunt. "Another Ibáñez Story." *New York Times* 11 Oct. 1926: 18.

——. "Hollywood Surprises New Swedish Actress." *New York Times* 28 Feb. 1926: X4.

——. "A Nathaniel Hawthorne Classic." *New York Times* 10 Aug 1926: 19.

——. "Persistent von Stroheim Conquered Film Magnate." *New York Times* 14 Dec. 1924: X7.

——. "The Screen." Rev. of *Flesh and the Devil. New York Times* (undated). *Flesh and the Devil* clips, LMPA.

——. "The Screen." Rev. of *My Best Girl. New York Times* (undated). *My Best Girl*, MHL.

——. "The Screen." Rev. of *Sunrise. New York Times* 24 Sept. 1927: 15.

Halsey, Stuart & Co. "The Motion Picture Industry as a Basis for Bond Financing." *The American Film Industry*. Ed. Tino Balio. Madison: U of Wisconsin P, 1976.

Hannoosh, Michele. *Baudelaire and Caricature: From the Comic to an Art of Modernity.* University Park: Pennsylvania State UP, 1992.

Harwith, John, and Susan Harwith. "Karl Struss: Man with a Camera." 5 Jan. 1977. *Sunrise* clips, MHL.

Hayne, Donald, Ed. *The Autobiography of Cecil B. DeMille.* Englewood Cliffs, N.J.: Prentice-Hall, 1959.

Hemingway, Ernest. *A Farewell to Arms.* New York: Bantam, 1929.

Higashi, Sumiko. *Cecil B. DeMille and American Culture: The Silent Era.* Berkeley: U of California P, 1994.

——. *Virgins, Vamps, and Flappers: The American Silent Movie Heroine.* Montreal: Eden, 1978.

Higham, Charles. *Cecil B. DeMille.* New York: Da Capo, 1973.

Hill, Joseph A. "Some Results of the 1920 Population Census." *Journal of the American Statistical Association* 18.39 (1922): 350–358. *JSTOR.* U of Oregon Library, Eugene. <http://www.jstor.org>, accessed 12 Apr. 2007.

Hilmes, Michelle. *Hollywood and Broadcasting: From Radio to Cable.* Urbana: U of Illinois P, 1990.

Hinkle, Beatrice. "The Chaos of Modern Marriage." *Harper's* 152 (Dec. 1925): 13.

"His Wife Laughed at His Appearance." *Bessemer Herald* 25 Oct. 1921: 6. NA, accessed 12 Apr. 2007

Historical Statistics of the United States Colonial Times to 1970s. Washington, D.C.: Bureau of the Census, U.S. Department of Commerce Bicentennial Edition, 1976.

"How Doug Made 'The Thief of Bagdad.'" *Photoplay* May 1924: 62–63.

Hynd, Alan, and Dorothy Calhoun. "News of the Camera Coasts." *Motion Picture News* Feb. 1927: 68; Sept. 1927: 51.

"Increases in B'Way Grosses." *Variety* 16 Nov. 1927: 7.

The International Jew: The World's Foremost Problem. Dearborn, Mich.: Dearborn Publishing, 1920.

Irwin, William. "They're Mean to Me." Unidentified clip, July 1931. Clara Bow clips, MHL.

It. Advertisement. *Motion Picture News* 18 Feb. 1927: 3.

Rev. of *It. Film Daily* 13 Feb. 1927. *It* clips, MHL.

Rev. of *It. Variety* 9 Feb. 1927: 14.

Jenkins, Alan. *The Twenties.* London: Heinemann, 1974.

"Joe and Sam Talk Show Stuff But Tell Each Other Nothing." *Variety* 7 Dec. 1927: 7.

"KDKA." *Hammond Museum of Radio.* 10 Feb. 2004. <http://www.hammondmuseumofradio.org>, accessed 13 May 2007.

Keaton, Buster, with Charles Samuels. *My Wonderful World of Slapstick.* New York: Doubleday, 1960.

Kerr, Walter. *The Silent Clowns.* New York: Knopf, 1975.

Kingsley, Grace. Rev. of *The Kid. Los Angeles Times* 21 Feb. 1921: II 7.

Kirby, Lynne. "Gender and Advertising in American Silent Film: From Early Cinema to *The Crowd.*" *Discourse* 13.2 (Spring/Summer 1991): 3–20.

Klumph, Helen. "Critics Agree 'Greed' Is Good." *Los Angeles Times* 14 Dec. 1924: C29–30.

Knopf, Robert. *The Theater and Cinema of Buster Keaton.* Princeton, N.J.: Princeton UP, 1999.

Koszarski, Richard. *An Evening's Entertainment: The Age of the Silent Feature Picture, 1915–1928.* Berkeley: U of California P, 1994.

Krämer, Peter. "The Making of a Comic Star: Buster Keaton and *The Saphead* (1920)." *The Silent Cinema Reader.* Ed. Lee Grieveson and Peter Krämer. London: Routledge, 2004. 279–89.

Krutch, Joseph Wood. *Modern Temper: A Study and a Confession*. 1929. Rpt., New York: Harcourt, Brace and World, 1956.

Kyvig, David. *Daily Life in the United States: 1920–1939, Decades of Promise and Pain*. Westport, Conn.: Greenwood, 2002.

Lane, Tamar. "Views and Reviews: *Smouldering Fires*." *Film Mercury* 19 Dec. 1924: 6.

Langley, Susan, and John Dowling. *Roaring '20s Fashions: Deco*. Atglen, Pa: Schiffer, 2006.

Larson, Edward J. *Summer for the Gods: The Scopes Trial and America's Continuing Debate over Science and Religion*. Cambridge, Mass.: Harvard UP, 1998.

Latham, Angela J. *Posing a Threat: Flappers, Chorus Girls, and Other Brazen Performers of the American 1920s*. Hanover, N.H.: Wesleyan UP, 2000.

Lawrence, Florence. "*Smouldering Fires* Scores at Premiere." *Los Angeles Examiner* 4 Jan. 1925.

"Leading Film Stars of 1927." *Variety* 7 Jan. 1928: 8.

Leuchtenberg, William E. *The Perils of Prosperity 1914–32*. Chicago: U of Chicago P, 1958.

Lewis, Sinclair. *Babbitt*. New York: Harcourt, Brace & Co., 1922.

——. *Dodsworth: A Novel*. New York: Harcourt, Brace & Co., 1929.

——. *Main Street*. New York: Collier and Son, 1920.

"Lillian Gish Opens Today at Columbia." *Washington Post* 23 Jan. 1927: F1.

Lindsey, Ben, and Wainwright Evans. *The Revolt of Modern Youth*. New York: Boni & Liveright, 1925.

Lipke, Kathleen. "Simplicity Keynote of Brown Film." *Los Angeles Times* 4 Jan. 1925.

Lippmann, Walter. *A Preface to Morals*. New York: Macmillan, 1929.

Loos, Anita. *Gentlemen Prefer Blondes*. 1925. Rpt., London: Picador, 1982.

Lowry, Carolyn. *The First One Hundred Men and Women of the Screen*. New York: Moffat, Yard, 1920.

Lukács, Georg. "Thoughts on an Aesthetic for the Cinema." Trans. Barrie Ellis-Jones. *Framework* 14 (Spring 1981): 2–4.

Lynd, Robert S., and Helen Merrell Lynd. *Middletown: A Study in Contemporary American Culture*. New York: Harcourt, Brace, 1929.

Maas, Frederica Sagor. *The Shocking Miss Pilgrim: A Writer in Early Hollywood*. Lexington: UP of Kentucky, 1999.

MacCann, Richard Dyer. *The Stars Appear*. Metuchen, N.J.: Scarecrow, 1992.

Maland, Charles J. *Chaplin and American Culture: The Evolution of a Star Image*. Princeton, N.J.: Princeton UP, 1989.

Manners, Dorothy. "What Do Men Want?" *Motion Picture Magazine* Aug 1927: 24.

Marchand, Roland. *Advertising the American Dream: Making Way for Modernity 1920–1940*. Berkeley: U of California P, 1985.

Marchetti, Gina. *Romance and the "Yellow Peril": Race, Sex, and Discursive Strategies in Hollywood Film*. Berkeley: U of California P, 1993.

"Marcus Loew Buys Metro Pictures." *New York Times* 6 Jan. 1920: 13.

Marcus, Steven. *The Other Victorians: A Study of Sexuality and Pornography in Mid-Nineteenth Century England*. New York: Basic Books, 1964.

"Marital Ties Cut." Unidentified clip, 22 Dec. 1927. Clara Bow clips, MHL.

"Mark of Zorro." *University of California San Diego History Server*. 8 Aug. 2004. <http://history.sandiego.edu/gen/filmnotes/markofzorro.html>, accessed 1 May 2007.

Marks, Percy. *The Plastic Age*. New York: Century, 1924.

"The Married Flapper." *Moving Picture World* 14 Oct. 1922: 595.

"Mary Lewis Wins Plaudits in Opera; Former Follies Girl Makes Her Debut as Mimi in 'La Boheme' at the Metropolitan." *New York Times* 29 Jan.1926: 18.

"Mary Pickford Weds Fairbanks." *New York Times* 31 Mar. 1920: 1.

"Mary Pickford Wins Divorce in Nevada." *New York Times* 4 Mar. 1920: 9.

May, Edith. "My Dream Comes True." *Cedar Rapids Evening Gazette* 27 Sept. 1920: 11. NA, accessed 27 Apr. 2007.

May, Elaine Tyler. *Great Expectations: Marriage and Divorce in Post-Victorian America*. Chicago: U of Chicago P, 1980.

Mayer, David. "Acting in Silent Film: Which Legacy of the Theatre?" *Screen Acting*. Ed. Peter Krämer and Alan Lovell. London: Routledge, 1999. 10–31.

McGowen, Roscoe. "Dupes and Madame Satan Flicker in Devilish Film." Rev. of *Flesh and the Devil*. *Daily News* 10 Jan. 1927. *Flesh and the Devil* scrapbook, MHL.

Meade, Marion. *Bobbed Hair and Bathtub Gin: Writers Running Wild in the Twenties*. New York: Doubleday, 2004.

Melnick, Ross. "Station R-O-X-Y: Roxy and the Radio." *Film History: An International Journal* 17.2 (2005): 217–33.

Mencken, H. L. "In Memoriam: W.J.B." *Baltimore Sun* 27 Jul. 1925. Rpt. in *Fitzgerald and the Jazz Age*. Ed. Malcom Cowley and Robert Cowley. New York: Charles Scribner's Sons, 1966.

Metcalfe, James. "What the Movies Do to Classics." *Wall Street Journal* 12 Aug. 1926: 10.

Miller, Nathan. *New World Coming: The 1920s and the Making of Modern America*. New York: Scribner, 2003.

Mills, T. F. "Allied Intervention in the Russian Civil War." 14 Oct. 2005. *Regiments*. <http://www.regiments.org/>, accessed 2 Apr. 2007.

Mintz, Steven, and Susan Kellogg. *Domestic Revolutions: A Social History of American Family Life*. New York: Free Press, 1988.

Mizejewski, Linda. *Ziegfeld Girl: Image and Icon in Culture and Cinema*. Durham, N.C.: Duke UP, 1999.

Montgomery, John. *The Twenties*. Rev. ed. London: Allen & Unwin, 1970.

Morris, Michael. *Madam Valentino: The Many Lives of Natacha Rambova*. New York: Abbeville, 1991.

Morrison, Patt. "Our Very Own Camelot." *Los Angeles Times* 30 Apr. 2006.

Mowry, George, ed. *The Twenties: Fords, Flappers and Fanatics*. Englewood Cliffs, N.J.: Prentice-Hall, 1963.

"Mrs. Stillman Bars Exile." *New York Times* 26 May 1921: 1.

"Much to Please in the New Henrietta." *New York Times* 23 Dec. 1913: 12.

Mulvey, Laura. "Visual Pleasure and Narrative Cinema." *Screen* 16.3 (Autumn 1975): 6–18.

"Musical Parade." *Los Angeles Times* 1 July 1922: II 9.

"My Adventures in the Midnight Follies." *Waterloo Times Tribune* 21 Nov. 1920: 7. NA, accessed 27 Apr. 2007.

My Best Girl pressbook, LMPA.

Rev. of *My Best Girl*. *Variety* 7 Nov. 1927. *My Best Girl*, MHL.

"Nazimova Plays Princess." *Waukesha Daily Freeman* 18 Jan. 1921: 6. NA, accessed 27 Apr. 2007.

Negra, Diane. "The Fictionalized Ethnic Biography: Nita Naldi and the Crisis of Assimilation." *American Film: Discovering Marginalized Voices*. Ed. Greg Bachman and Thomas J. Slater. Carbondale: Southern Illinois UP, 2002. 176–201.

"New Beauty Makes Debut Here Today." *Washington Post* 21 Feb. 1926: AF2.

"New and Old Films Whoop Up B'wy During Slow Week." *Variety* 28 Sept. 1927: 7

"The New Star." *Motion Picture Magazine* Jan. 1922: 55.

"The Newer Knowledge of Nutrition: The Use of Food for the Preservation of Vitality and Health." *Los Angeles Times* 4 Dec. 1921: III 3.

"1920 Open Year For All Radicals Palmer Declares." *Van Wert Daily Bulletin* 1 Jan 1920: 1. NA, accessed 12 Mar. 2006.

"1927 Amusement Taxes Total $17,835,818." *Film Daily* 27 Jan. 1928: 1, 8.

North, Michael. *Reading 1922: A Return to the Scene of the Modern.* New York: Oxford UP, 1999.

Nye, David E. *Electrifying America: Social Meanings of a New Technology.* Cambridge, Mass.: MIT Press, 2001.

O'Leary, Liam. *Rex Ingram: Master of the Silent Cinema.* London: BFI, 1993.

"1 January 1920." *NOAA Central Library U.S. Daily Weather Maps Project.* National Oceanic and Atmospheric Administration. <http://docs.lib.noaa.gov/rescue/dwm/data_rescue_daily_weather_maps.html>, accessed 1 May 2007.

"1,000 Bathing Girls on View in Pageant." *New York Times* 9 Sept. 1921: 12.

"P.D.C. Drops 3 Houses $23,700." *Variety* 9 Nov. 1927: 7.

Palmer, Niall A. *The Twenties in America: Politics and History.* Edinburgh: Edinburgh UP, 2006.

Palmer, Phyllis. *Domesticity and Dirt: Housewives and Domestic Servants in the United States, 1920–45.* Philadelphia: Temple UP, 1989.

"Pantages Pictures North Pole Society." *Los Angeles Times* 23 Jan 1921.

Paramount Theatre Program. *It* clips, LMPA.

Parchesky, Jennifer. "Lois Weber's *The Blot*: Rewriting Melodrama, Reproducing the Middle Class." *Cinema Journal* 39.1 (Fall 1999): 23–53.

Park, Robert E. "Urbanization as Measured by Newspaper Circulation." *American Journal of Sociology* 35.1 (July 1929): 60–79.

Parsons, Louella O. "Gilbert Weds Garbo." Unidentified clip, 14 Feb. 1927. Greta Garbo clips, MHL.

Peiss, Kathy. *Cheap Amusements: Working Women and Leisure in Turn-of-the-Century New York.* Philadelphia: Temple UP, 1986.

——. *Hope in a Jar: The Making of America's Beauty Culture.* New York: Owl Books, 1996.

Photo caption. *Photoplay* Oct. 1927: 19.

"*Photoplay's* Honor Roll for 1927." *Photoplay* Dec. 1927: 35.

"Picture Parade." Rev. of *Flesh and the Devil.* Mar. 1927: 60.

Pierce, Scott. "What It Costs to Be a Well-Dressed Flapper." *Motion Picture Classic* Mar. 1927. Clara Bow clips, MHL.

Pirandello, Luigi. *On Humour.* 1908. Trans. Antonio Illiano and Daniel P. Testa. Chapel Hill: U of North Carolina P, 1974.

"Plans Complete For Big 'Pep' Meeting Thursday Night at the Rex." *Bessemer Herald* 23 Oct. 1921: 1. NA, accessed 12 May 2007

"Police Hold Back Theatre Mob." *New York Telegram* 10 Jan. 1927. *Flesh and the Devil* scrapbook, LMPA.

"Producers Busy on Pictures to Thrill and Amuse." *New York Times* 27 Jan. 1924: X5.

Prouty, Olive Higgins. *Stella Dallas.* 1923. Rpt., London: Virago, 1990.

Quirk, James R. "My Estimate of Erich von Stroheim." *Photoplay* Jan. 1925: 27.

Ramsaye, Terry. "What the Pictures Do to Us." *Photoplay* Apr. 1927.

Rawson, Mitchell. "John Gilbert and Greta Garbo in Colorful Production." *Mid-Week Pictorial* 13 Jan. 1927. *Flesh and the Devil* scrapbook, LMPA.

"Reds Capture 3 More Towns." *Van Wert Daily Bulletin* 1 Jan. 1920: 1. NA, accessed 12 Mar. 2006.

Reid, Janet. "Are They Heroines to Their Costume Designers?" *Motion Picture Magazine* Feb. 1927: 110.

Reid, Laurence. Rev. of *It. Motion Picture News* 18 Feb. 1927: 587.

——. Rev. of *My Best Girl. Motion Picture News* 2 Dec. 1927: 1735.

——. Rev. of *Sunrise. Motion Picture News* 14 Oct. 1927. *Sunrise* clips, MHL.

Reid, Margaret. "Has the Flapper Changed?" *Motion Picture Magazine* July 1927: 104.

Rhodes, Chip. *Structures of the Jazz Age: Mass Culture, Progressive Education, and Racial Discourse in American Modernist Fiction*. New York: Verso, 1998.

"Richman to Face Large Balm Suit." Unidentified clip, 23 Dec. 1927. Clara Bow clips, MHL.

Robinson, David. *Chaplin: His Life and Art*. London: Collins, 1985.

——. "The It Girl." *Sight and Sound* (Autumn 1968). Clara Bow clips, MHL.

Ross, Steven J. *Movies and American Society*. Oxford: Blackwell, 2002.

Rothman, Stanley, David J. Rothman, and Stephan Powers. *Hollywood's America: Social and Political Themes in Motion Pictures*. Boulder, Colo.: Westview, 1996.

"Ruth Elder No Riot." *Variety* 23 Nov. 1927: 7.

Sann, Paul. "Uncle Sam's Water Wagon." *The Lawless Decade*. 1 Sept. 1999. <http://www.lawless.net>, accessed 22 Apr. 2007.

Adv. for *The Saphead. Van Wert Daily Bulletin* 8 Apr. 1921: 4. NA, accessed 3 May 2007.

"Scandal Hits Film Industry." *Variety* 16 Sept. 1921: 39.

Schallert, Edwin. "Etches Drama: *Smouldering Fires* Has Many Rare Moments." *Los Angeles Times* 5 Jan. 1925.

——. Rev. of *My Best Girl. Motion Picture News* 7 Oct. 1927: 1052.

——. Untitled. *Los Angeles Sun Times* 2 Dec. 1926. *Flesh and the Devil* clips, MHL.

Schatz, Thomas. *The Genius of the System: Hollywood Filmmaking in the Studio Era*. New York: Pantheon Books, 1988.

Schmied, Wieland. "Precisionist View and American Scene: The 1920s." *American Art in the 20th Century: Painting and Sculpture 1913–1993*. Ed. Christos M. Joachimide and Norman Rosenthal. Munich: Prestel, 1993. 47–59.

"The Screen." *New York Times* 19 Jan. 1920: 16.

"The Screen." *New York Times* 28 June 1920: 13.

"The Screen." *New York Times* 14 Feb. 1921: 16.

Seldes, Gilbert. *The Seven Lively Arts*. New York: Harpers & Brothers, 1924.

Adv. for *Sex Crushed to Earth. Monessen Daily Independent* 12 Nov. 1920: 3. NA, accessed 12 May 2007.

"'Sex Crushed to Earth' Stellar Picture." *Monessen Daily Independent* 13 Nov. 1920: 3. NA, accessed 12 May 2007

"Shadow Stage." Rev. of *My Best Girl. Photoplay* Dec. 1927: 52.

"Shadow Stage." Rev. of *Sunrise. Photoplay* Dec. 1927: 52.

"Shadow Stage." Rev. of *The Thief of Bagdad. Photoplay* May 1924: 54.

Silver, Charles. *Charles Chaplin; An Appreciation*. New York: Museum of Modern Art, 1989.

Skinner, Tina, and Lindy McCord. *Flapper Era Fashions from the Roaring 20s*. Atglen, Pa: Schiffer, 2004.

Sklar, Robert. *Movie-Made America*. New York: Random House, 1975.

——, ed. *The Plastic Age (1917–1930)*. New York: Braziller, 1970.

Slater, Thomas J. "A Woman Who Spoke Through the Silents." *American Film: Discovering Marginalized Voices*. Ed. Greg Bachman and Thomas J. Slater. Carbondale: Southern Illinois UP, 2002. 201–17.

Slide, Anthony. *Lois Weber: The Director Who Lost Her Way in History.* Westport, Conn.: Greenwood, 1996.

Smedley, Agnes. *Daughter of Earth,* New York: Feminist Press, 1987.

Smith, Julian. *Chaplin.* Boston: G. K. Hall, 1984.

Smith-Rosenberg, Carroll. "The Female World of Love and Ritual." *Disorderly Conduct.* New York: Knopf, 1985.

"'Sorrell's Sons' Strong Gross in 2nd Week at Rivoli." *Variety* 30 Nov. 1927: 7.

"The Spanish Dancer." *Film Year Book.* New York: Wid's Film and Film Folks, 1924.

St. Johns, Adela Rogers. "Clara Bow." *Liberty* 3 Aug. 1929. Clara Bow clips, MHL.

Stamp, Shelley. Commentary to *The Blot.* DVD. Harrington Park, N.J.: Milestone, 2003.

Starman, Ray. "James Cruze: Cinema's Forgotten Director." *Films in Review* 36.10 (Oct. 1985): 460–65.

Stearns, Harold. *America and the New Intellectual.* New York: George Duran, 1921.

Stenn, David. "Clara Bow: The 'It' Girl's Notorious House in Beverly Hills." *Architectural Digest.* Clara Bow clips, MHL.

Stewart, Jacqueline Najuma. *Migrating to the Movies: Cinema and Black Urban Modernity.* Berkeley: U of California P, 2005.

Stokes, Melvin, and Richard Maltby. *Identifying Hollywood's Audiences: Cultural Identity and the Movies.* London: BFI, 1999.

Strang, Lewis C. *Famous Actors of the Day, in America.* Boston: L. C. Page, 1900.

Streissguth, Thomas. *The Roaring Twenties: An Eyewitness History.* New York: Facts on File, 2001.

Stuart, Henry Longan. "Blasco Ibáñez in Tales of War and South America." *New York Times* 31 May 1925: BR9.

Studlar, Gaylyn. *This Mad Masquerade: Stardom and Masculinity in the Jazz Age.* New York: Columbia UP, 1996.

"Sudden Affluence." *New York Times* 6 Oct. 1921: 16.

Adv. for *Suds. Coshocton Tribune* 4 Oct. 1920: 12. NA, accessed 12 Mar. 2006.

"Suffrage Wins." *Waukesha Daily Freeman* 19 Aug. 1920: 1. NA, accessed 23 Apr. 2007.

Rev. of *Sunrise. Variety* 28 Sept. 1927. *Sunrise* clips, MHL.

"Sunrise Brings a New Day to the Movies." *Literary Digest* 3 Dec. 1927. *Sunrise* clips, MHL.

Susman, Warren. *Culture as History: The Transformation of American Society in the Twentieth Century.* New York: Pantheon, 1973.

Taylor, Frederick. *The Principles of Scientific Management.* New York and London: Harper & Brothers, 1911.

Tazelaar, Marguerite. "The Camera's the Thing." *New York Herald Tribune* 23 June 1929.

Telotte, Jay. "Keaton Is Missing." *Film Literature/Quarterly* 23.2 (1995): 91–98.

"Temptress." Exhibitor's Herald. 1 Jan. 1927: 57.

"The Theatre; What the Movies Do to Classics." *Wall Street Journal* 12 Aug. 1926: 10.

Thelin, John R. *A History of American Higher Education.* Baltimore: Johns Hopkins UP, 2004.

"Third Week for Film at Capitol." *New York Telegraph* 20 Jan. 1927. *Flesh and the Devil* clips, LMPA.

Thurber, James, and E. B. White. *Is Sex Necessary? or Why You Feel the Way You Do.* New York and London: Harper & Brothers, 1929.

Tibbetts, John. "Sternberg, *The Last Command." Cinema Journal* 15.2 (Spring 1976): 68–73.

——. "Vital Geography: Victor Sjostrom's *The Wind." Literature/Film Quarterly* 1.3 (July 1973): 251–55.

Tibbetts, John C., and James M. Welsh. *His Majesty the American: The Films of Douglas Fairbanks, Sr.* Cranbury, N.J.: A. S. Barnes, 1977.

Times Square Theatre Program. *Sunrise* clips, LMPA.

Turner, George, T. "A Silent Giant: The Hunchback of Notre Dame." *American Cinematographer* 66.6 (June 1985): 34–43.

"$248,296 in 4 Wks. Gilbert-Garbo Film." *Variety* 9 Feb. 1927: 7.

"286 Critics Select Ten Best Films." *Film Daily* 3 Feb. 1928: 1, 7.

Unidentified clip. Clara Bow clips, MHL.

Untitled clip. *New York Evening Graphic,* Jan. 1927. Greta Garbo scrapbook, LMPA.

"Van Wert Clothing Company." Advertisement. *Coshocton Tribune* 4 Oct. 1920: 12. NA, accessed 12 Mar. 2006.

Van Wyck, Carolyn. "Favorite Recipes of the Stars." *Photoplay* Oct. 1927: 101.

Vance, Jeffrey. *Chaplin: Genius of the Cinema.* New York: Henry N. Abrams, 2003.

"Victor Seastrom and 'The Scarlet Letter.'" *Christian Science Monitor* 30 Sep. 1926: 8.

Waldorf, Wilella. "The Big Screen." Rev. of *Flesh and the Devil. New York Evening Post* 15 Jan. 1927. *Flesh and the Devil* scrapbook, LMPA.

"Walker Fights Bar on Scandal Film Stars." *New York Times* 18 Jan. 1922: 3.

Wandersee, Winifred. *Women's Work and Family Values, 1920–1940.* Cambridge, Mass.: Harvard UP, 1981.

Watts, Richard Jr. "Flesh's Advocate." Rev. of *Flesh and the Devil. New York Herald Tribune* 16 Jan. 1927. *Flesh and the Devil* scrapbook, LMPA.

"What Was the Best Picture of 1927?" *Photoplay* June 1928: 80.

"When Your Boy Goes Camping." *Outlook* 18 June 1924: 125.

Whitaker, Alma. "Women Rave over Forum Photoplay." *Los Angeles Times* 9 Jan.1925.

Wilson, Angus, and Philippe Jullian. *For Whom the Cloche Tolls; A Scrap-Book of the Twenties.* New York: Viking, 1973.

Wilson, Joan Hoff, ed. *The Twenties: Critical Issues.* Boston: Little, Brown, 1972.

Winship, Mary. "Our Gang." *Photoplay* Mar. 1924: 40–41, 108.

Wolfe, Charles. "Vitaphone Shorts and the Jazz Singer." *Wide Angle* July 1990: 58–78.

York, Cal. "What's the Matter with Garbo?" *Photoplay* Apr. 1927.

Zolberg, Aristide. *A Nation by Design: Immigration Policy in the Fashioning of America.* Cambridge, Mass.: Harvard UP, 2006.

Adv. for *Zorro. Bessemer Herald* 25 Oct. 1921: 6. NA, accessed 12 Mar. 2006.

Zworykin, Vladimir K. "The Early Days: Some Recollections." *American Broadcasting: A Source Book on the History of Radio and Television.* Ed. Lawrence W. Lichty and Malachi Topping. New York: Hastings House, 1975. 53–56.

CONTRIBUTORS

MARK LYNN ANDERSON is an assistant professor of film studies in the Department of English at the University of Pittsburgh. He has published essays on the history of film education in the United States, the early Hollywood star system, and motion picture censorship. He is author of *Twilight of the Idols: Hollywood and the Human Sciences in 1920s America* (forthcoming).

MICHAEL ARONSON is an assistant professor of film and media studies in the Department of English at the University of Oregon. His first book, *Nickelodeon City* (2008), is a study of exhibition and moviegoing in Pittsburgh during the silent era.

JENNIFER M. BEAN is the director of cinema studies and an associate professor in the Department of Comparative Literature at the University of Washington. She is the author of *The Play in the Machine: Gender, Genre, and the Cinema of Modernity* (forthcoming) and coeditor of *A Feminist Reader in Early Cinema* (2002). She is currently working on a study of early film slapstick and modern theories of laughter, and editing a collection on the origins of American film stardom.

ANGELA DALLE VACCHE is an associate professor of film studies at the Georgia Institute of Technology in Atlanta. Her latest book is *Diva: Defiance and Passion in Early Italian Cinema* (2008). She is currently working on a book about André Bazin and the visual arts while developing a class on West African cinema.

LUCY FISCHER is Distinguished Professor of Film Studies and English at the University of Pittsburgh, where she serves as the director of the Film Studies Program. She is the author of *Jacques Tati* (1983), *Shot/Countershot: Film Tradition and Women's Cinema* (1989), *Imitation of Life* (1991), *Cinematernity: Film, Motherhood, Genre* (1996), *Sunrise* (1998), and *Designing Women: Art Deco, Cinema, and the Female Form* (2003), and the coeditor (with Marcia Landy) of *Stars: The Film Reader* (2004). Forthcoming is her edited volume, *Teaching Film* (with Patrice Petro). She is a former president of the Society for Cinema and Media Studies.

SUMIKO HIGASHI is a professor emerita in the Department of History at SUNY Brockport and visiting fellow in the Film Studies Program at Yale University. She is the author of *Cecil B. DeMille and American Culture: The Silent Era* and *Virgins, Vamps, and Flappers: The American Silent Movie Heroine*, as well as numerous essays on women in film and television, film as historical representation, and film history as cultural history. Currently, she is working on a study of the construction of stardom and femininity in the 1950s.

MARCIA LANDY is Distinguished Professor of Film Studies and English, with a secondary appointment in the Department of French and Italian Languages and Literatures, at the University of Pittsburgh. Her publications include *Fascism in Film: The Italian Commercial Cinema, 1929–1943* (1986), *Imitations of Life: A Reader on Film and Television Melodrama* (1991), *British Genres: Cinema and Society, 1930–1960* (1991), *Film, Politics, and Gramsci* (1996; with Amy Villarejo), *Cinematic Uses of the Past* (1996), *The Folklore of Consensus: Theatricality and Spectacle in Italian Cinema 1929–1943* (1998), *Italian Film* (2000), *The Historical Film: History and Memory in Cinema* (2001), *Stars: The Film Reader* (2004, coedited with Lucy Fischer), *Monty Python's Flying Circus* (2005), and *Stardom Italian Style: Screen Performance and Personality in Italian Cinema* (2008).

SARA ROSS is an assistant professor of media studies and digital culture at Sacred Heart University. She has published articles in *Camera Obscura*, *Film History*, *Aura*, and several anthologies, and is coeditor of Archival News for *Cinema Journal*. Her research interests include late silent film, romantic comedy, and the development of female characters in Hollywood.

MAUREEN TURIM is a professor of film and media studies at the University of Florida. She is author of *Abstraction in Avant-Garde Films* (1985), *Flashbacks in Film: Memory and History* (1989), and *The Films of Oshima: Images of a Japanese Iconoclast* (1998). She has published over eighty essays in anthologies and journals on a wide range of theoretical, historical, and aesthetic issues in cinema and video, art, cultural studies, feminist and psychoanalytic theory, and comparative literature.

GWENDA YOUNG lectures in film studies in University College Cork, Ireland, and is currently preparing a full-length study of American director Clarence Brown. She has published articles on American cinema and silent cinema in a range of U.S and European film journals and has coedited (with Eibhear Walshe) a collection of essays on the Irish writer Molly Keane (2006).

INDEX

CPSIA information can be obtained
at www.ICGtesting.com
Printed in the USA
BVHW030615180822
644880BV00005B/20